ENIGMAS: ESSAYS ON SARAH KOFMAN

ENIGMAS

Essays on Sarah Kofman

EDITED BY

PENELOPE DEUTSCHER

KELLY OLIVER

Cornell University Press | ITHACA AND LONDON

First published 1999 by Cornell University Press
First printing, Cornell Paperbacks, 1999

Printed in the United States of America

Library of Congress Cataloging-in-Publication Data

Enigmas : essays on Sarah Kofman / edited by Penelope Deutscher
   & Kelly Oliver
      p.   cm.
   Includes bibliographical references and index.
   ISBN 0-8014-2912-9 (alk. paper). — ISBN 0-8014-8141-4
(paper : alk. paper)
   1. Kofman, Sarah.   I. Deutscher, Penelope, 1966–   .
II. Oliver, Kelly, 1958–   .
B2430.k64e53   1998
194—dc21   98-39688

Cornell University Press strives to use environmentally responsible suppliers and materials to the fullest extent possible in the publishing of its books. Such materials include vegetable-based, low-VOC inks and acid-free papers that are recycled, totally chlorine-free, or partly composed of nonwood fibers.

Cloth printing   10 9 8 7 6 5 4 3 2 1
Paperback printing 10 9 8 7 6 5 4 3 2 1

Contents

Acknowledgments   vii
Foreword: Run, Sarah!   viii
Jean-Luc Nancy

Introduction: Sarah Kofman's Skirts   1
Penelope Deutscher and Kelly Oliver

I   LITERATURE AND AESTHETICS

1. The Imposture of Beauty: The Uncanniness of   25
   Oscar Wilde's *Picture of Dorian Gray*
   Sarah Kofman
2. Don Giovanni, or the Art of Disappointing   49
   One's Admirers
   Ann Smock
3. Kofman's Hoffmann   67
   Duncan Large

II   PHILOSOPHY AND METAPHOR

4. Suffering Contradiction: Kofman on Nietzsche's   87
   Critique of Logic
   Mary Beth Mader
5. Nietzsche and Metaphor   97
   Paul Patton

[v]

6.   Schemata of Ideology in *Camera obscura* and   109
     Specters of Marx
     Pierre Lamarche
7.   How a Woman Philosophizes   134
     Françoise Duroux

III WOMEN, FEMINISM, AND PSYCHOANALYSIS

8.   Rending Kant's Umbrella: Kofman's Diagnosis   143
     of Ethical Law
     Natalie Alexander
9.   Complicated Fidelity: Kofman's Freud (Reading   159
     The Childhood of Art with *The Enigma of Woman*)
     Penelope Deutscher
10. Sarah Kofman's Queasy Stomach and the Riddle   174
     of the Paternal Law
     Kelly Oliver
11. Eating Words: Antigone as Kofman's Proper Name   189
     Tina Chanter

IV   JEWS AND GERMAN NATIONALISM

12. Kofman, Nietzsche, and the Jews   205
     Alan D. Schrift
13. "Made in Germany": Judging National Identity Negatively 219
     Diane Morgan

     Notes   235

     Consolidated Bibliography   254

     Sarah Kofman: Bibliography, 1963–1998   264

     About the Contributors   276

     Index   279

Acknowledgments

The editors thank Keith Ansell-Pearson for organizing the Warwick conference on Sarah Kofman, where several of these chapters began. Also, we acknowledge the special efforts of the translators: Paul Patton, Duncan Large, and Lisa Walsh. Thanks also to Duncan Large for compiling the complete bibliography of Kofman's works. Thanks to Alexandre Kyritsos and Françoise Collin for their kind assistance in Paris. Finally, thanks to Galilée for translation rights for the English translation of Sarah Kofman's "L'imposture de la beauté" from *L'imposture de la beauté et autres textes,* Galilée, 1995, pp. 9–48.

Foreword: Run, Sarah!

JEAN-LUC NANCY

For Sarah, writing was what it should be, or perhaps what it is for anyone when it is considered, not in its particular qualities of style or voice, but above all in its bare gesture, in its delineation, its tracing, or (as she used to say) its scratching, not to say its scribble. In other words, before being the inscription and transmission of a thought, it was an attestation of existence. It may be that those who write are especially, if not exclusively, those who must attest to an existence, whether their own or that of another (not that these can always be separated), whether through lack of being or excess (not that these can always be separated). Sarah wrote for her living, as we say of those who make it their profession, but in her case, over and above the profession, it was not just a question of ensuring a subsistence but of attesting to an existence.

One day, Sarah told me how her arm had shown a reaction—the skin red and irritated—after she had rested it on her *Devenir- femme d'Auguste Comte*. "How I somatize!" she said. But she meant two things at once, one superficial, emotive, and nervous, the other more important: I identify myself through my writing, in particular through this writing the becoming-woman of a philosopher and through him no doubt that of all philosophers, which is also my own becoming-philosopher, my incorporation of philosophy. In this book, she wrote, "It is not a question of my attempting here to reduce philosophy to pathology or system to biography. It is rather a certain relationship of system to life which interests me: to see, not what the work *owes* to life but what the work *brings* to life; to grasp how a philosophical system can take the place of *délire*" (Kofman 1978a, 41). What interests me in

Translation by Paul Patton. A French version of this essay appeared in *Les Cahiers du grif* (new series): 3, 1997, 29–32.

Sarah's work, and what knitted much of the friendship between us, is this manner of relating "works" to "life," rather than the converse, and what followed from it: her interest in people rather than their productions, her estrangement from the play of roles in little public scenes. None of this meant that the works should not be taken into account, nor that her concern was not to be read, above all by her friends, just as she attentively read others.

But her primary concern, at least with her friends, was that she not be "read" in the sense of "assimilated" or "registered": it was rather that the other's reading return to her in the form of a story, with episodes, surprises, or comments. In the same way, she was interested in anecdotes in general; she said that they were "the equivalent of a touch which underlined the essential, the beauty, the one irrefutable thing, all that remained when the truth of the system had disappeared" (Kofman [1979] 1986b, 19). That is why I am recounting anecdotes about her. I cannot separate her from her anecdotes. This was her way of being absolutely faithful: forgetting nothing, not one "touch" on the part of her friends, since fidelity was for her the very course of life. Not "truth" but fidelity, the truth of fidelity, which has no final sense but the sense of its very course. Truth that returns to life and not the converse.

———

That writing relates to life, and relates it, does not mean the absence of thought nor even its secondary importance. It means that thought does not begin without this gesture of writing and also that, just as it is transmitted by it, so thought ends with this gesture. But also that "thought," finally, is caught up in life and relates to it, ending in it and therefore also capable of ending it: there is no life after thought. A life of thought is perhaps a life that does not already live enough, or that lives too much, or again, quite simply, it is a life that attests itself, inscribing that it took place.

In this gesture, therefore, an existence is attested. An existence, as a result, that is uncertain of itself, anxious for itself when it is not thereby attested. An existence that needs to have proof of its existence in this manner. This ontological argument states that writing demonstrates with its letters the necessity of the existence of its subject.

———

This gesture—make no mistake—is not only and not necessarily that of graphic writing nor that of literary writing. It is also that of spoken teaching, that which is called in French the *course*. Sarah was, as they say, a professor "from the heart." No doubt, preparing a course is by no means the same as writing a text. But Sarah paid scant consideration to the differences. Her books were often her courses, which is also a great philosophical tradition.

What there is of writing in a course must be in the nature of prose, in other words of the discourse that goes *prorsus,* straight ahead, *proversus,* turned toward the front (in opposition to *transversus*). It goes forward, from the front, without interruption: it has no thought of interruption, other than that which marks the end of the hour and which only inter-rupts in order to better ensure the continuity of the hours, week after week. It does not contract itself nor return itself *versus:* it makes no verse, or rather it only verses forward, always in the same direction. Its only con-cern is to run ahead of itself, to be delivered always further out in front. Its truth lies in its movement, not in its punctuation. Its truth is insatiable, the unappeasable course of the course, always a delivery ahead of itself.

Sarah would have been amused to learn (perhaps she knew) that Prorsa was a goddess of childbirth, Sarah who counted her books like so many children, she who wanted to make more of these children than her mother had made living children and who in fact made so many more. To make children: not to engender, which is a male affair and a question of signification, but to bear and give birth to, which is an uninterrupted course or uninterruption itself. A woman gives birth to her child through-out her life. It is not the emission of a signification; it is expression in Spin-oza's sense. These were Sarah's only children—the books, the courses, the course of the books—but they were what she wanted and it was through them that she never left infancy, that she endlessly prolonged a course of infancy, not her own but an absolute infancy of the course of life. She, who had no children, was very attentive to the children of others. Once we had exchanged news of our profession, books, and health, she never failed to inform herself about exactly what had happened to my children, and she forgot no detail.

Sarah was small. She joked about her little-girl size. But she also said, "Little Sarah doesn't give up without a fight." And she readily said "my little" to her friends (to me, for example: "my little Jean-Luc").

Prose, therefore course: "It follows its course," as Blanchot said of philo-sophical discourse. But Blanchot said this with an anxiety turned toward the notorious, pressing, and almost insupportable necessity of this course. Sarah, for her part, took pleasure in the interminable. She was not mobilized by the infinitely and frighteningly old hidden beneath the murmur. She was mobilized by the incessantly new, like the child who tries out prattle. She saw no end to her discourse, her course, or her books. No doubt, in this way too she was like all of us, but more than others she gave herself to the course; she became almost indistinguishable from it. Not that she identified herself with the university, or even with teaching. I am trying to speak of a larger, more important course—her personal *cante jondo*. She did not stop with the work, with the definite and, as it were, definitive form of a book. She was keen to finish a book, but in order to publish it (to launch it into another course, another circulation) and immediately to begin another (if it had not begun already). No doubt this rhythm and practice was not peculiar to her. But she brought to it a particular determination and an always awakened haste. As though, truly, the thing to do was to continue, not to punctuate, to activate the subject rather than to pose the object: in short, praxis rather than poiesis.

What is this interminable praxis of the course? What does it want to say? Perhaps it wants to say no more than the want-to-say. Perhaps it wants to say a want-to-say with no other end than itself. In consequence, a "will to will"—but equally a will that, ultimately, no longer wants, that is no longer a "want to say" in the sense that Derrida gave to his translation of Husserl's *bedeuten* (and that Sarah did not fail to employ: see, for example, Kofman 1986c, 64). In other words, a want-to-say that does not aim at the production of a conclusion, the establishment of a thesis, the *jouissance* of a signification. A "will to will" that would not be a "will to power" (if such may be conceived).

Sarah wrote little by way of conclusion to her books. Comparing final pages, we see that they are more like provisional interruptions than conclusions. Or she would write, "By way of conclusion, let us therefore leave the last word to laughter." Or she would conclude as though reporting, dating, and even multiply dating the end of her writing ("Terminating this book today, 25th of September, the day of Yom Kippur," a Jewish joke that ends with "You recommence already?"). How can we not hear Sarah laughing at her own conclusion, by way of conclusion, because she knows that she has already begun another book, the rest of the course (perhaps *Paroles suffoquées*, which appeared the following year).

This want-to-say is aimed more at the linkage of motifs, the connection of arguments, the production of documents, the continuous embedding of words and reasons, the indeterminate openness, and the floating of a significance. In Levinasian terms, which were hardly Sarah's, the "to say" rather than the "said." Could there be something of a Jewish voice in Sarah? Recital and commentary, a writing of the *biblia,* always in the indefinite plural? But Sarah was Jewish in the very manner that she attributed to Freud (and that was not without Levinasian and Blanchotian resonance): "If, after having written *Jokes and Their Relation to the Unconscious,* Freud burned his collection of Jewish jokes, renounced his Jewish heritage and identity, it was to better generalize that Jewish 'identity,' to confer it on all humanity and, with this gift full of risk, cause it to lose forever its supposedly assured identity" (Kofman 1986c, 197). One page further on Sarah draws her laughing conclusion with a Jewish *joke* that makes fun of *Jewish* jokes.

A "generalized" Judaism, a Judaism in incessant course of dissemination and therefore also "Greek." Sarah's Nietzsche is the one from whom she liked to cite "the Jews[,] . . . a people firmly attached to life—like the Greeks and more than the Greeks" (Nietzsche 1982, 72; quoted in Kofman 1994c, 55). A philosopher's Judaism, in the sense that instead of being governed by the law of a calling (or rather, while also being governed by it), it seeks to maintain fidelity to the phenomenon or the phenomena. In this sense, this practice ties together the observance of a law of phenomena and the observation of the phenomenon of law. It can never be finished because the law does not protrude and because, symmetrically, the phenomenon is not the manifest given. Like the phenomenon, the law presents itself ceaselessly.

——————

On the other hand, to want to say only the want-to-say can turn into a self-obsession, an energy of energy, a sterile and despairing "auto-nomie" (pure phenomenon of its own pure law). Sarah's discourse can no more be considered exempt than any other philosophical discourse. But this can also take a different turn: toward an always recommencing support for the possibility of meaning, for its very opening, or for its coupling, which is much more a condition of existence, infinitely more than any proposed conclusion or signification, founded or founding and sovereign in its order.

Linguists speak of a "phatic" function of language—in other words, of a function of simple opening and maintenance of the language exchange, the maintenance (*entretien*) of the exchange (*entretien*). Neither an apophatic (discourse of law) nor an apophantic (discourse of phenomena) but a phatic function: for example, when we say "yes," "huh," or "fine" only in order to punctuate and sustain the course of the dialogue (*entretien*). Weak words to sustain speech itself: they add nothing to the meaning, they do not connect, they hold open the place of speech. Sarah liked to speak; she insisted on the necessity of dialogue: "We must talk," "We haven't talked for ages," "So, tell me about your holiday."

In this sense, philosophy is responsible for the phatic function of the entire discourse of meaning—I mean for nonmythical discourse, for what does not itself produce its object but is produced in indefinite pursuit of "the thing itself," always already there, but never here. Philosophy maintains the opening of meaning. In other words, it does not allow sense to be deposited (nor to rest); it does not allow it to close in upon itself. When it does close the result is ideology (*Camera obscura*, inversion of the image), nonthought, when neither call to be heard nor phenomenon to save. The opening of sense is truth.

Truth, not finality. Sarah did not write under the impetus of an end: neither goal nor achievement, but so fleeting, always one foot in the next book. If she shared with her time the jubilation of endless interpretations and the multiplication of truths, this was against the backdrop of a more remote and severe truth, the name of which is necessity. She speaks of herself when she writes, "Thus, for Empedocles as for Freud there is no finality: a necessity reigns which merges into the repetition of the same in difference" (Kofman 1991a, 50). Sarah had the somewhat rare sense of sober necessity, without the grandiloquence of destiny and equally without bitterness: just a touch between sadness and joy. It is in this tone that she finally wrote on the first page of *Rue Ordener, Rue Labat:* "Maybe all my books have been the detours required to bring me to write about 'it'" (Kofman 1996, 3).

What "it"? In fact, "who," or rather, neither exactly the one nor the other: neither her pen nor her father, but a "same" to which she felt "obligated." Repetition of the same: not the catatonia of a "self" that withdraws into itself, but rehearsal (*répétition*) in the theatrical sense—an essay, sketch, or repetition of propositions that must each time be displaced and fashioned, "winding paths" that lead straight ahead. Attempts at identification for an identity always to come, or rather always to return from the immemorial. Attempts at the unidentifiable, not unlike the motifs of Lacoue-Labarthe, who wrote in a text on Artaud dedicated "to the memory of Sarah": "To write is to say how one dies. And it is thought itself" (Lacoue-Labarthe 1995). There is perhaps some Artaud in Sarah. For example, I believe I can hear her in this sentence: "To practice metaphysics is to undertake the meta, to add something extra to the immediate and rudimentary rusticity of one's being, not to raise oneself to the great universal conceptual ideas which leave the physical behind and give only the meta and nothing else" (Artaud 1956, 177)

But finally, *who, Sarah?* She wrote apropos of Nietzsche: "But who 'himself'? The Nietzsche that he would 'become[,]' . . . the promise that he represented? . . . But to say of someone that he promises is also to declare that he has not yet arrived at that which 'he' presages" (Kofman 1993a, 165). Sarah herself was perpetually suspended between her necessarily unfulfilled promise and her assurance, which was nothing other than that of "it," in other words, that of a primary errancy no less buried than the coming of the promise, that of an *Unheimlichkeit* of childhood in its entirety.

It is in this sense that she was a little girl who had to and was able to fashion for herself the identity of she who must constantly replay who she is—if that may be called "being"—constantly put it into play, try it differently. At once opinionated, stubborn, obstinate, never giving up. Sometimes that led to conflict. But this she sought only to end, on condition that she was recognized, not necessarily as being right, but as existing, and on condition that it was not she who was denied (and, for example, that I had not sought to poison her by allowing Trilling to smoke a cigar during a meeting).

To replay constantly, to revise the interpretation, to try another perspective, to be in the course of interminable analysis. Sarah represented this allegory: "Interminable Analysis Leaning over the Troubling Strangeness of Writing." But this allegory transforms itself into "Interminable Writing of Analytic Strangeness." Sarah never ceased to analyze the father of analysis and, in particular, to show how he attacks the woman in order to "fix and freeze her definitively in a type that corresponds with his 'ideal of femininity' " (Kofman 1985a, 222). A "type": did Sarah pay attention to the everyday sense of the word? She would have liked to laugh at it. ("*Un type*" is French slang for "guy.")

The woman, of course, is Sarah "herself" (once again, she would not have omitted the quotation marks). She is the one who runs throughout the analysis; she is the analysis "itself," the analysis of the analysis, the one who practices the "impossible profession" of analysis: "The plasticity of the 'ends' of the analytic profession makes of it more than a determinate technique, a sort of game with variable rules, adjusted to the temperament or to the underlying preferences of each player" (Kofman 1983b, 13). Her own rules, and her temperament, called for the interminable course of words, the unattainable infancy of meaning: "I spent my time reading everything anyone brought me: from the *Vermot Almanach* to *Life of the Ants* by Maeterlinck. In a notebook I kept a list of the words I didn't understand and looked up their meanings in the dictionary" (Kofman 1996, 76). There are those, male or female, who seek models in books, who only stop at certain chosen voices, and there are those, male or female, who seek an infinite renewal of meaning, an analysis more interminable than any turning over of the past.

With Sarah, the analysis of analysis—interpretation and dissolution—comes with its identification: it is the name of Nietzsche, in other words the one whom, along with Freud, Sarah analyzed and commented upon the most. Their two names run from one end to the other of her books, and the dedication to *Pourquoi rit-on?* is itself a program, moreover a difficult one: "with all my wishes for great Freudian if not Nietzschean laughter." The name of Nietzsche is the name of the master of the fiction of a "becoming himself" (Kofman 1993a, 165). He becomes himself in becoming "all the names of history." Sarah wants to lend herself to the play of all the names of Nietzsche; she espouses this plasticity, but she mixes with it the "becoming-woman" of all those names as the truth of every philosopher. It is as though all these names become a single name once more, Sarah, name of a woman or woman-name that names the plasticity of all the others. "*Ecce Mulier* Sarah," she wrote on my copy of *Explosions I,* and perhaps on others.

Neither a "philosopher" nor a "woman philosopher" but rather the woman for every philosopher, the philosophers' "rival" (Kofman 1985a, 222) but also the vita of their truth and their logic (Kofman [1979] 1986b, 223), their mother, their sister, and their lover, or rather, finally, philosophy "itself," that which makes fun of philosophy, or goes infinitely beyond it, or even goes without it, and embarks it upon a course more obscure and troubled than any discourse, but also more bare and more alive.

———

In other words, more mortal. The certainty of necessity is also that of a "text dominated by an investigation which is not, at any moment, complete without being immediately invalidated: in it the work of Eros is always undermined by the silent activity of the death instincts" (Kofman 1991b, 121). If speech does not accumulate a capital of significations, it brings forth that which must in the end suffocate it. It becomes itself the desire to have done with its own course. When Sarah used to say, toward the last days, that she could no longer even read, she was not giving a sign, an effect of something else: she was pointing to the thing itself. No longer to read (but also, for Sarah, no longer to listen to music, no longer to see paintings or films), no longer to write, no longer to live. She said to me, "Look, I read this book and already I can't recall what is in it." The next moment, I proved her wrong and she laughed, once again, a little. That was at her place, that last time, with Alexandre. It was the course stopped, interrupted with no possibility of resumption, or the same course finally precipitated clearly into its endlessness, into its insupportable absence of ending. A sort of clear madness that looks straight ahead into the truth and sees that it sees nothing there and that this cannot be said, nor can that which is affirmed in it (or that which is promised?). But it sees that an uninterrupted fidelity can nevertheless be spoken, in a voice of extreme suffering. As a result I say it anyway (seeing her again already on her way, frozen, and knowing that I will not make her laugh): run, Sarah!

Sarah Kofman's Skirts

PENELOPE DEUTSCHER AND KELLY OLIVER

French philosopher Sarah Kofman took her life on October 15, 1994, leaving a corpus of over twenty books: on Nietzsche, Freud, and Derrida; on Plato, Rousseau, Comte, and Kant; on Diderot, Shakespeare, Nerval, Wilde, and Hoffman; on Blanchot; and on her experience of the German occupation of France, as well as autobiographical pieces. Jacques Derrida wrote, in his homage to Kofman, that she had known and read Nietzsche and Freud, in every fold of their work, like no one else in this century (Derrida 1997, 137). She was a colleague of Derrida, Jean-Luc Nancy, and Philippe Lacoue-Labarthe, with whom she edited the Galileé Philosophie en effet publishing series over twenty years. She was recognized in her lifetime as a contemporary French intellectual, gave many radio interviews on her new publications, and caused a public debate about the need for state reform of tertiary institutions when university promotions were repeatedly withheld from her. She described herself as one of the "68 generation," a radical who had written a thesis under Deleuze, marginalized within the university system not as a woman but as a subversive philosopher connected with Nietzschean, Derridean, and psychoanalytic theory (Kofman with Ender 1993, 20). Well known as Kofman was, little was published on her philosophical work during her lifetime.

It is often the case in contemporary French academe that substantial commentary is not written on living philosophers. In her book on Derrida, Kofman dryly mocked this convention: "Death alone, this is how tradition would have it, legitimates commentary, the criticism of texts newly elevated to the dignity of an oeuvre of which it is now licit to bring to the surface the themes and the theses" (1984b, 15).

Only posthumously has it been possible to read sustained reflection by French intellectuals such as Derrida, Françoise Collin, Nancy, Monique Schneider, and others on Sarah Kofman. By contrast, Kofman's work had been the object of anglophone commentary for a long time before she died. Still, Kofman has been a consistently elusive figure, well known but hard to classify within Nietzsche studies, little discussed among psychoanalytic theorists despite the overwhelming role of psychoanalytic theory in her work, and equally difficult to classify from a feminist perspective, despite the feminist themes in her work.

A series of commentators such as Proust (1997) and Derrida (1997) have focused on Kofman's reconception of life, and in the Foreword to this volume, Jean-Luc Nancy writes that the connection between life and work is what he finds particularly interesting in Kofman's work. Though Kofman took the life/work opposition to be fundamental to the philosophical tradition, her most compelling interpretations of philosophers are informed by her intricate destabilization of this opposition. But because Kofman challenges philosophical conventions, her works can appear as maverick commentaries on individual philosophers, particularly when read in isolation from each other. This collection of essays on her work recuperates Kofman from the genre of commentators about whom one does not write commentary.

KOFMAN ON FREUD

The first works of Kofman to be translated into English were her two major works on Freud: her first book, *The Childhood of Art*, written in 1970 (translation 1988c), and *The Enigma of Woman: Woman in Freud's Writings*, written in 1980 (translation 1985a). *The Childhood of Art* is a little-known, intensely scholarly, and broad-ranging interpretation of Freud on art, literature, and aesthetics, "so rich, so acute, so exemplarily lucid in its reading of Freud," recalls Derrida (1997, 152). *Childhood* is a fascinating dossier that analyzes every instance in which literary works and artwork serve as figure, example, or object of interpretation for Freud. Kofman embarks from Freud's ambivalent declarations concerning the limits of the application of psychoanalysis to art. She opens out an immense reading that moves to a Freud for whom the primary processes of dream work are found to be parallel to those concealed in literary work and artwork. The question of art ingeniously becomes the occasion for a book-length construction of Freud as a sustained theorist of the psychic as "trace," "différance," or "textuality," deconstructing oppositions between origin and representation, creator and creation, primary and secondary processes, life and text. Kofman realizes a scrupulous reading that entirely rethinks Freud.

Most anglophone readers first came to know Kofman through her second major book on Freud of a decade later, *The Enigma of Woman*. As Monique Schneider clarifies, Kofman makes her own intervention into the Freudian text, "impertinently" disengaging its implicit content of internal contestation. Her intervention is grounded in a concept of the text as a mobile network of thoughts, and her project is to constitute the mobility of this network, rather than "catching the text out in flagrante delicto" (Schneider 1997, 40). Kofman is suspicious of moments when the traditional philosopher tries to stabilize the network of thoughts at work in his text into a consistent, controlled line of thought, for example, in authorial metastatements explaining the real intent of the text. She argues that the exposure of phallocentrism, while crucial, should not suppress the mobility of a text. The politics of exposing phallocentrism should operate in tandem with a politics of exposing textual heterogeneity.

KOFMAN AND FEMINIST PHILOSOPHY

Kofman was entirely resistant to any suggestion that hers was a feminine voice, resistant to the concepts of *écriture féminine* and *parler femme*. There has been great interest in those contemporary theorists grouped, if erroneously, within a series labeled as New French Feminisms. Kofman's work resists inclusion in that series. Kofman never wrote about female desire, never tried to remetaphorize femininity or to speak the feminine: "I don't accept that there's a writing somehow 'proper to women.' I'm a partisan of clarity, of rational, well-constructed texts" (Kofman with Jaccard 1986, 7). As Hermsen comments, she also does not work "with or on" female writers (Kofman with Hermsen 1992, 65). There is no sense in which Kofman engaged with the work of women philosophers, historical or contemporary. It might seem, then, that Kofman has little to say to feminist concerns, and she was not involved in the feminist movement. But she identified the substantial work she achieved on the positioning of women in the history of philosophy as housing her feminist position: "My position as a woman philosopher marks itself in this manner, and my feminist position can be found in these kinds of readings" (Kofman with Ender 1993, 14).

Kofman suggested that her feminist engagement could be seen in her specific philosophical methodology, and indeed in the very fact that she wrote. Above all, Kofman suggested that her feminism was evident in her interest in demonstrating how the great masculine masters were governed by the irrational domain of their sexual economy.

The male philosopher's pretension to a transcendence of his sexual economy is sustained, Kofman would also add, at women's expense. The history of metaphysics is one that sustains such binary oppositions as that between the intelligible and the sensible, and one that also associates women with the sensible (Kofman with Ender 1993, 17). In this sense, the pretensions of philosophy to transcend the domain of the sensible are sustained at the expense of the feminine, which serves as the figure of that from which the male philosopher would distance himself. It is at this point that Kofman's feminism comes together with her project of destabilizing the pretensions of traditional philosophers. Kofman wanted to discredit philosophy's traditional self-image in favor of an alternative conception of philosophical writing.

INTERPRETING THE PHILOSOPHER'S SEXUAL ECONOMY: THE DEBT TO PSYCHOANALYSIS

Kofman developed a methodological approach to philosophical texts that involved analyzing a philosopher's sexual economy. This methodology, she explains (Kofman with Ender 1993, 12), first began with her work on Auguste Comte's *Aberrations: Le devenir-femme d'Auguste Comte* (1978a). Kofman argues that Comte's sexual economy interconnects with the production of his positivist system. A paranoid position with regard to femininity connects with his conceptualization of three ages in which women are denied access to the valorized positivist age. But Comte's sexual economy is described by Kofman as mobile. In a later phase of his work, a melancholic identification with his dead love, Clotilde de Vaux, interconnects with a philosophical position less excluding of femininity (Kofman with Jardine 1991, 105). Such a reading is particularly significant, Kofman argues, in the context of a philosopher who is presented in the university tradition as particularly objective, scientific, and rigorous, divorced from the domain of the drives.

Kofman describes herself straightforwardly as following a psychoanalytic approach in her reading of Comte (Kofman with Ender 1993, 13), and in the case of her readings of Kant and Rousseau, Kofman's debt to a psychoanalytic approach is again evident. This is emphasized in secondary material on these readings. Whether critics are impressed by this aspect of the reading (Fermon 1997, 103), or wary of it (Tahon 1997, 83), or neutral with respect to it as Natalie Alexander is in Chapter 8, the view that Kofman is psychoanalyzing the philosophers is uncontested. Kofman also describes in numerous contexts her identificatory relationship with Freud, and so we are unsurprised to see some form of analysis of the philosophers apparently being undertaken. This raises an important issue in the interpretation of her work, namely, the relationship between the psychoanalytic and deconstructive approaches.

In *Le respect des femmes* (Kofman 1982b, partially translated in Kofman 1982a and 1989b), Kofman herself expresses wariness of a simple psychoanalytic reading of Rousseau that would class him as hysteric or paranoiac (1982b, 150n). She also expresses wariness of any approach that would sustain a simple opposition between the "life" and the "work" of an author, as if the latter should be seen as an expression or translation of the latter. As she writes, if the "life" writes itself in texts, it is itself also a text (18). Kofman should not be seen as reducing texts by reference to an author's pathological case history, life, psyche, neurosis, paranoiac personality, unconscious, or drives, understood as outside of, or governing, or explaining the text. Kofman finds in her earliest work on Freud a theoretical apparatus that precisely destabilizes such oppositions. The works of an author and the relationship between them, as she glosses Freud, cannot be understood *from* the author's life (Kofman 1988a, 88). For Freud, says Kofman, the life is not extratextual. Therefore, so long as one does not consider the author or the author's life as an extratextual domain "explaining" the life, it is entirely appropriate to read text and life intertextually (Kofman 1988c, 102).

Kofman's deployment of psychoanalytic readings is not grounded in a confidence in a split between text and author, or a split between text and "psychobiography." To the contrary, each of her readings is grounded in a project to destabilize separations between rational philosophy and the author's life, blood, drives, and desires. It is Kofman's contention that these domains cannot be severed. She undermines the philosopher's pretension to free himself or herself from such murky domains through the life of the mind.

ANALYZING THE RETURN OF METAPHYSICS

Kofman's readings of Freud and Nietzsche operate quite differently from her interpretation of the libidinal economy of traditional philosophical texts. However, we have seen Kofman's argument that figures of femininity serve as blind spots, indicating weak points in philosophical arguments (Kofman with Hermsen 1992, 65). If this is true of Comte and Kant, what shall we say of Freud and Nietzsche? What do figures of femininity indicate to Kofman in the work of philosophers such as Freud and Nietzsche who do not pretend that philosophy is distanced from sexual economy? It is interesting that Kofman still offers a symptomatic reading of such philosophers. Freudian and Nietzschean metaphors of femininity are symptoms of a lurking metaphysics that can be unveiled in the work of writers Kofman takes to be antimetaphysical.

How does Kofman argue this of Freud and Nietzsche? Although Freud destabilizes oppositions between origin and representation, Kofman argues that his material on femininity subtly reinstates this opposition and is therefore a blind spot in his work. Freud's unstable texts reconstitute a position he has also undermined, that there is an original truth to women (women as castrated) that is repressed by the child. Exposing Freud's phallocentrism in *The Childhood of Art*, Kofman also exposes a lurking metaphysics in Freud that undermines his most deconstructive position on psychic textuality. (See Chapter 9 of this volume.)

Kofman argues that Nietzsche puts under erasure the opposition between masculine and feminine (Kofman with Jardine 1991, 108) and, she adds elsewhere, the oppositions between art and science, unconscious and conscious, and so on (Kofman 1973, 60). This project of putting metaphysical oppositions under erasure is one that she claims can be understood as interconnecting with Nietzsche's sexual economy, which she locates in his self-presentation as "possess[ing] a double system of evaluations that comes from his mother on one side, and from his father on the other" (Kofman with Jardine 1991, 108–109). This Nietzsche is presented at length in Kofman's massive works, *Explosion I* and *Explosion II* (1992, 1993a, translation forthcoming). In an early work, *Nietzsche and Metaphor* (1993b), which is discussed by Paul Patton in Chapter 5 and Alan Schrift in Chapter 12, one constant theme is her emphasis on a Nietzsche who mocks the philosopher's confidence in truth, a Nietzsche for whom truth originates in an abyss of metaphor. This is a truth about truth for which Nietzsche has the stomach, but not many other philosophers, who instead treat truth as a woman they hope to unveil, to win, though they don't know how to begin. However, it is the philosopher's sexual economy that constitutes the blind spot in the philosophical text. Although Kofman regards both Freud and Nietzsche as having importantly deconstructed metaphysical concepts, she believes that vigilant readings still must address sites in their work where metaphysical concepts return. She argues that their discussions of women and femininity are particularly symptomatic of such a return and so bear close philosophical scrutiny.

KOFMAN'S LIFE

Kofman took her life shortly after the publication of her autobiographical narrative, *Rue Ordener, Rue Labat* (translated 1996). At the end of her life, and after *Rue Ordener*, she felt herself disastrously unable to continue to read or write. *Rue Ordener* and an earlier work, *Paroles suffoquées* (Stifled words) (1987b), recount Kofman's experience of the German occupation, the removal of her father, his death in a concentration camp, the avoidance of capture through concealment of her and her mother in Paris with a Christian woman (Mémé), the trouble this caused for her relationship with her mother, and her eventual turn to philosophy later in her teens. (See Kelly Oliver, Chapter 10, and Tina Chanter, Chapter 11, in this volume.)

After the publication of this short autobiography, and particularly after her death, commentators were struck by the extent to which themes presented in *Rue Ordener* echoed themes Kofman had repeatedly located in the vast number of philosophers and literary writers she studied throughout her corpus. Kofman opens her autobiography with the suggestion that her works of philosophy have been a way of recounting "ça." She left her life as though daring commentators to read her own philosophical works as Kofman herself had read so many other philosophers, reading the life as text in interconnection with the literal texts. If Kofman had worn the masks of Freud and Nietzsche, she provoked her commentators to wear the mask of Kofman.

Thus, Jean-Luc Nancy in the Foreword suggests that Kofman's readings of Freud stage her taking the father to task for having paralyzed the girl. Kofman, he suggests, "never ceased to analyze the father of analysis, and in particular to show how he attacks the woman in order to 'fix and freeze her definitively in a type that corresponds with his 'ideal of femininity.' . . . The woman, of course, is Sarah 'herself.'" Derrida reflects on Kofman's first work, *The Childhood of Art*. Now, he suggests, it strikes him as an "anamnèse autobiographique[,] . . . une autobiogriffure": "All of the positions—of the father, the mothers, of the substitution of the mothers, of the laugh and of life as a work of art—can already be recognized there, rigorously assigned" (Derrida 1997, 152).

The connection between the psychic life, the text of the life, the text of the psyche, and the philosophical texts may be the single strongest implicit and explicit theme in the nascent genre of "Kofman studies." Kofman will have had the last laugh if her death has provoked interpretations of her philosophy influenced by her philosophy, Kofmanian interpretive masks in philosophers from whom she certainly desired the recognition. Kofman, who loved jokes, might have laughed to see

Derrida unexpectedly offering so very Kofman-like an interpretation of *The Childhood of Art,* in memoriam.

Will such forms of commentary recognize Kofman the philosopher? Complex methodological issues are involved in how Kofman's philosophy is to be read in terms of her life. The degree to which it mattered to Kofman that she be read and recognized as practicing serious, rigorous philosophy is evident in her interviews. It is particularly germane, then, to pose the question of how successfully she has been and will be read as a philosopher. Thinking of the persona Sarah Kofman is not inappropriate to thinking about the philosopher. The question is not whether, but how, we should figure the life and identities of Sarah Kofman. For it is already possible to begin interpretative work concerning the strategies that are seen in the posthumous figuring of Kofman by commentators.

One image of Kofman that has been seen is that of the gay, taunting, impudent girl. For example, Schneider refers to her impertinent reading of Freud (Schneider 1997, 42), Proust to her playfulness as a woman philosopher (Proust 1977, 8), and Smock to the way she "liked to play the role of the mocking girl whose laughter interrupts the philosopher at his desk" (Smock 1996, x). Another image is that of the child Kofman, again an image overdetermined by Kofman, who left a narrative of childhood as one of her final works. The image of the philosopher as a little girl emerges in Nancy's evocation in the Foreword of Kofman as "mobilized by the incessantly new, like [a] child" and "able to fashion for herself the identity of she who must constantly replay who she is," and in Jean Maurel's "Enfances de Sarah" (1997), in which Maurel emphasizes the childhood stolen from Kofman, the child dormant in her, reading this into multiple titles and themes in Kofman's philosophical work (*Camera obscura; Explosion II: Les enfants de Nietzsche; The Childhood of Art; Comment s'en sortir?* and so on). Some of the most frequently recurring posthumous figurings of Kofman have included the insolent girl, the traumatized child, and the figure of tragedy. (Collin [1997, 20] offers an important counterpoint by emphasizing Kofman's Sadeian cruelty.) Turning to the narrative of Kofman's life, commentators often find catastrophe: the trauma of Kofman's childhood, the tragedy of her suicide. At an homage to Kofman held by her colleagues at the Sorbonne, Elisabeth de Fontenay suggested that it is precisely Kofman's suicide that provokes one to reflect on the relationship between her life and work, or between her work and her two deaths, the one that she narrowly escaped as a child, the other of 1994. Françoise Armengaud suggests that Kofman's death in 1994 could be thought of as the Holocaust having finally caught up with her, killing her with the delayed action of a time bomb (Armengaud 1997).

It is not surprising that many of the commentaries that interconnect Kofman's life with her work tend to interpret her philosophical writing in terms of the life of a traumatized child or woman: these are memorial essays responding to the death of a contemporary. This is also an appropriate response to Kofman's complex theorization of the life-text interconnection. But given a tendency to read the work of women philosophers through marginalizing lenses, such interpretations are not without their risks. A sudden preoccupation with a tragic "Kofman" persona may inhibit strong interpretation of her philosophy. How can the connection be made without danger to our perceptions of Kofman as a philosopher? Perhaps by incorporating the challenge from Kofman—and many others, including Nietzsche—to the fiction that philosophy is a domain of dispassionate rationality disconnected from the drives and the body of the philosopher.

THE STRUCTURE OF THIS BOOK

This book is divided into four parts: "Literature and Aesthetics," "Philosophy and Metaphor," "Women, Feminism, and Psychoanalysis," and "Jews and German Nationalism."

LITERATURE AND AESTHETICS

Enigmas begins with a previously untranslated essay by Kofman herself, "The Imposture of Beauty: The Uncanniness of Oscar Wilde's *Picture of Dorian Gray.*" This chapter was originally published as the first chapter in *L'imposture de la beauté et autres textes* (1995b). In this essay, Kofman develops four major themes: bad influence, the mirror stage, the screen, and mourning.

Kofman discusses the importance of influence in Wilde's *Picture of Dorian Gray.* She points out that Dorian Gray recognizes himself in his portrait for the first time only after Lord Henry "judges the picture to be a wonderful work of art and a wonderful likeness." This suggests that it is Lord Henry's influence that leads Dorian Gray to recognition. But influence is only effective when it touches on something from Dorian's childhood that makes him susceptible. In Kofman's analysis, it is this influence that creates "an artificial being who lives a borrowed life." In *The Picture of Dorian Gray,* influence is always bad influence because it produces mere copies or impostures, artificial beings, like Dorian Gray, living borrowed

lives. Ultimately, Kofman suggests, Oscar Wilde is exercising his own seductive influence over the reader, making the reader accept the impossible and the incredible even while creating the uncanny sensation that
necessarily calls it into question.

As in much of her other work, Kofman's analysis of Wilde's story turns
around the figure of a screen. We might be tempted to say that the appearance is on one side of the screen and the reality on the other, if it
weren't for the multiplication of screens in Kofman's reading. With *The
Picture of Dorian Gray*, the imposture of beauty—the idea that beauty is
eternal—serves as a protective screen for the fragile, perishable nature
of beauty. The painting of Dorian Gray, hidden behind its own screen,
protects Dorian from aging and from his sins, ultimately protecting him
against change and loss. And, most importantly, the picture of Dorian
Gray serves as a screen for another picture, the picture of his mother as
a bacchante.

Here, Kofman insists that the mother cannot be ignored. Behind the
scenes of Dorian's desire for eternal beauty is his beautiful mother. As she
does so often, Kofman reminds us that the masculine figures she is analyzing (be it Nietzsche, Freud, or the fictional character Dorian Gray) are
the sons of mothers. Rather than face the loss or death of his mother, Dorian incorporates her. Rather than give her up through the processes of
mourning, he makes his mother himself.

Kofman concludes that a double reading of the Wilde story is possible,
"one reading serving as a golden mask for the other." The most obvious interpretation, the moral interpretation—that the guilty never escape the all-
seeing eye of conscience—is merely a screen for another, more dangerous
reading. Like an Apollonian mask covering over the terrors of the Dionysian,
the moral interpretation recuperates order. Yet on the other side of the
screen, Kofman sees a more dangerous moral to this story, an antimorality
moral. She suggests that *The Picture of Dorian Gray* can be read as the lesson
that "the excessive, mutilating puritanism that society imposes can only lead
anyone who refuses to submit to it to adopt a morbid solution (that of
melancholy) and to regress to the narcissistic stage of magic and animism."

Because society, with the voice of the paternal grandfather, had condemned Dorian's mother, marked her with the scarlet letter, she loses her
beauty. But Dorian refuses to accept society's condemnation; he refuses to
lose his beautiful mother. Rather than mourn her loss and reconcile himself to the puritanical codes of his paternal grandfather, Dorian incorporates the image of his beautiful mother into himself, Kofman argues. He
saves her image from tarnish and decay by making her beauty his own and
transferring all of her moral and physical blemishes, along with his own,

onto the painting. In the end, then, the picture of Dorian Gray is a screen, an Apollonian mask, for the Dionysian picture of the mother as bacchante. Oscar Wilde's text itself becomes an imposture, a screen, that enjoys "tricking his readers by serving them up the picture of Dorian so as better to conceal the other picture, which secretly haunts them."

But the art of constructing screens and wearing masks is not for the weak at heart. Only those strong enough to wear masks because they know that they need them acknowledge that the changing, decaying turmoil of reality—this Dionysian "truth"—is too powerful to bear. The strength of life depends on serious playing at the surface: in Chapter 1, Kofman says, "The aestheticism of Wilde's hero can be understood by using the categories that Nietzsche sets up in *The Birth of Tragedy*, where he systematizes the teaching of the Greeks, who knew that one must remain on the surface and be superficial out of profundity, that one must not try to look 'beneath the skin,' and that on the contrary one must camouflage 'artistically' everything that is distressing and liable to make one feel sick."

The Dionysian face that is too terrible to see, that needs to be masked, is the face of death. The face of death is also, of course, the face of life. And this is precisely what Dorian Gray (and so many other male heroes that Kofman analyzes) cannot face: life is death. The artist and those who can live artistically recognize the Dionysian face by masking it. On the other hand, those who merely turn to art or go to the theater to escape life, death, and ultimately themselves are the weaklings who, like Dorian Gray, mistake faking it for making art. They are content with fakes that distract them from everything terrifying about life (death), whereas the stronger artistic sorts take their plays more seriously and realize that every mask risks bringing them face to face with life, death, and themselves, even as those same masks make it possible to live (and die) with the Dionysian flux.

In Chapter 2, engaging texts by Kofman—*Don Juan ou le refus de la dette*, *Mélancolie de l'art*, "L'imposture de la beauté," *Séductions: De Sartre à Héraclite*, and *Autobiogriffures*—and Louis-René des Forêts, Ann Smock explores relationships between strong and weak art, artist and audience, laughter and seriousness, life and death.

Smock frames her analysis of Kofman's work with des Forêts's story of an oboe player named Frédéric Molieri who one evening fills in for the lead singer in a production of Mozart's *Don Giovanni* when the baritone breaks down during the performance. Without any previous experience on stage, this oboe player steps out of the pit and into the opera. His performance is so dazzling that the opera director immediately asks him to sign a contract. Although Molieri reluctantly signs the contract, he insists that he cannot guarantee that he will ever again be able to repeat his performance.

Smock explores the nature of the risk that Molieri took by climbing onto the stage and the continued risk he took every subsequent time he did so. She reads des Forêts's story as a tale of the risks of art and the even greater danger of the faker replacing the artist. If art isn't dangerous, it is not effective; it is not strong art. If the audience of performance or writing is lulled into complacency, then art becomes fake and we become numb to life. Why would we become numb to life? Smock's essay seems to ask. Her answer is that we become numb to life when we are afraid to face death. The fear of death and the fear of life ultimately amount to the same thing. In order to engage life, the artist must be willing to risk death every time he or she steps onto the stage.

Art is doubly dangerous. It requires that we risk our lives and ourselves— we could say face our lives and ourselves—or it can become a flimsy crutch, always threatening to break and send us crashing to the floor. Smock suggests that Kofman describes the danger that art poses if it becomes a crutch because art, writing in particular, like Hoffmann's Murr the cat, can tear narcissism to shreds and leave the individual without any metaphysical or egological foundation. Following Kofman, Smock insists, if beauty, and not some fraud, is really what you prize above all, then you'll be as willing to cast aside that mask as cherish it. Perhaps you'll toss it nonchalantly out just because you love it.

Smock tells us that Kofman knew the risks of great art and the necessary connection between art and life, that she wouldn't settle for complacency or faking it. And ultimately, when it comes to death (and life, for that matter) there is no faking it. Smock asks if we are up to dying, up to dropping our masks and playing our parts. Her taunting is itself Kofmanian, reminiscent of Kofman's analysis of Dorian Gray's love of theater in Chapter 1, where she says that what was unforgivable about Sybil was that "by her suicide she should show—without shame, without a mask—that death is not just a game and that in life, unlike in the theater, it is never possible to 'take one's moves again.'"

Embroidered throughout Chapter 2 are allusions to Kofman's own death, which, like her life and work, continues to menace her audience. In Smock's essay, des Forêts's character of Molieri seems to pose as Kofman's double. Once the greatest opera singer in all of Europe because he risked everything (and nothing) by stepping out of the pit and onto the stage, Molieri ends his short but brilliant career by turning in a lewd, disgusting, and hugely disappointing performance as Don Giovanni, the role that his own performance had defined for that opera house. Smock suggests that Molieri would no longer stand for the complacency of his audience, who came to be entertained without taking any risks themselves. His final, disappointing performance provokes them into confronting not only Molieri and the opera director, but also themselves and the purpose of art itself. Molieri's last performance (like Kofman's?) is an outrage, but an outrage that demands a self-reflexive response.

Chapter 3, Duncan Large's "Kofman's Hoffmann," takes up the theme of the double in Kofman's analyses of E. T. A. Hoffmann's fiction in three of her texts: "The Double Is/and the Devil," "Vautour rouge," and *Autobiogriffures*. Large argues that in "The Double Is/and the Devil," Kofman critically engages with Freud's all too schematic reading of the psychosis of Hoffmann's hero in "The Sandman," Nathaniel, as precipitated by the return of a repressed infantile castration anxiety. Large suggests that Kofman goes beyond Freud's reading in two ways: first, employing Freud's own concepts, Kofman recuperates the feminine characters whom Freud occludes (Nathaniel's mother, the Sandman as maternal); second, Kofman goes beyond the Freudian scheme and reinstates the *uncanny* as something much more than a simple "theme" or "concept." Large argues that Kofman compensates for Freud's excessively neat solution to its problems by opening up the question of Hoffmann's writing that Freud himself has repressed.

Large points out that this deconstructive emphasis on the textuality of Hoffmann's writing is sustained in the next study, "Vautour rouge," where Kofman diagnoses five textual levels in order to argue that Hoffmann's writing bears a "double stamp," which in turn produces a proliferation of self-relativizing narrative perspectives. In this analysis, Kofman draws on another Freudian concept, that of deferred action. Large maintains that here, in contrast to her analysis of "The Sandman," she also links the text's Dionysian proliferation of perspectives explicitly to Nietzsche, and in the latter part of her study she focuses on the marginalized figure of the hairdresser Pietro Belcampo/Peter Schoenfeld, whom she reads as Nietzsche's double, his laughter cutting through all the novel's metaphysical intricacies.

Large suggests that the textual doubling reaches its extreme in Kofman's final Hoffmann study, *Autobiogriffures*. Here, Kofman turns to Hoffmann's *Life and Opinions of Murr the Tomcat,* in which the operative conceit is that a self-educated tomcat is writing his autobiography on sheets that he has ripped out of his master's own life story. Kofman suggests that with this text, Hoffmann's work deconstructs the fundamental opposition between madness and reason. Large describes how it is in the (meta-)mimetic relation between representations of psychosis and the means of representation themselves that, for Kofman, Hoffmann is at his most Nietzschean.

In addition to tracing the influence of Nietzsche, Freud, and Derrida in Kofman's readings of Hoffmann, Large also concludes that Kofman's analysis of the intimate relation between textuality and madness in all three of her studies of Hoffmann's writings lays the groundwork for her subsequent explorations of the same nexus in the writings of Comte and Nerval (in the late 1970s) and ultimately those of Nietzsche himself, when in the *Explosion* books she squarely confronts the "madness" of Nietzsche's *Ecce Homo*.

PHILOSOPHY AND METAPHOR

Mary Beth Mader, in Chapter 4, also takes up the theme of the relationship between madness and reason, between suffering and logic. She delineates, develops, and extends Kofman's reading of Nietzsche's criticisms of Aristotelian logic in her essay "Les présupposés de la logique" from *Nietzsche et la scène philosophique*. Mader delineates Kofman's account of Nietzsche's genealogical and ontological arguments against Aristotelian logic. Kofman explains that Nietzsche's critique of logic consists of two prongs: logic is but a salve for the psychic pain of contradiction (the genealogical argument) and logic's law of identity actually falsifies the true changing nature of the world (the ontological argument). Mader argues that while Kofman's insight that logic is a species of catharsis can be profitably extended, her prioritization of Nietzsche's genealogy-over-ontology argument is misleading.

Extending Kofman's analysis, Mader suggests that we can embrace logic as a cathartic ordering practice when it is unburdened of its pretensions to veridicality without demonition. Mader argues that Kofman does not embrace the depth of Nietzsche's criticisms when she claims that his criticisms render logic only a tragic drama. Mader maintains that only someone committed to the illusion that logic *should* provide us with the truth about reality could read its source in human tragedy as a demotion.

Mader suggests that if the fictional nature of tragic drama does not delegitimate it, the falsifying nature of logic as catharsis should not delegitimate it either. She argues that the traditional ontological import of the laws of logic would be left behind without regret in a thorough Nietzschean understanding of logic, while their existential import makes them all-but-inevitable medicine. Mader concludes that it is not their existential import that causes them to succeed as ordering practices, though it is this ordering capacity that permits their therapeutic function. Like Nietzsche, Kofman is concerned with philosophy as therapy.

In Chapter 5, Paul Patton offers further interrogation of Kofman's analysis of Nietzsche. He discusses Kofman's *Nietzsche and Metaphor* in the context of other influential views, notably those of Derrida and Deleuze, about the nature of concept and metaphor and their place in philosophy. He argues that Kofman's work was important in that it was among the first to address the question of metaphor in Nietzsche: not only his constant use of metaphors throughout his writing, but also the manner in which he employed the concept of metaphor in his early theorization of the nature of human thought and knowledge.

Patton suggests that Kofman's discussion of Nietzsche's operational use of metaphor is especially significant in view of the manner in which his dissolution of the opposition between metaphor and concept in the essay "On Truth and Lies in a Nonmoral Sense" has inspired both Derrida's defense of generalized metaphoricity and Deleuze's dismissal of the concept of metaphor.

Patton retraces the argument of Nietzsche's "On Truth and Lies in a Nonmoral Sense" to show the sense in which he can only be said to employ a metaphor of metaphor in describing human language and thought and its relation to the *thing itself.* This implies a certain indeterminacy in the problem that Nietzsche identifies, which might be rendered determinate in more than one way. Patton suggests that the work of Derrida and Deleuze may be seen to follow the lead of this argument by refusing to admit any philosophical concept of metaphor and eventually by reconceptualizing the nature of concepts.

In Chapter 6, Pierre Lamarche traces another genealogy of influence and legacy between Kofman and Derrida. Lamarche begins with a discussion of Kofman's resistance to being called a Derridean. Reminiscent of Kofman's later analysis of influence (which is always bad) in Oscar Wilde's *Picture of Dorian Gray,* Lamarche quotes Kofman: "If I think 'as a Derridian,' just then I'm not thinking anymore." If anything, Lamarche's chapter shows how Kofmanian Derrida is in his *Specters of Marx.* Lamarche points out that Kofman's first chapter of *Camera obscura* (1973), on Marx, was first presented in Derrida's seminar on religion and philosophy, twenty years before Derrida's *Specters of Marx.* But of course, as Lamarche suggests, the genealogy of influence is more complicated.

In the first section of the chapter, Lamarche explores Kofman's focus on the relationship between ideological and religious metaphors in Marx's *German Ideology* and *Capital* in her essay "Marx: Black Magic." Lamarche argues that Kofman shows how Marx employs a series of metaphors that both modify and displace, but also uphold and expand upon, the notion of ideology formation as an inversion of base/superstructure, implied by the initial reference to the camera obscura metaphor. Note that once again Kofman engages in a psychoanalytic reading of Marx's texts in order to uncover a primary repression buried within them. Lamarche points out that although Kofman endorses the heterogeneity of Marx's texts, she points to his nostalgia for the ideological values of light, clarity, transparency, and truth betrayed through the metaphor of the camera obscura.

In the second section of the chapter, Lamarche presents a powerful engagement between Kofman's *Camera obscura* and Derrida's *Specters of Marx,* referring to their "common sensitivity." Lamarche shows how Derrida's reading of the centrality of the notions of specter and spectrality in the analysis of ideology, and the relationship between ideological and religious metaphor, were anticipated by Kofman. Lamarche connects Derrida's reanimation of Marx's argument that ideology is itself a specter with a body of sorts to Kofman's analysis of this body as a fetish for real equality and freedom. Here again Kofman searches for the pathology of her analysand, in this case Marx.

Lamarche concludes that although Derrida is to be congratulated for resuscitating a particular specter of Marx in order to deconstruct the ideology of the New World Order, he fails to "capitalize" on what Kofman identifies as the heterogeneity of Marx's work. This opening up of a reworking and unworking of texts, in this case Marx's, is what Lamarche sees as Kofman's legacy.

In Chapter 7, Françoise Duroux also discusses Kofman's legacy. Like Patton and Lamarche, she traces lines of influence; unlike them, however, she takes up the question of Kofman's status as a *woman* philosopher and how that affects her place in the history of philosophy. Duroux argues that Kofman is not just a professor like so many other professional philosophers; rather, she is an inventor because her philosophy "constructs another system, a countersystem in the polemic between the greats." Kofman is an innovator because she doesn't follow the rules of philosophical propriety.

Duroux says that in a sense, Kofman digs around in the dirty linens of the philosophers, looking for "the *motivating forces* of their construction: the *economy* of a concept, the *motives* of a system, the *interest* of the speculation." Kofman doesn't take her philosophers' words at face value but insists on making us face the pathology of their systems. In this way, Duroux suggests, Kofman commits a crime against philosophy by restoring the conditions of its production, not only the historical and social conditions but also the subjective and psychic conditions.

Duroux asks a series of provocative questions about why it is mostly women who engage in this "inappropriate" kind of analysis, which seems to require an aptitude for disrespect. She suggests that this lack of philosophical propriety is the result of "women who philosophize from within woman's situation rather than through its abandonment." The "crime against philosophy," then, is taking sexual difference seriously, even showing it off, lifting one's skirts like one of Kofman's favorite figures, Baubô.

Ultimately, Duroux sees in Kofman's readings of the philosophers a search for woman and, more particularly, the search for the mother. Kofman reads in Kant, Rousseau, Comte, Nietzsche, and others a system of thought produced through pathology, the system as the gain of illness, which "serves as a defense against insanity." Kofman's work is concerned with this precarious border between philosophy and madness.

At the conclusion of the chapter, Duroux asks us to consider Kofman's own defense, a defense that is shattered when Kofman turns her critical eye toward herself in one of her last books, her autobiographical *Rue Ordener, Rue Labat*. There, the double and doubled mother steps out of the shadows of her own motivation for looking for her/them in the writings of the philosophers. The theme of the double and doubled mother will return repeatedly in the next section.

WOMEN, FEMINISM, AND PSYCHOANALYSIS

In Chapter 8, Natalie Alexander takes up one of Kofman's philosophers, Kant, and shows how Kofman exposes his ethics as a defense against the mother. Like Lamarche and Patton, Alexander focuses on Kofman's analysis of metaphors and the relationship between metaphors and concepts. Like Mader, Alexander sees Kofman's reading strategy as a type of diagnosis for the sake of therapy.

Alexander analyzes Kofman's diagnosis of Kant's ethics in *Le respect des femmes (Kant et Rousseau)* in terms of three reading strategies: an aesthetic or rhetorical approach, a skeptical approach, and a therapeutic approach. Discussing the aesthetics or rhetoric of Kofman's text, Alexander centers her exploration on Kofman's metaphor of respect as an umbrella that distances us from wet and unpleasant natural elements, whose fabric can be torn and mended again because it is a manufactured artifice, a simple machine that people can control to protect themselves. Kofman argues that respect for women plays a crucial role in constituting Kant's moral philosophy, yet this respect, like an umbrella, serves to distance and protect men from women.

Alexander identifies the skeptical deconstructive strategy of juxtaposing and overturning opposites in Kofman's discussion of a series of opposites in Kant's ethics between wife and whore, pursuit and resistance, nature and humanity, dignity and utility, reason and inclination. Anchored in the figure of the mother, Kant's ethics moves around a sexual economy that distinguishes between women worthy of respect and those who are not respectable but are available for use. Kofman identifies Kant's disgust with animal vice and nature with an abhorrence of female sexuality. Alexander argues that throughout *Le respect des femmes* Kofman has been constructing a diagnostic genealogy with which she can trace the pathology that gives rise to Kant's ethics.

Like her analysis of Hoffmann in "The Double Is/and the Devil" and her reading of Oscar Wilde's character of Dorian Gray in "The Imposture of Beauty," in *Le respect des femmes* Kofman insists on returning the mother as double and doubled. Just as she reads Dorian Gray as the son of his mother, she reads Hoffmann's hero in "The Sandman," Nathaniel, as the son of his mother. So too she reads the great philosophers as sons of mothers. She traces this maternal genealogy through Kant, Rousseau, Freud, Nietzsche, and others, all the while diagnosing how it becomes pathologized within a patriarchal sexual economy. In Kofman's readings of the history of philosophy, the double mother becomes a symptom of a perverse sexual economy.

Obviously, Kofman's various readings of the pathologies of the philosophers rely on Freudian psychoanalytic theory. But as Penelope Deutscher argues in Chapter 9, Kofman undercuts the fundamental concepts of Freudian theory even as she employs them. Deutscher centers her analysis on two of Kofman's texts on Freud: *The Childhood of Art* and *The Enigma of Woman*. Through her readings of these two texts, Deutscher defends Kofman against the critics of her work who claim either that she identifies excessively with Nietzsche, Freud, and Derrida or that her engagements with them are not faithful enough. Deutscher shows how Kofman uses the theories of these thinkers against each other in order to produce her own philosophy.

Taking up Kofman's interpretation of Freud's musings on femininity, Deutscher demonstrates some of the ways in which Kofman turns Freud's own concepts back onto Freud, thereby seemingly endorsing those concepts, and at the same time calls his concepts into question through this turning. Kofman uses Nietzschean and Derridean strategies in order to displace the Freudian vocabulary. Deutscher proposes that by engaging these thinkers together, rather than confusing them, Kofman challenges them and the history of philosophy.

Specifically, Deutscher suggests that although Kofman seems to appeal to the Freudian concepts of castration and fetishism in *The Enigma of Woman,* she also undercuts those concepts. Deutscher concludes that by extending the Freudian notion of the instability of psychic truths to women, Kofman complicates the concept of castration and uncouples the Freudian association between truth and the castration of women.

In Chapter 10, Kelly Oliver also complicates Kofman's fidelity to Nietzsche and Freud by turning Kofman's concepts back onto Kofman's own work. Looking for screens, masks, and impostures (what Kofman often refers to as apotropaic figures) in Kofman's work, Oliver explores the ambiguous and double figure of the mother in her work on Nietzsche and Freud. Oliver argues that although in much of her work Kofman describes the ways that males come to terms with identification and separation with their mothers as symptoms of various pathologies, thereby challenging the Oedipal scenario as a normalizing operation, in other places she reinscribes these same figures within an Oedipal scenario and classic family romance.

Oliver diagnoses Kofman's ambiguity with regard to the Oedipal situation and family romance by turning to Kofman's autobiographical book, *Rue Ordener, Rue Labat*. Finding analogies between Kofman's analysis of Nietzsche's and Freud's relationship to the mother and Kofman's own relationship to her mother, Oliver situates Kofman between maternal and paternal laws, both operating within a patriarchal economy that demands the mother's suicide. (Oliver asks us to remember Jocasta, while Tina Chanter, in Chapter 11, asks us to think of Antigone and Kofman herself.)

Analyzing Kofman's descriptions of her relationship to Jewish food prohibitions during World War II, Oliver delineates and complicates the relationship between maternal and paternal law. She shows how even while Kofman is caught within the sacrificial economy of the Oedipal scenario and family romance, her work and life upset that economy. Oliver concludes that Kofman's "fidelity to her philosophical fathers has as its apotropaic counterpart her resistance to a paternal law that requires matricide and her own fantastic maternal genealogy that insists on turning her philosophical fathers into sons of mothers."

The tension between maternal and paternal authority is also a central focus of Chapter 11. Like Smock, Tina Chanter begins her essay in the theater; this time it is not the cavalier hero Don Juan whom we see but the overly serious Antigone. Chanter frames her analysis of Kofman's work and her relation to philosophy with a discussion of Antigone, in particular Kofman's review of Philippe Lacoue-Labarthe and Michel Deutsch's 1978 production of the play *Antigone*.

Through her subtle analysis of Kofman's "L'espace de la césure," and "Autobiographical Writings," Chanter creates an analogy between Kofman and Antigone, both of whom are caught between two laws and ultimately find suicide as their only way out. Like Oliver, Chanter identifies the tension between the two laws, maternal and paternal, in Kofman's account of her relation to her family's attempts to keep kosher during the war. Chanter identifies Kofman's desire with breaking the maternal command and loosening or suspending the paternal authority. Young Sarah wanted what was forbidden. Yet the circumstances during the war and her substitute maternal figure, who changed her diet and blamed her poor health on the food of her childhood, complicate the border between the pure and the forbidden.

Chanter relates this complicated space between the maternal and paternal authority of Kofman's childhood to her position within the academy, when after writing nineteen books she was not even the equivalent of a tenured professor, a fact that left her bitter. Chanter suggests that Kofman occupies a space between maternal and paternal authority, in a double bind that leaves her swinging to and fro: "The universality of her judgments, and the way she undercuts their universality each time she utters them, would be extraordinary if this swinging to and fro in a double bind, trying to justify herself as on a par with the male establishment and yet not simply allowing herself to be assimilated into it, were not so very familiar." Chanter's analysis here takes us back to Oliver's suggestion that within a patriarchal economy, maternal authority necessarily undercuts itself; maternal authority is authorized only insofar as it makes universal judgments and undercuts them at the same time.

Chanter points to a relationship in this in-between space between mourning and the law. She concludes that Kofman's illness and vomiting are the symptoms of her substitution of mourning for law. For Kofman, as for Antigone, "mourning 'becomes' the law, in the decorative sense of adorning it, but it also becomes subject to it, undergoing transformation of and by it." We are reminded of Kofman's diagnosis of Oscar Wilde's *Picture of Dorian Gray,* where in a perverse economy that prohibits mourning—Antigone is sentenced to death for engaging in its rituals—puritanical morality leads to neurosis. Mourning, its rituals, and fetishistic substitutions take the place of law when the law prohibits mourning. Mourning, like the food that Sarah vomits, like the maternal authority that regulates it, is both required and forbidden.

JEWS AND GERMAN NATIONALISM

In Chapter 12, Alan Schrift examines the last of Kofman's five books on Nietzsche, *Le mépris des Juifs: Nietzsche, les Juifs, l'antisémitisme.* Schrift discusses and critically assesses Kofman's defense of Nietzsche against the charge of anti-Semitism. While Schrift agrees with Kofman that Nietzsche was not the *reichsdeutsch* anti-Semite that his sister and others wanted him to be and that too many readers on both sides of the English Channel have thought him to be, he is not persuaded by Kofman's account that "in order for Nietzsche to become-Nietzsche, he had to become a Jew."

Schrift says that Kofman may be correct in suggesting that "ultimately Nietzsche becomes who and what he is by settling accounts, once and for all, 'with the Germany of the Reich, with his mother and his sister, and with the paternal substitutes who had been, among others, Wagner and Schopenhauer.' " And he thinks that she may be right as well to conclude that to settle these accounts meant settling accounts with the anti-Semitism that was perhaps their central unifying feature. But he remains skeptical of her general conclusion that Nietzsche's anti-Semitism can be regarded as a youthful excess that he eventually outgrew. Instead, Schrift offers several alternatives to this conclusion that suggest that although Nietzsche is not the racist anti-Semite that the Nazi ideologues tried to make him out to be, his attitude toward the Jews is at best ambivalent and deeply problematic.

In Chapter 13, Diane Morgan takes a different tack in diagnosing Kofman's reading of Nietzsche's *anti*-anti-Semitism in *Le mépris des Juifs*. Beginning with Kofman's analysis of Freud's essay "Negation" in her *Métier impossible*, Morgan explores Kofman's innovations concerning Freud's notion of negativity as it relates to self and national identity. Morgan reads two types of negation in Kofman's Freudian account: first, negation that works with the pleasure principle by expelling or denying elements that threaten the stability of identity, and second, negation that transforms the self-preserving instinct into an instinct for mastery that turns against the subject.

Morgan argues that Kofman's innovation concerning Freud is to see how the first, self-preserving type of negation turns into the second, self-destructive type of negation, especially in the drive to unify one's own thinking and life. She points to Kofman's readings of Freud and Nietzsche, which turn on that point where their own negations move from self-affirming to self-denying, where identification becomes identity; in Nietzsche's case this is when his identification with Wagner, Zarathustra, Dionysus, and Christ becomes his mad idea that he actually *is* Wagner, Zarathustra, Dionysus, and Christ.

Morgan extends Kofman's analysis of the psychic operation and economy of identification through negation when she considers the relationship between self-identity and national identity. Both self- and national identity operate through a series of identifications and negations. For example, Kofman denies Nietzsche's anti-Semitism by reading Nietzsche's own denials of his relation to his mother and his sister. Morgan complicates Kofman's conclusions by turning Kofman's concepts back onto her own texts. What of Kofman's own denials and identifications?

Following Kofman, Morgan concludes the chapter with the provocative suggestion that the attempt to unify one's own biography and biology, that is to say one's own life, through creating a fantastic genealogy that denies disparate aspects of one's personality and collapses ambivalence, contradiction, and diversity into identity, ultimately leads to death. Morgan turns to Kofman's own autobiographical story, *Rue Ordener, Rue Labat* (the story of two mothers, one Jewish and denied and one French and affirmed), in order to diagnose Kofman's own dangerous negations in the process of self- and national identity.

In a sense, Morgan's reading of Kofman takes us back to Kofman's reading of Oscar Wilde. Kofman identifies two types of negation, one that makes us stronger and one that makes us weaker, in Nietzschean terms, one that is life-affirming and one that is life-denying. Kofman also identifies two types of art, one that makes us stronger and one that makes us weaker, one that is life-affirming and one that is life-denying. What do art and negation have in common? The life-affirming art, negation, and identity face everything difficult in life, but with a sense of humor; they can laugh at themselves. But laughing at oneself is a risky business. It shouldn't be taken too far or an impropriety appropriate to opening life becomes a domineering sense of propriety that once again clamps down on life. If we are not careful, laughter at our own seriousness becomes the kind of serious laughter that belittles life and makes it seem worthless.

Perhaps it is appropriately disrespectful—keeping in mind Kofman's critique of respect and her insistence on troubling philosophy—to conclude with one of Kofman's favorite doubles, the figure of Baubô. Kofman sees Baubô as the female double of Dionysus, who represents fecundity and the eternal return of life. Baubô has a sense of humor. She takes life seriously by laughing at it. Recall that Baubô makes Demeter, the goddess of fertility, laugh by pulling up her skirts and showing her a drawing of Dionysus on her belly. Kofman says that "the belly of the woman plays the role of the head of Medusa. By lifting her skirts, was not Baubô suggesting that she go and frighten Hades, or that which comes to the same, recall fecundity to herself? By displaying the figure of Dionysus on her belly, she recalls the eternal return of life" (1988a, 196–197).

Kofman was continually lifting her skirts by exposing the male philosophers and their fears of woman and her fecundity. Her work makes us face the pathology of philosophy and of our own relation to life and ourselves. At every turn Kofman's texts confront us with our own ambivalence about feminine sexuality and the maternal body. Often they leave us mired in ambivalence, doubles, apotropaic figures, contradictions, enigmas, riddles, and screens covering screens, but always in search of the psychic means to multiply life in the face of death. Kofman's work forces us to reflect on the relationships between philosophy, literature, writing, and life. Her work and life continually remind us of the risk of taking life seriously, of the necessity of exposing ourselves, and of the need to laugh.

PART I

LITERATURE AND AESTHETICS

The Imposture of Beauty: The Uncanniness of Oscar Wilde's Picture of Dorian Gray

SARAH KOFMAN

Man must not have the opportunity to see his own face, for that is the most terrible thing. Nature has presented him with the gift of not being able to look at it, just as he cannot look into his own eyes.

It was only in the waters of rivers and lakes that he was able to behold his face. And the very position he had to take up was symbolic. He had to lean over and bend down in order to perform the ignominious act of seeing himself.

The inventor of the mirror imprisoned the human soul.
—Fernando Pessoa, *The Book of Disquiet*

Let us be merry; let us outwardly be happy. A handsome mask is better than an ugly face. Then why, poor fools, do we snatch it off?
—Théophile Gautier, Albertus, sec. LXXII (Gautier 1903, 254)

Translation by Duncan Large. Translator's Note: An abridged version of the original French text was published (as "L'imposture de la beauté") in *Autrement* (série "Mutations") 148 ("Le visage," October 1994), 191–214. The present translation is based on the full French version, "L'imposture de la beauté: L'inquiétante étrangeté du *Portrait de Dorian Gray*, d'Oscar Wilde," first given as a paper in April 1994 at the Centre for Critical and Cultural Theory, University of Wales, Cardiff, and published posthumously in Kofman 1995b (9–48). A number of textual corruptions have been clarified by consulting the author's typescript; errors in quotation and referencing have been corrected where necessary.
    All page numbers within the text refer to Wilde 1981.

BAD INFLUENCES

He is young, wonderfully handsome, innocent, and pure. This is how Lord Henry perceives him when they first meet, immediately linking body and soul together to form an undivided unity, establishing a relation of sign to signified between the inside and the outside in a most Hegelian fashion.[1] The physical perfection of youth (the finely-curved scarlet lips, the blue eyes, his crisp gold hair) reflects and expresses a moral perfection: frankness, candor, purity. A true physiognomist, he *reads* in his face "something . . . that made one trust him at once. All the candour of youth was there, as well as all youth's passionate purity. One felt that he had kept himself unspotted from the world" (15).

His face is perfectly beautiful, as only a child's face can be—one not yet ravaged by the marks of time, whose features bear no trace of the destructive passions or of the manifold human interests and their devastation (Hegel 1975, 1:151).

Perfectly beautiful, and a perfect likeness of the portrait of a "young man of extraordinary personal beauty" (1) painted by the painter Basil Hallward, which his friend Lord Henry has the opportunity of seeing *before* he encounters the original. Clamped to an easel, set up on display[2] from the start as a kind of frontispiece, the picture of Dorian Gray, placed at the head of the book and in its title, indicates its true hero.

By inverting the traditional hierarchy between the model and the copy, this privileged placement demonstrates uncannily (*unheimlich*—and in this text we shall never escape from *Unheimlichkeit*) the primacy and originality of the double, which absorbs the model and captivates the reader. (The name of the "original," which indicates the reality of the referent, is provided by the painter only belatedly: first so as not to give it away to Lord Henry and to "keep" it wholly for himself, but also in order to emphasize that art is primary and not a crude copy of life or the real.)

Between the model and his double, the text establishes not a mimetic relation of represented to representation but instead a relation of "sympathy" (106), in the magical sense of the term. And relations of magical "influence" are what link the characters to one another, especially the painter to his model.

The painter Basil, who adores Dorian passionately, was bewitched by him the moment their eyes first met.[3] As though he were being acted on by a spell, a subtle influence, he found himself seduced, suddenly fascinated by someone who "stole his soul" and changed the meaning of his life and art in a devilish and "fatal" (6) way. Like Alcibiades, who could sense a hidden *agalma* beneath the ugliness of Socrates' face,[4] the painter Basil devotes his life from now on to searching for the "secret" of a face and its beauty (no less enigmatic than Socrates' ugliness), which he must "grasp" at any price. He can no more be parted from Dorian than from his own shadow. Only in his presence—under his "influence"—can he paint his most beautiful works and find in a plain woodland the *wonder* he has always looked for and always missed. Utterly "absorbed" (6) by Dorian, so much so that he loses the self-control and self-possession that have hitherto been his,[5] Basil senses that the secure limits to his narcissism and identity are wavering: he is on the verge of a crisis tearing apart the unity of his being, dispossessing and emptying him of it to the benefit of his "double," on whom he has projected all his narcissistic overvaluation of himself. What it is that possesses and captivates him, he says, is not so much the apparent beauty of the young man as what it indicates—the secret wonder he is seeking, unwittingly at first, and of which the visible beauty of Dorian is just a shadow or a mere pattern (36). This wonder is ideal beauty, the idea of beauty such as might be contemplated by the initiate in Plato's *Symposium*,[6] who is sent into unimaginable raptures at the end of the dialectic: an un-changing, eternal, marmoreal beauty that nothing can taint, wither, or ravage and that, in contrast to visible beauty, is not destined to decay.

At first Dorian is unaware of his beauty, a beauty fit to *ravish* the soul, de-spite Basil's repeated praise of him, which he laughs at (25). The subtle in-fluence he exercises on him is not reciprocated, and Basil feels he has given away his soul to someone for whom he is merely a "flower to put in his coat" (12), an ephemeral ornament, something simply to flatter his vanity. It is only when Lord Henry judges the picture to be a wonderful work of art and a wonderful likeness (24) that Dorian Gray recognizes himself for the first time in his picture, and the sense of his own beauty comes on him like a revelation.

The formidable influence that Lord Henry exercises over Dorian from the first moment of their meeting awakens him to an awareness of himself and his beauty, an awareness that it has a sovereignty that needs no expla-nation because it is a divine right, "the wonder of wonders" (22). But Lord Henry also awakens him to its evanescence by inviting him to pick life's roses[7] before youth and beauty—one's only precious possessions—begin to decline: "What the gods give they quickly take away. You have only a few years in which to live really, perfectly, and fully" (22).

Lord Henry plays the role of the devil and the serpent. By his poisonous, wily words, his musical voice and hands, he fascinates Dorian, enthralling and hypnotizing him, arousing in him an insatiable, ravenous curiosity for life that he has never felt before, a mad hunger for knowledge that will only increase with gratification: the more he knows, the more he will desire to know (128). Lord Henry strives to make Dorian taste the forbidden fruit of the tree of knowledge. As in the book of Genesis, which is being parodied here, the primal scene of seduction actually takes place in a garden—that belonging to Basil (who, like God, finds himself tricked by the devil)—a garden of delights full of trees, roses, and lilacs, of honeysuckles and the blossoms of a laburnum the color of sweet honey, "whose tremulous branches seemed hardly able to bear the burden of a beauty so flamelike as theirs" (1, the start of the book).

Like a dead man's soul being tugged at by an angel and a devil fighting over it,[8] Dorian's soul, which has not yet lost its purity and innocence, becomes the object of desire for two men who want to attract it in opposite directions: one on whom he himself "exercises" an influence but who has had no effect on him, the other who, by revealing the mystery of life to him, does indeed seize hold of his soul and makes a devilish attempt to re-create him in his own image under the effect of his "bad influence" (and he recognizes that every influence is bad to the extent that it creates an artificial being who lives a borrowed life at the cost of fulfilling his own nature—not thinking his natural thoughts, or burning with his natural passions, reduced to becoming an echo of someone else's music and to acting a part that has not been written for him [17]).

Lord Henry takes a perverse, exultant pleasure in this power of re-creation, by which he sets himself up as a rival to God (and to Basil):

> There was something terribly enthralling in the exercise of influence. No other activity was like it. To project one's soul into some gracious form, and let it tarry there for a moment; to hear one's own intellectual views echoed back to one with all the added music of passion and youth; to convey one's temperament into another as though it were a subtle fluid or a strange perfume: there was a real joy in that. (35)

But this "influence" can only be felt because it reaches and touches a secret chord that Dorian felt vibrating before only in his boyhood, when he did not really understand it. It makes him become aware of what he himself unwittingly already is, of what he really can become: a being filled with passions and desires that, until now, he has been able to satisfy only in his dreams and that the moral and religious prohibitions of puritan society have kept repressed and castrated.

Although Lord Henry's whole being attracts and enchants him (43), it is nevertheless his low, languid voice that, like a hypnotist's, fascinates him (when he is with him, he asks him to talk to him all the time and says that no one talks so wonderfully as he does [43]), and it is his hands—*cool and white,* "flower-like," he says (21)—that, as he speaks, move like music and seem to have a language all their own, casting a strange, captivating spell over him. Dorian Gray repeatedly emphasizes the special seductive force exerted on him by voices: Lord Henry's and that of "the first woman he loved," the actress Sibyl,[9] whose love might have led his soul in a quite different direction:

> I never heard such a voice. It was very low at first, with deep mellow notes, that seemed to fall singly upon one's ear. Then it became a little louder, and sounded like a flute or a distant hautbois. . . . You know how a voice can stir one. Your voice and the voice of Sibyl Vane are two things that I shall never forget. When I close my eyes, I hear them, and each of them says something different. I don't know which to follow. (50)

"He [Lord Henry] was conscious . . . that it was through certain words of his, musical words said with musical utterance, that Dorian Gray's soul had turned to this white girl and bowed in worship before her. To a large extent the lad was his own creation. He had made him premature" (57), not needing to wait till life or a work of art disclosed to him life's secrets.

Lord Henry's wily words, with a music of their own "as sweet as that of viol or of lute" (19), give plastic form to things that have hitherto been formless in him and make them exist in reality through their magic:[10] "He was dimly conscious that entirely fresh influences were at work within him. Yet they seemed to him to have come really from himself" (18).

THE MIRROR STAGE

So Lord Henry's insidious, enchanting words, which inspire Dorian to a hedonistic carpe diem, play the part of a revealing mirror and expose Dorian to himself for the first time, making him *see* the fascinating beauty that Basil's picture magnificently reflects, awakening in him an unquenchable desire to preserve it forever. Before the devilish seduction scene Dorian was splendid, but as Lord Henry can guess by looking at the picture (3), *he did not think.*[11] He had kept his beauty only because, like a child, or like Adam before the Fall, he was unconscious: he was not yet self-divided, had not yet been "tainted" by any duplicity.

When Narcissus first gazes at the beauty of his own face reflected in a river, he fails at first to recognize it as his own representation and falls madly in love with it, but Dorian Gray perceives his specular double and recognizes it as such the first time he sees it, becoming intensely jealous of it as if it were a rival more favored than himself, because it at least is destined to keep its beauty for all time. The picture strikes him a sudden and violent blow not so much on account of its flattering likeness to himself as because this is merely the sign that it has robbed, stolen, devoured his essence.[12] He is struck by it as though by a knife thrust that makes him differ from himself, makes him lose his secure identity, and reduces him to impotence:[13]

> When he saw it . . . a look of joy came into his eyes, as if he had recognized himself for the first time. . . . The sense of his own beauty came on him like a revelation. He had never felt it before. . . . Then had come Lord Henry Wotton with his strange panegyric on youth, his terrible warning of its brevity. . . . Now, as he stood gazing at the shadow of his own loveliness, the full reality of the description flashed across him. Yes, there would be a day when his face would be wrinkled and wizen, his eyes dim and colourless, the grace of his figure broken and deformed. The scarlet would pass away from his lips, and the gold steal from his hair. The life that was to make his soul would mar his body. He would become dreadful, hideous, and uncouth.
>
> As he thought of it, a sharp pang of pain struck through him like a knife. . . . He felt as if a hand of ice had been laid upon his heart. (24f.)

This knife thrust, which makes a corpse of him from the outset, heralds and prefigures the final knife thrust against the malign double, which (as in all the fantastic tales of the German Romantics) is in reality aimed at himself and kills him, while the rival remains for eternity in all his wonder and beauty:

> He seized the thing, and stabbed the picture with it. . . . When they [the servants] entered, they found hanging upon the wall a splendid portrait of their master as they had last seen him, in all the wonder of his exquisite youth and beauty. Lying on the floor was a dead man, in evening dress, with a knife in his heart. He was withered, wrinkled, and loathsome of visage. (223f.: end of the text)

The whole text is played out between these two knife thrusts. In between is the story of Dorian Gray's passion for the impossible, his desperate attempt to reappropriate his fantastic self-sufficiency and narcissistic security, which the double has tainted. The anticipation of the loss of his youth and beauty, prompted by the sight of the double[14] and intolerable to his fragile narcissism, makes him utter a wish, an impious prayer: that he should be exchanged for his portrait. At any price:

"How sad it is! I shall grow old, and horrible, and dreadful. But this picture will remain always young. . . . If it were only the other way! If it were
I who was to be always young, and the picture that was to grow old! For
that—for that—I would give everything! Yes, there is nothing in the
whole world I would not give! I would give my soul for that!" (25f.)

As a prostitute, one of Dorian's victims, points out, he sells his soul to the
devil (and Dorian becomes more and more convinced that he does have
a soul, that it is a terrible reality, that it can be bought, and sold, and
bartered away, poisoned, or made perfect [215]) in order to keep his
pretty face (193) and remain forever the "Prince Charming" of his youth.
The uncanniness begins not at the point when Dorian Gray utters this
prayer, but when he believes in its effectiveness, in other words when he
believes, like the child at the narcissistic stage,[15] in the omnipotence of his
desires and his thoughts, believes that by his words alone he has been able
to have a magical influence on the deity. Even to the extent of acknowledging the possibility, then the reality, of his wishes being fulfilled.
    Thanks to the magic of art—the only field, according to Freud,[16] in
which magic can still be practiced with complete freedom—the benevolent readers, who might imagine that they have surmounted the narcissistic stage long ago, abide by the convention imposed by the author (another
contract with the devil), who exploits his seductive influence to make them
identify with the hero, while they are reading, and accept the impossible or
the incredible, though not without subjecting them to the effect of *Unheimlichkeit*, since Wilde makes sure he leaves the readers in doubt as to the
genre he has adopted (by contrast with what happens in children's fairy
tales, which admit to being what they are, for there must be a doubt and a
debate about the reality, or otherwise, of the incredible if uncanniness is to
come into play).[17] For example, he raises doubts about the purely subjective and imaginary nature of the picture's "transformation" by making the
painter at one point a witness to it. But by restoring the picture's beauty to
it *in fine*, and by displaying the face on the corpse of Dorian Gray, he also
leads us to think that the whole metamorphosis might only have been an
insane hallucination caused by a delirium of introspection. And it is this
"also" that is decisive for the effect the text produces.

SCREEN

If readers, by submitting to convention, gain the strange pleasure
that uncanniness provides, the sign of a return in them of what they thought
they had surmounted, what does Dorian Gray gain once his contract with

the devil is fulfilled? His picture, originally a benign double—he looks in delight at the splendor and beauty of his youth that it depicts—becomes, after his mad "prayer," a malign and fatal (122) double, which he forces to assume the burden (220) of age and his sins. While he himself, reduced to his visible appearance alone, preserves himself intact, the picture becomes the projection of his soul, the mirror (222) (or the conscience) in which everything he wants to protect himself from comes to be reflected. It becomes a monstrous image of the part of himself that he has rejected and detached, a critical authority projected outside of himself in the form of a double (as Freud notes, this is a new "content" that the double can assume with the development of the ego). A monstrous living soul that from now on will never stop badgering him with horrible reproaches, and from whose criticism he will ultimately be able to find release only by stabbing it (223).

Previously the fatal picture represented the "diary" of his life (154), a kind of hieroglyphic writing to which he alone knew the secret, a record of vice written in blood, in "scarlet letters": red, vermilion (with which the painter signed his picture [24]), and purple are its dominant colors, which gradually supersede the whiteness of the original purity. After the painter is murdered and his corpse reduced to nothingness, the canvas of the picture—a mocking parody of the *vera iconica* of Christ—becomes a shroud from which the blood spilled by the crime oozes drop by drop:

> He saw the face of his portrait leering. . . . On the floor in front of it the torn curtain was lying. He remembered that the night before he had forgotten, for the first time in his life, to hide the fatal canvas, and was about to rush forward, when he drew back with a shudder.
>
> What was that loathsome red dew that gleamed, wet and glistening, on one of the hands, as though the canvas had sweated blood? How horrible it was! (173f.)

Then, because he can no longer stand the look on this face, the gaze of the Other on himself, and he wants to eliminate from it every sign of maleficent passion, in the belief that simply changing his life, reorienting it henceforth toward the good, will be enough to erase the terrifying and degrading traces of the crime, determined to "convert," he drags the purple hanging from the portrait, free from terror for the first time. But:

> A cry of pain and indignation broke from him. He could see no change, save that in the eyes there was a look of cunning, and in the mouth the curved wrinkle of the hypocrite. The thing was still loathsome—more loathsome, if possible, than before—and the scarlet dew that spotted

the hand seemed brighter, and more like blood newly spilt. Then he trembled. . . . And why was the red stain larger than it had been? It seemed to have crept like a horrible disease over the wrinkled fingers. There was blood on the painted feet, as though the thing had dripped— blood even on the hand that had not held the knife. Confess? Did it mean that he was to confess? To give himself up, and be put to death? He laughed.[18] (221f.)

The fulfillment of Dorian Gray's prayer, which correlates to a fetishistic disavowal of the real that he cannot *see*, is intended to ensure that he benefits by escaping all blemishes: those of age and of thought, of the passions, suffering, and pleasure. Those caused by the marks from the hot branding iron of infamy and by the vices that gnaw into the soul like worms eating away at a corpse. Blemishes that affect the freshness and brilliance of the complexion, wrinkling it like the fading, broken flower that is nevertheless the very symbol of ideal beauty. As in the poems of Ronsard, in Wilde's text there is an abundance of flowers, whose dazzling beauty and verticality mask their fragility and transience, making one forget their foul-smelling origins.[19] They are the symbol of the evanescence of human beauty and its imposture, for all that it makes us believe in the illusion of its eternity and serves as an "Apollonian" mask, a screen protecting us from an intolerable "Dionysian" reality. An imposture of beauty because, by its very splendor, it appears to protect us from the loss of our narcissistic securities, from any fall, any flaw, failure, defilement, degradation, corruption—from the ruin, the defeat with which, in reality, beauty itself is fatally threatened.

And at first it does indeed seem as though the devil's bargain succeeds in maintaining intact the beautiful external and internal image that Dorian Gray's extremely fragile narcissism requires, and his magical belief in his omnipotence and immortality along with it. The mask of his beauty, which (by contrast with the ugliness of the Socratic Silenus, which conceals a wonder inside) conceals his inner ugliness from everyone's eyes, spares him both from the "marks" of time and sin and from remarks that might blemish him and taint his infallibility. Emblematically, this protective mask saves his life, for when Sibyl's brother thinks that he recognizes in Dorian, twenty years after his sister's death, the man who scorned her and caused her suicide, he abandons all thought of avenging her and killing him when he notices by the light of a street lamp Dorian's youth and beauty, sure signs for him of his innocence: Dorian could not be the man Sibyl called her "Prince Charming";[20] no need even to check who he is.[21]

What is more, at first Dorian Gray gloats triumphantly when he looks at himself in the mirror given to him (and this is no accident) by the devilish seducer and compares the image he sees reflected in it to that of his rival, who continues to decay and wither, while he preserves his beauty and his youth untainted:

> He would examine with minute care, and sometimes with a monstrous and terrible delight, the hideous lines that seared the wrinkling forehead or crawled around the heavy sensual mouth, wondering sometimes which were the more horrible, the signs of sin or the signs of age. He would place his white hands beside the coarse bloated hands of the picture, and smile. He mocked the misshapen body and the failing limbs. (128)

> When the blood crept from its face, and left behind a pallid mask of chalk with leaden eyes, he would keep the glamour of boyhood. Not one blossom of his loveliness would ever fade. . . . Like the gods of the Greeks, he would be strong, and fleet, and joyous. What did it matter what happened to the coloured image on the canvas? He would be safe. (106)

He breaks off his most distant journeys so that he can come—furtively and in secret, like a thief—and find enjoyment in this contrast, which fascinates him and makes him more and more curious about the corruption of the picture (whose enigma he attempts to solve by giving himself over to endless speculations on the relations between the soul and the body):

> He himself would creep upstairs to the locked room, open the door with the key that never left him now, and stand, with a mirror, in front of the picture that Basil Hallward had painted of him, looking now at the evil and aging face on the canvas, and now at the fair young face that laughed back at him from the polished glass. The very sharpness of the contrast used to quicken his sense of pleasure. He grew more and more enamoured of his own beauty, more and more interested in the corruption of his own soul. (128)

Thus, unlike the fantastic hero of the novel Lord Henry gave him[22] (a true double with whom he identifies to the extent that he sees in him a kind of prefiguring type of himself and regards the work, of which he has nine copies, as containing the story of his own life, written before he has lived it),[23] he himself, at the beginning, has none of

> the grotesque dread of mirrors, and polished metal surfaces, and still water, which came upon the young Parisian so early in his life, and was occasioned by the sudden decay of a beauty that had once, apparently, been

so remarkable. It was with an almost cruel joy—and perhaps in nearly every joy, as certainly in every pleasure, cruelty has its place—that he used to read the latter part of the book, with its really tragic, if somewhat over-emphasized, account of the sorrow and despair of one who had himself lost what in others, and in the world, he had most dearly valued.

For the wonderful beauty that had so fascinated Basil Hallward, and many others besides him, seemed never to leave him. . . . He had always the look of one who had kept himself unspotted from the world. (127)

The difference between him and the hero of the novel is illuminating: what Dorian Gray's mask triumphantly protects him from is the danger of melancholy, of the impossibility of mourning a loss, a danger that catches up with him when, turning his attention to embroideries and tapestries and totally absorbing himself in them, he reflects with sadness on the ruin that time brings on "beautiful and wonderful things," a feeling that he immediately anticathects with the idea that he, at any rate, has escaped that: "Summer followed summer, and the yellow jonquils bloomed and died many times, and nights of horror repeated the story of their shame, but he was unchanged. No winter marred his face or stained his flower-like bloom. How different it was with material things! Where had they passed to?" (137f.).

Yet his narcissistic triumph can only be completely assured if he "forgets" the accusing face of his double and conceals it from the sight of any possible witness. *Esse est percipi.*[24] Dorian takes a whole series of preventive, precautionary, obsessive measures in order to stop anyone from gaining access to it and to shield it from sight: he banishes the picture to a room situated at the top of the house and locks the door; he wraps it, as in a curtain (140), in an old purple satin coverlet that "had perhaps served often as a pall for the dead" (118f.), in order to hide this terrible object that has a corruption of its own, worse than the corruption of death itself (119). After he discovers its first transformation, following his abandonment of Sibyl, he puts the picture behind a large screen, "of gilt Spanish leather, stamped and wrought with a rather florid Louis-Quatorze pattern." He scans it curiously, "wondering if ever before it had concealed the secret of a man's life" (94).

Before he leaves the room—not to enter it again for weeks, so that he can forget the hideous painted thing by letting himself be absorbed by life—he steals a glance at the picture, which seizes him with horror and forces him, to avoid suffocating, to open the window and turn his back on his "conscience" (92).

The defense used by Dorian Gray (whose "golden" Christian name, Apollonian like the screen, conceals the Dionysian grayness of his soul,[25] as emphasized by his surname?) is always to escape behind protecting screens, starting with those of his eyelids. After the murder of the painter, he "crushed with dank hands his burning lids as though he would have robbed the very brain of sight, and driven the eyeballs back into their cave" (167): a magical means of getting rid of the body so as to stifle his terror, even before he has the body pulverized (by his chemist friend Alan Campbell) and transformed into a handful of ashes so that no vestige, no trace, remains (168).

Feeling hounded and pursued by his double despite all these precautions, his imagination making him *see again*, despite himself, each hideous and horrible detail of his crime, haunted by shadows of his crime, who peer at him and mock him from the most silent corners and most secret places (200), Dorian has only one way of escaping this unrelenting persecution that condemns and punishes him—to try to "buy oblivion" (184) at any price, to strive "to forget, to stamp the thing out, to crush it as one would crush the adder that had stung one" (185), destroying the memory of his former sins with brand-new ones committed in appalling bolt-holes, in opium dens, in the ugliness of the real, for "memory, like a horrible malady, was eating his soul away. . . . He wanted to be where no one would know where he was. He wanted to escape from himself" (188). And from the "wild terror of dying" (199). In order to forget, he collects rare, beautiful, luxurious things for a season: "These treasures, and everything that he collected in his lovely house, were to be to him means of forgetfulness, modes by which he could escape" (140).

But all these measures to which he has recourse in order to forget, and that serve as an anticathexis for his terror of himself and of death, are also (as Freud noted with regard to an etching by Félicien Rops)[26] a means of making the repressed return. Such is the case, for example, with the opium of books with which he drugs himself for a while. Especially those by Théophile Gautier, who is quoted and alluded to at several points in *The Picture of Dorian Gray,* and whose aesthetic of art for art's sake, of a purely ornamental and gratuitous art, Wilde seems to adopt, setting himself against any realism or moralizing and grafting his text, through the voice of Lord Henry,[27] onto that of this French poet who influences him—an intertextuality (even plagiarism) that again breaks down the well-defined "narcissistic" limits of a "corpus" with a determinate author. This conception of art for art's sake does not stop him from making art play a pharmaceutical role that destroys its supposed gratuitousness—for it is in an attempt to "forget" that Dorian Gray immerses himself in *Émaux et Camées* (*Enamels and Cameos*) and in particular the "lovely stanzas upon Venice" (164),[28] that Venus of the Adriatic, a poem that glorifies marmoreal, impassive, pagan beauty, although Gautier knows that it is a surface mask intended to remedy time's degradation and blemishes by hiding them, and to conceal the hideous face of death.[29]

So after murdering the painter, Dorian Gray immerses himself in Gautier as if he were a drug, but the intolerable then returns in the very thing that was meant to make it tolerable, for the poem on Venice puts him in mind precisely of Basil, with whom he stayed in that city. "Poor Basil! what a horrible way for a man to die! He sighed, and took up the volume again, and tried to forget" (164). Immediately before, as he turned over the pages, he had come across the poem about the hand of Lacenaire,[30] as if by chance: "The cold yellow hand, '*du supplice encore mal lavée*,' with its downy red hairs and its '*doigts de faune*'" had made him glance "at his own white taper fingers, shuddering slightly in spite of himself" (164).

Again, in order to try to forget, he had begun sketching, first flowers, and bits of architecture, and then human faces. "Suddenly he remarked that every face that he drew seemed to have a fantastic likeness to Basil Hallward" (163). It is precisely in order not to see the face of the Other imposing itself upon him—despite himself, and in every effort he makes precisely to escape it—that he goes over to his bookcase and takes out a volume of Gautier at hazard: "He was determined that he would not think about what had happened until it became absolutely necessary that he should do so" (163).

From a more general perspective, although he tries to escape the gaze of his conscience by detaching it from himself and banishing his double to the most distant point, where it is confined to a locked room, shut out from the sunlight (105), and veiled,[31] he cannot in fact remain separated from such an important part of his life, and he returns—even taking a morbid pleasure in doing so—to look at himself more and more often in this magic mirror that, having revealed to him the beauty of his body, reveals to him the ugliness of his soul, and in which he follows his mind into its secret places (106), making it the guide to his life. Though at first he uses as a pretext for his returns the desire to reassure himself that no one has come and stolen his picture or his secret, he very quickly realizes that he is fascinated by the progressive decomposition of his picture, the visible symbol of the degradation that sin brings about. His finite curiosity (105)—his original sin—is stronger than his need to hide from his depravities, and it spurs him to find a perverse enjoyment in the spectacle of the decay of his soul laid bare: with no sense of shame, as only an innocent child, or Adam before the Fall,[32] might look at himself if he felt the need (but he has no interest in doing so). A sinful curiosity, for what Dorian hopes is that he can have a perfect awareness of the events in his life while they are happening and someday even see the change taking place before his very eyes (105). His delight in looking at himself is perverse and devilish, truly blasphemous, for God alone ought to be able to have perfect knowledge of what he has created.[33]

Like every pervert, Dorian Gray can derive the fullest enjoyment only when he is in the presence of a third party, a witness to whom he can display the degradation of his soul as he mocks it in triumph. This witness has to be the "creator" himself, the painter Basil, rival to God[34] and as proud as He is of his creation and its original splendor, which he thought he would see endure eternally, and whose modification and corruption he cannot acknowledge without observing it with his own incredulous, horrified, paralyzed eyes, without feeling sick and dizzy:

"I wonder do I know you? Before I could answer that, I should have to see your soul. . . . But only God can do that."

A bitter laugh of mockery broke from the lips of the younger man. "You shall see it yourself, to-night! . . . Come: it is your own handiwork. Why shouldn't you look at it? . . ."

There was the madness of pride in every word he uttered. He stamped his foot upon the ground in his boyish insolent manner. He felt a terrible joy at the thought that some one else was to share his secret, and that the man who had painted the portrait that was the origin of all his shame was to be burdened for the rest of his life with the hideous memory of what he had done. . . .

"I shall show you my soul. You shall see the thing that you fancy only God can see. . . . Come upstairs, Basil. . . . I keep a diary of my life from day to day, and it never leaves the room in which it is written. I will show it to you." (152–154)

"You are the one man in the world who is entitled to know everything about me. You have had more to do with my life than you think. . . . So you think that it is only God who sees the soul, Basil? Draw that curtain back, and you will see mine" . . . ; and he tore the curtain from its rod, and flung it on the ground.

An exclamation of horror broke from the painter's lips as he saw in the dim light the hideous face on the canvas grinning at him. There was something in its expression that filled him with disgust and loathing. . . . Yes, it was Dorian himself. But who had done it? . . .

It was some foul parody, some infamous, ignoble satire. He had never done that. Still, it was his own picture. . . . Why had it altered? . . . His mouth twitched, and his parched tongue seemed unable to articulate. . . .

The young man was leaning against the mantelshelf, watching him with that strange expression that one sees on the faces of those who are absorbed in a play when some great artist is acting. There was neither real sorrow in it nor real joy. There was simply the passion of the spectator, with perhaps a flicker of triumph in his eyes. (155f.)

The surface [of the picture] seemed to be quite undisturbed, and as he had left it. It was from within, apparently, that the foulness and horror had come. Through some strange quickening of inner life the leprosies of sin were slowly eating the thing away. The rotting of a corpse in a watery grave was not so fearful. (157)

Dorian's childish triumph is short-lived. Momentarily moved by the painter who, faced with his blasphemy, invites him to pray to God, to undo by prayer what prayer has brought about, to believe in the biblical verse that leads even the greatest of sinners to hope that their crimes will be pardoned and completely wiped away—"'Though your sins be as scarlet,[35] yet I will make them as white as snow'" (158)—seized by a boundless loathing for the man who now shares his secret and whom he holds responsible for his degradation, he stabs him repeatedly. He is aware, once again, only of the theatrical effect of a body falling to the ground, waving grotesque stiff-fingered hands in the air, and listens only to the drops of blood falling on the carpet (159). He does not even glance at the man he has just murdered. He refuses to see the look on his face and sums the whole thing up with "The friend who had painted the fatal portrait to which all his misery had been due, had gone out of his life. That was enough" (159). The man who loved him so much has become for him a "thing . . . seated in the chair, straining over the table with bowed head, and humped back, and long fantastic arms" (159). A kind of "hideous puppet" (23), a scarecrow from which he will now try to escape.

But killing the author of the picture still does not destroy the picture, the other scarecrow. In order to forget it, like the hero of his novel he now avoids all mirrors—and crushes beneath his heel, like a child, the one Lord Henry gave him (220), in which at first he was happy to look at his image—for he can no longer tolerate his beauty (which, as he now understands, has been but a mask to him) and his youth, this imposture, without a feeling of loathing. They were what ruined him, stained him, spoiled him. Troubled by the living death of his soul, making the picture the scapegoat for everything that marred his life ("It was the portrait that had done everything" [221]), he can avoid the sight of it only by stabbing it, too—his last magical means of erecting, once and for all, a screen between himself and his conscience, between himself and the reality he has never stopped denying.

THE IMPOSSIBILITY OF MOURNING

> *Les grandpères ont toujours tort.*
> —The Picture of Dorian Gray, p. 49

One might wonder why Dorian Gray makes such a cult of beauty,[36] and why he chooses an aesthetic mode of life that makes him transform his life into a work of art[37] and view every happy or unhappy event like a spectacle.

Emblematically, the first woman he loves, whom he compares to a Tanagra figurine (75), is an actress, and he loves in her only the multiple roles she plays, whether male or female:[38] by turns Rosalind or Juliet, Desdemona, Ophelia, or Imogen. Like the narrator in Gérard de Nerval's *Sylvie,* he loves this new Aurélia above all from afar, separated from her by the footlights, and worships her like a goddess set on a pedestal of gold (77–80). He sees her as a divine magician transforming the audience as she likes: "They sit silently and watch her. They weep and laugh as she wills them to do. She makes them as responsive as a violin. She spiritualizes them" (81). And her magic might have had a benign influence on Dorian had she not unfortunately taken it into her head to "really" love him, thenceforth abandoning all theatrical artifice and becoming a real, all too real object, of no further value to Dorian because, loving him, she can no longer play at love, and because she therefore loses all her poetry and can no longer inspire either his imagination or his curiosity: she, Sibyl Vane, is now nothing but a vain "wounded thing" (88), a "trampled flower" (87). Dorian sees the end of his "love" for Sibyl—which prompts the actress's death, to which he remains insensitive—as merely the end of a tragedy in which he has taken a great part (100). The actress's death, as Lord Henry implies, was simply her last role:

> You must think of that lonely death in the tawdry dressing-room simply as a strange lurid fragment from some Jacobean tragedy, as a wonderful scene from Webster, or Ford, or Cyril Tourneur. . . . To you at least she was always a dream. . . . The moment she touched actual life, she marred it, and it marred her, and so she passed away. Mourn for Ophelia if you like. Put ashes on your head because Cordelia was strangled. . . . But don't waste your tears over Sybil Vane. She was less real than they are. (103)

Looking at the past from an artistic point of view, becoming the spectator of his own life, is a ruse that enables Dorian to escape suffering (110). It is enough for him simply not to talk of terrible things to deprive them of their reality (107), just as it is enough for him to tear up the newspaper announcing the actress's death to obliterate, magically, the woman he finds intolerable because she is too hideous, too horribly real: "How ugly it all was! And how horribly real ugliness made things!" (124).

Art, the mask of Apollonian beauty and serenity, has a pharmaceutical function: it makes the Dionysian "real" tolerable and prevents us from having to die of "truth." The aestheticism of Wilde's hero can be understood by using the categories that Nietzsche sets up in *The Birth of Tragedy,* where he systematizes the teaching of the Greeks, who knew that one must remain on the surface and be superficial out of profundity, that one must not try to look "beneath the skin,"[39] and that on the contrary one must camouflage "artistically" everything that is distressing and liable to make one feel sick.

Dorian loves the theater because, as Diderot stresses in the *Paradox on Acting,* it relies on a collection of conventions, artifices, and rules of good taste that exclude anything that might displease the audience and safeguard them from the natural cacophony, from everything excessive, unwieldy, discordant, misshapen. He cannot forgive Sibyl for really dying a *real* death—what bad taste!—and not being a good actress and simply *acting out* a different death in order to please him. What is unforgivable is that by her suicide she should show—without shame, without a mask—that death is not just a game and that in life, unlike in the theater, it is never possible to "take one's moves again."[40] That she should fall from the divine pedestal of gold on which he had placed her and reveal her human, all too human fragility, reveal the fact that she was not a goddess but a wounded thing, ruined forever.

Dorian does not succeed in mourning the eternity of beauty, like the poet whom Freud talks about in "Vergänglichkeit" ("On Transience"), for whom the fragility and evanescence of beauty seem necessarily to devalue it and to give rise to a feeling of disgust at the fleetingness of this world, or at any rate a revolt against it, the sacrilegious impossibility of admitting that the splendors of nature and art are destined to fade away into nothing: the claim that beauties cannot but be somehow perpetuated, shielded from any destructive influence.

Now according to Freud this demand that beauty should last forever does not relate to anything real and is simply an effect of our desire. As Wilde puts it, it seems, on the contrary, that in all beauty there is a fatality— precisely that of being defeated[41] and ruined. What Freud disputes is that the transience of beauty should devalue it, since limiting the possibility of an enjoyment, on the contrary, actually raises its value by making it scarce: "The beauty of the human form and face vanish forever in the course of our own lives, but their evanescence only lends them a fresh charm. A flower that blossoms only for a single night does not seem to us on that account less lovely" (Freud 1916, 305f.). Nor does the brief duration of works of art detract from their value as such either, for they are, by their nature, linked to a specific society and period.

Why then can the poet who is Freud's companion for a day not tolerate—any more than Dorian Gray can—the thought of the transience that is beauty's destiny? Freud's reply is the following: he had a kind of foretaste of mourning over its decease, and, since the mind instinctively recoils from anything that is painful, he felt his enjoyment of beauty interfered with by thoughts of its loss.

In "Vergänglichkeit," Freud is puzzled at the feeling of pain produced by mourning, the loss of the object:

> Why it is that this detachment of libido from its objects should be such a painful process is a mystery to us and we have not hitherto been able to frame any hypothesis to account for it. We only see that libido clings to its objects and will not renounce those that are lost even when a substitute lies ready to hand. Such then is mourning. (Freud 1916, 306f.)

So those who, faced with the loss of possessions, devalue them because they have proved incapable of resisting the vicissitudes of time are in a state of preemptive mourning for a loss. A state of mourning that is enigmatic because it cannot have an economic explanation (the libido, once free, could replace the lost objects with objects that are equally or still more precious), and because in any case a bout of mourning, however painful it may be, comes to a spontaneous end someday: when it has renounced everything it has lost, it consumes itself. Only once mourning has been surmounted can we admit that our experience of the fragility of beauty does not after all diminish the high regard in which we hold it; only then does it become possible to cathect the libido in other beautiful objects, in the knowledge that they are perishable. (For Freud, since the mourning of loss must end by itself, it would be as well to move on right away. For the danger of an endless bout of mourning is that it makes the libido narcissistically turn in on itself, on the closest object, at the expense of what is distant. It prevents Eros from extending itself by restricting its cathexes to oneself, one's family, one's fatherland, nation, or race. The libido can no longer be cathected by sublimating itself in "cultural property." An endless bout of mourning is dangerous for civilization.)

The case that Freud does not consider in this text (he will do so later in *Mourning and Melancholia*) is the one in which mourning is impossible—a pathological case of melancholy, which is precisely that of Dorian Gray. Dorian Gray fails to mourn beauty. *His* beauty, to be sure, but behind his own, what he does not manage to tolerate—such is my hypothesis—is the loss of his mother's beauty, with which he identified. Yet I do not think I am reading the text in too psychoanalytic a way, improperly, doing violence to it. Wilde himself provides some indications that point in this direction. I have not yet highlighted the fact that the room to which Dorian banishes his picture, behind a screen, to conceal it from everyone's eyes, is not just situated at the top of the house. It is the room in which he spent the majority of his boyhood and adolescence. Here it is that he "exhibits" (without exhibiting) his picture, the progressive blemishing of his soul, deliberately, monstrously scorning and mocking the stainless (122) "rose-white" (219) purity of this boyhood and the man who strove to preserve it for him by his stern prohibitions: his grandfather, the representative of the Law, who seems to have played a decisive role. He cannot stand this grandfather because, he says, the grandfather transferred the inordinate hatred that he felt for his mother and her beauty onto him as a child. The mother's fatal beauty led her into a passion for a man of a lower class (32), a penniless young fellow, "a mere nobody," who was killed in a duel more or less caused by the grandfather a few months after their marriage—and she herself, having stopped speaking to her father, died within a year of this "bad business" (33).

So Dorian's mother was an uncommonly beautiful woman who risked everything for a mad passion. Hidden behind Dorian's exquisite beauty (35) is the tragedy for which his grandfather was essentially responsible. Is it not to gain a victory over this man whom he hates twice over—he robbed him of his parents' love and is also the stern representative of the Law—that Dorian, who was reduced in his boyhood to impotence and submission, should attempt to make himself omnipotent by magic? Is it not because he was particularly badly treated that later on, as if by way of revenge, he needs to be a malign, pernicious influence on the young people around him, experiencing a terrible joy in depraving them and driving them to despair (219), using his spells to put them at his mercy, and dictating his terms to them in turn? The scene with his friend Campbell is emblematic in this respect. Having summoned Campbell to dispose of Basil's body "chemically," he cannot bear the way he resists obeying him in spite of all his entreaties, or the moral lesson he serves him up, an intolerable attitude that reminds him precisely of his grandfather: "You treated me as no man has ever dared to treat me—no living man, at any rate. I bore it all. Now it is for me to dictate terms" (171).

This man who is no longer alive was an image of death to him even while he was living. Not only because he caused the death of his parents, but because with his whole body he presented the sight of a man marked and withered by age: marks that Dorian noticed and kept an eye on all the more intently because he cannot have stopped wishing the stern old man dead. Is his later horror of aging not due to his refusal to become like this hated grandfather, a real counterexample, someday? Is his devil's bargain with the picture not a way of trying to gain a victory over him by preserving forever an image that is intact and without blemish, a youth and a beauty that are indestructible, while the face painted on the canvas, hidden from everyone's eyes under its purple sheet, becomes brutish, bloated, and squalid? Growing more and more like his grandfather's face (as he fantasizes about it, at least):

> The cheeks would become hollow or flaccid. Yellow crow's feet would creep around the fading eyes and make them horrible. The hair would lose its brightness, the mouth would gape or droop, would be foolish or gross, as the mouths of old men are. There would be the wrinkled throat, the cold, blue-veined hands, the twisted body, that he remembered in the grandfather who had been so stern to him in his boyhood. (122f.)

Blue-veined hands that he hates because they are castrating and emblematic of death, prefiguring what his own hands will become—criminal hands like those of Gautier's Lacenaire. Contrasting with the memory of these hands are the white, musical hands of Lord Henry, which are particularly fascinating and call to mind the hands of a woman, hands he has lost forever—those of his mother, whose portrait displays the beauty he himself has inherited. He is afraid that the other members of the family whose portraits he can see might have passed on to him poisons, which would effectively have marked him in advance with corruption and which he feels threatening him in the faces of all those ancestors whose lives are inseparable from his own:[42]

> He used to wonder at the shallow psychology of those who conceive the Ego in man as a thing simple, permanent, reliable, and of one essence. To him, man was a being with myriad lives and myriad sensations, a complex multiform creature that bore within itself strange legacies of thought and passion, and whose very flesh was tainted with the monstrous maladies of the dead. He loved to stroll through the gaunt cold picture gallery of his country house and look at the various portraits of those whose blood flowed in his veins. . . . Had some strange poisonous germ

crept from body to body till it had reached his own? Was it some dim sense of that ruined grace that had made him so suddenly, and almost without cause, give utterance, in Basil Hallward's studio, to the mad prayer that had so changed his life? (143)

Dorian's narcissistic fragility, which makes the limits of his body and of his individuality insecure, makes him believe that his inheritance is not only from his physiological relations but, to a still greater extent, from literary ancestors and from all the peculiar and terrifying characters who have trod the world stage making sin wondrous and evil subtle. It seems to him that their lives have mysteriously been his, a feeling shared by the hero of the novel Lord Henry gave him. Through some magical transmission, through the influence of these real or imaginary characters on him, he feels that he has been (to parody Nietzsche) all the depraved figures in history.[43]

Though he cannot work out conclusively which of them has passed on which poison to him, one thing he is sure of is that he has inherited his beauty from his mother alone—a beauty that is utterly pagan and Dionysian, described as that of a bacchante affirming the sensuality and cheerfulness of life, the beauty of a loving mother who protected him with her smile:

> And his mother with her Lady Hamilton face, and her moist wine-dashed lips—he knew what he had got from her. He had got from her his beauty, and his passion for the beauty of others. She laughed at him in her loose Bacchante dress. There were vine leaves in her hair. The purple spilled from the cup she was holding. The carnations of the painting had withered, but the eyes were still wonderful in their depth and brilliancy of colour. They seemed to follow him wherever he went. (144)

And yet the beauty that the picture displays has been lost; the beloved mother is dead, and her death has deprived the child of her smile too soon. Is it not because of the impossibility of mourning this loss, the loss of his mother's beauty and of her smile, that Dorian tries to save her for all eternity, incorporating in himself forever the beauty of his mother that was passed on by her? Is it not in "reparation" for and of his mother, to conceal her blemishes from everyone, that he wants to "keep" his youth and beauty untainted, so as to keep her intact in himself, as beautiful as in her portrait? In order to gain a victory over the hated grandfather, who detested a mother so beautiful, did he not, by means of his devil's bargain, want to be the Infant savior of his mother?

A memory of her blemishes, due not so much to age, since she died young, nor to the passions, but to the impossibility of satisfying them fully because of a stern, "castrating" father who cruelly deprived her of any enjoyment by arranging the death of the object of her mad passion. The fact that in all this what is at stake is indeed the salvation of his mother's withered body, saved by hiding it behind a mask of eternal beauty—this is proved by, among others, the passage in the text where Dorian is fascinated by ecclesiastical vestments, above all by those of the Bride of Christ, when he says she "must wear purple and jewels and fine linen that she may hide the pallid macerated body that is worn by the suffering that she seeks for, and wounded by self-inflicted pain" (139).

From a more general perspective, in the Pietàs where the Virgin is represented holding a blood-soaked Christ on her knees, one can say that art performs an inversion: it displays the bleeding body of the Son so as better to hide that of the mother, as if the Son, in order to "save" the mother, were taking her wounds on himself.[44] Wilde's originality is to relate the Virgin's wounds to the ascetic ideal,[45] which spoils lives and arrests their growth—mars them by castrating them (74), preventing them from blossoming out in all their fullness. Through the voices of Lord Henry and Dorian,[46] he expresses a new hedonism: immaculate perfection and harmony consist in refusing renunciation and incompleteness (216); real degradation is not to be found in vices but in the mutilation of the passions.

When Lord Henry seduces Dorian in Basil's Edenic garden, he exhorts him not to let himself be ruined by prohibitions but to live the wonderful life that is in him, to be always searching for sensations and afraid of nothing (22). Under his influence, Dorian will turn life into the greatest of the arts by seeking to invent a system of life that might find its highest fulfillment in the spiritualization of the senses:

> As he looked back upon man moving through History, he was haunted by a feeling of loss. So much had been surrendered! and to such little purpose! There had been mad wilful rejections, monstrous forms of self-torture and self-denial, whose origin was fear, and whose result was a degradation infinitely more terrible than that fancied degradation from which, in their ignorance, they had sought to escape, Nature, in her wonderful irony, driving out the anchorite to feed with the wild animals of the desert and giving to the hermit the beasts of the field as his companions.
>
> Yes: there was to be . . . a new Hedonism that was to recreate life, and to save it from that harsh, uncomely puritanism that is having, in our own day, its curious revival. . . . It was never to accept any theory or system that would involve the sacrifice of any mode of passionate experience. . . . Of

the asceticism that deadens the senses, as of the vulgar profligacy that dulls them, it was to know nothing. But it was to teach man to concentrate himself upon the moments of a life that is itself but a moment. (130f.)

My hypothesis is that if Dorian Gray tries to keep intact in himself his mother's beauty as it is fixed by the picture representing her as a bacchante (not an insignificant detail), this is an attempt to restore to her her Dionysian completeness beyond the ascetic ideal to which her father, the emblem of puritan society, subjected her.

A double reading of *The Picture of Dorian Gray*—this text in which the double is the only thing at issue—is thus possible, one reading serving as a golden mask for the other. On the first reading, the story of the degradation of the painting, the mirror of Dorian's soul, which culminates in his death, would be a kind of fantastic moral tale: the eye of conscience pursues the criminal always and everywhere; in spite of all the precautions he takes in order to hide from it, he can escape it only by killing himself. This would be the story of a monstrous, proud passion (the passion for the impossible, the desire to emulate a Greek god and keep the brilliance of youth and beauty for all time [220]) and its punishment. The beauty of Wilde's writing and his aestheticism would then be a mask for his "deep" moralizing. But this reading could not be Oscar Wilde's. According to the treatise that he sets out in the Preface, art must not have any moral goal, but instead a purely ornamental value, and it must seek simply to create what is "beautiful."

This moral interpretation that seems at first sight to emerge from the text serves as a cover (a golden screen) for another reading that can be heard, mutedly, in Lord Henry's musical and devilish voice as it leads the way to a new hedonism. The lesson of *The Picture of Dorian Gray* would then be the following: the excessive, mutilating puritanism that society imposes can only lead anyone who refuses to submit to it to adopt a morbid solution (that of melancholy) and to regress to the narcissistic stage of magic and animism. Dorian Gray does not succeed in mourning the loss of his mother's beauty, and her "beautiful image" has been withered by society, marked with a scarlet letter. This is why he incorporates it into himself to keep it fetishistically intact and immaculate. He magically transfers[47] the blemishes on his mother, and his own indiscernible ones, onto his picture, which is hidden behind a screen.

A "morbid" solution adopted by Dorian Gray (and Oscar Wilde?), then, for he is precisely not this "complete" man, the new hedonistic ideal. Though his mother was able to be a bacchante, following in the train of Dionysus, he himself is not really beautiful or strong enough to truly affirm life, to dare to reveal himself and look at himself naked. His fragility forces him to become an impostor and to hide behind the protecting mask of youth and beauty. Dorian Gray is not Nietzsche's Dionysian Oedipus, daring, if only for a moment, to look at the "truth" without veils or masks.[48]

Agreeing to look at one's face in a mirror, in all its nakedness, in the knowledge that its beauty is transient and destined to decay (thus following Socrates' advice, according to Xenophon)—for this one must have surmounted and gone beyond the mirror stage. But Dorian Gray seems to have become fixed on it, or at least to have regressed to it.

In conclusion I would say, then, that the picture of Dorian Gray, fascinating as it is, serves as a screen for the other picture, that of his mother, which is even more seductive and uncanny. Foregrounded right from the first page of the text, and displayed in the title, it is the former—more than Dorian Gray himself—that is the impostor: an "Apollonian" impostor masking another, "Dionysian" picture, which is less open to view. The imposture of beauty is also the imposture of the "author" of the text, who likes tricking his readers by serving them up the picture of Dorian so as better to conceal the other picture, which secretly haunts them.[49]

Don Giovanni, or the Art of Disappointing One's Admirers

ANN SMOCK

At the edge of the old cemetery in Linz, carved upon four adjacent, moss-covered tombstones four names, four epitaphs, eight indecipherable dates that increase the perplexity of the young foreigner passing through and confronted with this insoluble enigma, a long stake in his fist, hooded against the chill like a knight at a tournament beneath a steely sky threatening snow.

—Louis-René des Forêts, *Ostinato*

My title alludes to Sarah Kofman's essay on Molière's *Dom Juan:* "L'art de ne pas payer ses dettes" (Kofman and Masson 1991, 63–121), and to a story by des Forêts called "Les grands moments d'un chanteur" (des Forêts 1960), whose protagonist, a certain Frédéric Molieri, briefly the most fabulous singer in all of Europe, takes upon himself the role of Don Giovanni in Mozart's great opera and eventually treats his scandalized admirers to much more than they ever bargained for. Or, as they might have put it (outraged as they were), made them pay far, far too much for an extraordinarily disappointing evening at the opera.

Molière's insubordinate Dom Juan is likewise breathtakingly irreverent where obligations and accountability are concerned. He won't, as Sarah

---

Sarah Kofman introduced me to *Ostinato* before its publication as a single book, when it was still appearing intermittently, in pieces, in various reviews.

Kofman emphasizes, consider himself bound by any engagement at all, and this is because he's in permanent rebellion against the derisory conception, constantly pressed upon him, of life as a loan and of God as the supreme banker, who prudently keeps track of everything he gives lest he forget to collect all that's due him in the end. Such a calculating God could only be taken seriously by people who are equally vulgar. Sarah Kofman stresses this with relish. Only coarse, conniving people would credit a divine creditor. Molière's Dom Juan is a nobleman and above bookkeeping; he's an unbeliever and he scoffs at bargaining. If life really were a divine gift, then God wouldn't keep track of it but would forget it; he wouldn't count out one's allotted days but would lose count and would scarcely think to claim some equivalent in exchange. Were there such a thing as grace, it certainly would not be anything to count on or reckon with. On the contrary, it would be incalculable, unforeseeable, without regard for what is due to whom.

Dom Juan refuses to pay his debts, Sarah Kofman maintains, because he won't dignify with any sort of reverence the least edifying of social bonds, the one tying a debtor to a creditor, which is the pathetic, commonplace model for religious devotion. He doesn't deign to feel obligated for life and is as oblivious to what he has coming to him as to what he owes. Scornful of the bargain at the basis of moral seriousness and ethical responsibility, he simply won't acquire the anticipatory memory that Nietzsche says enables humans to pledge the future ahead of time and commit it in advance to making good on a deal struck sometime in the past, thereby dimming the future's gleam of indeterminacy and faithfully renouncing everything startlingly new.

Dom Juan the forgetter of promises delights in the seductive charm of the fortuitous encounter. And if Molière's play—constructed, Sarah Kofman observes, as a series of more or less happy chance events—nonetheless seems ultimately to denounce this daringly haphazard insouciance and to make Dom Juan the scoffing debtor pay, it's in a mocking parody of tragedy. For only vulgar credulity could see in the portentous arrival of a glorified bill collector a tragic denouement: only a servile and superstitious temperament like that of the valet, Sganarelle, who, as the final curtain falls upon the scene he's long predicted—the ultimate tit for tat—noisily laments that his wages are still owing. A refined ear, Sarah Kofman says, can hear Dom Juan laughing in Hell at his servant, whose so-called Heaven, so often evoked, cares absolutely nothing for him after all.

No doubt it's true that Dom Juan's soul is at stake in Molière's play, but to Sarah Kofman what Molière suggests is that laughter is the only salvation. I admired in her voice that cynical, defiant, laughing note—her impudence, scattering grave philosophy's truths, boldly greeting instead beautiful, uncanny signs and figures, "diablement trompeurs" (Kofman 1985b, 42). Even in her last desperate weeks, I believed that her laugh might save her. I recall the aggressive lightheartedness with which she was sometimes capable of regarding all that wounded her—the high-spirited malice in her writing, her mind's fierce *désinvolture,* worthy of a song remembered by des Forêts, a song that poured from the throat of a bird perched high in a chestnut tree just outside the window of a chapel: its liquid trills mounted effortlessly high above the choir's *Magnificat,* defying the solemn religious hymn of praise with gay impertinence and reminding the listener of rebels who stand all alone against authorities everyone else obediently acknowledges (des Forêts 1963, 127–131). These insurgents obstinately refuse to settle for anything less than victory, even though they know perfectly well that winning is at best an illusion. They believe in it all the same, defiantly, and of course they are not so foolish or self-serving or weak as to believe in it for a minute. They're defeated and indomitable, utterly unbeatable and beaten inevitably—"des battus imbattables," to borrow an expression of Sarah Kofman's (Kofman 1995b, 129).

It's their beauty that suffuses the entire *récit* that des Forêts calls "Les grands moments d'un chanteur." It's the magnificent impenitence of Mozart's Don Giovanni. Face to face at the end of the final scene with the devastating revelation of sin and death that he has himself provoked by the sheer force of his insolent disbelief, still unrepentant, the noble libertine flings five times his glorious "*No!*" in the face of the phantom judge, whose reality he thus openly acknowledges while he proudly disdains to acknowledge anything whatsoever. In des Forêts's story, this unflinching recognition of defeat that savagely recognizes no such thing stuns operagoers in all the great capitals of Europe with its beauty during the brief but sensational singing career of Frédéric Molieri, who makes his unexpected debut in the role of Don Giovanni—and who soon thereafter, no less unexpectedly, once again in the role of Don Giovanni, defies the expectations of his admirers with an appallingly tasteless performance, flouts the complacent sensibility of those he calls "faux raffinés," and withdraws from the stage.

Molière's Dom Juan, Sarah Kofman writes, laughing at all contractual arrangements, nonetheless enters into a contract with himself: a contract of "radical atheism," she says. This contract commits him to breaking all contracts and every commitment. Frédéric Molieri's sensational opera career involves, in my view, just such a bold and paradoxical engagement. His debut, unforeseen and indeed utterly implausible yet absolutely magnificent, occurred when a celebrated Viennese star, who was engaged to sing the title role in Mozart's *Don Giovanni* by the opera company for which

Molieri worked as an obscure but honorable member of the oboe section, fell to pieces at the end of Act I. At the last minute, Molieri stood in for him. He was, altogether unexpectedly—magically, it almost seemed—a huge success, and the opera director, practically weeping with relief and gratitude as the final curtain fell, pressed him to sign a contract right away, to continue as principal singer for the rest of the season. But Molieri was reluctant. He said that he couldn't be sure he'd be able to reproduce his initial success. Some observers apparently felt that he was just being coy, but the narrator says that for his part he found Molieri's prudence perfectly legitimate. "Comment s'engager à donner," he rhetorically inquires, "ce qu'on ne possède pas et qui, à tout moment peut vous faire défaut?" (How could you commit yourself to deliver something you don't possess, which is liable at any moment to fail you?) (des Forêts 1960, 21).

Now one can't always count on the pertinence of the narrator's perceptions, but here his remark is interesting: it suggests that a serious performer can't really be expected to guarantee anything and, indeed, that such an expectation—which is actually quite commonplace, especially among opera lovers who flock to performances of stars with enormous reputations—betrays a rather timid conception of art. Or quite a trivial one, scarcely worthy of the grandeur of serious performers who, far from ensuring that the audience gets its money's worth and comes away from the theater overcome with delight as anticipated, risk everything every time. More precisely, they risk exactly what they don't have in their possession or at their command: their role. To *play* a role—really to play it, according to this serious way of thinking—would be to stake it, the way bold gamblers might laughingly bet a sum of money they never could come up with in a million years. Great actors are those who make a promise they have no means of keeping, who just make it anyway and trust to luck. To act (*jouer*) would be to enter a game such as poker and take your chances. Indeed, the narrator wonders at one point in his account whether, just before Molieri went on stage for the first time, the thunderclaps that punctuate the music in the last scene before the Intermission in Mozart's *Don Giovanni* hadn't rung in his ears as an invitation to try his luck ("une invitation à tenter sa chance") (des Forêts 1960, 16).

Acting, understood in the way I suggest, would require the audacity to be utterly irresponsible and not a bit serious. However, note this: Frédéric Molieri took on the role of Don Giovanni—he assumed this risk—in an emergency, at a moment the narrator describes as one of those at which every act engages the total responsibility of its author. At such times, the narrator observes, most people tend to fly into flurries of anxious indecision, debating at length with themselves and others about what to do rather than doing anything at all. That is certainly how the director of the opera company and just about all the stagehands and performers behaved on the evening when the famous singer performing the role of Don Giovanni declared himself unable to continue after the end of Act I. By comparison, Frédéric Molieri, who took action in that crisis, appears to be quite a serious and responsible person after all—but chiefly about being irresponsible and unserious. Not hesitating to assume a responsibility that the Viennese star had proved unwilling or unable to bear even to the end of the evening, let alone to the end of his engagement with the opera company—not shrinking, that is, from taking on the obligation that the other singer, willingly or not, had dropped—Molieri plays Don Giovanni, proud libertine who drops all his responsibilities. He assumes the role that consists of assuming nothing whatsoever and shoulders an obligation that involves shrugging all duties off, and he plays that part to the hilt ("jusqu'au bout").

Though strongly attracted ever since childhood to the theater, up until that evening he had never played a role, never even tried acting. Indeed, he had a kind of aversion to making any sort of public appearance at all. He didn't show any signs of ambition, preferring, we learn from the narrator, to leave everything up to chance rather than count on his own efforts. To satisfy his parents, he'd learned to play the violin and the oboe and had pursued a respectable but modest career as an orchestra musician. I think it likely that on the night of his unanticipated debut in the role of Don Giovanni, something made him decide all of a sudden to go ahead and play his own role: the role of one who never undertakes any effort to earn anything (any sort of notice or acclaim), who no doubt cares very little for anything that could ever be won or deserved by dint of effort, and who would only be interested in what might come to him purely by chance. Life, for instance.

The role of a noble, then, and a libertine, indifferent to the wages of sin or of virtue. The role, moreover—inasmuch as it is Molieri's own—of one who has no role and never goes onstage, never makes public appearances. "Ne se produit pas," one would say in French. "Se produire: jouer, paraître en public au cours d'une représentation" (play a part, appear in public; literally, produce oneself, cause oneself to exist or to be born). Molieri's role is that of one who doesn't do so, who doesn't do anything in the way of causing himself to exist. No doubt his name, Molieri, is meant to suggest that of the author of Dom Juan—the subject, one might say, of the complex utterance that the whole drama constitutes.

Indeed, when, just the afternoon before his astonishing singing debut, Molieri lets a violinist friend of his in on the unsuspected fact that he has a gorgeous voice, he does so by hiding behind a bush as they stroll together on the banks of the Main in Frankfurt. From his hiding place he imitates that afternoon, "à s'y méprendre," first the voice of the singer slated to sing Don Giovanni that night, then the voice of the one who is to take the role of Leporello, and so on. Molieri demonstrates to his friend by way of this little scene the ploy of the person who, as it is bitterly remarked in another text of des Forêts (des Forêts 1963, 152–153), never shows up even to be congratulated no matter how much everyone shouts "Author! Author!" and who is without a voice except insofar as he arranges to get it into persons, as it were, or "im-personated," by distributing it among a number of dramatis personae. Molieri demonstrates to his friend the status of the person—*personne*—whom (is it from politeness?) we call the first. Who is content—he has his reasons!—to remain an unfulfilled, empty promise. Nothing but a name.

This is the role of Don Giovanni. Or, rather, it is the act of playing it— the daring act of coming out into the open, onto the stage, and into the bright lights and gambling it—that makes it that magnificent role. The act of playing it: by this I mean the assumption of full responsibility for the sheer irresponsibility of it, the serious commitment to honor by whatever means necessary, should it ever come to that, the absolutely groundless pledge that it consists of. The act of playing a role is the act of staking it, rashly—the act of staking imprudently exactly what one doesn't have in one's possession—with every intention of taking the consequences, whatever they may be. Molieri plays his own role in just this way, and thereby he makes it that glorious and risky role, the role of Don Giovanni, insouciant forgetter of engagements, obligations, promises, and debts of every sort, who tends not to show up to make good on his word; who doesn't care how much this carelessness will cost him and without flinching pays the highest price; who, even when Heaven itself calls, does not answer to his name; and who never shrinks for an instant from answering for that, without remorse.

GRAVE INSOUCIANCE

Everyone, it is more than once suggested in different texts by des Forêts, loves to identify with Don Juan. Proud, unbending, and at the same time never above a feast, a dance, a serenade—seriously unserious—he is manifestly blessed with the special grace of children, who play vehemently, with utter commitment and also at the same time for no purpose, with perfect detachment, taking themselves lightly and doing so seriously. To win, to lose; victory, defeat; happiness, despair—none of this is of great consequence, des Forêts writes in *Ostinato*. All that counts is to play, to play the

game, to plunge into it and play it with everything you've got, for no reason whatsoever except to laugh (des Forêts 1997, 183).

Sarah Kofman often evoked such grave lightheartedness. In keeping
with our deep thoughts we should be superficial, she says, in her essay on
The Portrait of Dorian Gray, which she entitled "L'imposture de la beauté,"
or "Beauty's Fraud" (Kofman 1995b, 9–48). In it she refers to Nietzsche
and to the Greeks as he characterized them in *The Birth of Tragedy:* they
knew that art is just a mask, but far from presuming to pry behind the fair
appearances with which the healing god Apollo disguises the Dionysian
"real," they kept to the surface of things. Not, one gathers, because they
were weak, but rather because they were strong: strong enough to grant
themselves illusions and to fall for the luminous deceptions that enchanted them. In keeping with their lucidity, they duped themselves,
never failing to love life and affirm it. Similarly do the rebels in des Forêts's
work believe in happiness and victory, which they are by no means so weak
as to believe in for a minute. Without hope they obstinately refuse ever to
abandon hope; they stake everything upon life's triumph. And when Don
Giovanni disdains to acknowledge the defeat of joy with a vehemence exactly proportionate to his unflinching recognition of death's victory, it is
then that the splendor of art, exemplified in "Les grands moments" by
Mozart's masterpiece, reaches its full intensity.

Dorian Gray couldn't stand the horror that life's inevitable rout inspired
in him, Sarah Kofman writes; he couldn't bear to know that youth's gorgeous perfection is an ephemeral appearance. Above all, he couldn't stand
to contemplate the ruin of his lovely mother's passionate existence. By
preserving his own beauty, like some indestructible fetish, he sought to
save her. But Sarah Kofman considers that Dorian Gray wasn't strong
enough or beautiful enough to love his beautiful mother, whose portrait,
mentioned at the very start of the story, shows her as one of the maenads.
He was neither strong nor beautiful enough, Kofman writes, to dare to be
seen without a mask or even for an instant to look on himself naked. He
wasn't deep enough, you might say, to be a shallow aesthete.

Dorian Gray hadn't the profundity you need to love a mere illusion or
the strength required to depend on a mirage for strength. He was really
just a fake: "Sa fragilité le contraint à devenir un imposteur et à se dis-
simuler derrière le masque protecteur de la jeunesse et la beauté" (His
fragility forced him to become an imposter and to hide behind the protective mask of youth and beauty) (Kofman 1995b, 48). Such beauty is
nothing but a fraud for those who, not lovely enough to do without disguises, require it for protection. Moreover, it falls in with obscurantism,
enforcing ignorance, nourishing hysteria. In her essay on *La religieuse*

(Kofman 1990b, 9–60), Sarah Kofman stresses how Diderot employs the "charm" supposedly proper to women in general, and characteristic in particular of the alleged author of his text (Suzanne, a young nun cloistered against her will), as a seductive veil behind which he develops a scathing critique of religious institutions. Literature, called into service thus as a cover, is like a captivating woman, adept at concealing things, coy, and also "innocent," which is to say intellectually stunted. Protected by Suzanne's charming exclamations of utter incomprehension as by a fool-proof alibi, Diderot describes women who delight in loving each other, oblivious of men. The pretty nun's alluring, feminine, "poetic" foolishness serves to distract readers pleasantly while Diderot boldly denounces the institutions that deny a decent education to women. But Sarah Kofman denounces *him* for maintaining nevertheless a conception of art as tranquilizer and of woman as alluring idiot. He contributes to annexing the "power" of art to that of ignorance, ever more "fascinating" than knowledge. A different literature, and a new woman, both of them freed from the desire to fascinate and seduce, remain to be invented, Kofman writes.

You'll reduce art to a crutch, I hear her say in various texts, if, not being bold enough to dispense with it, you are therefore not up to being helped by it. But for those with heads clear enough to be deceived by a mirage, beauty is no fraud, and if, from your awareness that art will never hold you up, you gain the strength gracefully to lean on it—if thus you stake everything upon beauty—it will give you nothing to reproach it for, even when it lets you fall.

Don Juan made just such an unlikely wager and stuck with it to the bitter end, and I suppose that if any of us dared to play our own role, it would be that of Don Giovanni. But who would ever be so bold, the narrator asks early in "Les grands moments," as to assume at a moment's notice the honor of that part, and the risk? Molieri got the chance to, unexpectedly one night, pretty much the way that on some night or morning or afternoon, as luck would have it, each one of us was born. Got the chance to live, that is. Maybe fewer of us than one would ordinarily think rise to the occasion. Well, at least we can all attend the opera. And from safe in the dim recesses of the auditorium rapturously listen, forgetful of ourselves, to a voice that—especially when the star performer has the quasi-supernatural power of a Frédéric Molieri—comes to us, as the narrator aptly puts it in "Les grands moments," all unaltered straight from the other world.

I think it is for each of us our own voice, which is to say the voice that reaches us from beyond the obstacle to it, and to ourselves, that we are— the voice that would be our own if ever we dared to come out from the shadows, emerge from behind the protective screen or the disguise that our survival is. If ever we dared to shed the role or mask that our person is. If ever we were mad enough—which of course we are not!—to rise up out of the audience and rush to intervene in the action on stage (*"We're* not crazy!" opera lovers stoutly declare in des Forêts's text). Yet Frédéric Molieri did rise up one night from the pit ("la fosse d'orchestre"). Something seems to have made him decide to abandon his cover, to drop his disguise and take up his part, to remove his mask and assume his role. Or I might put this the other way around: assuming his role, he finally got round to departing from it. No doubt his name, Molieri, is also meant to remind us of the great playwright who died on stage in the role of *le malade imaginaire.* So perhaps I should not have said that Molieri got a chance to play his part (and cause it thereby to be the great, dangerous part of Don Giovanni) pretty much the way that on some night or another, as luck would have it, each of us was born, but rather the way that at some time or another each of us will die. If we are up to it. If we dare to grab the chance and try our luck without costumes, wigs, or makeup, *à visage découvert,* as it were.

I should also, perhaps, have said that when the thunderclaps sounded in the music just before the intermission of Mozart's *Don Giovanni* and Molieri heard in them, according to the narrator's surmise, an invitation to try his luck, he heard in fact a challenge equivalent to the one the exuberant unbeliever, the noble cynic Don Giovanni, issues to the stone Commander when he invites the statue to dinner.

Indeed, issuing an invitation, or making an appointment, or agreeing to a rendezvous are acts that receive a somewhat disquieting emphasis in "Les grands moments." And if as his sensational singing career develops Molieri becomes more and more exasperated by his public, I suspect that it is because of his admirers' shallow, thoughtless interpretation of such acts, in particular the act of buying a ticket to the opera: committing oneself, that is, to being there at the theater and to meeting someone there if—however unlikely this may seem—that person should really show. If Molieri comes to detest his fans, I think that it is because they entertain so frivolous a relation to opera, taking their own role, when they attend, so lightly, never really engaging themselves in the act of being there. They do come, though, with appalling regularity; they are disgustingly confident of having a nice time at Molieri's performances and don't appear to think that they run any risk at all of disappointment—especially since he has become so famous. This dogged trust in him, this persistent belief that he will not surprise them with anything other than the anticipated brilliant performance, is just the public's habitual way of never taking him seriously, I expect he thinks, and of never believing in him, or in opera, at all. He refers to them as "faux raffinés": they purchase their tickets like some vulgar Don

Giovanni who'd invite the Commander to dine without any sense of the danger involved, feeling perfectly safe, never for an instant taking seriously even the remote possibility that the stony judge might, against all odds, accept and rather drastically interrupt the dinner hour on the appointed evening.

This ignoble interpretation of the role of Don Giovanni is in fact the one Molieri treats his audience to in the scandalously blasphemous last performance of his career. It is the performance his complacent public deserves. Bit by bit, starting toward the middle of Act I, he introduces into his interpretation a few tasteless gestures, an occasional gratuitous sentimental flourish; then some show-offy virtuoso embellishments; then, since his fans, so hard to disappoint, delighted with anything, have barely started to stir uncomfortably in their seats, a few wrong notes; then, at last, whole passages sung gratingly out of tune. By the time the terrifying final scene of Mozart's masterpiece arrives the audience is fully roused; indeed, it shouts its incredulous disgust as, staggering and waving his arms around before the advancing stone figure of the Commander, Molieri cries out in a ludicrously melodramatic voice, laughing at the same time, like a vulgar drunk entertaining himself by pretending to be scared to death of something he doesn't for a minute take seriously, knowing as he does that it is just a delusion brought on by too much wine. Thus does Molieri show his admirers, in his horrendous final performance, the trivial excuse for art that, loving him, they have loved—the cowardly travesty of bold rebellion. Thus does he hold a mirror up to their disbelieving faces and let them look their fill upon the only Don Giovanni their petty souls are able to love.

DISPOSSESSION

This is just the sort of devastating artistic effect that delighted Sarah Kofman and drew her to literature. Writing, she was happy to observe, is very apt to prove a disaster for self-love. It has a diabolical tendency to undermine your "identity," cut your ego to pieces, confound your "genius." In the little book she wrote on Hoffmann's autobiography of a cat (*Die Katze Murr*), she mischievously stresses "feline writing" ("l'écriture de chat"), which scratches out the metaphysical opposition between intelligence and instinct and writes art straight into life itself, tearing human, all-too-human, narcissism to shreds in the process and scratching up our edifying monuments—Science, Reason, the alleged proofs of our so-called mastery—products, in fact, of our *ressentiment* and jealousy (Kofman [1976] 1984a). We humans all want to be king of the beasts; we want to be loved like a god. And it is by no means only on the unlikely occasions when a cat takes up the pen that our effortful attempts to command such adulation are at risk. For all writing worth anything is barbed and feline and a menace: let it be as linear, as logocentric, as you like, Sarah Kofman says, and it is still sure to dispossess you; it has no respect for propriety or property (Kofman [1976] 1984a, 139).

THE RISKS OF OPERAGOING

When Frédéric Molieri gave his admirers such a disagreeable shock at the end of Mozart's *Don Giovanni,* one might say that he called them, just as the Commander calls Don Giovanni in the opera's final scene. Molieri called his fans back to themselves—back from the self-forgetfulness, the complacent rapture they habitually enjoy at the opera (he reminded them rudely of themselves). He called them to come to, wake up, remember their role, and make good on their frivolous promise to meet him at the opera. He invited them to come out in the open and answer for their highly dubious claim to be there at all in the dim, shadowy auditorium. If they had suspected that they stood a chance of being unmasked thus and judged at the opera—if they had thought that they ran any risk of discovery by loving art—no doubt they would have stayed at home. But they didn't think that they had anything to fear. They weren't believers. They considered opera to be a well-produced mirage whose willing victims they were delighted to be from time to time of an evening; they assumed that they could enjoy the occasional thrill of self-recognition for the mere price of a ticket and without any danger of actually encountering anyone, or finding anyone out. In their sanguine view, nothing ever really comes of art. I wouldn't say that Molieri was exactly a believer in opera any more than his trivial admirers were. But I think that he thought something ought to come of art. I think that when he unexpectedly took to the stage, he decided suddenly to gamble everything on the chance that out in the bright lights and in the role of Don Giovanni he could, perhaps, even just once, *embody* an insignificant nothing, an empty promise, a mirage, and command a stunned, incredulous belief in it.

In any case there is much in "Les grands moments" to suggest that simply going to the opera—just showing up there of an evening—is really a rather dramatic act and that members of an audience are, in this sense, actors too, even though they don't usually play their role. Among all the invitations and appointments made rashly or fearfully or imperiously and then kept or just barely missed or broken in "Les grands moments," there is one especially memorable rendezvous at the opera, made by the narrator and his old friend Anna Fercovitz. It rather strongly suggests that to go to the opera is to answer a mysterious summons without quite knowing what to expect, but to answer anyway, to take a chance.

Anna Fercovitz, whom the narrator hasn't seen for a very long time, unexpectedly appears before him at a moment near the beginning of the story when he happens to be feeling particularly dazed and disoriented. Like a figure in a dream bearing an enigmatic message, she presses a pink ticket into his hand, saying, "Come without fail. Let nothing prevent you." Then she disappears. Moreover, when they meet later and talk about the performance they've attended together, the narrator has the vague impression that he is being tested, and one might very well feel that he is undergoing a sort of interview or trial, to see if he is equal to performing some function, or an audition, like Moliere's hasty one just before he went on stage for the first time, to see if he is up to playing some role. He is surprised by Anna's tone of voice, which, he says, makes it sound from time to time as if she were delivering an ultimatum to him. All this could easily make one suspect that attendance at the opera involves an unforeseeable chance—one last chance, in fact—if one is up to the occasion, to accomplish something one has put off far too long. Maybe it's to honor an engagement or pay a debt, or perhaps it's rather to incur some obligation, give one's word. It's to die, perhaps, or else to live.

Of course, people generally just purchase their reserved seats in the ordinary way and expect, based on the established reputation of the company and the composer, to get their money's worth. They are perfectly confident in the theatrical structure that *bolsters* the subject, as Sarah Kofman says (Kofman 1985b), arranging for him to be "bien assis" and to blissfully dominate the scene where suffering and death are "represented." Propped up securely, he cleanses himself of the intolerable and spares himself the madness of dispossession. Nevertheless, it could be that whoever puts on evening dress and takes his place in the auditorium responds—boldly perhaps or perhaps rather timidly (limiting the risks involved to a strict minimum), or perhaps just thoughtlessly, without any real awareness of the danger involved—to the attraction exerted by the peril of discovery. What if, some evening, that person—the so-called first—who never shows, who really can't afford to, does, after all, turn up? What if it turns out that someone actually does live under his name? What if he emerges and proves unmistakably to be he? Perhaps to act (*jouer*) is to ask for, or call upon, oneself—indeed, to go further and brazenly provoke an answer, running the risk that one really will receive a response, and really will appear, before one's very eyes.

It's that risky adventure, of discovery, I think, that draws people to the theater: they come there to find themselves, as it were, at the risk of finding themselves out—taking themselves by surprise, coming upon someone they'd never expected, in whose reality they don't believe, and, quite against their better judgment, recognizing themselves. Spontaneously affirming in spite of themselves, when caught thus unawares, what they had no intention of acknowledging, as if they'd proved unable to resist the pressure brought by teachers and priests and parents and, forsaking their pride, just babbled out the creed that those authorities dictated, or as if they'd turned out unable to withstand torture and had shamelessly talked. Or had succumbed to the temptation to drink and abandoned all dignity on one of those occasions when people gather round a table imbibing and communing, faces red, eyes bulging. For really, one comes to the theater to meet someone and confide in him or her, at the risk of denouncing oneself. *Se découvrir:* to discover oneself, and also to let oneself be known. To confide, to tell a secret. To uncover, disclose, expose oneself to the inspection of someone else, or of many others. Quite possibly to make an embarrassing public spectacle: *s'exhiber. S'exhiber sur les planches.*

This scornful expression for crude acting applies to the overwrought Viennese star whom Molieri replaced at the last minute on the night of his debut—the overheated singer who got completely carried away during the agitated party scene at the end of Act I in Mozart's opera and performed as if he actually were drunk and had forgotten he was in a public place. This unhappy artist had ignored the conductor and run away with the tempo; he'd performed as if all he could think about was getting through his role as fast as possible, the way sometimes, when facing a grave risk, one can't stand to do anything but throw oneself headlong into it, eyes tight shut, in hopes of just getting the whole thing over with fast. Likewise, when you have to abandon your cover and venture onto dangerous terrain, you are apt to find the tension and suspense of stealthy maneuvers unbearable and to just rush out into the open, yelling. Or when you are engaged in some action such as writing, or such as living, as des Forêts says in *Ostinato:* some risky action that you've undertaken without any idea what the point of it could be and that probably won't find its resolution except in death. When the shadow of that "monstrous figure" falls across your path, then "foncer droit les yeux fermés [est] l'unique recours contre le dégoût qu'elle inspire et la peur d'avoir à l'affronter" (to charge straight ahead, eyes closed, is the only recourse against the horror death inspires and the fear of having to confront it) (des Forêts 1997, 105–106).

I expect at any rate that Molieri takes to the stage on the off chance that Anna Fercovitz will meet him there: I suppose that for him *se découvrir* means above all to confide in Anna and that he boldly undertakes to ask her for himself, as it were. He challenges her to recognize him, I think—invites her to answer him, defies her to judge him. Provoking her hatred and braving her contempt, he dares her to believe in him.

Things are difficult between them. Molieri tells the narrator that the public loves him for what he is not and for what deserves no admiration—and this is painful enough—but that with Anna Fercovitz things are more difficult still, because she cannot bring herself to hate him for what he is. He must sense that while most of his admirers misguidedly adore him as a mere entertainer, a person of no substance whatsoever, utterly dependent on the love and approval of others, who spends his evenings seducing one hall-full of strangers after another (a low, dependable Don Juan), Anna recognizes him for what he is, which is to say, *in credible.* From the stunning rigor with which he incarnates Don Giovanni, she must see how unbelievable he is—how utterly fantastic. After all, when he complains that there are no male roles quite to his liking and that he wants to sing Carmen and Lulu, she laughs and says why not, what's to prevent you?—as though she knows he could play any role, since he has none of his own, and be anybody at all, since he is no one, and sing soprano if he wants, since he is not a man. But she can't reconcile herself to the contempt for him that she manages to express intermittently; she thinks he is *fabulous,* although she can only state this in stiff and affected phrases that don't appear to convince even her; that surprise the narrator, who remembers her as the most endearingly frank, untheatrical of women; and that make Molieri himself impatient.

When will she ever show him that she knows who he is? He must wish she would, for example, turn away from him, disgusted once and for all, as any reasonable woman would turn away from the jilting cheat whose deceitfulness he has not hesitated to assume. He must wish she would turn away, for he always seems to be trying to disappoint her, and often he appears to find her reluctance to be displeased discouraging, if not indecent (one evening the narrator sees him recoil with unmistakable disgust when she happens to touch his arm in the course of an awkward conversation, and on another occasion he crudely mocks her for pursuing him, treating her as a woman one simply can't shake off). But it seems she can't quite bring herself to answer his invitation to hate him for what he is—which is how he begs her to love him, love him for what makes her hate him. She lurches between intoxication and disgust, euphoria and humiliation, all the way to the end. Whatever it is that inclines her toward him seems to have turned her into a *comédienne* who tirelessly contrives to avoid the discovery she cunningly angles for even though this wretched artfulness clearly makes her miserable.

And the singer himself: how could he convince her of his rigorous responsibility, which consists in taking it unapologetically upon himself to be unworthy of trust and perfectly unbelievable? Perhaps if she could witness a blatant demonstration of irresponsibility on his part, a lamentable exhibition like the sloppy and overwrought performance by the singer he replaced the night of his debut, who didn't bother to adhere to the demands of his role but flapped about the stage in a ludicrous effort to impress his spectators and win their love. Barring such an embarrassing failure, Molieri surely won't succeed, except in prudently covering up exactly what he longs to show. But does he really want the discovery he wants? I don't suppose so. And no doubt it vexes him still more that he should prove thus unable to be serious about being taken seriously. He is like a truth whose sole proof lies in its doubtfulness, a secret whose discovery disguises it. Disappointment is the *condition* of an encounter with him—an encounter happy beyond belief. Indeed, with his awful last performance he does contrive to extract from all his admirers this incredulous tribute: *it can't really be you.* "What is this semblance we encounter?" they angrily exclaim. "Who is this shadow, this pale ghost?" (des Forêts 1960, 50).

UNRECOGNIZABLE BEAUTY

Molieri tries to win for art—for beauty, that mirage, and for himself, that hollow promise—the response at once utterly skeptical and absolutely confident that Sarah Kofman, following Nietzsche, imagines the Greeks were strong enough and beautiful enough to accord life's insubstantial splendor. In particular he asks Anna Fercovitz not to mistake beauty for the fraud it is not—the reassurance, the shield, the seductive mask—but to recognize the sheer nothing that it is—the pure illusion, the lie. He asks her to love him, in other words, without masks or veils or illusions, but naked, for the sake of what it is that makes her hate him. That he should ask her is, in itself, magnificent. But by what traits is such magnificence to be recognized? By its "own," "repulsive" ones alone. And what resources would you call upon within yourself if you had to answer someone whom you loved and who asked—indeed, it would be just exactly this that would make you love him!—that you hate him instead and prove in this way the glad persistence of your love?

I expect that Molieri demands of Anna Fercovitz what Sarah Kofman expects from the Nietzschean, Dionysian Oedipus that poor Dorian Gray was not. Kofman reads at least two "lessons" in Wilde's story, and I propose one here for des Forêts's: strength and beauty are no one's attributes, they cannot be attested to, they have no proper form. Perhaps they inhere in the distortions and cross-outs, the lamentable claw marks and rips that Kofman links to writing, always "déappropriante." Maybe it is a measure of that devilish, feline energy that Frédéric Molieri should be revealed at his noblest on the night he shows himself to be a clown, mugging for laughs and begging for love. Indeed, he does finally get everyone who ever loved him to hate him. One easily imagines the desperate sort of joy he must feel to wreck his chances thus—to seize, as he does, a lucky occasion to ruin them.

LUCK

But luck, Maurice Blanchot writes—*la chance*—is just another name for *le hasard*, which isn't good or bad. It is just chance. Nevertheless, *la chance*, in French at least, is good. Which leads Blanchot to say that good or bad, luck is just luck, always good (Blanchot 1973, 40). You might put it this way: luck is neither good nor bad; it is just good. It's good regardless of whether it is or isn't. Its goodness, that is, doesn't really count one way or the other in the matter of its being good.

Now in a different story by des Forêts, called "La chambre des enfants" and published in the same collection with "Les grands moments" (des Forêts 1960), a schoolboy states that if it weren't for the masters at his school—if it weren't for all the drama (the inspections and interrogations, the praise and scolding, the rebellions, confessions, and punishments) that the presence of the masters guarantees—he and his fellow pupils would, of course, still do all their chores, but they wouldn't do them well and they wouldn't do them poorly; they would just do them. I don't suppose that this performance would be of any interest to anyone or that there would be anything to say about it. I suppose it would be quite like the "nothing" about which Molieri is amused to observe the narrator at the end of "Les grand moments" getting so distraught, as he anxiously presses the retired singer to explain his whole story: his gorgeous voice, its sudden quasi-magical revelation, its no less sudden unaccountable loss, and his spectacular fall from his fabulous pinnacle of fame. Such *bonheur*, such *malheur*; such victory, such defeat. "Is it true you've renounced singing?" the feverish narrator asks Molieri. And "Is it painful for you?" And "If you could, would you sing again?" Molieri mildly suggests that his questioner leave off dramatizing, since he, Molieri, has not renounced anything; he is just unable to sing so he is not singing. "There is nothing to say about it," he adds. "It is of no interest to anyone." "If you couldn't walk anymore, would you go on walking?" (des Forêts 1960, 54).

Anna Fercovitz suspected, at the height of Molieri's career—when she was struggling and failing to find the right words and tone of voice to say that he was a great singer, a noble heart, and her lover—that he was "insignificant": that he didn't sing well, I suppose, and didn't sing poorly; he just sang. This must be what she longed to discover (that there was nothing to discover, to think, or to say about the whole business), since this is no doubt what she felt intuitively to be incomparably beautiful. Certainly it is what she dreaded to think yet feared she did think after all, inasmuch as she couldn't quite think it (thinking instead that Molieri was great, that he was horrible, and so on, just what people do routinely think, sparing themselves much thought). She kept trying to get her friend the narrator to formulate a clear judgment of the singer (though she also went out of her way to prevent him from doing so), and once, when she'd extracted from him a rather stiff declaration that such a marvelous voice couldn't possibly be disappointing, he saw her disconsolately draw her neck back into her shoulders like a person who despairs of ever being understood: "Oh, his voice, yes, of course," she mutters impatiently (des Forêts 1960, 38).

Anna must feel that Molieri's voice—his marvelous voice, his disappointing voice—is really a red herring in the whole affair, the whole bewildering affair of his marvelous voice. She must sense that its beauty is something like luck's goodness, which doesn't matter one way or the other in the matter of luck's being good. This is not for a moment to deny that she *extracts* "marvelous" from her interlocutor, or that she often accuses him despairingly of finding Molieri "disappointing" and finally decides to break off with the singer because she thinks her friend the narrator finds him "insignificant." After all, words are our masters in everything; even to keep quiet we have to have recourse to them, and they will always say too much or too little (des Forêts 1988). They will always say marvelous or disappointing, gorgeous or insignificant. But Molieri's beautiful voice must have been similar to Anna's lovely face, which, despite her having grown quite a bit older by the time of her affair with Molieri since the narrator's earlier friendship with her, is still lovely, as the narrator observes, though this doesn't appear to give her any confidence for, as he also dimly perceives, beauty is not an advantage in her affair with Molieri. I don't suppose that beauty is a disadvantage, either; I expect that insofar as this affair concerns beauty, beauty doesn't matter one way or the other. Anna Fercovitz must have sensed just exactly that insignificance in Molieri's voice—the lovely insignificance of beauty.

As far as her judgment is concerned, then—her judgment as to what Molieri is and what he isn't (a marvel, a disgrace, a noble heart, a coward)— as far as her decision is concerned, it isn't a matter of any decision at all one way or the other. Rather, it's a matter of the swift stroke with which a judgment might retract its pertinence, suspend itself, and suddenly just hang there. It's a matter of the decision whereby a decisive word—for example, *marvelous,* or perhaps *disgraceful*—might abruptly just annul its significance in the affair that, in the very same movement, it would decide. Between Frédéric Molieri and Anna Fercovitz, it's a matter of a trenchant word like that, which would simply hang there then, like the words *good* and *beautiful* when, designating their perfect irrelevance, those words have their full, their stunning meaning.

Molieri's voice must have communicated with dubious words like those, I think: with the words required to remove those words from language—the words that mean they have no meaning. *Unbelievable* words that stun you, words you can't take seriously. Questionable words to send you lurching between wonder and bitterness. *Perplexing* words, really, like the names upon tombstones. Insoluble enigma.

Kofman's Hoffmann

DUNCAN LARGE

The fact that Sarah Kofman devoted six of her twenty-seven books to Freud and five to Nietzsche is ample indication of their importance to her thinking, so it is not surprising that it should be her work on these two writers that was first to be translated into English (and other languages) and that has in turn provided the basis for the reputation she has rapidly acquired in recent years outside of France. Yet one should not lose sight of the fact that the fascination she showed from the beginning to the end of her career with the "literary" effects of philosophical and psychoanalytic writing was counterbalanced by a complementary philosophical and psychoanalytic concern with more specifically literary writing—from the studies collected together as *Quatre romans analytiques* (1974) through to her essay on Wilde's *Picture of Dorian Gray*, "L'imposture de la beauté" (1995b, 9–48). Her trajectory in between spans books on Nerval (1979), Shakespeare (1990a), and Molière (Kofman and Masson 1991), but the literary writer for whom she showed the greatest and most sustained interest was the German Romantic novelist and story writer E. T. A. Hoffmann.

This chapter addresses the three studies of works by Hoffmann that Kofman published in the mid-1970s, relatively early in her philosophical

My thanks to Roger Stephenson and Keith Ansell Pearson for giving me the opportunity to present earlier versions of this chapter as papers to the Centre for European Romanticism at the University of Glasgow and the Centre for Philosophy and Literature at the University of Warwick. A highly condensed version of parts of its argument was published in Large 1995, 451–453.

career. Whereas her first book, *L'enfance de l'art,* published in 1970 (translation 1988c), had been devoted to Freud and the visual arts, her second book on Freud, *Quatre romans analytiques* (translated as *Freud and Fiction,* 1991b), focuses on his relation to literature, and the longest of its essays, "The Double Is/and the Devil: The Uncanniness of *The Sandman* (*Der Sandmann*)" (Kofman 1991b, 119–162), is a reading of Freud's reading of what is probably (not least because of Freud's attentions) Hoffmann's most famous story. Kofman's initial approach to Hoffmann, and to writing on literature in general, is mediated through Freud, but of the four writers addressed in *Freud and Fiction* (Empedocles, Hebbel, Jensen, and Hoffmann), it is Hoffmann alone who engages her attention thereafter,[1] for in successive years she followed up this initial study with two longer ones devoted to the German writer's two novels: "Vautour rouge" (Kofman 1975), a long essay on *The Devil's Elixirs* published in the influential collective volume *Mimesis: Des articulations,* and *Autobiogriffures* (Kofman [1976] 1984a), a short book on *Life and Opinions of Murr the Tomcat.*

My interest in these works here is not so much in their outstanding quality as interpretations of Hoffmann—which Hoffmann studies have so far, unfortunately, failed to register[2]—as in the light they shed on the development of Kofman's own critical method. Of the three, only one ("The Double Is/and the Devil") and a half (of *Autobiogriffures*) have so far been translated into English, and "The Double Is/and the Devil" is the only one to have attracted critical attention, from those such as Lis Møller in *The Freudian Reading* (Møller 1991) who echo Kofman's interest. But by taking the three studies together I want to argue that they show Kofman moving away from Freud's agenda and pursuing her own concerns. More specifically: coming as they do after her first two books, *L'enfance de l'art* and *Nietzsche et la métaphore,* which was published in 1972 (translation 1993b), they form part of her ongoing dialogue with Freud and Nietzsche; indeed, each exemplifies the (consciously cultivated) dialogue within her writing *between* Freud and Nietzsche, a dialogue that, in the "Rhapsodic Supplement" to *Explosion II,* Kofman herself characterizes as the specificity of her critical method:

> Freud and Nietzsche, these two rival "geniuses" whom I have always needed to keep together so that neither of them could ultimately win out over the other or over "me": continually playing with the one and the other, and playing the one off against the other, within "myself," I prevent each from gaining mastery (reading Freud, I read him with a third, Nietzschean ear; reading Nietzsche, I understand him ["je l'entends"] with my fourth, Freudian ear). (Kofman 1993a, 371f.; cf. Kofman with Hermsen 1992, 66)

Kofman's studies of Hoffmann in the mid-1970s, I shall argue, demonstrate the emergence of this method not simply as a way of reading Nietzsche and Freud, but as a way of reading that is more generalizable in its application.

In the importance Kofman ascribes to literature, she of course takes after both Freud and Nietzsche: the former drawing on literary examples even as he attempts to establish psychoanalysis as a "scientific" discipline,[3] the latter adjudging the most important German books (apart from his own) to be not Kant's *Critiques* or even Schopenhauer's *The World as Will and Representation* but rather Eckermann's *Conversations with Goethe* ("the best German book there is" [Nietzsche 1986, 336]) and the poetry of Heinrich Heine (Nietzsche 1992, 28).[4] Yet Kofman's inquiry is also a valuable instance of that typically deconstructive concern to undermine any generic divisions into "philosophical" and "literary" texts by addressing the textuality of all texts: the "effects of writing" in even the most "philosophical" of productions, and correlatively the philosophical interest that even the most "literary" of works can repay. Together with Derrida and the other philosophers in the group associated with the Philosophie en effet series, Kofman rejects any narrow definition of philosophy "proper" ("la philosophie") in favor of a broader conception of "the philosophical" ("le philosophique"), which counteracts such attempts to divide philosophy off from its traditional "others."[5] In Kofman's early Hoffmann studies, then, and in "The Double Is/and the Devil" in particular, the figure of Derrida can be seen as a further point of triangulation. In 1973 she published an important essay on Derrida entitled "Un philosophe 'unheimlich'" (1984b, 11–114), which leaves many "traces" in her work on Hoffmann: her "real encounter" with Derrida (Kofman with Jardine 1991, 108, 111; Kofman with Ender 1993, 11) gives birth to a deconstructive approach that at once both establishes and evades Nietzsche and Freud's agonal embrace.

THE REPRESSION OF WRITING
("THE DOUBLE IS/AND THE DEVIL")

"The Double Is/and the Devil" represents the first full working out of a reading of Freud's reading of Hoffmann already adumbrated in *The Childhood of Art* (1988c, 6–8, 97f.) and "Un philosophe 'unheimlich'" (1984b, 57 n. 6, 71–73). In choosing "The Sandman" as the subject of her first Hoffmann study, Kofman is led by Freud's 1919 essay "The 'Uncanny'" ("Das Unheimliche"):[6] all her readings of Hoffmann will in one sense complement this essay, Freud's only engagement with the German writer,[7] by extrapolating Freud's interest in Hoffmann to other works that he leaves relatively, or entirely, uncommented. More productively, though, as Kofman signals at the outset of the Introduction to *Freud and Fiction,* her aim—in *Freud and Fiction,* but also beyond it—will be to *supplement* Freud's analyses (with all the Derridean force of the term):

> The four essays which follow, grafted onto four of Freud's literary interpretations . . . , are in fact rewritings of the texts from which they stem. In pushing the Freudian interpretation to its limits, in the most faithful way possible, they effect displacements which allow them, I feel, to "surmount" a purely analytic kind of reading. (1991b, 3)[8]

Through her own polyperspectival strategy in reading "The Sandman," Kofman will recuperate its perspectivism from the monologism of Freud's reading, a strategy that is more faithful to the psychoanalytic method Freud in a sense sells short, and that at the same time allows Kofman to critique that method, its evasions and aporias. By "grafting" her critical analyses onto Freud's, she draws attention to the very limits of the Freudian inquiry itself, and especially to Freud's systematic repression of precisely those "literary" qualities of the texts he subjects to scrutiny.

Freud himself was aware of (certain of) the limits of psychoanalysis as an approach to the products of artistic creation: in the closing chapter of his study "Leonardo da Vinci and a Memory of His Childhood," he defensively tries to forestall "the criticism . . . that I have merely written a psychoanalytic novel" (Freud 1910, 134). But Kofman mischievously borrows this formulation for the (French) title of her own study (cf. Kofman 1988c, 157–159), for Freud is more of a "novelist" than he himself is prepared to admit (Kofman 1991b, 3–8), and his interpretations of all these works, she argues in Nietzschean mode, are forceful, violent *appropriations.* Such is the character of any reading, and yet Freud's is, for Kofman, an extreme case—his readings are akin to the appropriations of the "pre-Socratics" by later philosophers, an analogy on which she dwells in the section entitled "Aristotle and the 'Pre-Socratics,'" which precedes the studies in *Freud and Fiction* "proper" (Kofman 1991b, 9–19).[9]

In his essay "The 'Uncanny,'" Freud first approaches the term *unheimlich* obliquely by considering a number of dictionary definitions for its apparent opposite, *heimlich.* These cluster around two main senses, "familiar"/"homely" and "concealed"/"secret," so that *unheimlich* emerges as the familiar that temporarily appears to be foreign, or the secret that comes to light, as in the definition by Schelling that retains Freud's interest for the rest of the study: "'Unheimlich' is the name for everything that ought to have remained . . . secret and hidden but has come to light" (Freud 1919, 224, ellipses in original). Equipped with this definition, Freud then proceeds to an analysis of various evocations of the uncanny, beginning with Hoffmann's "The Sandman": here he interprets the hero Nathaniel's ultimately suicidal psychosis as deriving from a repressed infantile castration anxiety that periodically resurfaces in his adult life at the sight of the optician Coppola, an "uncanny" double of the lawyer Coppelius (the "Sandman" of the story's title) who, during one traumatic incident in Nathaniel's boyhood, apparently threatened to put out his eyes with burning coals. "The prefix '*un*' is the token of repression," Freud goes on to conclude (Freud 1919, 245; cf. Freud 1925, 235f.).

Such is Freud's neat solution to the complexities of the story, but what he himself calls his "predilection for smooth solutions and lucid exposition" (Freud 1919, 249) leaves Kofman less than satisfied. In "The Double Is/and the Devil," she argues that by seeking to isolate a single definition for the concept of "the uncanny" in Hoffmann's story—and then insisting on it, especially in the face of an earlier definition by Jentsch that the uncanny involves an irresolvable moment of intellectual uncertainty such as that provoked by the "living doll" Olympia—Freud is *mis*appropriating the text in the interest of his own interpretative schematization.[10] His desire to isolate "the uncanny" as a universalizable concept is in any case already the first false move for Kofman, since "uncanniness" invades the text to such an extent that it necessarily eludes fixation within a traditional conceptual framework of binary oppositions, even one as relatively nuanced as Freud's. For although Freud derives a paradoxical semantics of the term that always already includes its apparent opposite, he still short-circuits its complexity, the other potential meanings that he even explicitly acknowledges—its magical associations, for example (Kofman 1991b, 146)—only in order to pass over them again. In deriving his "master concept," it seems that Freud is already taking shortcuts, a strategy that for Kofman is but typical of his whole procedure in this analysis, his compulsion to account for every phenomenon adequately and completely, to arrive at his analytic telos of "scientific" certainty ("psychoanalysis leaves no remainder" is his watchword [Kofman 1991b, 122]).[11]

In many other ways that Kofman tracks down in the course of her close reading of Freud's discussion, it is shown to exhibit this tendency to abolish uncertainty or indeterminacy too readily and prematurely, to foreclose on the disclosure of the text's truly "uncanny" potential: when he unproblematically reduces Coppola and Coppelius to "one and the same" figure, for example; when he discounts the possibility that the uncanniness of the Sandman and that of the automaton Olympia might actually derive from the same instinctual reaction; when he wraps up the end of the story without allowing it an ambiguous openness. Kofman's response to these evasions on Freud's part is on the one hand eminently deconstructive: she points, for example, to the duplicities of Freud's own interpretative strategy, such as when he discounts Jentsch's interpretation only to reintroduce intellectual uncertainty as an operator into his own analysis at other levels (Kofman 1991b, 125). What is more, Kofman pays close attention to precisely those marginal features of the text where its fault lines are more evidently discernible: footnotes, acknowledged selections and omissions, and so on (cf. Kofman 1984b, 17). As an example, the all-too-cursory plot summary that Freud gives of Hoffmann's story in one of his more substantial footnotes (Freud 1919, 232 n. 1) omits to mention the detail—"essential, like all details" (Kofman 1995a, 144)—that the Sandman plucks out the eyes of little children, in the traditional rendering, in order to feed "his" own, a feminization of the Sandman figure (as maternal) that Freud leaves out of account because it would otherwise disrupt his system of gender attributions. As Kofman brilliantly demonstrates in her essay on Freud's interpretation of Jensen's *Gradiva,* the selective and slanted plot summaries with which he prefaces his analyses of literary texts—ostensibly included simply to refresh the reader's memory—are always carefully constructed in order to vindicate the invariably thematic interpretations to come.[12]

Such close attention as Kofman devotes to every aspect of Freud's text, though—including, indeed especially, the marginal—is itself an orthodox psychoanalytic procedure (her concern with detail is a paraphrase of Freud in *The Interpretation of Dreams*), and in "Un philosophe 'unheimlich'" she brings together deconstruction and psychoanalysis in precisely this respect: "It is perhaps in the quality of the attention he pays to texts that Derrida is closest to psychoanalysis and its way of listening. . . . [Derrida's way of listening] has its eye on the slightest details, on everything that is discarded by the logocentric tradition, considered to be a negligible and secondary remainder" (Kofman 1984b, 92). "The Double Is/and the Devil" in fact exhibits a doubly psychoanalytic technique that works on the level both of the Hoffmann story, for which it seeks to provide a more adequate interpretation, taking account of more of its (specifically *textual*) effects that Freud chooses to omit, and on the level of Freud's interpretation, which is itself subjected to a psychoanalytic critique.

On one level, then, Kofman's interpretation of Hoffmann's story reinstates the figure of the mother (Nathaniel's mother, the Sandman as maternal figure) whom Freud so systematically occludes. Nathaniel's psychotic symptoms derive, for Kofman, not so much from a fear of the return of the castrating father figure, the crux of Freud's analysis, as from a repressed desire for his mother that issues into a confrontation with the emergent death drives within him. By reorienting her psychoanalytic interpretation in such a way, by applying a category (the death drives) that Freud himself, at the time of his composition of "The 'Uncanny'" in 1919, was only in the course of formulating in response to his experience of the First World War, a category that would only surface in his writings with *Beyond the Pleasure Principle* in 1920 and subsequently, Kofman is situating Freud's analysis as a transitional text, the internal contradictions reflecting its position on the cusp of Freud's break with the bipartite psychic model and his turn to the tripartite divisions of the 1920s and 1930s.

But beyond this historical contextualization, Kofman is also making a more specific claim about the nature (and especially the inadequacies) of Freud's essay: his unitary, reductive reading of "the uncanny" as a symptom of the return of the repressed serves as a feint, a repression of the death drives on Freud's *own* part. The symptom of this is not only the deceptive and inadequate neatness of Freud's reading, but also the excessively thematic character of his representation of the operation of "the uncanny" in the story (Kofman 1991b, 128–132). Working against such a reductive and distorting thematic concentration, Kofman inflates the "concept" of the uncanny to the point where it incorporates not only, paradoxically, its own status as (but) quasi-concept, but also the effect of Hoffmann's text (as text) and of writing itself. Ironically, then, Kofman reinstates the question of writing, of the textuality of Hoffmann's story, as precisely the repressed element that Freud "brackets" in characterizing the uncanny as (merely) the return of the repressed. In the third part of his study, Freud introduces a distinction between real and fictional instances of the uncanny, arguing that although in fiction many more instances of it are to be found than can be accounted for by his "general contention that the uncanny proceeds from something familiar which has been repressed" (Freud 1919, 247), nevertheless, as far as real life is concerned, his definition still holds—thus conveniently "forgetting" that this definition was itself derived from a work of fiction. Freud constantly distances himself from the "diabolical" order of the fictional in Hoffmann's text, Kofman argues: "Taking most of his examples from fiction, Freud does not take into account the specificity of this realm, a specificity which is subsequently acknowledged" (Kofman 1991b, 128). She counters this by reading Hoffmann against Freud and deriving in the second half of her essay a number of characterizations of writing from Hoffmann's story itself. The opening sequence of letters, which Freud passes over in his effacement of questions concerning the narrator and narrative perspective in general, serves Kofman (again in Nietzschean mode) as a paradigm case of Hoffmann's perspectivism, which she links in to the rest of the story via the motif of the *Perspektiv* or telescope (Kofman 1991b, 134). Epistolary form—the necessary interreference or intertextuality of the individual letters (Kofman favors the term *enchevêtrement* or "inter-weaving" [160])—becomes metonymic of writing itself in its fragmentary plurality, its "supplementarity," a term borrowed from Derrida (137), and in its association with repetition, the death drives, the "diabolical duplic-ity" of literary mimesis (141–144).[13] In short, writing itself has an "un-heimlich" effect.

Small wonder, perhaps, that Freud should seek to evade this effect and adopt what Kofman terms an "apotropaic" defense mechanism (Kofman 1974, 180;[14] cf. Kofman 1975, 162; Kofman [1976] 1984a, 151): by con-fronting the specificity of writing head-on at the close of her essay on Freud and "The Sandman" (reprised in her Postscript), Kofman is both making good (or at least better) Freud's psychoanalytic model and going beyond it, establishing the parameters of her own subsequent inquiries.

DIABOLICAL DOUBLES ("VAUTOUR ROUGE")

Both of Kofman's subsequent essays on Hoffmann (like *Nietzsche and Metaphor* before them) open with the question of writing and the specificity of Hoffmann's plural style. Inverting Freud's order of priorities, Kofman from now on will approach Hoffmann's works from the perspec-tive of their problematic textuality, and it is only on this basis that she will perform her own readings of Hoffmann's troubling "themes." We have al-ready seen her borrowing a number of key Derridean characterizations of writing—"graft," "supplement"—as well as extending the Freudian con-cept of the uncanny to "accommodate" it, and all of these effects are pred-icated, for Kofman, on a "diabolical mimesis," an originary doubling that, in turn, opens up the space for potentially infinite repetition. In "Vautour rouge," appropriately enough her contribution to the collective volume *Mimesis,* Kofman continues and develops this line of argument, arguing that writing, and Hoffmann's writing in particular, bears a "double griffe" (Kofman 1975, 98)—a "double stamp" (although the formulation also resonates with "double greffe," "double graft")—and in the first section of this essay, entitled "L'enchevêtrement" (Kofman 1975, 97–113), she em-phasizes the "interweaving" of narrative strands that she had begun to ad-dress in her earlier study.

Freud refers to the narrative complexity of *The Devil's Elixirs* at one point in "The 'Uncanny,'" but it is again mentioned only in order to be swerved away from immediately afterward as he once more narrows down to a thematic reading, reducing doubling to the motif of the doppelgänger, and heads off into a consideration of the existing theoretical positions on the subject, starting with Otto Rank's famous study. Once more, then, Freud is selecting and summarizing, "raiding" one of Hoffmann's works for a specific, ascertainable "motif" in order only to discard the rest:

> Hoffmann is the unrivalled master of the uncanny in literature. His novel, *Die Elixiere des Teufels,* contains a whole mass of themes to which one is tempted to ascribe the uncanny effect of the narrative; but it is too obscure and intricate a story for us to venture upon a summary of it. Towards the end of the book the reader is told the facts, hitherto concealed from him, from which the action springs; with the result, not that he is at last enlightened, but that he falls into a state of complete bewilderment. The author has piled up too much material of the same kind. In consequence one's grasp of the story as a whole suffers, though not the impression it makes. We must content ourselves with selecting those themes of uncanniness which are most prominent, and with seeing whether they too can fairly be traced back to infantile sources. These themes are all concerned with the phenomenon of the "double," which appears in every shape and in every degree of development. (Freud 1919, 233f.)

The construction of Hoffmann's novel is, indeed, bewilderingly intricate, and I offer the briefest of summaries here in full recognition of its inadequacy. The novel is presented (by an anonymous "editor") as the autobiography of an eighteenth-century monk, Medardus, who chances upon an ancient vial among the relics in his monastery and drinks the "Devil's Elixir" it contains; thereafter he becomes progressively more wayward, morally and geographically—he is forced to flee the monastery and embarks on an itinerant life of the passions. He is periodically possessed by the forces of evil and is pursued by an eerie double, the "mad" Count Viktorin, before finally returning in repentance to his monastery, where he dies in mysterious circumstances.

Whereas Freud seems content to "fall into a state of complete bewilderment" at all these (and, of course, many more) goings-on, Kofman plunges in and celebrates the richness of the novel's excesses. At the opening of "Vautour rouge" (subtitled "Le double dans *Les élixirs du diable* d'Hoffmann"), her reading of the double privileges the multiple framings of the narrative itself before she goes on to address, as Freud does, the multiple instances of the doppelgänger as motif. She distinguishes five narrative strands or "hands" at work: not only that of the "editor" and the two parts of the novel itself but also the intercalated story of Medardus's ancestor, the painter Francesko, which "uncannily" foreshadows his own, and the final pages appended after Medardus's death as a "Nachtrag" (supplement) by the monastery librarian (Kofman 1975, 98f.), to which one could add the letter by Aurelia to her abbess, which Medardus reads in the second part. Far from weakening Hoffmann's text, Kofman argues, the fissured heterogeneity of its style—which is to some extent attributable to the contingencies of its two-part production but by no means wholly ascribable to them, and which many other critics have found to a greater or lesser extent rebarbative—is its strength. It is also the reason Kofman chooses it as a paradigm text: "Heterogeneity: is this not the very character of every text?" (Kofman 1975, 98).

Such heterogeneity, the paradoxical primacy of intertextuality in Hoffmann's text, radically undermines such notions as authenticity or originality of expression. Writing itself is a system of diabolical, spectral doubles, each "haunting" the rest, Kofman argues, so the multiple levels of Hoffmann's text render, for example, the question of the extent to which *The Devil's Elixirs* is a "rewriting" of "Monk" Lewis of secondary importance. Kofman is more concerned to attend to a pluralized *reading* strategy that might in some sense be adequate to the text. What is required, she argues, is a recognition of the necessity for *at least* a double reading in response to it. She produces, in fact, a tripartite scheme of possible interpretations, which she terms "realist, 'psychoanalytic' (interpretation through visions, dreams, hallucinations, projections), theological" (Kofman 1975, 105, cf. 108), applying this model by way of example initially to the function of the old painter's manuscript in the text, but going on to claim that "Medardus's manuscript suggests at least this triple reading always, for every event" (105).

The sense of the "at least" becomes clearer in a later, slightly different definition, in which "theological" modulates into "metaphysical, Hegelian, or Schellingian" (113), and this is now subordinated not so much to a Freudian, "psychoanalytic" interpretation as to an ironic, parodic, *Nietzschean* one:

> There is a reading that doubles the first and comes to undermine it from beneath, a parodic doubling/lining ["doublure"]: this sees the triumph of a madness and a Dionysian intoxication that are unsublatable. Theological and tragic visions are effaced in the interest of an ironic vision of events: the laughter of the madman makes all meaning, every assured direction ["sens"], burst open. (Kofman 1975, 113)[15]

Kofman's hierarchization of interpretations is in any case a Nietzschean gesture,[16] but it seems as though a Nietzschean reading of Hoffmann might itself have the last laugh. Let us analyze her interpretative model here in more detail.

Kofman's initial response to the heterogeneity of Hoffmann's perspectivistic style, as we have seen, is to focus on the narrative of the old painter—the story of the "good" double of the novel's hero, Francesko, which, coming at the end of his (and the text's) peregrinations and revealing what Freud calls "the facts, hitherto concealed from him," marks in a sense the *terminus ad quem* of his personal trajectory and the teleology of the text, yet which also marks the *terminus a quo* of both, in that it is chronologically prior to and "prefigures" or "haunts" the whole narrative of Medardus's life. Such an uncanny textual presence lends itself to a psychoanalytic interpretation, and indeed Kofman expands on its problematic temporality by bringing it under the Freudian "quasi-concept" of *Nachträglichkeit* (retroaction) or, in French, the effect of the *après-coup*. Kofman argues similarly that Medardus's apparently idyllic childhood—the "lost paradise" with whose description the novel opens—is itself fantaastic, always already lost because tainted by doubling. It is "constructed nostalgically in the time of the *après-coup*. Presence is always already riven by a tear, a difference" (Kofman 1975, 119). Kofman explicates such self-difference by introducing the Lacanian concept of the mirror stage in the formation of the ego, arguing, "The necessity of passing by way of a double to become oneself reveals a structure of 'fallibility,' the condition of all the subsequent 'faults,' and of the indefinite proliferation of doubles" (118).[17] Furthermore, by arguing that Hoffmann already constructs his text, *avant la lettre,* with a "latent" and a "manifest" content—"the manifest text being the originary double" (101)—Kofman advances the claim that Hoffmann's text both prefigures and already supplements psychoanalysis itself (cf. Agacinski et al. 1976, 21).

The Derridean, deconstructive strain in Kofman's analysis of *The Devil's Elixirs* is apparent from the ways in which she expands on her characterization of writing in this essay—by reference to such philosophemes as "the 'graphics of supplementarity'" (Kofman 1975, 100), phonocentrism (117), and (developing her analysis of Jentsch's notion of "intellectual uncertainty" in the previous essay) undecidability (163; cf. Kofman 1984b, 85). In the central section, "The Devil's 'Pharmacy'" (Kofman 1975, 132–138), she draws on Derrida's "Plato's Pharmacy" (Derrida 1981, 61–171) to characterize Hoffmann's writing, in turn, as a *pharmakon:*

> The theme of the double in the *Elixirs* could never, then, be a theme like any other, and the logic of the double could never be the logic of identity or of truth. Writing, which is at least double, *pharmakon,* both remedy and poison, cannot simply be an elixir of life: although it produces decodable effects of meaning, through its intervals ["écarts"], its aphorisms, it is always to some extent diabolical, an ambiguous power of truth and lie. (Kofman 1975, 111)

Writing ("l'écriture") is a "tissu d'écarts" (Kofman 1975, 112, cf. 98), Kofman writes—a tissue or text composed of intervals, distances, gaps, deviations, indeed differences—echoing the title (*Écarts*) of the collective volume on Derrida's work to which "Un philosophe 'unheimlich'" was her contribution (cf. Kofman 1984b, 21). Nor does this designation apply to writing alone, for all mimetic practices are riven by such "écarts," Kofman argues, turning, in the section entitled "Painting and Eloquence—The Abuses of Resemblance" (Kofman 1975, 120–132), to "the gap ['écart'] between the model and the painted object" (120), which "the imposture of mimesis" (127, 130–132) in general seeks to conceal.[18]

But it is the Nietzschean voice that speaks (or rather laughs) loudest in Kofman's analysis of *The Devil's Elixirs*, as the space opened up by the heterogeneity of Hoffmann's writing that Freud signally failed to address opens onto parody, "mad doubling," and madness itself. In this context the marginal, comical double figure of the hairdresser Pietro Belcampo (in German Peter Schönfeld) is key to Kofman's analysis. The "laughter of the madman" quoted earlier is his: "Laughter of the innocent Belcampo/Schönfeld/Nietzsche, burlesque double of the monk Medardus who is gnawed away by bad conscience. Triumph of humor and irony" (Kofman 1975, 113). Kofman describes Belcampo/Schönfeld as "like Nietzsche, his own double ['sosie'], capable of having a double evaluation on everything" (Kofman 1975, 157; cf. Kofman 1988a, 187), and his is the last laugh heard resonating in Kofman's analysis of the text (as in the text itself), for in her conclusion she explicitly goes beyond a psychoanalytic reading and ends her account under the sign of this Nietzschean figure:

> It is the figure of Belcampo/Schönfeld who, rid of the devil and of bad conscience, makes the text burst apart and prevents it from being "sublated" by philosophy or psychoanalysis. Belcampo and everything in Medardus which is Belcampo. Belcampo whose "Nietzschean" reading of events parodies the theologico-Hegelian reading just as the art of hairdressing parodies fine art. (Kofman 1975, 162f.)[19]

"A HOFFMANNIANISM WITHOUT RESERVE" (AUTOBIOGRIFFURES)

Kofman's more Nietzschean reading of Hoffmann is extended and developed in the last of her studies, *Autobiogriffures*, where she reads Hoffmann's characterization of his eponymous hero, Murr the Tomcat, as even more Nietzschean than that of Belcampo/Schönfeld. Murr, as Kofman points out, is a kind of parodic philology professor who is most at home in ancient Greek (Kofman [1976] 1984a, 79) and dreams of lecturing on Aeschylus, Corneille, and Shakespeare (62). Murr grafts his family tree onto the noble lineage of Tieck's Puss in Boots—in Kofman's analysis, he is "Murr the Tomcat, an autobiographer who feels the need to affirm himself by declaring his noble titles, loudly proclaiming the name of the supposed father (at the same time parodying the fantastic or fanciful genealogies which 'heroes' narcissistically draw to a close)" (15f.)—just as Nietzsche, in *Ecce Homo*, will dream of his own "fantastical genealogy," claiming to be descended from Polish nobility and creating a father for himself more to his taste than his biological father (Nietzsche 1992, 11–12; cf. Kofman 1994a).

Leaving aside such "biographical" points of comparison, though, what Hoffmann's novel achieves, Kofman argues, is an "inversion of traditional values" (Kofman [1976] 1984a, 84) of precisely the kind that she tracks in her earlier study of Nietzsche and metaphor. There she argues that Nietzsche's use of metaphor has a doubly subversive effect: on one level he inverts the traditional (Aristotelian) privileging of concept over metaphor and on another he also inverts the already existing metaphoric hierarchies of traditional metaphysics (Kofman 1993b, 105; cf. Kofman 1973, 60f.; Kofman 1988a, 180–190; Kofman with Hermsen 1992, 70). But where Nietzsche, in the essay "On Truth and Lies," uses the metaphors of the beehive and the spider's web to debunk the grandeur of man's conceptual edifices, Kofman shows how, in *Murr the Tomcat*, Hoffmann radicalizes this subversion of the (Aristotelian, Cartesian) opposition of animal to human—Nietzsche's designation of man as a "metaphorical animal" (Kofman 1993b, 25)—by pushing it to its limits and enacting it with the ironic fiction of a tomcat *writing* the very text we are reading.

By its linear nature, the tomcat's autobiography—like *The Devil's Elixirs* before it (cf. Kofman 1975, 113)—mocks the traditional formula of the autobiography as *Bildungsroman*, and yet at the same time the "rhapsodic," fragmentary organization of *Hoffmann's* text is such that Murr's self-narrative is continually breaking off to give way to the interleaved autobiography of his master, Johannes Kreisler (the operative conceit here is that Murr has ripped up sheets of Kreisler's existing text to use for his own writing, and that an editor has inadvertently bound them all between the same covers). The result is that the book *Murr the Tomcat* is, in Kofman's words, "an unclassifiable, atopic book belonging to no determinable genre: a bastard text that mixes with the life of the cat 'pages that are quite foreign to it, belonging to a book that was to have contained the biography of Kapellmeister Johannes Kreisler.' A book that is about neither a man nor an animal, that, furthermore, breaks the order of the logos—a book with neither beginning nor end, in which chronological order is undone" (Kofman [1976] 1984a, 72).

The formula of the double autobiography, such a perspectivistic pluralization on the textual level, Kofman argues, reflects the radical subversion of the "subject of autobiography": "Such a 'rhapsody' . . . effaces the signature of the proper name and of the single author" (74f.). That way madness lies, one might suspect, and indeed the ultimate metaphysical opposition Kofman sees deconstructed in *Murr the Tomcat* is the opposition between reason and unreason—the split and pluralized identity of the text mirroring the madness of Murr's double Kreisler (and *his* spectral double Ettlinger).

As before, though, it is the "schizophrenia" of the text that Kofman is keenest to pursue, arguing that in *Murr the Tomcat* Hoffmann takes to its extreme the parodic potential of writing as bearing a "double griffe" or "double stamp," which we saw her developing in her analysis of *The Devil's Elixirs.* Taking up the question of "plagiarism" where she left off in considering the relation of the earlier novel to Lewis's book *The Monk,* she develops the notion of originary intertextuality by considering the relation between *Murr the Tomcat* and Tieck's *Puss in Boots*—itself "grafted onto" Cervantes, and so on (Kofman 1981, 16)—for since Tieck is actually cited periodically/parodically by Murr, as we have seen, Hoffmann's text has about it a self-consciousness, a self-reflexivity that makes it legitimate to argue, as Kofman does, that the novel is "about" intertextuality: "*Murr the Tomcat* is thus above all a text, and a text on writing as generalized grafting ['greffe généralisée']: Murr grafts his individual life onto that of his whole species, just as Hoffmann grafts his text onto Tieck's" (Kofman [1976] 1984a, 17). Developing ("citing"/"grafting onto") Derrida's remarks on the generalized "iterability" of language in his controversial 1971 paper "Signature, Event, Context" (Derrida 1982, 320f.; cf. Derrida 1988), Kofman argues that Hoffmann's writing has a "deliberate citational quality"— Murr's narrative is a patchwork of pastiche that even opens on a parodic quotation from Goethe's *Egmont*—a "citationality" that has the effect of "effac[ing] the signature of the proper name": "This 'citationality' metonymically gives voice to the general putting-into-quotation-marks which every text and every language constitutes" (Kofman 1981, 18; cf. Russo 1987, 107f.).

As if to emphasize this point, Kofman herself weaves into her study numerous quotations on the subject of cats, animality, and autobiography by a wide variety of writers from Lucretius to Borges.[20] Her own playfulness is at its most pronounced in this study, and she certainly rises to the challenge posed by what is, in Barthes's terms, Hoffmann's most "writerly" text, punning and neologizing away with irrepressible inventiveness (Kofman [1976] 1984a, 22, 38), not least in the title of her study, where she inflates the term "griffe" to the point where it explodes into "mad" polysemous plurality. Winnie Woodhull, the translator of the only section that has so far been rendered into English, has the following to say in her opening translator's note:

> Some remarks are in order regarding Kofman's highly overdetermined ti-
> tle, *Autobiogriffures,* which I have translated as *Autobiogriffies.* Suggesting
> "autobiography" (the text written about the cat Murr [= "auteur-biogra-
> phie"?]) as well as "biography" (the text written about Johannes Kreisler
> [= "autour-biographie"?]), *"autobiogriffures"* also contains the word *"grif-
> fures,"* meaning slight wounds, or scratches, from *"griffe,"* meaning claw
> (or, in English, a claw-like ornament [clasp]). *"Montrer ses griffes"* is to act
> aggressively. *"Griffe"* can also mean a signature stamp or seal. *"Griffe"* sug-
> gests *"greffe,"* meaning a graft; *"griffures"* suggests *"biffures,"* or lines used to
> cross out textual material to be suppressed. *"Griffonner"* means to write in
> a confused, barely legible manner. In French, one who writes illegibly is
> said to have *"une écriture de chat,"* to write in "chicken scratch" (or literally,
> "cat scratch"). A related word pertinent to Hoffmann's heterogeneous
> text is "griffon," a mythic composite figure. (Kofman 1981, 20)[21]

This playful polysemy of Kofman's title reflects the polyperspectivalism of Hoffmann's text, to which she has already referred in her study of "The Sandman" as an example of Hoffmann's proto-Nietzschean deconstruction of the madness-reason opposition (Kofman 1991b, 134, 136). But of her Hoffmann studies it is in *Autobiogriffures* that Kofman most sustainedly explores the configuration of uncanny doubling and proliferation, inversion and subversion, "madness" and textuality, and it is no coincidence that her most Nietzschean Hoffmann study should thus represent such a clear link between the concerns of *Nietzsche and Metaphor* and the two late *Explosion* books. At the end of "Vautour rouge," Kofman argues that Hoffmann the author, while inevitably splitting himself and investing himself piecemeal in his characters, remains sufficiently detached—"à l'écart," one might say—to play one off ironically against the others and avoid lapsing into madness himself. The same is true, she argues in *Autobiogriffures,* in the more extreme case of the split narrator in *Murr the Tomcat,* and, in the *Explosion* books, it holds even for Nietzsche, the most radical case of all, for in *Ecce Homo* Nietzsche splits himself off from *all* his previous metaphoric self-representations in order to affirm them *après-coup* in one great fantastic roll call (cf. Kofman 1992, 11–43). Kofman defends both Hoffmann and, more urgently, Nietzsche from the charge of madness by showing how although a "mad" self-doubling is the very prerequisite of artistic creation, of literary creation in particular and of autobiography par excellence, nevertheless the metaphoric distance separating the "author" from his multiple textual investments is maintained throughout these writings, which thus serve a therapeutic-apotropaic function in displacing that most crucial, most fateful of "écarts" (cf. Large 1995).

TRAVELS IN ATOPIA

In conclusion, then, just as Kofman will continue to interrogate, and to interrogate through, Freud, Nietzsche, and Derrida—her "masters of suspicion" (in Ricœur's phrase), to each of whom, as we have seen, she precisely denies mastery through their mutual relativization—so, too, she will continue to explore the problems she first addresses in the series of early Hoffmann studies on which I have been concentrating. Questions of uncanniness, the double, and diabolical mimesis will continue to "haunt" Kofman's texts thereafter: she is occupied with the question of madness and textuality not only in the *Explosion* books but also in her studies of Auguste Comte (1978a) and Gérard de Nerval (1979), and Hoffmann will constantly recur as a point of reference in her writings, right up to "L'imposture de la beauté," where the uncanny double is invited to Kofman's philosophical feast one final time.

In her three Hoffmann studies, Kofman repeatedly describes Hoffmann's disorienting, uncanny, perspectivistic writing as "atopic" ("atopique") (Kofman 1975, 97; Kofman [1976] 1984a, 72), a term that she applies equally to the work of Freud (Kofman 1983b, 23f.), Nietzsche (Kofman 1993b, 5), and Derrida (Kofman 1984b, 18),[22] the three writers (among others) whose perspectives she strategically exploits in her readings, as she puts into practice the pluralized reading strategy that is a feature of all her writings—from *The Childhood of Art* (Kofman 1988c, 1–22) to "L'imposture de la beauté" (Kofman 1995b, 47f.; cf. Kofman 1984b, 99–114; Kofman 1985b, 24; Kofman 1989c). I have argued that over the course of the three studies she moves away from an initial critique of Freud's readings of Hoffmann to the affirmation of a more Nietzschean, "Dionysian" potential in Hoffmann's work, all the while developing Derridean characterizations of the function of textuality in order to stress the link (which Freud himself marginalizes) between the thematic and textual levels, the effects of Hoffmann's pluralized style. She highlights the playful self-referentiality of Hoffmann's writing: its parodic relation to the business of writing itself ("editorial" conventions, narrative perspective) and to all the various generic traditions (in "The Sandman," the epistolary novel and the supernatural tale; in *The Devil's Elixirs,* the detective story and the Gothic novel; in *Murr the Tomcat,* the "animal story" and the "educative" novel; in both novels, the autobiography and the *Bildungsroman*). She also follows Nietzsche, for her the philosopher of laughter par excellence,[23] in stressing the humor in the works themselves: the closing words of the first chapter in *Nietzsche and Metaphor,* describing Nietzsche's philosophy as one that "by combining all the 'genres' in its writing, deletes all oppositions with one great burst of laughter" (Kofman 1993b, 5), describes the effect of Hoffmann's writing for Kofman, too. In "Vautour rouge," as we have seen, she lets "Belcampo/Schönfeld/Nietzsche" have the last laugh; in *Autobiogriffures* laughter not only has the last word but *is* the last word (Kofman [1976] 1984a, 152).

But Hoffmann's humor not only passed Freud by in the earnestness of his inquiry into "The 'Uncanny'"; it was also lost on Nietzsche himself, who was prepared to accept the conventional perception of Hoffmann as "Schauer-Hoffmann," a writer of sensationalist Gothic horror stories, and, given his violent dislike of Romanticism, to dismiss him accordingly.[24] Above all, then, Kofman's studies remain "faithful" not so much to Freud, Nietzsche, or Derrida as to the spirit of Hoffmann himself: perhaps one should write not of "Kofman's Hoffmann" but, in her own manner, of Kofman/Hoffmann, of her own readings as parodic doubles. The "certain mimeticism" with regard to Derrida's style that Kofman discerns in her own productions from the early 1970s (Kofman with Jardine 1991, 108) is a feature of her relation to every writer: she cannot write on a (male) author without in some sense identifying with him and adopting his style (Kofman with Ender 1993, 10)—"loving" him (Kofman 1993a, 371)—and in the three studies I have been examining it is her love for Hoffmann that emerges most strongly of all.

PART II

PHILOSOPHY AND METAPHOR

Suffering Contradiction: Kofman on Nietzsche's Critique of Logic

MARY BETH MADER

In the essay "Les présupposés de la logique," or "The Presuppositions of Logic," from the volume *Nietzsche et la scène philosophique* (Kofman [1979] 1986b), Sarah Kofman offers a reading of Nietzsche's critique of Aristotelian logic. In particular, she addresses Nietzsche's arguments against the three laws of logic, focusing primarily on his treatment of the law, or principle, of noncontradiction. This chapter argues for an alternative prioritizing of Nietzsche's arguments against Aristotelian logic than that presented by Kofman, while proposing that her insight about logic as a species of catharsis might be deepened.

At first glance, it seems insignificant, though slightly amusing, that this principle is also commonly called the principle of contradiction. But this ambiguity or, even, duplicity points to a thought implicit in the rest of this chapter: that the notion of contradiction depends upon the notion of identity. In the present case, the production of an apparent contradiction can demonstrate the role of identities in the generation of contradictions. I have said that one principle is called by two different names. Is it not a contradiction to say of something that it is both the principle of contradiction and the principle of noncontradiction? According to either principle it should be. In deriving this contradiction from the question of the name of the very principle at issue, we can see that the meaning of the term *contradiction* is both fixed in and shared by the two principles. It is on the issue of the meaning of the term *principle* that the divergence takes place. In one case, the principle names a prohibition; in the other, it names a requirement. At this point, philosophers traditionally spot the identity elsewhere: in one state, the state of being contradictionless, that is aimed at by two different, but ultimately synonymous principles. That is, the principles attempt to describe or preserve one and the same contradictionless state. In this way, the contradiction is eliminated; it is seen to have been merely "apparent." And it is the identity of the contradictionless state that both permits and eliminates the apparent contradiction.

So a bit of the immensely more complicated relations between the notions of contradiction and identity is glimpsed in this example of the question of the name of the law prescribing or describing a contradictionless state. To accord with Nietzsche's view that the principle is a contingent interdiction, it will be called the principle of noncontradiction in this chapter, since that name lends itself more readily to an interpretation of the principle as a prescriptive one. One of the aims of this chapter is to suggest that Kofman's reading of Nietzsche's critique of Aristotelian logic can be improved by attending to the dependence of the notion of contradiction on that of identity. Doing so shows both that Nietzsche's genealogical argument is best seen as a pointed refutation of Aristotle's defense of the principle of noncontradiction and that a separate ontological Heraclitean argument proposed by Nietzsche most directly calls into question that principle itself.

NIETZSCHE'S SUSPICION

In *Metaphysics,* book 3, Aristotle argues against what he takes to be Heraclitus' denial of the principle of noncontradiction. Aristotle writes:

> For the same thing to belong and not to belong to the same thing and in the same respect is impossible. . . . This then is the firmest of all principles. . . . For it is impossible for anyone to believe that the same thing is and is not, as some consider Heraclitus said—for it is not necessary that the things one says one should also believe. But if it is not possible for contraries to belong to the same thing simultaneously . . . , then obviously it is impossible for the same person to believe simultaneously that the same thing is and is not; for anyone who made that error would be holding contrary opinions simultaneously. That is why all those who prove go back to this opinion in the end: it is in the nature of things the principle of all other axioms also. (Aristotle 1971, 7–8)

The principle as it is advanced by Aristotle is that one cannot ascribe contradictory properties to one and the same thing, at one and the same time, or that one cannot both affirm and deny of a thing that it has a particular property. Aristotle gives several arguments for why one ought to accept the principle but does not think that it is susceptible to demonstration, since it is so basic and ultimate a principle. His arguments are aimed mainly at showing others why a person who denies the principle cannot actually be engaging in anything that we could recognize as thinking or as signifying. (Indeed, to Aristotle, such a person resembles a "vegetable.") Though we can report that we believe a contradiction, such reports must be false; it is not possible to hold "contrary opinions simultaneously." For the purposes of this chapter, two points are especially important: that Aristotle formulates the law in terms of "same thing" and "same respect" and that his argument for the principle rests on the alleged impossibility of believing a contradiction.

Kofman delineates Nietzsche's arguments against this Aristotelian view of contradiction in the essay under consideration here. Her reading of Nietzsche's genealogical diagnosis of the principles of logic is this: the principles of identity and noncontradiction, Nietzsche argues, are merely tools to generate a soothing grid of stable categories that humans impose on a chaotic world of becoming. They are a fictive overlay, the origins of which we forget, that works as a sort of ontological fixative for us. Their seeming incontrovertibility is not an indication of their necessary truth, but proof of the limits of human imagination and needs. We are simply so constituted that chaos and contradiction amount to suffering; logic and the language in which it lives are invented as the cure for this suffering, as a means of mastering disorder. Logical necessity is thus a vital need. If there is any necessary truth associated with logic, it is that we need it in order to live. Our inability to tolerate life without it demonstrates our weakness rather than the truth of logical principles.

NIETZSCHE'S EPISTEMOLOGY

Nietzsche's essentially skeptical epistemology, or what Habermas has called his "theory of knowledge" (Habermas 1971, 295), does imply that he cannot appeal to any nonhuman ontological entity in virtue of which logic is able to satisfy a human need for regularity and order. Though the question of Nietzsche's views on the possibility and nature of knowledge is a complex and contested one, it is safe to say that he is relentlessly skeptical of all previous philosophical attempts to justify or to found traditional claims to knowledge. In the posthumous collection of Nietzsche's writings, *The Will to Power,* he states: "We have measured the value of the world according to categories *that refer to a purely fictitious world*" (Nietzsche 1968b, 13). And later, in allusion to Kant's metaphysics: "We have no categories at all that permit us to distinguish a 'world in itself' from a world of appearances" (488). So seeking something that corresponds to our logical laws in virtue of which they can work to order, regardless of our acceptance or denial of their necessary truth, is, of course, out of the question. Nietzsche's critique of knowledge precludes his being able to appeal to any entities that would permit traditional epistemological claims in support of his view that logic is essentially a falsifier.

WHY IS LOGIC A FALSIFICATION?

It seems that Kofman understands Nietzsche's genealogical account of the human origin and motivation for logic as an argument for the claim that logic is a falsification of reality. She writes that for Nietzsche, logic, insofar as it is an "anthropomorphic fiction," "falsifies the 'real' to render it formulatable and foreseeable" (Kofman [1979] 1986b, 124). However, though it may frequently appear to be Nietzsche's argument that what is a fictional human creation, that is, a product of human imagination, is therefore falsifying, this does not comprise his argument at its most powerful or plausible. He may agree that in many cases what is a product of human imagination is falsifying, but it is not falsifying because, or solely because, it is a product of human imagination.

More importantly, if we can never test the traditional fiction/nonfiction distinction, as Nietzsche holds, so that the use of the words *truth* and *falsity* becomes extremely problematic, if not impossible, the alleged falsifying nature of logical laws equally fails to follow from the claim that those laws are fictional human creations. That we have no criterion of truth does not show or imply that every supposed logical truth is false. It shows, rather, that the previously cherished distinction between truth and falsity as independently established must be abandoned. From not ever being able to know if some statement is true, we cannot any more conclude that it is false, though we might well conclude that the entire issue is a waste of time. In sum, the notion that there might be some reason besides our need for logic that accounts for logic's ability to order in a soothing manner is not more implausible than the supposition that human need alone accounts for that ordering ability.

Kofman and Nietzsche hold that the motivation for, and the aim of, logic is the mastery of painful disorder. This means that Nietzsche believes logic to be efficacious in some manner *on its way* to providing a cathartic and survival value; logic soothes only by virtue of its ordering function. This raises the following question: does this logic order for us, assuming it does, because we take it to be independently true, because we take it to be ontologically necessary, or does it order regardless of what status we give it, independently of our belief in it? It would seem that Nietzsche would accept the latter part of the disjunction, namely, that logic in some sense "works," regardless of what status we give it, since he himself uses logic and orders "things," though he considers logic to have a fictional status. His own employment of logic, therefore, tends to show that it works as an ordering practice regardless of the status we accord to it. However, that it orders regardless of the status we give it does not show that it does so merely because of our constitution, merely because of our need for regularities and our constitutional, instinctual, physiological, inherited intolerance of chaos and contradiction. We can grant that it is an error to conclude from our vital need for regularities, and from logic's ability to satisfy this need or "to work" by ordering, that logical principles are true independently of that need or that they encode or formulate some deep ontological nature of the world, or that they are ontologically necessary. However, from granting this we should not suppose that our need alone explains the particular capacity of logic to satisfy that need.

For Nietzsche, our treating logic as not only true, but as true necessarily, or as made true independently of human beings, constitutes a doubled mistake: not only do we believe that a falsification is true, we believe that it is true entirely independently of ourselves and of our need. This distinction makes sense for Nietzsche because he holds that it is possible to believe that logic is "true," in the sense of its being a useful falsification, and he can employ it, as he does persistently, even though he does not take its "truth" to amount to anything inseparable from our needs and capacities as a particular type of animal.

In her interpretation of, and expansion upon, Nietzsche's views, Kofman calls logic a species of catharsis, making reference to Aristotle's celebrated theory of tragic drama as catharsis (Aristotle 1967, 25).[1] For present purposes, what is pertinent in her identification of logic as a form of catharsis is her restriction of logic to merely catharsis. She writes: "If it is true that catharsis has as its aim to discharge man of pity and terror, thus, in the final analysis, of the unbearable (suffering, death, the ambiguity of existence), logic (and all of the speculative) could well be *but* a particular case of catharsis" (Kofman [1979] 1986b, 123). Kofman repeatedly stresses the notion that logic is "only" or "merely" or "but" something that expresses and satisfies a human need. However, though Nietzsche would likely agree that logic is a species of catharsis, his genealogical argument about the vital necessity of logic does not, in itself, support his view that logic is a falsifying fiction. Surely it is the nature of the need and, thus, of the logic needed, not the fact that logic derives from and satisfies a need, that renders a logic falsifying. Making this distinction permits the following question: is it possible to imagine a human need that, though it is a need, would not be a need for a logic that falsifies? That is, is it possible to have a human need for a logic that does not, by ordering, deny the unordered state of that which is being ordered, including the state of the orderer?

NIETZSCHE'S GENEALOGICAL ARGUMENT CONTRA ARISTOTLE

Nietzsche's genealogical argument about the utility of the human fiction of logic must be understood strictly in the context of the Aristotelian arguments for the necessary logical truth of the laws of logic. That is, it is better understood as an attempt at a specific rebuttal of Aristotle's position than as a positive argument for the claim that logic is falsifying. Nietzsche is not claiming that the fact that something is humanly created or useful or soothing to human beings demonstrates that it is falsifying. Rather, against Aristotle's position, his genealogical argument aims to show the more limited claim that the fact that something is useful to us, or seemingly inevitable in human life, does not show that it is true or true necessarily. (Recall Aristotle's claim that the impossibility of disbelieving the law of noncontradiction implies the logical necessity of that law.) With the genealogical argument, Nietzsche is pointing out that it is a mistake to conclude from the fact that something is useful or seems inevitable or incontrovertible that it is true or true necessarily. Aristotle argues that because logic is inevitable it is true necessarily. By providing a genealogical explanation for the inevitability of logic, Nietzsche counters that the fact that logic is inevitable does not imply that it is true necessarily.

But if neither the intensity of devotion to a belief or practice nor its seeming inevitability show that belief to be true, why should either one show the belief to be false or falsifying? It doesn't; Nietzsche advances a quite different, Heraclitean, argument for the claim that logic not only is not shown to be true by our devotion to it but can be shown to be falsifying for other reasons.

NIETZSCHE'S HERACLITEAN ARGUMENT

Nietzsche holds that what we take to be logical necessity is in fact mere human need; so-called logical necessities are actually moral needs. But needs for what? An advocate for logical necessity could agree in part, saying, "Sure, we have a human need: for logical necessity! Our need for logical necessity doesn't show that there is not that sort of necessity, any more than our need for it shows that there is that sort of necessity (as you, Nietzsche, have pointed out)." The Heraclitean argument begins to meet this sort of objection to the genealogical argument.

The genealogical argument is Nietzsche's explanation for why *we hold* logic to be true though it falsifies. But what exactly is his argument for the claim that logic falsifies? Basically, Nietzsche advances an ontological argument against the law of identity on which Aristotelian logic is founded. That is, logic is held to be falsifying because it misrepresents the fundamentally Heraclitean nature of reality to which Nietzsche subscribes. Though Kofman acknowledges this other Heraclitean argument, she doesn't take it to play the role I am suggesting it does.

Heraclitus' philosophy was remarkable for its insistence on the reality of change in the world. For Heraclitus, the most fundamental characteristic of reality was that it is forever changing; this "continual transition" (Nietzsche 1968b, 281), to use Nietzsche's phrase, was symbolized for Heraclitus by the dynamic element of fire. His doctrine of flux is often expressed in the following quote, found in Plutarch and attributed to Heraclitus: "One cannot step twice into the same river, nor can one grasp any mortal substance in a stable condition, but it scatters and again gathers; it forms and dissolves, and approaches and departs" (Williams 1989, 11).

A similar philosophy of a world of becoming is articulated enthusiastically by Nietzsche. In *Twilight of the Idols,* he writes: "But Heraclitus will always be right in this, that being is an empty fiction. The 'apparent' world is the only one: the 'real' world has only been *lyingly added*" (Nietzsche 1968a, 36). His view rests on an acceptance of the Heraclitean conclusion that the testimony of the senses indicates a world of "plurality and change" (37) but is not therefore false. He writes: " 'Reason' is the cause of our falsification of the evidence of the senses. Insofar as the senses show becoming, passing away, change, they do not lie" (37).

What happens to the status of Aristotelian logic, then, in a Heraclitean framework? Nietzsche's view is that this logic cannot live up to the conditions of a Heraclitean world and therefore, at the very best, will consist in a massive distortion. He writes in *Human, All Too Human:* "Logic rests on presuppositions with which nothing in the actual world corresponds, for example on the presupposition that there are equivalent things, that a thing is identical at different points of time" (Nietzsche 1984, 19). Also, in *The Will to Power,* Nietzsche writes: "Logic is bound to the condition: assume there are identical cases" (Nietzsche 1968b, 277).

Kofman notes this argument from *The Will to Power* (Nietzsche 1968b, 279), in which Nietzsche proceeds to dissect the "self-identical 'A'" of logic, the "A" of the familiar formulation of the law of identity, A = A. All propositions of logic presuppose self-identity as a condition of the world, but we have no evidence that this is the case, in other words, that there are such things as cases and things at all. In fact, the testimony of our senses even appears to lean toward the opposing conclusion, that all is flux and that identities are illusions "pasted on" to the authentic universe of becoming. At bottom, then, logic is a simple prejudice in favor of sameness, unverifiable and, given a Heraclitean ontology, profoundly misleading. Thus, Nietzsche traces the seeming ultimate firmness of Aristotelian logic to a mere assumption, the assumption that there are identities in the world and thus that the law of identity and those laws that rely on it are ontologically, and therefore logically, justified.

My criticism of Kofman's explication is that though she mentions Nietzsche's Heraclitean argument against the notion of identity that undergirds Aristotelian logic, she appears to find Nietzsche's genealogical argument the more important of the two arguments. I find, however, that the genealogical argument by itself is insufficient to establish the claim at issue — that logic falsifies — though it may well be acceptable as an account or an explanation of why not everyone agrees with Nietzsche about logic's misleading quality. Nietzsche's frequent declarations that our animal needs make logic a vital human necessity should not occlude the point that it is actually his Heraclitean ontological argument that supports the view that logic falsifies. The genealogical argument is an answer to the Aristotelian argument for logic's logical and ontological necessity based on its seeming inevitability, but it simply cannot establish the different claim that logic is not only a fiction, but a falsifying fiction.

To establish that claim we require the Heraclitean argument against the law of identity, which teaches that logic misleads in a double fashion. It misleads because it fails to respect the Heraclitean nature of the world, but it further misleads because it claims a faulty status for itself as independently and necessarily true. For Nietzsche, then, we have gone wrong twice in our estimation of logic. Not only are alleged logical truths not true; they are not true necessarily. He sees that logic makes two sets of claims: a set of claims about an extralogical world and another set of claims about those initial claims. That is, logic claims to truly capture some deep aspects of an extralogical world, but it also reflexively claims something about its own status: that its claims about the order of an extralogical world are themselves true necessarily. Interestingly, Nietzsche's work shows that one doesn't have to accept either type of claim in order to employ logical laws.

Nietzsche's dramatic turning of our attention from the alleged logical and ontological necessity of the laws of logic to the human investment in the truth value of those laws comes not only as a result of a rejection of traditional epistemologies in favor of a souped-up skepticism derived from the Kantian critiques of theories of knowledge, but also from his own positive Heraclitean view, or assumption, that we live in a world of becoming, change, and contradiction.

Clearly, for Nietzsche, logic satisfies human needs because it falsifies certain intolerable life conditions. Kofman's essay makes it too easy to suppose that Nietzsche holds the converse as well: that logic falsifies these life conditions because it satisfies human needs. Instead, logic falsifies because it orders the unordered and conceals both this ordering and that which is ordered. So logic falsifies not because it satisfies human needs but because of the distorting nature of those needs. This implies that different needs could generate different logics—and perhaps nonidentity logics of becoming and change—in addition to Aristotelian logic. It is Nietzsche's Heraclitean argument against the law of identity that most profoundly undermines Aristotle's formulation of the principle of noncontradiction.

THAT SAID . . .

Kofman's characterization of logic as a kind of catharsis prompts the following two points. First, if the construal of logic as a species of catharsis is fully accepted, then the qualification of it as *but* catharsis is unnecessary. If the traditional logician's view of logic as the formulation of ontologically, rather than genealogically, necessary truths is abandoned, then logic as catharsis should not be classed as any sort of demotion for logic, as the term *but* seems to imply. Only if we retain the logician's ranking of logic, or a nostalgic wish for this ranking, would we hold that logic as catharsis represents a diminishment of logic.

Second, we can perfectly well drop the claim that logic formulates ontological truths about a real world and still employ logic as an ordering practice that soothes. It is plain that Nietzsche himself does this, and indeed, his frequent arguments for the biological origins of the devotion of human beings to the laws of logic imply their vital inevitability. He never disagrees with Aristotle's claim that these laws have an inevitability; he just proposes a very different explanation for the inevitability and refuses the conclusions Aristotle draws from that inevitability. What is important here is that neither logic's ordering capacity nor its cathartic function depends on the claim that logic formulates ontological truths about a real world. We can, indeed, embrace logic as a cathartic ordering process when it is unburdened of its pretensions to veridicality and do so without loss. We can truly grant to logic the status of tragic drama, the cathartic function of which does not render it "only" tragic drama. If the fictional nature of tragic drama does not delegitimate it, it is not clear why the falsifying nature of logic as catharsis should do so for a Nietzschean thinker, especially when it works to order and, thus, to soothe, regardless of whether we hold it to be expressing ontologically necessary truths.

In a thoroughly Nietzschean understanding of logic, the traditional ontological import of the laws of logic would be left behind without regret, while their existential import would make them all-but-inevitable medicine. But it is certainly not their existential import that causes them to succeed as ordering practices, though it is this ordering capacity that permits their therapeutic function.

Nietzsche and Metaphor

PAUL PATTON

Sarah Kofman's *Nietzsche and Metaphor* (Kofman 1993b)[1] represents an important moment in the development of French interpretations of Nietzsche. These interpretations have played a significant role in the revival of interest in Nietzsche throughout the humanities and social sciences. Kofman was among the first to draw attention to the question of metaphor in Nietzsche: not only to his constant use of metaphors but also to the manner in which he deployed the concept of metaphor in his early theorization on the nature of human thought and knowledge. Kofman argued that Nietzsche "inaugurates a type of philosophy which deliberately uses metaphors, at the risk of being confused with poetry" and that in his early work he employs a notion of metaphor as a "fundamental operator" in his attempts to reformulate the relations between philosophy, art, and science (Kofman 1993b, 16–17).

The great merit of Kofman's study is to have analyzed Nietzsche's use of metaphor from the perspective of his views on the nature of thought and language. In doing this, she was at the forefront of those interpretations that led to a renewed appreciation of Nietzsche as the creator of a style that was "neither purely conceptual nor purely metaphorical, neither scientific nor artistic" (Miller 1985, 47). A first version of Kofman's study was presented to Derrida's seminar at the École Normale Supérieure during the period 1969–1970, in the immediate aftermath of May 1968. Twenty-five years later, the importance of the translation of Kofman's study lies in the fact that it affords us the opportunity to revisit a much earlier and more inchoate stage of the contemporary debate on the place of metaphor in the text of philosophy.

Kofman's discussion of Nietzsche's operational use of metaphor in "On Truth and Lies in a Nonmoral Sense" is especially significant in view of the influence of this essay on other views about the nature of philosophy and its differences from both science and art. Both Derrida's defense of generalized metaphoricity and Deleuze's dismissal of the concept of metaphor may be traced back to this Nietzschean problematic. In his work alone and with Guattari, Deleuze repeatedly denies the existence of metaphor in philosophy and affirms only the creation of new concepts. Although Derrida draws attention to the play of metaphor in texts of philosophy, he argues in "White Mythology" both that the concept of metaphor is a philosophical concept and that it is thoroughly imbued with metaphor. Like Deleuze, he denies the existence of any principled distinction between concept and metaphor, preferring to use the rhetorical term *catachresis* to refer, by analogy, to the philosophical invention of new concepts.[2]

Nietzsche opened up a rich field of problems with regard to the differences between metaphor and concept and their respective roles in thought and language. With the rediscovery of this field in the work of Kofman and others, the sense of these problems had to be determined anew in order to find novel ways of resolving them. As often occurs with work produced in the first throes of a revolutionary shift in thought and sensibility, Kofman's own manner of determining the sense of these problems may not in the end have been the most productive. Her analysis was not without its own internal tensions, in part because of the manner in which it tended to fix the forgetting of metaphor and the relations between concept and metaphor in Nietzsche's account into a psychoanalytic frame.

In "On Truth and Lies," Nietzsche adopts the perspective of a transcendental anthropology in order to suggest that what we take to be knowledge is only a product of human invention that we have no reason to suppose is "congruent with things." Since we have no way of stepping outside our perceptual mechanisms and scientific concepts in order to compare the results with reality itself, Nietzsche is careful to point out, we equally have no reason to suppose that categorial distinctions such as the contrast between individual and species do not "correspond to the essence of things." To do so, he says, "would of course be a dogmatic assertion and, as such, would be just as indemonstrable as its opposite" (Nietzsche 1979, 84). Nietzsche's anthropological perspective enables him to reduce the difference between art and science and to argue that all attempts to divide up and simplify the "mass of images" that stream from the human senses are the work of man as "an *artistically creating* subject." Words and concepts no less than images or sensory impressions appear as the products of human invention: at most they are a different form of art. Not only is there no question of a criterion of "correct perception"; here the idea of correctness is out of place. Between the world as such and our representations of it "there is, at most, an aesthetic relation" (Nietzsche 1979, 86).

As Maudemarie Clark notes, Nietzsche here relies upon a theory of perception and knowledge that is consistent with Kant's view of human sensibility and understanding (Clark 1990, 82, 86). Nietzsche writes:

> All we actually know about these laws of nature is what we ourselves bring to them—time and space and therefore relationships of succession and number. . . . All that conformity to law, which impresses us so much in the movement of the stars and in chemical processes, coincides at bottom with those properties which we bring to things. (Nietzsche 1979, 87–88)

Kofman concurs with this Kantian reading when she suggests that, for Nietzsche, the senses and thought together create the images through which we perceive the world and "space and time are not real; they exist only for a sentient being who sees everything through these two fundamental metaphoric forms" (Kofman 1993b, 28).

For Kant's metaphor of a Copernican revolution in the domain of metaphysics, Nietzsche substitutes his own figure of man as the eternal reason spider, spinning out of himself the "rigid and regular web of concepts" upon which he relies for the guidance of his life and conduct. With reference to this web of concepts, he writes: "We produce these representations in and from ourselves with the same necessity with which the spider spins" (Nietzsche 1979, 87). Kofman comments that this metaphor "highlights the fact that the concepts are constructed from man himself just as the spider creates its web from its own substance" (Kofman 1993b, 69). However, in addition, she reads it as a condemnation of the man of reason, whom she presents as a kind of vampire feeding off the lifeblood of the senses in order to give it back in the form of a lifeless conceptual web. In support of this reading, Kofman cites the following passage from the Kröner edition of *Nietzsche's Werke:*[3] "In the last resort, we achieve nothing more by cognition than the spider achieves by weaving its web, hunting and sucking the blood of its prey" (Kofman 1993b, 72). At the end of "On Truth and Lies," Nietzsche portrays conceptual thought as a no less effective means of ruling over life than the more artistic constructions of intuitive cultures. For Kofman, however, the arachnoid metaphor conveys a condemnation of conceptual thought as such. In general, she argues, "The metaphor of the spider is attached to the metaphors of the rag, the ghost, and sickly pallor to indicate that the concept is hatred of life and the death of desire" (Kofman 1993b, 71). As I propose to show in what follows, her reading of the arachnoid metaphor thus reproduces *en abîme* a critical stance toward the concept that recurs through *Nietzsche and Metaphor.*

The terms of this condemnation of the concept include not only the opposition between life and death but also that between identity and difference. She says, "The concept is a transition from the analogous to the identical, from diversity to unity" (Kofman 1993b, 37). In its literal or rhetorical sense, metaphor involves drawing attention to similarities between different things. Thus, a poet can equate old age with a "withered stalk" or a novelist can equate the soul of an obsessed man driven toward a single goal with a locomotive whose path is "laid with iron rails." Just as ordinary metaphor can be said to involve the imitation of one image in another (a person's soul, a locomotive), so Nietzsche argues that language involves the imitation of mental images in sound. These mental images are themselves the imitation of a nerve stimulus. Concepts then involve the iteration of this same process: a word becomes a concept when it is imitated in a general term that "simultaneously has to fit countless more or less similar cases." It is at this point, Nietzsche argues, that the difference between metaphoric and conceptual use of language intervenes: "A word becomes a concept insofar as it simultaneously has to fit countless more or less similar cases. . . . Every concept arises from the equation of unequal things." One leaf is always different from another one, so "the concept 'leaf' is formed by arbitrarily discarding these individual differences and by forgetting the distinguishing aspects" (Nietzsche 1979, 83).

However, similarity is not identity. Concepts may discard or "repress" the differences between things, but in the case of metaphor these individual differences are not forgotten. The difference between literal and metaphoric language is that in the former case we forget that there are only similarities or likenesses between things: "Truths are illusions which we have forgotten are illusions; they are metaphors that have become worn out and have been drained of sensuous force, coins which have lost their embossing and are now considered as metal and no longer as coins" (Nietzsche 1979, 84).

Nietzsche argues that the drive to fabricate images in response to sensation is the "fundamental human drive" (Nietzsche 1979, 88). As such, Kofman argues, it is an unconscious activity that consciousness can only represent to itself metaphorically, that is, by analogy with its own conscious activities (Kofman 1993b, 25). Moreover, she points out, Nietzsche employs two metaphors to describe this activity: an analogy with visual art and an analogy with metaphor. Kofman calls these the artistic model and the rhetorical model, respectively, and suggests that they involve two distinct and opposing ways of characterizing the results of the primary aesthetic activity. The artistic model is present in *The Birth of Tragedy* and is the more constant model throughout Nietzsche's writings. Art is deserving of our ultimate gratitude, he writes in paragraph 107 of *The Gay Science* (Nietzsche 1974, 163), because it enables us to accept with good conscience the fact that untruth and error are inescapable features of the human condition.

The artistic model is a "good model," Kofman suggests, because it implies the creation of forms that are products of human sensibility, just like the world that we observe and contemplate. With respect to human knowledge, this model then "allows the opposition between reality and appearance to be unequivocally effaced" (Kofman 1993b, 32). The rhetorical model, by contrast, is a bad model, since it reestablishes the opposition between reality and appearance. Kofman writes, "To call this artistic construction metaphor is to carry on referring 'our' world to another which would be the world *proper,* the thing 'in itself' " (Kofman 1993b, 33). Kofman argues that the rhetorical model is at best a "detour" in the development of Nietzsche's thought, albeit a necessary stage in the "generalization of metaphor" that occurs along with the development of the will-to-power hypothesis in his later writings. These writings represent a "generalization of metaphor" in the sense that they offer a nonrepresentational view of human thought and knowledge without any implicit reference to a "proper" object or referent. The role played by metaphor in the early writings is taken over in the later writings by the concepts of "text" and "interpretation." As a result, the "proper" itself becomes no more than an interpretation and "the notion of metaphor becomes totally 'improper' since it is henceforth no longer referred to a proper but to an interpretation. To continue using this notion as a key concept might have been dangerous because of its metaphysical implications, and it is understandable that Nietzsche should have abandoned it after making strategic use of it" (Kofman 1993b, 17).

However, Kofman's case for incompatibility between the artistic and rhetorical models is open to question both at the level of the text and at the level of principles. With regard to Nietzsche's text, it is not obvious that in "On Truth and Lies" he sees the artistic and the rhetorical models as being in conflict with one another. Indeed, it is precisely because of the metaphoric genesis of language and concepts that Nietzsche calls man an "artistically creating subject." At one point, he even collapses the two figures into one, referring to the "artistic process of metaphor formation" (Nietzsche 1979, 88). At the level of principles, the opposition of the two models and her implicit criticism of the rhetorical model rely upon the claim that it preserves the idea of the proper, the idea of a thing in itself that is misrepresented by human thought and perception.

But this is to presuppose both a particular theory of metaphor and a particular interpretation of Nietzsche's operational use of metaphor to describe the unconscious activity of man as an artistically creating subject. Kofman does argue that in *The Birth of Tragedy* Nietzsche assumes an Aristotelian concept of metaphor, according to which metaphor consists in giving something a name that properly belongs to something else, but only in order to reverse the relationship between concept and metaphor (Kofman 1993b, 15). Her suggestion that the Nietzsche of *The Birth of Tragedy* could not maintain an Aristotelian definition of metaphor only serves to highlight the implausibility of the claim that the rhetorical model of thought and language preserves an idea of the proper.

Consider Nietzsche's characterization of the genesis of language and concepts as a process of metaphor: "To begin with, a nerve stimulus is transferred into an image: first metaphor. The image, in turn, is imitated in a sound: second metaphor. And each time there is a complete overleaping of one sphere, right into the middle of an entirely new and different one" (Nietzsche 1979, 82). What is the sense of metaphor here? In this passage, Nietzsche describes a process that is anterior to both literal and metaphoric uses of language. Necessarily, he employs "metaphor" metaphorically in order to describe this process. Since, on this account, this process is the precondition even of literal language use, on which metaphoric use depends, it must be taken metaphorically and not simply in the rhetorical sense given by Aristotle. Moreover, since we are dealing here with a metaphor of metaphor, we need to ask what aspect of the rhetorical process is being considered analogous to this primary artistic activity.

Given Nietzsche's careful agnosticism with regard to whether or not human categories correspond to the essence of things, what matters to him in the figure of metaphor is not the reference to the proper. Equally, given his account of language and concept formation, it cannot be that what is at issue in this primary metaphoric process is giving something a name that belongs to something else. For this would suppose the metaphysical equivalent of a literal language, one that would designate things as they are in themselves, apart from human capacities and interests. But it is precisely Nietzsche's claim that there is no such literal system of metaphysical representation, no Logos. It is true that he relies upon the belief in such a Logos, and in the possibility of truth in the sense of metaphysical correspondence with the nature of reality, in order to suggest that what we take as truths are illusions. Maudemarie Clarke argues that far from rejecting the notion of truth, in this essay Nietzsche relies upon a metaphysical correspondence theory of what would constitute truth in order to claim that we have no reason to suppose that human experience gives us truth in that sense (Clark 1990, 83). But this is only a conditional acceptance of the idea of truth as correspondence for rhetorical effect. It enables Nietzsche to assert that man "forgets that the original perceptual metaphors are metaphors and takes them to be the things themselves" (Nietzsche 1979, 86).

Throughout "On Truth and Lies," Nietzsche remains agnostic about whether or not human categories correspond to the essence of things. From the anthropological perspective of this essay, all we have is the metaphysical equivalent of metaphoric language, where this is understood to involve the translation of sensory impressions into language and thus the indirect presentation of phenomena that have an impact upon our senses. Hence the proliferation of metaphors in Nietzsche's text to describe this originary metaphoric process: Chladni's sound figures that represent sound waves in air by means of patterns in sand, the painter without hands expressing his vision in song. Kofman herself points out that Nietzsche offers only a number of mutually complementary metaphors to describe this activity, "none in itself sufficient to describe it 'properly'" (Kofman 1993b, 40). However, what is common to all these cases is the transfer or "carry-over" ("Übertragungen") of a signal from one domain to another. Peter Heckman writes that for Nietzsche in this context, "a metaphor is a translation from one dimension to another" (Heckman 1991, 310).

Nietzsche's metaphoric representation of unconscious artistic activity amounts to a necessarily fluid and indeterminate characterization of the metaphysical status of language. It is precisely this fluidity that enables him to undertake what Kofman calls a strategy designed to fill the abyss opened up by the metaphysical tradition and to "delete the opposition between concept and metaphor" (Kofman 1993b, 25). However, the same fluidity also allows for the possibility that the problem might be resolved in other ways. The argument of "On Truth and Lies" is that rational and intuitive means of representation are equally products of this same transformative activity. Each has its advantages and disadvantages, but there is no epistemological ground on which to privilege one over the other. There is no question of the proper or adequate representation of one thing by another: all signs are equally improper.

It is even a matter of indifference, in relation to this problematic, whether we say that concepts are derived from this primary metaphoric process or that metaphors are produced according to the logic of concept formation: the imitation of one thing by means of another is common to both. Neither from the fact that Nietzsche views the drive toward the formation of metaphors (in this metaphoric sense) as the fundamental human drive nor from the priority of this originary metaphoricity can we derive any priority or hierarchy in the relations between metaphor and concept, or for that matter between art and science. Both have their origins in originary metaphoricity. Thus we can say with equal justice that the concept of metaphor is irreducibly metaphoric and that the metaphor of metaphor is a protoconcept.

Here we have reached a critical point in the problematic field of an originary metaphoricity. To go beyond this indeterminate problematic field and refigure the understanding of philosophical, scientific, or artistic thought, the field must be determined in some particular manner. At this undetermined point, a choice arises. On the one hand, we can retain the traditional concepts of concept and metaphor, the former with its commitment to identity and its implicit hostility toward difference implied in the forgetting of particularity, the latter with its impropriety and its vitality. On the other hand, we can refigure these concepts in such a way that identity and propriety are no longer among the defining properties of concepts. The latter path leads to the conclusion that the difference between concepts and metaphors can no longer be sustained at the level of principle. It leads to the forgetting of the forgetting of difference and particularity that was supposed to distinguish concept from metaphor. It leaves no place for the Aristotelian concept of metaphor.

This latter path is the one followed by Derrida and Deleuze. As Derrida argues in "White Mythology," the concept of metaphor is irreducibly metaphoric: transposing or carrying over the name of something onto something else already involves a spatial as well as a proprietary metaphor. On the other hand, the proper or literal use of language involves the same metaphoric movements, since it is defined as a means of conveying what might be conveyed by other means or what might not be conveyed at all and yet still exist.

In turn, the metaphoric character of the concept of metaphor affects the concept of concept. Deleuze denies the existence of metaphor in any sense other than that which coincides with the creation of new concepts. If there is no proper relation to the object, and if concepts are always defined in relation to the particular problem field in which they operate, then the transposition of a term from one field of application to another is never just the metaphoric use of language, but the creation of a new concept. Throughout their collaborative work, Deleuze and Guattari deny that they engage in a metaphoric use of language. There is no such thing as metaphor, they claim, just the deterritorialization that is involved in the transfer of a term to a completely foreign domain. In other words, there is only the creation of concepts, which is coextensive with the practice of philosophy.

Such creations may be more or less successful, but there is no difference in principle between the more and less durable outcomes of this process. Concepts, like artwork, will always involve what Nietzsche calls "a suggestive transference, a stammering translation into a completely foreign tongue" (Nietzsche 1979, 86). "Stammering" and "stuttering" are precisely the terms Deleuze and Guattari employ to characterize the creative use of language. The creation of a new style or new concepts involves a kind of stuttering, not by the speaker but by the language itself: "It's easy to stammer, but making language itself stammer is a different affair; it involves placing all linguistic, and even nonlinguistic, elements in variation" (Deleuze and Guattari 1987, 98). Far from seeing the concept as parasitic upon the primordial life of the senses or the sensory, the Deleuzian resolution of the Nietzschean problematic draws attention to the life of the concept and beyond that to the nonorganic life that is common to both art and philosophy.

In their different ways, both Deleuze and Guattari and Derrida are concerned with thinking through the implications of Nietzsche's account of language for the concepts of metaphor and concept. Kofman also points to the manner in which Nietzsche's genealogy of moral concepts "reveals the 'becoming' inherent in each concept" (Kofman 1993b, 86). Nevertheless, her overall argument offers no way beyond the opposition between concept and metaphor. Rather, it retains the traditional concepts of both concept and metaphor in order to undertake a "Freudian-Nietzschean" critique of conceptual thought from the perspective of originary metaphoricity. Kofman reinstalls the abyss between concept and intuition that metaphysics had carved out, only now in the form of the opposition between concepts and originary metaphoricity. By further specifying metaphor in Aristotelian terms as parasitic upon the identity of the concept and its proper relation to its object, she is able to carry the opposition back into the realm of originary metaphoricity itself in opposing Nietzsche's artistic and rhetorical models of this process. In effect, Kofman's account imposes a particular determination of the sense of Nietzsche's metaphoric use of the notion of metaphor and, on this basis, condemns the rhetorical model as an inadequate expression of the primary unconscious drive identified by Nietzsche.

Two further elements are essential for this criticism of the rhetorical model. The first is the rhetoric of a post-'68 celebration of difference in opposition to the violence of identity. Much of Kofman's analysis of the relations between concept and metaphor is clothed in the language of this rhetorical politics of difference. Metaphoricity understood in these terms, she argues, implies "the loss of individuality and the reduction of differences" (Kofman 1993b, 34). The second element is Kofman's restoration of the abyss by imposing a Freudian model of the relation between concept and originary metaphoricity. On this basis, she seeks to portray the concept as the sworn enemy of difference and as a repressive agency in the service of reactive forces. Not only is this argument open to question; it also produces several tensions in her own text.

Consider her discussion of the "forgetting" that accompanies concept formation. Nietzsche employs a series of metaphors that suggest that this forgetting is simply the result of natural processes and the passage of time: concepts as coins from which the embossing has worn away so that they can no longer function as coins, concepts as the "residues" of metaphors or as "hardened and congealed" metaphors (Nietzsche 1979, 84–87). By contrast, Kofman insists that this cannot be a merely empirical forgetting, as suggested by Nietzsche's metaphors. The forgetting of metaphor cannot be understood to mean simply a linear and empirical genesis of the concept, since this would imply that it is an event that takes place in "linear historical time," whereas Nietzsche's typological conception of history already marks "a break with the traditional concept of time." Kofman therefore calls for "a new concept of forgetting" and argues that "the forgetting of metaphor does not occur at a specific point in time. . . . It is originary, the necessary correlate of metaphysical activity itself" (Kofman 1993b, 25). Thus, whereas primary metaphoric activity is instinctive and unconscious, conceptual thought is conscious and predicated upon the necessary forgetting of its metaphoric origins. Indeed, Kofman suggests that the concept plays a privileged role in the forgetting of metaphor, namely, the role of a force of anticathexis that sustains the originary repression of metaphoricity by installing a system of secondary repression: "It allows a system of secondary rationalizations to be set up after the event, effacing the fact that metaphorical activity is originary, at the origin of all knowledge and activity" (35).

To characterize conceptual thought as founded upon the repressed unconscious of originary metaphoricity is not necessarily to condemn it. However, Kofman folds the psychoanalytic model of the relation between concept and metaphoricity onto a genealogical account of the forces involved in the repression of metaphors. In the terms of Nietzsche's account in *On the Genealogy of Morals,* forgetting is the result of a perspective shift that accompanies the appropriation and transformation of old evaluations by new forces. The forgetting of metaphor in particular is presented as the result of the triumph of reactive forces, as another expression of the same relative weakness that gave rise to moral judgment: "It was the same forces which repressed metaphor in favor of the concept and imposed the morality of the herd, for the same reasons: the neediness of a certain type of life, that of the greatest number, which was not strong enough, not 'bad' enough to will its perspective as such" (Kofman 1993b, 57). The implicit critique contained in this account is especially apparent in the analogy drawn between the genesis of the concept and that of justice. What the genesis of the concept and that of justice have in common above all is the establishment of equivalences or the imposition of equilibrium: "Man invents equivalences as he does analogies" (44). Moreover, in each case Kofman suggests that the metamorphosis is carried out by violent means, by the exercise of force upon the primary differential relations of language or society. Kofman writes: "In both cases the same metamorphoses and the same forgettings take place. Indeed it is the same metaphorical activity, reducing differences and assimilating the similar, that is at the origin of the genesis both of 'justice' and of the concept" (43).

This parallel between justice and the concept in Kofman's text enables her to transpose the barbarism and violence that Nietzsche discovers behind the institution of morality and justice onto the institution of the concept. In each case, those who fail to measure up are sanctioned, by punishment or by exclusion: "Those who misuse the concept—the liar, the artist, the dreamer—are excluded from the city" (Kofman 1993b, 46). In each case, the violence of the origin is forgotten and differences are sacrificed: "The triumph of justice and of the concept go hand in hand with the abandonment of individual perspectives" (48). Kofman even goes so far as to claim that while justice and the memory that sustains it give us the capacity to make promises, and along with this conscience, responsibility, and the preconditions of personal identity, nonetheless "these gratifications are merely a deception, for this violent process culminates in the triumph of the collective over the individual. The 'proper' is subjected to the social norm just as impressions and images are branded by the concept" (47).

Kofman's suggestion that the fixation of metaphors into concepts offers merely illusory gratifications appears to reverse the traditional hierarchy of concept and metaphor in precisely the manner she rejects in the Introduction to *Nietzsche and Metaphor*. She argues there that it is more Nietzschean "to write conceptually in the knowledge that a concept has no greater value than a metaphor and is itself a condensate of metaphors . . . than to write metaphorically while denigrating the concept and proposing metaphor as the norm" (Kofman 1993b, 3). In general, her account of Nietzsche's style in the end presents him as a philosopher who creates neither concepts nor new metaphors. Rather, he appears as one who plays with and parodies the established concepts and metaphors of philosophy: "Nietzsche reiterates old metaphors rather than inventing new ones" (185). Whether or not this is all that Nietzsche does, it certainly does not exhaust the possibilities opened up by his "conceptual" deconstruction of the opposition between metaphor and concept. In the closing paragraphs of "On Truth and Lies," Nietzsche alludes to the possibility of a free intellect that would "speak only in forbidden metaphors and unheard-of combinations of concepts" (Nietzsche 1979, 90). The Deleuzian and Derridean resolutions of the Nietzschean problematic take up this suggestion in a manner that points, not to the reversal of the hierarchy or the critique of concepts in favor of metaphors, but rather to the cultivation of a different "sense" of truth, and thereby perhaps to a different exercise of conceptual thought.

Schemata of Ideology in Camera obscura and Specters of Marx

PIERRE LAMARCHE

*C*amera *obscura: De l'idéologie* was Sarah Kofman's third book, appearing as part of the Philosophie en effet series in 1973.[1] In the Introduction to the English translation of *Nietzsche et la métaphore*, Duncan Large notes the extent to which the Philosophie en effet group was, or at least was perceived to be, dominated by the theoretical influences of Jacques Derrida (Kofman 1993b, xxxvi n. 52).[2] What Kofman refers to as her "vrai rencontre" with Derrida had taken place while she was coediting the Philosophie en effet series in collaboration with Derrida, Jean-Luc Nancy, and Philippe Lacoue-Labarthe, and of her relation to these figures, Kofman has said in an interview with Alice Jardine: "We are all four very different, over and above our profound community of ideas. But assimilation being easy, particularly where a woman is concerned, one must sometimes clarify certain things" (Jardine and Menke 1991, 108).[3] The main clarification Kofman is referring to is the one vis à vis her relation to Derrida, to whom she has often been subordinated. In this interview, she underscores the fact that her work on Nietzsche and Freud in the 1960s—a decisive double engagement that, of course, has formed the basis of her entire

I would like to thank Kelly Oliver, Harry Cleaver, and especially Robert E. Ramirez, all of whom were crucial, in different ways, to the execution of this project.

oeuvre—was done "before having either read or met Derrida. My later reading of Derrida allowed me to generalize the type of reading I had done in isolation on these two authors" (108). Later in the interview, in a question "relating to [Kofman's] own work," she is asked, "As a philosopher and a Derridean, how would you . . . ?" (111). Alice Jardine admits that the question was "a sort of trap, but not meant to be wicked." The substance of the question is not significant. The "trap" is in Jardine's qualification of Kofman as both "philosopher" and "Derridean," and it is to the application of these qualifiers that Kofman responds in her answer. While accepting the former, Kofman protests that the qualifier "Derridean" is inappropriate as applied to her own thought, or indeed in general (it implies, among other things, a "Derridean" canon that Derrida himself would vociferously resist). Furthermore, in a line that is often referred to in discussions regarding Kofman's relation to Derrida, she notes, "If I think 'as a Derridean,' just then I'm not thinking anymore" (111).

Nonetheless, it is interesting to observe that in this same interview—conducted in 1988, after years in which she struggled against the tendency to dismiss her work as derivative of Derrida's—Kofman begins by suggesting that, as a writer, her main referents "are the great thinkers on writing: Blanchot and Derrida" (104). Blanchot, who, with the exception of *Paroles suffoquées,* is seldom referred to by Kofman,[4] and Derrida rather than Deleuze, who, if one wishes—for whatever reason, for better or for worse—to identify the contemporary figure who seems to have had the greatest influence on both Kofman's writing and her thinking, appears better situated than Derrida.[5]

Be that as it may, it is in a text that is codedicated to Derrida, and that opens with a chapter on Marx, that one can arguably locate Kofman's work at the site—both spatial and temporal—of its most intense engagement with Derrida. *Camera obscura* appears in 1973, and this year also sees the publication of "Un philosophie 'unheimlich,'" Kofman's essay focusing on Derrida's relation to Freud and psychoanalysis, which was reprinted in *Lectures de Derrida.* Kofman tells us in the final footnote of *Camera obscura* that the book was first presented in Derrida's seminar on religion and philosophy at the École Normale Supérieure, and she thanks Derrida, whom she owes, "notably, for having suggested that for Marx, religion is the form of all ideology" (Kofman 1973, 76).[6] The issues of the religious and ontotheological dimensions of Marx's writing and their relation to his account of the genesis and function of ideology will be treated at length by a certain Derrida precisely twenty years after the appearance of this footnote in *Camera obscura,* in his *Specters of Marx.* Derrida's reading—particularly of how the notions of the specter and spectrality figure the analysis of ideology, and of the relationship between ideological and religious metaphor in Marx—are in many ways anticipated by Kofman's work.

THE INVERSION OF THE CAMERA OBSCURA

Ideology, as the story goes, was born in the Bastille during the Reign of Terror. The imprisoned French revolutionary aristocrat Antoine Destutt de Tracy conceived of *idéologie* as a science of ideas that would weaken the stranglehold held by the Catholic church's intelligentsia over the vast majority of France's uneducated masses by demonstrating the falsity of the worldview concocted by the intelligentsia. Ideology was thus intended as a liberating, scientific inquiry that would expose the incoherence and baselessness of the superstitious fantasies spun by the priests in the service of maintaining the dominance of their own, and the nobility's, position over the masses. It was a science of demystification that would lay bare *the truth*, in opposition to the manipulative system of distorted ideas of the priestly caste. Ironically, it was another revolutionary, Napoleon, no less, who, after assuming the mantle of emperor, began to skirmish with de Tracy and his fellow *idéologues*, referring to them as dreamers and windbags and seeing in them a threat to his own authoritarian rule. And so by the time of Marx's early writings, the notion of ideology had already begun to take on the negative connotations of a speculative idealism, which is precisely what ideology was supposed to exorcise. And it is this kind of connotation that Marx, of course, exploited.[7]

Similarly, the camera obscura had, in the Renaissance and early Enlightenment, been conceived of as a scientific apparatus that would lay bare the world in a perfect, though inverted, reproduction. The device consists of a darkened chamber that admits light from outside through a convex lens embedded in a pinhole, projecting an image onto a screen placed at the lens's focal point. To correct for the inversion produced by the lens, a second lens can be introduced that *inverts* the inversion. The camera obscura can be as small as a portable box and as large as a building that many people at a time may enter in order to see a carousel of images projected on the walls by a rotating, periscopic viewer. The image in the camera obscura can be traced directly onto a secondary medium, allowing a transparent copy of the object of study to be made—a kind of Renaissance Xerox. No longer would artists and illustrators be limited by their drawing ability in attempting to render the world around them. The camera obscura would allow them to trace the external world, in *true* perspective, proportion, and form, without fear of the distortion inherent in the distance between the visual impression and the hand that attempts to reproduce it. But this instrument of transparency and clarity, linked to the faith of the Renaissance and Enlightenment in the transparency and clarity implicit in the visual, optical paradigm—the immediately *apparent*—becomes, as Kofman notes, a metaphor of occlusion and mystification in Nietzsche, Freud, and Marx, just as ideology, after its emergence as a supposed science of demystification, becomes regarded with more and more suspicion, gradually metamorphosing from the *true* science of the early *idéologues* like de Tracy to the false obscurantism of, say, Marx's *The German Ideology* (hereafter *GI*).

Sarah Kofman's *Camera obscura: De l'idéologie* opens with a quotation from Nietzsche's *Philosophenbuch:*

> What does man really know about himself? Can he even once perceive himself, completely, as if displayed in an illuminated glass case? And nature, does she not hide most things from him, even his own body, in order to keep him shut up—far away from the coils of his intestines, the swift current of his blood, the complex vibrations of his fibers—within a proud, phantasmagoric consciousness? She has thrown away the key: and woe to the fatal curiosity that would love to gaze through a cleft in the chamber of consciousness (*Bewusstseinszimmer*), far outside, and sense that man rests upon the merciless, the greedy, the insatiable, the murderous, in the indifference of his ignorance, hanging in dreams, as it were, upon the back of a tiger. (Kofman 1973, 11)

The aphorism glitters with all the poeticism of the Nietzsche who heralds the collapse of the Enlightenment subject: of the dream of a clearsighted consciousness, apprehending itself in the stability of the unified cogito, thence understanding and subduing the world around it. Who dreams this dream hangs on the back of a tiger, ignorant of the seething reality hidden below, pullulating with its drives and currents, carrying the dreamer precariously aloft. The connection between this sketch of the immolation of a unified, transparent subjectivity and the issue of ideology, especially in Marx, is clear. Read straightforwardly—which here would be to say, without art—the aphorism undoes an equally artless reading of Marx's conception of the task of ideology critique. If ideology is at bottom a false consciousness—a speculative idealism that naturalizes and legitimates bourgeois domination under capital—then the task of ideology critique is to oppose this false consciousness with a true consciousness that sees things *as they really are*—the consciousness of the proletariat as the last revolutionary class, restoring, or instituting, a truly natural world of social relations not based upon domination and exploitation.

But to say that consciousness itself is always already phantasmagoric—
an illusion, a dream, a lie that makes one sort of life possible—is to say that
all consciousness is false consciousness. To see things truly would be to see
a festering chaos of "insatiable," "murderous" impulses as the counterpoint to the dream work of the stable, unified subject. Thus and so, there
would be no clear, transparent consciousness of a sane and sensible natural order of pristine sociality outside of the inverted and fully idealized
world of liberal free-market democracy that could be offered as an alternative to the ugly reality of social relations mystified and obscured by
bourgeois ideology. One lie is as good as the next; thus there would be no
stable position grounded in *the truth* from which to launch a criticism of
false consciousness and of the desperate world false consciousness ob-
scures. *Bonne nature,* in one sense, would always only be the nightmare of
the dreamer, and never a corrective to a phantasmagoric dream world.

And so Hobbes's lies—which might be used to legitimate the promise of
liberal democracy by offering up a nasty, brutish, and necessary alternative—
would be at least as legitimate as Proudhon's utopian dreams. Here we see
the germ of the reactionary, conservative Nietzsche pilloried by some of the
more orthodox brands of leftist theorists, who paradoxically maintain a
zealous commitment to the philosophical, ontological categories of truth
and falsity—a zealousness mocked by Marx himself. Although Kofman is
no Marxist in any sense of the word,[8] she will refuse to set Marx up as the
naive defender of truth against the scandalous Nietzsche, which for Kofman, of course, could only be to Nietzsche's advantage. Kofman's readings
are more subtle than this, more attuned to both the difficulties and the possibilities that are opened up by the *heterogeneity* of his texts.

The metaphor of the camera obscura appears in *GI* as a "perfect" analogy for the process of inversion that takes place in all ideology. By the
time of *Capital,* however, Marx's depiction of the genesis and function of
ideology has clearly been altered. The stakes involved in this shift are the
subject of the first chapter of *Camera obscura,* "Marx: Black Magic." Kofman, of course, is not the first to notice Marx's change of position from
GI to *Capital.*[9] The strength of her reading is the stress she places on the
multiplicity of metaphors strategically assembled by Marx in his articulation of both (1) the metaphors of the camera obscura and ideology and
(2) the element that brings them together analogously—the *inversion.* By
paying careful attention to this play of metaphors that animates the analysis in both *GI* and *Capital,* Kofman shows how the second text modifies
and displaces, but also upholds and expands upon, the reading of ideology given in the first—a reading that was never as simple and naive as it
has been depicted.

In the course of a few sentences in *GI*, Marx lays out the metaphor of the camera obscura as a direct analogue of the formation of ideology, but then, as Kofman stresses, he immediately modifies and corrects it with a series of other metaphors.[10] This familiar passage begins as follows: "If in all ideology men and their circumstances appear upside-down as in a camera obscura, this phenomenon arises just as much from their historical life processes as the inversion of objects on the retina does from their physical life processes" (Marx 1977, 164; Kofman 1973, 13).

Already, the mechanical model of the camera obscura has been coupled to the optical metaphor of the eye; the camera obscura functions just like an eye that reflects the world in transparent, but inverted, form on the retina. Stated in this initial and simple form, the ideological inversion described through the specular metaphor of the camera obscura can best be understood in relation to Marx's criticism of Hegelian idealism. Ideology depicts reality—that is, material, social relations—as being determined by consciousness, just as Hegel viewed the material world as being determined by the idea. Specifically, bourgeois ideology depicts notions such as the free labor market, democratic rule, and equality under the law as determining the material relations of society, thus underwriting and guaranteeing the egalitarian nature of society and legitimating bourgeois liberal democracy and an economy organized around the principle of capital. This conception inverts the materialist view of base/superstructure that sees material, social relations as themselves determining consciousness, culture, and ideology. In this view, it is bourgeois domination under capital that is at the root of bourgeois ideology, which then secondarily seeks to legitimate this domination.

Thus far in *GI*, and in Kofman's reading, the metaphor of the camera obscura illustrates the straightforward vertical inversion of the base/superstructure relation inherent in Marx's conception of ideology. Limited to the bounds of a straightforward, specular metaphor, ideology appears to be something like a false consciousness: a picture of the world stood on its head, where down is up, white is black, imprisonment is freedom, tyranny is democracy, and so on. The answer would be to simply turn the image right side up, invert the inversion, expose the ugliness false consciousness turns upside down and calls beautiful, and then oppose this with the *truth* about how social relations should function. But again, Kofman stresses the fact that Marx immediately, indeed in the very next sentence of the text, expands his analogy of the process of ideological inversion using another metaphor: "A second metaphor clarifies the first and describes the inversion of the inversion undertaken by Marx: 'In direct contrast to German philosophy which descends from heaven to earth, here we ascend from earth to heaven.'" (Kofman 1973, 14).

This second metaphor makes it clear that ideological inversion is hierarchical because it substitutes an imaginary basis—ideals, slogans, "heaven"—for the real basis of social relations, the "earth." The metaphor also appends the strict, spatial inversion implied by the specular reflection of the camera obscura with what Kofman refers to as "a supplementary religious connotation: a slight displacement bringing to light the privilege of religious ideology as an exemplar, seen as constitutive of ideology as such" (Kofman 1973, 14). And so here we have a hierarchical inversion supplemented by a religious metaphor that underlines the distinction between real material, social processes—sociality as such—and all ideal, imaginary, superstructural formations—"ideology as such." A third metaphor, that of "chemical sublimation," is then immediately adjoined, in order to complete the account of ideological inversion introduced by the camera obscura metaphor (17–18).

The specular relation connoted by the camera obscura metaphor implies the dependence of ideology upon its material base. There is no reflection in the camera obscura without something real to reflect. But the metaphor is in itself insufficient to account for the apparent autonomy of ideology, that is, its supposed independence from material, social relations, an independence necessary for it to be conceived of as standing above social relations, somehow determining and guaranteeing them, as, for example, the telos guiding our social development and underwriting its egalitarian form, or at least guaranteeing that equality and freedom are matters of minor adjustment and are waiting for us just around the corner. And so Kofman notes that "the camera obscura, and all of the other specular metaphors, imply a relation to the real. Marx is thus forced to couple them to the chemical metaphor of sublimation[,] which describes a process of idealization along with the volatilization of the constitutive elements; hence the "forgetting" of the process of genesis, and the illusion of autonomy" (Kofman 1973, 18).

This final metaphor of chemical sublimation, accounting for ideology's apparent autonomy, allows Kofman to initiate a wordplay that will, with elaboration, launch the discussion of ideology in *GI* into *Capital* and beyond to Nietzsche and Freud, eventually carrying us all the way to Derrida's *Specters* and instigating a true schema of ideology, which, as it turns out, will be a gathering of ghosts. Conceived of as independent from, and determinative of, material relations, and thus cut off from the process of its own genesis, ideology becomes severed from reality and is locked inside the darkroom of the camera obscura:

So everything happens as if the key to the darkroom had been thrown away, and the idea shut in ["l'idée abandonée au logis"], imprisoned, forced to narcissistically revolve around itself. A reflection cut off from its source, and, ever since, capable only of engendering reflections of reflections. Simulacra. Fetishes. (Kofman 1973, 18)

L'idéologie is also *l'idée au logis:* "the idea shut in," imprisoned, with the key to the darkroom thrown away and forgotten. When it posits itself as independent from, and constitutive of, social relations, ideology cuts itself off from its very source and thus dehistoricizes itself. But ideology can only turn its back on—can only *veil* and *forget*—its source by making of itself, and of its metaphysical system, a fetish, engendering other fetishes. A simple example, and one that operates from the moment that capitalist means of production are introduced, is that of the notion of the free labor market, which multiplies forms of pseudolegitimating ideals as it is spun into the demand for the individual's right to work, against the injustice of being forced to bargain collectively, all of this grounded in the transhistorical value of the subject's desire to maximize its freedom. Collective bargaining had been a practical adjustment, subsequently incorporated into the ideology of the free labor market when the freedom and egalitarianism of this aspect of the wage labor system were exposed as a lie. The ideal, or "ideologem" in Derrida's usage, of the free labor market now spins itself a new fetish, a new ideologem—the *right to work*—to answer the readjustment of power relations that has occurred in favor of the workers through the vehicle of collective bargaining.

The ideal of the right to work continues to obscure and distort the truth of the labor market. And just so, the ideal of the free labor market itself, severed and locked away from its genesis in a system organized around the domination of capital, is a fetish that veils the vastly unequal bargaining positions, the inordinate preponderance of power on one side of the equation within the real labor market, the constraint on the worker to operate within the logic of the wage-labor system, the inescapableness of the wage form, perhaps most significantly the historical contingency of capitalist means of production, and on and on. This ideal of the free labor market is a "shut-in": one who is unwilling, or unable, to venture into the clear light of day and see the world for what it really is, one who is locked away, safely under key—the object of a perverse, fetishistic fantasy that has something to do with the phantoms of something like justice and rightness. All of the history, and all of the real effects, of the wage-labor system are forgotten in the ideology of the "free labor market."

And so the forgetting of its genesis locks ideology inside its darkroom, its camera obscura. The key has been tossed, just as Nature has thrown away the key to the chamber of consciousness, leaving man "hanging in dreams." Is ideology's forgetfulness then an *aktive Vergesslichkeit?* A primal repression? Kofman will relate the structure of ideology both to the forgetfulness that is the first principle of consciousness in *On the Genealogy of Morals* and to the metaphor of the watchman guarding the entrance to consciousness in Freud's "A Note on the Unconscious in Psychoanalysis."[11]

In order to reconcile the difference between the specular metaphor that implies ideology's dependence upon its material base and the metaphor of sublimation that emphasizes its apparent autonomy, locked inside its camera obscura, Kofman makes recourse to a passage from "Theses on Feuerbach," in which religion stands in for the form of *all* ideology:

> Feuerbach starts out from the fact that religion makes man a stranger to himself, and divides the world into a religious world and a secular world. His work consists in resolving the religious world into its secular basis. He does not see that this work, once completed, leaves the most important issues unresolved. The fact, notably, that the secular basis detaches itself from itself and establishes itself as an independent realm in the clouds can only be explained by the cleavages and self-contradictions within this secular basis. The latter must, therefore, in itself be both understood in its contradiction and revolutionized in practice. Thus, for instance, after the earthly family is discovered to be the secret of the holy family, the former must then itself be destroyed in theory and in practice. (Thesis IV, quoted in Kofman 1973, 19)

And Kofman, continuing to multiply the Freudian/Nietzschean imagery of her analysis, concludes:

> Nothing, then, serves to uncover the family secrets concealed in the darkness of rooms: the appearance of autonomy can ultimately be explained "by the self-contradictions of the secular base." Thus, the "concept" of ideology, with all that attaches it to the Greek *eidos* and to the gaze, remains speculative, Feuerbachian. The inversion of the inversion cannot invert anything. Only the transformation of the real contradiction can displace or resolve problems. (Kofman 1973, 20)

Is this a criticism of Marx? Has Kofman's analysis of the text revealed a fatal paradox in the binary logic of Marx? Has the dreamer Marx lost his grip on the tiger beneath him, leaving his ideology critique squarely within the realm of ideology, of abstract speculation to this or that end? Kofman herself asks with regard to her own reading, "Are there contradictions then in the 'text' of Marx?" (Kofman 1973, 20). But of course the value of

exposing theoretical contradictions seems to have been severely undermined by Marx's analyses of ideology: "Only the transformation of the *real*
contradictions can displace or resolve problems" (Kofman 1973, 20, emphasis added). What is accomplished by uncovering a purely theoretical
contradiction in an analysis that exposes another contradiction in theory?
Certainly not the recuperation of the latter: of bourgeois ideology. Kofman claims that the contradictory elements of Marx's varying elaborations
on the concept of ideology point not to a theoretical inadequacy (what is
the significance of pure theoretical speculation at this point?) as much as
to the *heterogeneity* of his texts, to the multiplication of metaphors that allows each of them to be displaced and reevaluated by turns, deeply prob-
lematizing an entire system that privileges, and fetishizes, a particular
metaphoric hierarchy—the *ideal* over the *material*. Such privileging finds
its most obvious and sweeping expression in the gesture of proclaiming
ideology's autonomy over the society it purportedly structures. And perhaps, though this is not mentioned by Kofman, this same heterogeneity
points also to the various Marxes apparent in his texts: to the theoretician
and to the polemicist, for example. Would not the polemicist Marx employ, without hesitation, rhetorical flourish to strategic, political ends, regardless of strict, theoretical inconsistency?

By now, the simple reading of *GI* that relates ideology to mere reflections
and echoes, inexplicably detached from their material base, has been ex-
ploded. Kofman will show how *Capital* expands upon the account of ideology given in *GI* by picking up on and extending the play of metaphors that
is already very much at work in *GI*: the *specular/optical* metaphor indicating
the inversion, but in *Capital* identified as an inappropriate metaphor to describe ideological inversion, since it is incapable of accounting for autonomy, and the metaphor of *sublimation,* signifying the forgetting of the
source of ideological constructs in concrete social relations. But the concentration in *Capital* is on the *religious,* indeed the *occult,* metaphor, which
illustrates the hierarchical transformation of the inversion, the appearance of autonomy lacking in the specular metaphor, and the strangeness,
the psychosis if you will, of the world of commodity exchange. The intersection of these movements of autonomy, hierarchy, and psychosis is the
realm of a spectral play of metaphors, engendering phantoms and
fetishes, intervening in a space of *appearance* between flesh and word.

In the chapter on the commodity from volume 1 of *Capital,* the commodity form stands in for an ideological construct par excellence. Marx's
task is to illustrate how the form of all value becomes equivalent to exchange value, reducing qualitative differences in human labor to mere
quantities of homogeneous labor-time, and thus how the social relation in-

volved in the process of commodity exchange becomes mistaken as a trans-action solely between *things:* the commodities themselves, which are the repositories of abstract labor-time, as opposed to the products of real human labor. Again, it is a question of explaining an apparent autonomy, the autonomy of reified, fetishized objects, the independence of commodities from the human beings who produce, exchange, and make use of them:

> A commodity appears, at first sight, a very trivial thing, and easily under-stood. . . . The form of wood, for instance, is altered, by making a table out of it. Yet, for all that, the table remains that common, sensible thing, wood. But, as soon as it steps forth as a commodity . . . it not only stands with its feet on the ground, but, in relation to all other commodities, it stands on its head, and evolves out of its wooden brain grotesque ideas, far more wonderful than "table turning" ever was. (Kofman 1973, 23; Marx and Engels 1996, 81)

"Table turning" (*table tournante*) is the French euphemism for the séance. The bizarre world of commodity exchange is also described here as "phan-tasmagoric," "fantastic," and enveloped in a "cloud of mystery"; the connec-tion between the occult, secretive, enigmatic, "ethereal" elements of reli-gious ideology and the ideology of the commodity form is stressed by Kofman as she reinscribes the play of specular, chemical/subliminal, and re-ligious metaphors in *Capital* within the general economy established by *GI*. And of course, the whole process by which the commodity becomes alien-ated from the social relations of its production and exchange is discussed under the explicit heading, "The Fetishism of Commodities and the Secret Thereof." The chapter opens the English-language edition of *Capital,* the book that is the pinnacle of Marx's scientific methodology and the most dis-tant from the speculative, philosophical early writings he had, supposedly, settled accounts with in *GI*. Nonetheless, here, at a critical juncture of *Capi-tal,* Marx chooses the example of a table to illustrate an ordinary commod-ity. Why not the coat that he uses as the general example of a commodity elsewhere in the chapter? The metaphor of the *table tournante,* with its spiri-tual, occult overtones, was clearly built into the choice. Because of the need to account for the hierarchical inversion inherent in ideological formations and for ideology's appearance of autonomy (here, the autonomy of the com-modity), Marx cannot easily settle his spectral, metaphysical accounts.

Pace those who might be tempted to read the language of the chapter on the commodity as retrograde, an insignificant throwback to the poetic early Marx, Kofman's point is that the shift in the account of the process of ide-ology formation from *GI* to *Capital* is largely consistent. If the proliferation of religious metaphors in this chapter is the signal that the commodity form must be analyzed as an ideological construct—as Kofman argues, picking up on Derrida's suggestion—then this elaborate metaphoric play is a necessary component of the discussion and a clarification and elaboration of the account of ideology given in *GI*. It cannot, and need not, be wished away as an aberration. Let us here recall that Marx's texts are *heterogeneous;* purity and pristine consistency are values of bourgeois metaphysics, not the polemicist Marx. Not the Marx who seeks to put a weapon in the hands of the working class.[12]

Just as with *GI,* the discussion of *Capital* culminates in a Freudian/Nietzschean meditation on the notion of the *idée au logis.* And here, in *Capital,* it becomes crystal clear that the key to the chamber—the key thrown away and forgotten in the *ideology* of ideology—cannot be uncovered, and consciousness' fog cannot be raised, by a simple overturning of ideology's metaphysical hierarchy. It can only come through the theoretical *and* practical transformation of the entire base/superstructure complex.[13] The metaphor of the camera obscura now becomes the sign of a fully Freudian repression, and here a certain mimeticism becomes necessary:

> Thus, the camera obscura isolates consciousness, separating it from reality. Locked inside itself, it constructs a kind of neoreality analogous to that experienced by psychotics. Marx describes this world as phantomlike, fantastic, phantasmagoric, or also as *fetishistic.* This last term seems able to be taken in a technical, psychoanalytic sense: for Freud, fetishism implies both the recognition and the denial of reality, and the construction of a substitute for it—the fetish. . . . The darkroom functions like one who is unconscious, and who is able, or unable, to tolerate the sight of this, or that, reality. What refuses to see ideology? Who refuses? . . . The camera obscura is the unconscious of a class, of the dominant class which, in order to be able to maintain its domination indefinitely, wants to veil the historical character of its domination; the historic as such, the processes of production ["genèse"], the qualitative differences in labor, difference itself.

> And furthermore, nothing would be of use to lift the veil and expose the real in its transparency. . . . [This] would be to forget that transparency itself is also a product of history, and not a given that would exist prior to ideology. . . . For Marx, obscurity is primary, and cannot be overcome by theory[,] by pure and simple demystification. . . .

> Clarity comes to pass in time, after the fact ["la clarté advient dans le temps de l'après coup"], conquering not through the resolution of theoretical oppositions, but through revolutionary practice (Kofman 1973, 31–33).

And so the shift in the account of ideology from *GI* to *Capital* makes explicit what had only been hinted at in *GI*, and what had been obscured by the overly specular nature of the camera obscura metaphor taken by itself: ideology does not give a mystified reflection of a transparent world of social relations; it reflects a world already transformed and enchanted, "reflection of a reflection, fantasy of a fantasy" (Kofman 1973, 25). Within capital, the world of real, concrete social relations is always already a phantasmagoric, distorted, opaque realm—always only the nightmare of ideological dream work. This enchanted phantasmagoria is the unconscious of the dominating class that seeks to perpetuate its domination through the veil of ideology, which veils what is already veiled. And there is no simple, transparent picture of the real world—of a natural, untrammeled social order—to oppose to it. Theory can be critical, can reveal lies—internal, immanent contradictions—but it cannot oppose lies with the truth. Truth happens in the process of the transformation of social relations, which opens a space for individuals to develop their own possibilities. This account of ideology is critical; it bridges the gap between the purely mechanical, specular inversion of reality implied by the camera obscura metaphor and the desire to confound and mystify the world on the part of a class that cannot tolerate either the lie given to its ideals by the perversity of social relations under capital or, critically, the historical contingency of this social configuration. It is a desire born in the need to repress a vexing reality, to hang, in the indifference of ignorance, above the tiger lurking beneath bourgeois ideology.

For Marx, then, obscurity is primary, particularly the obscurity and mystification of real (which here would be to say *false*, in the sense of truncated, impoverished, or reductive) social relations under capital, and there can be no *light* without the work of practical transformation. In the following chapter, on Freud—"The Photographic Apparatus"—the metaphor of the camera obscura, in the more contemporary guise of the photographic camera, is tied to the primal repression of the unconscious; the unconscious—which is not part of "fully lived" consciousness and may or may not come to consciousness—is primary to psychic life, just as photography first requires a negative, which may or may not be developed, before there can be a positive print. In "Nietzsche: The Chamber of the Painters," the metaphor is tied to the primacy of forgetting in the genesis of consciousness and to the metaphor of the veil. Unlike Freud, and especially Marx, no "nostalgia for clarity" is tied to Nietzsche's use of the camera obscura metaphor (Kofman 1973, 60). For him, it becomes a sign of generalized perspectivism and the death knell for the illusion of transparency within any regime of discourse. In this way he is different from Marx, who, though he is under no illusion that the discourse of purely theoretical ideology critique can of itself usher in the day of, or give us the blueprint for, undistorted, transparent social relations, nonetheless maintains a nostalgia for this ideal and a hope for its future: the hope of a future to come, with light and clarity, dispelling capital's dreary, psychotic mists. The hope of a future in which, to begin with, sociality as such, "difference itself," as Kofman notes, has supplanted the idols—the phantoms, the *eidola*—of a dominating class as the true basis of all things. This "nostalgia for clarity" that Nietzsche escapes also signals the ideal of the *scientific* Marx: science, with its perfect eye reflecting the world clearly and transparently, as Marx endeavors to do in his post-philosophical writing. Marx maintains a distinction between science and ideology, even though he knows that science—clarity and light, the camera lucida—can never, in and of itself, overturn ideology's camera obscura. And he maintains a nostalgia for the *ideological* values of light, clarity, transparency, and truth, even though he sees through them.

But would Nietzsche's *aktive Vergesslichkeit* then, on Marx's terms, leave intact a de facto truth embedded in the world of social relations under the domination of capital—that is, in the world of radically disproportionate possibilities (for many, now as then, the future is severely truncated)—one that figures all possible perspectives and inscribes them within the logic of capital, despite the fact that there may be no explicit privileging of this truth, since none is required? Would Nietzsche's forgetting lead us to forget our own historical position, out of which grow only certain possible alternative perspectives cultivated in the fetid soil of the phantasmal substantial/ unsubstantial bodies that traverse the politic: the great disciplinary factories of Western society, like the school and the prosthetic guardian of mass media? Would it then foreclose on the possibility of a *true* rupture, grounded in the explosive remembering of something like a Benjaminian historical materialism? This is a sin for which Nietzsche has historically been chastised by those on the left, and such castigation has been visited upon his sons and daughters. It would seem to ignore the obvious retort that the intransigence of a particular social configuration, the world as fait accompli, is the first thing the vital consciousness is likely to willfully forget—to cast aside along with the multiplication table that was memorized with such charming naïveté. The retort, of course, leaves us with a drastic tension provided by Walter Benjamin's challenge.

The account of Marx's reading of ideology that resolves ideology into a Freudian fetish, emanating from the collective unconscious of the bourgeois class, bears a family resemblance to the reading given by, arguably, the foremost Marxist contemporary of Kofman in France: Louis Althusser. What I consider to be a more appropriate reading of ideology formation, one more faithful to Marx's own reading, is suggested here by Kofman.

More appropriate, in part, because it is less ambitious, in the sense of be-ing more suspicious of the work of mere critique—of the "class struggle" carried on at the level of theory, as Althusser once referred to philosophy. Note that this suspicion is the direct result of Marx's own insistence that ongoing work of practical struggle is required to accomplish what theo-retical polemics alone cannot. And of course, Kofman's concern is with the play of metaphors in certain passages of Marx's texts, rather than with how his entire legacy may bear on particular historical developments or how to rethink Marx as a whole in order to account for the foreclosure of certain possibilities during the course of the twentieth century.

Kofman has deconstructed Marx's concept of ideology in its metaphorically/metaphysically charged etymology and in its *play:* in ide-ology's connection to the Greek *eidolon*—the phantom, the specter—with its connection to *eidolatria*—idolatry, the idolization/idealization inher-ent in the fetish—the ghostly, unsubstantial vestige of a vexing reality. But she has also connected *ideology* to the *form,* the *idea* of that which is seen, the *eidos,* thus underscoring ideology's connection to the visible, the *ap-parent,* to faith in what would be seen through a perfect eye, like the eye of the camera obscura. And so Kofman has also brought to light the betrayal of that faith, through her elaboration of Marx's reading of ideology's ap-parent as a phantom or ghost—the mark of the occult, the supernatural, which is the mark of spiritual and religious metaphor, with all of its related phantasmagoric connotations, the spectral, and the "spooky" (*es spukt;* "it spooks," as Jacques Derrida will show). And most significantly, Kofman has analyzed the notion of ideology as it figures the *idée au logis:* the idea im-prisoned in consciousness, a certain domestication shrouding some rather uncomfortable family secrets and again invoking the critical connection to the fetish, and to unconscious repression.

So whither the "practical transformation" that makes possible the pro-cess of ideological demystification and deconstructs the opposition be-tween theory and practice, between material and immaterial? Kofman has left us at (Marx's?) impasse. For the Derrida of *Specters,* the clue may reside precisely in that element of the "concept" of ideology "that attaches it to the Greek *eidos* and to the gaze" (Kofman 1973, 20).

THE SPECTER OF KOFMAN
IN DERRIDA'S SPECTROLOGY

Specters of Marx is, very generally speaking, a critique of *The End of History and the Last Man*, by Frances Fukuyama, and of the notion of a New World Order inaugurated after 1989. Fukuyama's book, and the discourse of the New World Order, both announce the triumph of Western liberal democracy over the dark forces of socialism and communism and thus declare the victory of a certain ideology over all pretenders. We are now at the end of history, with the one true ideology instantiating itself rapidly around the globe. The chapter "Apparition of the Inapparent" from *Specters* offers a meditation on Marx's conception of ideology, with the outline of an avenue of resistance to what Derrida claims to be the self-proclamation of victory on the part of the ideology of Western liberal democracy.

Sarah Kofman's name appears, once, in a footnote, in *Specters of Marx* (Derrida 1994, 194 n. 33).[14] One is tempted to think, with regard to this, of Marcelle Marini's observation in another interview from *Shifting Scenes:*

> Similarly, regarding quotation, I think that there are other obstacles for women: at least in France, women are quoted infrequently. Perhaps in general we function less according to quotation here than in the United States, but women are certainly quoted much less frequently. . . .
>
> There is a kind of forgetting, an effacing of women, even by women (although more generally by men). (Jardine and Menke 1991, 154–155)

And here, if nothing else, the question of *forgetting* seems to press. Kofman's own acknowledgment of Derrida in *Camera obscura* is deferential, but not entirely clear. Again, he is thanked, "notably, for having suggested that for Marx, religion is the form of all ideology" (Kofman 1973, 76). A critical suggestion, and one that animates much of Kofman's analysis of Marx. And this notion is certainly critical to Derrida's own analysis of ideology in the chapter "Apparition of the Inapparent." One wonders about the dynamics of Derrida's seminar, which took place two decades prior to *Specters.* I am in no position to assign credit for the ideas in either book, nor am I particularly interested in doing so, for the methodology apparent in both analyses very much bears the original mark of each thinker. But at the very least, the affinities between the accounts (and there are, of course, many differences) suggest a common point of view, perhaps a common *sensitivity*, brought to these accounts of Marx on ideology. I would suggest that Derrida picks up on, and expands upon, Kofman's reading, a reading that had used Derrida's clue to pick up on, and expand upon, the reading of ideology given by Marx in *GI* and *Capital.* I want to argue for the usefulness of reading "Apparition of the Inapparent" in and through the analysis laid out in *Camera obscura.*

And so I am not entirely satisfied with Fredric Jameson's assessment of the reason for Derrida's insistence upon the connection between religious and ideological metaphor in Marx. Jameson notes Derrida's linkage and attributes it to his interest in a "postmodern aesthetic religion" that helps to illuminate "the specificity of our own time" (Jameson 1995, 98–99).[15] What, precisely, Jameson means by "postmodern aesthetic religion" is never clearly articulated; from the few clues he gives it would appear that his reading ignores the link between Derrida's analysis of ideology and Kofman's work in *Camera obscura,* and thus also the dynamics of Derrida's seminar at the École Normale Supérieure over twenty years ago.

Once again, it is to the element of the concept of ideology "that attaches it to the Greek *eidos* and to the gaze" that Derrida will turn to in his analysis of ideology, picking up on the theme announced by Kofman. The *eidos* is the form, figure, shape, or that which is seen, and it figures the *eidolon,* which is the phantasmal, ghostly, unsubstantial specter of the seeable: "The 'phantasma,' which the *Phaedo* (81d) or the *Timaeus* (71a) do not separate from the *eidola,* are figures of dead souls, they are the souls of the dead: when they are not hanging around funeral monuments and sepulchers (*Phaedo*), they are haunting the souls of certain living persons" (Derrida 1994, 147). The *eidolon* is the specter of all we hoped would be clear, concrete, and immediately *apparent;* it is the ghost of the *eidos.* But for Marx, and for Kofman and Derrida reading Marx, spectrality, unsubstantiality, obscurity reign, just as much as in Nietzsche's Apollinian dream world, in which dreams alone—the unsubstantial, the unconscious—are grasped immediately. If ideology is "a fantasy of a fantasy," then it is a ghostly reflection of the ghost of that which is seen, of that which is apparent and would think itself real.

Ideology is a Borgesian/Baudrillardean simulacrum. It is all about specters, which here would be specters of specters, ghosts of ghosts, fantasies of fantasies. According to Derrida, Marx is afraid of ghosts and wants to banish them from sight, wants to exorcise their very real, very substantial, very material effects. *GI* and the chapter on the commodity from *Capital* are clear indications that vis à vis ideology, Marx wants to hunt down these specters and eradicate them, just as much as the holy alliance of European powers was seeking to exorcise the specter of communism, which in 1847 was haunting Europe with more than a weak messianic power. Derrida gives a long tour de force reading of the chapter on the commodity from *Capital,* paying very close attention, of course, to the metaphor of the *table tournante.* The passage returns to, and multiplies several times over, Kofman's themes of the play of the occult metaphor and its relationship to the notion of the fetish. However, whereas Kofman had concentrated on the short passage following the deployment of the camera obscura metaphor in her discussion of *GI,* Derrida is concerned with Marx's virulent criticism of Stirner.

It is the mark of all specters that they are "sensuous nonsensuous" (Derrida 1994, 151, 192 n. 19), that they appear to be substantial, but (in fact?) are not. Stirner tries to exorcise the specters of ideology by incorporating ideology's ideals into the body of each individual member of society. Those who take the ideals of society as their own and incorporate them into themselves have made the specter live in a material body and banished the specter of the ideal: its sensuous nonsensuousness. By claiming ideology as their own ("These are *my* ideals, the ideals of my society; I make them live in my activity as a sovereign individual"), their sheer ideality is erased. But for Marx, this is not enough. The specters of ideology have already been given a body, a "given, or rather lent, borrowed body[,] . . . a technical body or an institutional body" (Derrida 1994, 127). Here, a whiff of Althusser, and of Foucault.[16]

These institutional, technical bodies, these prosthetic bodies, would, here and now, correspond to all of the shimmering apparatuses that modern Western, liberal democratic society has promulgated for itself—from district gerrymandering to (the now maligned) affirmative action, to unemployment insurance and job retraining, to Derrida's personal vendetta: the entire system of Western jurisprudence (complete with its prisons)— to make its ideals a reality, the reality that contemporary ideologues have presented to us as a fait accompli: Western, liberal democracy standing over and above the slag heap of failed "Marxist" regimes, as the glimmering paradise the soothsayers always said it would be and had been. The New World Order has made good upon, actualized, given a "lent, borrowed body" to the promise of its ideology.

So, as Derrida notes well: "Marx is very firm: when one has destroyed a phantomatic body, the real body remains" (Derrida 1994, 131). Here the real body is the specter of ideology; the "phantomatic" ideals that are supposedly *incorporated* into the institutions of Western society, institutions that give the ideals life, causing them to guarantee that the sunny idealism of Western democracy will seal the fate of society, now at the end of its history: a fate that is nothing less than the actualization of freedom for all, now and forever, amen, according to one particular ideologue—a certain Fukuyama. Thus, one cannot banish the specters, erase the sheer ideality of ideology, precisely because ideology *is* a specter; it is sensuous nonsensuous; it has something like a body, a body that Althusser might call "state apparatuses," or that Foucault might call "disciplines."

This is clearly a rereading, and a reanimation, of the point that Kofman punctuated in *Camera obscura*. Critique alone cannot banish the phantasmagoria of ideological formations, since this phantasmagoria *lives* in the virtual bodies that act upon the body of society, in ideological apparatuses: "For Freud, fetishism implied both the recognition and the denial of reality, and the construction of a substitute for it: the fetish" (Kofman 1973, 31). Kofman's fetish is the lent, borrowed body of something like Foucault's disciplines, which can distort the ideals of bourgeois ideology from the very moment they are put into material practice (cf. note 16). And so "practical transformation" is what is needed. If theoretical critique is immanent—if it argues that apparatuses, in practice, contradict their own ideals—then the critique itself calls for nothing, necessarily, more than an alteration of those apparatuses, which has thus far always only been a perpetual fine-tuning that constantly defers the process of radical transformation, buying time for the powerful to alter and exploit any new configuration that was supposed to lead to the actualization of society's ideals. If theoretical critique is transcendental—attacking the ideals themselves—then it is vacuous unless it offers an alternative to the status quo, which could only be either a utopian telos or a real process of somehow tearing down the apparatuses and institutions that have been delegitimated and creating something new. Again, in either case, stress must be placed on the practical movement of dismantling delegitimated institutions and reconstructing a revitalized social body.

Not only does the cagey Marx show how Stirner's attempt to banish ideology's specters has left the institutions of an exploitative society intact; he also shows how Stirner's attempt to incorporate ideology into the living body of the individual—in the thickness, solidity, and clarity of its ipseity—merely incorporates one specter within the body of another. Stirner tries to incorporate the ideals of liberal democracy into the body of another ideal of liberal democracy: the clear-headed, bright-eyed, Enlightenment cogito—the legendary transcendental "I" (Derrida 1994, 136–139). But in Derrida's view, and this is his reproach, Marx's fear of ghosts speaks of his nostalgia for just such a body—a living, breathing incarnation of the sovereign ego that would *really* exorcise these ghosts. It is a nostalgia for the Enlightenment subject—indeed, for the subject of Western liberal democracy. But such a subject is, phantomatically, forged in the fires of capital precisely by the bad ghosts of ideology, appearing on the stage first as tragedy and second, in Marx's dreams, as farce.

Again, as Kofman suggested, Marx maintains a troubling nostalgia for clarity and light, though he sees these, truly, as a dream. He believes that he can oppose the bad ghosts in the name of the good ones—the ones in (all of our?) dreams. He wants "to denounce, chase away, or exorcise the specters but by means of critical analysis and not by some countermagic. But how to distinguish between the analysis that denounces magic and the countermagic that it still risks being?" (Derrida 1994, 47). As Jameson indicates, reading Derrida reading Marx, "[Marx] wants to get rid of ghosts[;] he not only thinks he can do so, but that it is also desirable to do so. But a world cleansed of spectrality is precisely ontology itself, a world of pure presence, of immediate density, of things without a past: for Derrida, an impossible and noxious nostalgia, and the fundamental target of his whole life's work" (Jameson 1995, 103).

If Derrida wants to lay to rest Marx's bad ghosts, where is the *real* exorcism, the *true* denouncement, the "practical transformation" of society? In a sense, this has always been a false question. It has always carried with it the air of a plea for ontology, of a utopian schema, carefully and scrupulously laid out, all the pieces clearly identified and put into place. Such utopian idealism is precisely what Marx's scientific turn was supposed to eradicate forever in a storm of anti-idealist polemic. One wonders if Kofman and Derrida have both underestimated the cunning of the incendiary, "scientific" Marx, who had what is now referred to as a reality check for the fatuous ideologues who lauded the freedoms of liberal democracy while women in London bathed their children in open sewers. Today, there are many more dreamers whose spectral ideals legitimate a social body fully traversed by relations of power and domination. Their prosthetic apparatuses, their *disciplines,* are their fetish. As long as such ghosts retain their power, there is much to be afraid of, and so the fervor of the ghost hunter may find its source in the horrors of the *present,* and not in a nostalgia for *presence.*

Be that as it may, Derrida himself does indeed retain the hope of a practical transformation (and by now, the implicit dichotomy of base/superstructure should be sufficiently imploded, with the faithful among us maintaining, with Althusser, the determinism of economics "in the last instance"). The hope is borne by the sensuous nonsensuousness of two specters: a new International and what gives this International its strength—a persistent, Benjaminian *weak messianism.*

Derrida's call for a new International sounds as if it would be the call for a countertendency geared directly toward what Marx would refer to as "practical transformation," as if it is intended to get something done, to intervene, within the social body. It is an International that itself has banished the specters of an ontologized Marx, tied to fictions of the fully present, such as class, party, dictatorship of the proletariat, and, one would assume, the "I"—the full Enlightenment ego:[17]

The name of the new International is given here to what calls to the friendship of an alliance without institution among those who . . . continue to be inspired by at least one of the spirits of Marx[,] . . . even if this alliance no longer takes the form of a party or of a workers' international, but rather of a kind of counterconjuration, in the (theoretical and practical) critique of the state of international law, the concepts of State and nation, and so forth: in order to renew this critique and especially to radicalize it. (Derrida 1994, 85–86)[18]

However vague, obscure, *spectral* is Derrida's description of the workings of this new International, it is at least clear that, as he conceives of it, he himself has been working on it for the past decade, most notably for English readers in *The Other Heading* and "Force of Law." Perhaps this is merely confirmation that Derrida's long-awaited intervention into the political has indeed been taking place, spearheaded, it would seem, by his rereadings of Benjamin and Levinas. Much work is left to be done, not least by Derrida himself, to flesh out how, precisely, these clearly fascinating pieces of writing are intended to intervene, or perhaps are intervening, within what I will still, naively, call the practical arena.

Derrida's second hope is linked to a kind of question that appears at the very beginning of *Specters,* in Derrida's exordium: "Someone, you or [I], comes forward and says: *I would like to learn to live finally.*" He then clarifies: "Will we ever know how to live and first of all what 'to learn to live' means? And why 'finally'?" (Derrida 1994, xvii). The passage is evocative of many of the central themes of the book: how to learn to be vital, to live in the face of death—the death announced, for example, by Fukuyama's new end of history—hence how to live *finally.* How to make the (good) ghosts live, the ghost, for example, of Marx, who, par excellence, has shown us what it means to be vital. How, then, to revitalize the social body, to initiate the practical transformation that we all, friends of the good ghost, hope for. But how to do so in a way not tied to the repressive (in Derrida's view) ontologies of the subject that are soiled with all the filth of Western liberal democracy, with its ideology standing above and sanitizing the prostrate, decaying bodies of so many. Hence, how to escape the ghost of death that, supposedly, Marx himself could not escape, how to live, finally, without recourse to the nostalgia of clarity and of the "I," the untrammeled subject, free in its unity and coherence. And so how to shatter the dream world that leaves us hanging in the indifference of ignorance, on the back of a tiger that is our vital selves.

How to live, finally? For Derrida, it would seem that the most plausible response to this question is linked to Benjamin's revitalization of the anti-utopian, anti-idealist spirit of Marx, his announcement of a weak messianic power through which future generations will redeem the past—will redeem, for one, the catastrophic past that was Benjamin's present at the moment he took his life. The power is *weak* in that it advances from an unfigured future, and its promise seems threatened by the dark days of Europe, circa 1940, and by our own New World Order. Nonetheless, it is a *persistent* messianism that survived all through the ashes of the Holocaust, and that survives today because "never in history has the horizon of the thing whose survival is being celebrated (namely, all the old models of the capitalist and liberal world) been as dark, threatening, and threatened" (Derrida 1994, 52). Threatened by the specters of Marx. Recall from the final addenda of "Theses on the Philosophy of History":

> We know that the Jews were prohibited from investigating the future. The Torah and the prayers instruct them in remembrance, however. This stripped the future of its magic, to which all those succumb who turn to the soothsayers for enlightenment. This does not imply, however, that for the Jews the future turned into homogeneous, empty time. For every second of time was the strait gate through which the Messiah might enter. (Benjamin 1968, 264)[19]

How to live would then be to mourn the dead, while keeping faith with an absolute future that refuses to be ontologized. The future is the strait gate through which the absolute Other will return, for the first time. In it, all that has been repressed—"difference itself" (Kofman 1973, 31, after Marx)—will live and exorcise the bad ghosts. This is inescapable.

Derrida's new International, which gains its strength from the weak but persistent messianic power of all that has been excluded and that will, ineluctably, return, once again has banished the specters of an ontologized Marx. It keeps faith with Marx's good ghost:

> We would distinguish this spirit from the other spirits of Marxism, those that rivet it to the body of Marxist doctrine, to its supposed systemic, metaphysical, or ontological totality, . . . to its fundamental concepts of labor, mode of production, social class, and consequently to the *whole history* of its apparatuses (projected or real: the Internationals of the labor movement, the dictatorship of the proletariat, the single party, the State, and finally the totalitarian monstrosity). For, let us speak as "good Marxists," the deconstruction of Marxist ontology does not go after only a theoretico-speculative layer of the Marxist corpus but *everything* that articulates this corpus with the most concrete history of the apparatuses and strategies of the worldwide labor movement. (Derrida 1994, 88–89, emphasis added)

To echo Aijaz Ahmad, such glad tidings "leave me speechless." Indeed, and again: who is afraid of ghosts here? Derrida is "bound to" the specter of an ontologized Marx "in a troubling way" (cf. note 18). He wants to root it out, hunt it down, and eradicate it and everything that has issued from it. Derrida is bound to the vision of a good ghost pitted against a bad one. The bad ghost is the specter of the ontologized Marx of the class struggle, the Internationals of the labor movement, of histomat and of diamat (more properly Engel's ghost), and so on. Against this is the good ghost, to whom Derrida wishes to ally himself and with whom deconstruction in general supposedly keeps faith. This good ghost has at least two aspects. First, it is the specter of the radical critic (Derrida 1994, 88). With regard to the discourse of radical, Marxian critique of ideology and culture, a certain Negative Dialectics has arguably always already surpassed what Derrida has to offer us, here in *Specters,* at least, though it is also certainly true that Adorno is dead, dead as a doornail, and Habermas sits on his throne, inaugurating a program of reconciliation.

The second face of the good ghost is, again, a Benjaminian weak messianism, compelling enough if it stands for an openness to the absolute Other, to the return of difference, but for these very reasons structurally indiscernible. Of its *substance* we cannot speak; we must pass on in silence. Well and good, truly, but . . . This ontology—if he prefers, this *hauntology*—that Derrida binds himself to, out of fear of the ghost of an ontologized Marx, out of fear of both good and bad ghosts, still lacks, for one, a theorization of what I will—entirely problematically, hopelessly naively—refer to as the ongoing work of "practical struggle" occurring everywhere, all of the time. This accusation, if that is the correct word for it, calls for a detailed account of what, precisely, the new International is intended *to do.* This, one may notice, is in large part the question of how to combat a certain all-powerful ideology, wherein the entire edifice of Western jurisprudence represents the most distant goal thus far achieved on the straight path to an absolutely free egalitarian society, which is supposedly just within our grasp.

Or perhaps we could see an engagement on Derrida's part with the largely deontologized, largely self-deconstructed Marxism of the now quarter-century-old Autonomist movement, centered around the work of Tony Negri, Sergio Bologna, and others. Autonomism theorizes the "revolution" as the ongoing project of the refusal of the imposition of work, and of the subsequent process of (indeterminate, open-ended) self-valorization. The Autonomist movement is largely contemporaneous with what is called poststructuralism and seems to share much common ground with it. It is perhaps more closely related to poststructuralism than even the Negative Dialectics of Adorno, which of course is often noted as bearing more than a family resemblance to deconstruction.

Michael Ryan has noted these affinities in his *Marxism and Deconstruction* (Ryan 1982, 73–80).

Or perhaps we could see simply a new reading, a rereading, a re-rereading, of the cunning of Marx—a cunning that appears to have been underestimated by both Kofman and Derrida. A reengagement with Marx the polemicist, ontological and economic categories intact as part of the polemical arsenal. A reengagement with the Marx who risks all—including being guilty of the charges against him that he is afraid of ghosts and that he maintains a nostalgia for clarity—in order to further his political project of advancing workers' struggle. Would Derrida ever risk a deconstruction of the political stakes of using class analysis, of using the labor theory of value—the notions of surplus value and unpaid labor—and so on? Would he risk an analysis of the stakes of strategically invoking the idea of a working class struggling against the imposition of work, a strategic intervention that might constitute an attempt to support the struggle of individuals seeking to escape their own ontologization and to develop their own possibilities? What, precisely, is so very spooky about such categories and such a strategy? (cf. Jameson 1995, 94–95).

While I can only applaud Derrida's ongoing, passionate, and elegant calls for, as one example, a notion of justice as an absolute responsibility (here and now) to the absolute Other, there appears to me to be a great deal missing from his analysis in *Specters*. Derrida's work in picking up and expanding upon the play of Marx's spectral metaphor, the work that Kofman lays the groundwork for, is clearly provocative and fascinating. Nonetheless, Derrida seems to foreclose upon numerous possibilities for opening himself up to what Kofman crucially recognizes to be the heterogeneity of Marx's texts. Kofman herself chooses not to develop these possibilities. Her interest in Marx is limited to his position as a precursor to Nietzsche and Freud in the historical movement away from Enlightenment faith in the possibility of the eye without a point of view—the eye of God—and toward suspicion of any claim to a universal perspective. Marx stands at the threshold of the movement that sees perspectivism as primary and the claim to a God's-eye point of view as a signal of phantasmagorical, fetishistic obscurity.

But Derrida's project in *Specters* is much more ambitious than this. While he has admirably shown how Marx's revitalized specter can offer us the tools for dismantling the ideology of the New World Order, because of the ambition of *Specters* the absences within the text are more acutely felt. The greatest absence issues from Derrida's refusal to open up to the heterogeneity of Marx's ontology—a heterogeneity, again, that Kofman recognizes but does not develop at any length. There is an absence, then, of any attempt to work with, and rework, and unwork Marx's classical categories—to reevaluate them and uncover new possibilities within them. Instead, Derrida chooses to exorcise these supposed bad ghosts of Marx. Perhaps, then, it is left to others to carry on the work of opening up Marx's heterogeneity, the work that Kofman announces and that we friends of a certain substantial spirit of Marx must collectively advance:

> The *German Ideology*, like *Capital*, reinscribes a system of traditional oppositions, mythical and ideological; yet these same texts open up displacements in such a way as to make it possible to depart from them, in order to embark on the work of deconstructing the system of oppositions they remain dependent upon. (Kofman 1973, 34–35)

How a Woman Philosophizes

FRANÇOISE DUROUX

There are professors, and there are inventors. The majority of those who make a career of philosophy are professors. Their professional activity consists of commenting upon "the great philosophers," that is, the inventors.

Inventors are rare. There are not many innovative philosophies, and it should be recognized that in the pantheon of philosophers, there are few if any women. To invent a philosophy supposes and requires a project, a systematic "ambition," to which, said Simone de Beauvoir, women are little disposed. For "ambitare," according to Otto Weininger, is the product of a disposition reserved for conquerors and prostitutes. It is interesting to re-mark that this ambition can be proclaimed without the fulfillment of its conditions: it does not suffice, for example, to call oneself a "new philoso-pher" to be an inventor. Men, however, have had this pretension.

On the other hand, there have been women who have philosophized without claiming to construct a "system" and who have, however, inno-vated. Sarah Kofman, like Hannah Arendt, is among these.

Translation by Lisa Walsh. From Françoise Duroux, "Comment philosophe une femme," *Les Cahiers du grif* (new series): 3, 1997, 87–105.

WHAT CONSTITUTES THIS INNOVATION?

Innovation does not enter into the rules of the game; it constructs another system, a countersystem in the polemic between the greats. There exists, to my knowledge, one exception: Luce Irigaray wrestles with the texts of the greats (*Speculum de l'autre femme*) in order to attempt a countersystem (*Ethique de la différence sexuelle*).

Neither does innovation respect the rules of the "professors," those who make the history of philosophy in the form of courses and respectable, "appropriate" theses. Whoever "does philosophy" begins by reading, reading the greats. From there, several paths are open. The first path is to take up the challenge and construct an *other* system. The second is to enter into the systems and comment upon them: this is the serious history of philosophy.

The third path is to judge that the second position is insufficient and the first impossible, and thus to flee: this is the position taken by Simone de Beauvoir when she abandons the charge to Sartre and privileges him to "make a philosophy," declaring that literature is better suited to her feminine disposition. She, who received second place in the philosophy *agrégation* just behind Sartre and of whom de Gandillac had said, "She *is* philosophy," gives up. "It is toward literature that I should orient myself," she says, because "my ease in entering into a text comes precisely from my lack of creativity." She feels incapable of taking "this concerted delirium that makes up a system" to term. But it is also because she cannot manage to be a "disciple" that she finds refuge for her "intellectual ambition" in the realm of literature (Beauvoir 1962).

Sarah Kofman takes a fourth path, one that disturbs the well-established equilibrium between the scholarly exercise of reading (certainly authorized to bluestockings) and the audacity of the creator (forbidden to them). She reads; she does not claim to construct a system that is anti-Hegelian, anti-Marxist, and so on. Therefore she is going to read, but otherwise: this is what disrupts and makes her a bit disagreeable to the philosophical community.

When she approaches a "great" text, a great author, it is not to make an intelligent, conscientious, respectful exegesis of the type with which we are familiar through the works of Guéroult, Hippolyte, and many others. Neither is it to analyze the tournaments of champions: "Leibniz criticizes Descartes." Rather, it is to seek behind them, at the depths of the thinking of a system, the *motivating forces* of their construction: the *economy* of a concept, the *motives* of a system, the *interest* of the speculation. The Freudian vocabulary will be recognized—oh how inconvenient to the affirmative gaze of free and disinterested thought.

This method leads to an unusual, if not inconvenient, approach: a rooting about in the lives of theoreticians, which not only manifests a suspicious disrespect but above all contradicts certain conventions of evidence, those of philosophy's status. It suffices, in effect, to consider that a philosophical concept depends above all on its *disconnection*, on the fact that the concept and the system are uniform, pure, exempt from all contingency, in other words, that the concept moves in a transparent universe, outside vulgar realities. The Philosopher would be miraculously exempted from temptations of power, sex, money, fashion, and so on. (The example of our contemporaries is enough to debunk this myth.) Sarah Kofman thus commits an act, if not an offense, of "crime against philosophy" when she passionately seizes theories to restore them to their conditions of production, not only the historical and social ones, which would be acceptable in their "objectivity," but also the subjective ones. That a great philosopher might be a man like others, to whom things happen, who has feelings, loves, hates, and that his thoughts might be thereby "affected," this is what interferes with the principle of disconnection.

It is through this subtly internal treatment of the genesis of theories that Sarah Kofman maintains a new, disturbing, inconvenient position. For her, it is not a question of crudely linking system and biography, gossip and theory, but a search for how an articulated thought is intertwined with a subjective structure and history. It is men and women who make history, and it is men and women who make philosophy: not pure minds.

How does Sarah Kofman proceed in returning the thoughts to their author? I must note in passing that it is mostly women who have a tendency to give themselves over to this sort of analysis. It would be appropriate to ask why: an aptitude for disrespect? A de facto marginality in relation to the consensus of a factually masculine community? In any case, like Sarah Kofman (no doubt undeliberately like her), Monique David-Ménard presented us with an unanticipated Kant, his madness in pure reason, far from the debates that stimulate the post-Kantians (David-Ménard 1993). For my part, through a similar approach, I read Spinoza in his own passions.

I did not then know the *Aberrations,* the Auguste Comte of Sarah Kofman, and it is only after the fact that I gauged the proximity of our approaches. The spirit of the times? A familiarity with psychoanalysis? Or yet, not a "feminine" position, but one of women who philosophize from within woman's situation rather than through its abandonment. The result was an unplanned convergence on a rather important point: the tracking, within a conceptual elaboration, of the presence of he—or rarely she—who has the ambition to think, the connections (as opposed to the principle of dis-connection) between the conceptualization that is produced and its con-texts. Sarah Kofman uncompromisingly intertwines the threads of deter-minations, conceptual or otherwise, that produce a philosophical text.

Philosophers, generally and as a matter of principle, do not treat sexual difference. Generally, this is demonstrated by the record. As a matter of principle, it refers back to the philosophical "position" of disconnection, which supposes that the thinker—because he is a man—produces pure thought, freed from passions and earthly attachments. To be clear, he shits in all innocence. As a result, in the monuments of theoretical thought, there is little mention of women: as a matter of principle sexual difference does not constitute a theoretical object because it would risk jamming the direct line of communication with Being, the Pope, and the Others.

There is little mention of women, but this is not out of the question in that sexual difference does make a reappearance from time to time, as ex-ample, appendix, accident, supplement, exception. The system digests it. It is even constructed to make sexual difference disappear, but it reap-pears, as a rift, a rift in reason that religion has effectively closed, but that philosophy has difficulty reading. And it is fascinating to observe how "thinkers," each in his own way, negotiate this treatment.

It goes without saying that the "readings" done by the official historians of philosophy have complete latitude in validating the burial of the ques-tion: a system has its bases and one simply cannot speak of sexual difference or what the system might imply or presuppose about it. Plato's *Republic* can be read without taking into account the difficulties to be encountered upon the transition from the equal education of men and women to the necessary division of duties and spaces. Kant can be read with no regard for the several paragraphs in the *Metaphysical Foundations of Morals* where he treats sexuality and marriage. These texts can even be integrated with the licentious levity that affected one of my professors at the Sorbonne: a pro-cess of nullification. Spinoza can be read, as Matheron does, as reducing jealousy to rivalry for the king's love, no joke. Rousseau's *Social Contract* can be read without mentioning *Emile, The New Heloise*, or the *Confessions*. One is thereby at ease. The system has digested a question that remains, how-ever, at its heart.

The reconstitution from sparse fragments of the underground logic of the operations determined by this question, where sometimes what should be silenced is expressed, such has been the work of Sarah Kofman on sev-eral decisive and treacherous texts. I experienced this sort of work by hav-ing performed it on Spinoza: pieces of the *Ethics,* aporias from the *Political Treatise* that the *more geometrico* is called to repudiate. Kofman had already done this sort of work, on Comte, Kant, and Rousseau. (Nietzsche remains a case apart.) The work consists in reintroducing sexuality, and thereby the question of sexual difference, in what she calls the "economy" of a thought that claims to be "pure."

What are the gains and strategies used to obtain this result: purity? And how does the treatment of sexual difference constitute the almost invisible operator of a conceptual mechanism? What are the implications of this analysis of philosophical ideas in terms of "economy," "gains," "interest of speculation"—metaphors that are dear to Freud, but costly to the fantasies of theoreticians: libidinal economy, gains of neurosis, cost of repression, and so on.

In Kofman's readings of Comte, Kant, and Rousseau, one question is insistent: the search for woman, or rather, the search for the mother. Kant's categorical imperative (gluttonous superego), Rousseau's "Maman," and Comte's Virgin-wife are interpreted as so many figures whose incorporation into the system permits a triumph over irrationality ("avoir raison de la déraison"). The gain of illness is the production of the system, but the system serves as a defense against insanity.

One might, then, hypothetically come full circle: *Rue Ordener, Rue Labat.* Sarah between two mothers: the question that had penetrated her life and that she had kept at a distance by transferring it, through a "philosophical operation," onto an analysis of the figures of several great thinkers, by putting their thought to the question in order to find out what she attributed to life, how she allowed for the possibility of living, if not healing—how, reciprocally, the gain of illness is included in theoretical production.

The autobiographical plunge, practiced in vivo, undoubtedly induces an earthquake. Philosophy protects. The plunge causes the philosophical position to explode: Sarah Kofman's suicidal plunge into her own melancholy, which she had located so well in Comte. After she had written and published this book, she complained of no longer being able to write. Until then, she remained alongside the madness of men who think, and her own. The objects: Kant, Rousseau, Comte; the instrument: Freud. And then identification: Nietzsche.

From Comte's *Aberrations* to Nietzsche's *Explosions,* the same search, led with constancy, persists. It is on Comte (Kofman 1978a) that she tests her method and sharpens the instruments borrowed from Freud *cum grano salis* (with a grain of salt). The Nietzsche "case" differs, because Nietzsche and his fate constitute an Ariadne's thread, the example to follow in order to philosophize and scratch out autobiography ("autobiogriffer"); what she is looking for in the philosophers, the point of madness, is not, in his case, deciphered between the lines but erupts in shattering declarations.

We can do better than to make the hypothesis that Kofman consistently writes her autobiography under the auspices of philosophy. She does not keep a "journal." She does not say "I," as Simone de Beauvoir becomes so meticulously attached to doing. Nietzsche, Kofman says, "feels no affinity with these buffoons whose low and vulgar souls alone prize so-called sincerity." But in the "philosophies" of philosophers, she is going to search for the echo, the resonance, of her question. It is a long, patient, passionate work of masonry in which, questioning the breaking points of Comte, Kant, Rousseau, and finally Nietzsche, she says much more about herself than any anecdotal, introspective, expurgated, reviewed, and corrected autobiography could. In Nietzsche she finds the subversion of the genre of autobiography: "What every great philosophy has been to this day: the confession of its author, a sort of involuntary memoir which wasn't taken as such."

Autobiography is written after the fact to put the pieces back together, to trace the trajectory of someone, Nietzsche, for example, who has always *been* through metamorphoses and, above all, from a double origin. Just as Sarah has two mothers, Nietzsche has two languages, two countries. Thus he cannot write an appropriate autobiography, an account of childhood with an ascribable mother and father. He even invents a fantasized genealogy. *Ecce Homo* breaks with the appropriate and conventional tone of autobiography. Whereby Sarah Kofman authorizes herself to be inappropriate and to put popular psychology in its place to better restore philosophy to the nonanecdotal biography of its author. Because if a philosophy can be cut off from anecdote, it is less legitimate to disconnect it from the imaginary, fantasized biography of the same author and from the symbolic position that follows: a major inconvenience from which, Kofman notes, Heidegger wards her off. In effect, for him it is a question of preserving Nietzsche from madness by ceasing to "leer in the direction of the man" in order to return him to the history of thought, "blind," she says, "to that madness that threatens all thinkers, all thought, all subjects." To save (Nietzsche's) thought to the detriment of life—this is the metaphysical operation.[1]

But life is not synonymous with Confession, and from *Ecce Homo*, Kofman arrives at a conception of autobiography not as "sincere avowal" (an exhibition incompatible with the "modesty of a god"),[2] but rather as affirmation: "a selective account capable of making assessments and taking count through the succession and the intertwining of masks and doubles: an account capable of standing up to and against the deafness of contemporaries, to and against the isolation that produces madness, the very existence of he who 'writes such good books.'"

Contrary to Rousseau, Kant, and Comte, Nietzsche appears as a figure of identification in whom the point of madness is not a symptom of denial but, on the contrary, a site of articulation between life and philosophy. Madness, then, becomes a mask among others, or the ultimate mask, a figure of the solitude of a thought that only tolerates the heights of the Engadine, heights that the century's ordinary cultivated men are unable to tolerate. Like Nietzsche, Sarah is sensitive to the climate. Like Nietzsche, illness makes her a shrewd and cunning psychologist who does not hesitate to rummage about in the corners—ill in good health, because for the philosopher, illness is an object of scientific curiosity.[3] But this reciprocally implies that the philosopher necessarily has the philosophy of his or her person, that is, of his or her body.

PART III

WOMEN, FEMINISM, AND PSYCHOANALYSIS

CHAPTER EIGHT

Rending Kant's Umbrella:
Kofman's Diagnosis of Ethical Law

NATALIE ALEXANDER

A renewed interest in the history of philosophy, in particular that of the early modern period, has recently emerged among philosophers, especially among Continental, postmodern, and feminist thinkers. Characteristic of the postmodern mood and methods within which she works, Sarah Kofman offers readings of canonical figures that upset traditional interpretations, overturn hierarchies, and set out to transform one's thinking. It is already past time to look carefully at those of Kofman's works that treat of the history of philosophy, because in addition to her better-known works on the thinkers who most influenced her—Nietzsche, Freud, and Derrida—Kofman has written about several philosophies from ancient and early-modern periods (Kofman 1978a, 1990b, 1982b). This chapter focuses on her reading of Kant's ethical imperative of respect for human dignity.

Kofman undeservedly remains a little-known figure in the United States. While the works of other French women theorists have been translated and extensively discussed, Kofman's work, though of recognized merit, has

I gratefully acknowledge the assistance I have received on this project from my writers' group—David Christiansen, Janet Davis, Martha Edwards, Rebecca Harrison, and Bill Hutton—as well as from my student assistants—Kelly Barbour, Mark Dodds, Karl Kopitske, and Robyn Reed—and the unflagging support and encouragement I have received from the editors of this volume. Any infelicities in this essay are, of course, my own.

received less attention. That her work has not yet become well known among both Continental and feminist philosophers in the United States has hampered our understanding of the traditions within which she works and has denied us insights into the historical questions she poses.[1]

In *Le respect des femmes (Kant et Rousseau)*, Kofman argues that "respect" for women plays a crucial role in constituting the moral philosophies of both Kant and Rousseau (1982b, 13–20).[2] She also argues that despite the obvious contrasts between their ethics, the same sexual economy, an economy of domination, is at play in both at the root of their moral theories. In this chapter, I explore Kofman's interpretation of Kant by which she identifies and describes the sexual economy that inaugurates Kant's ethics. Kofman traces the gender issues lurking in the origins of Kant's ethical theory, carefully drawing out the relations between his a posteriori writings concerning respect for women and his great a priori principle of ethics that mandates a rational respect for all rational agents. In order to develop a strong reading of Kofman's text, I successively develop three approaches to her deconstructive interpretation: I begin with an aesthetic/rhetorical approach, then deepen my reading by drawing out a skeptical approach, and finally, through a therapeutic approach, enrich my reading of Kofman's genealogical diagnosis of Kantian ethics.

RESPECT IS AN UMBRELLA

At first glance, Kant's and Rousseau's treatment of women could not be more different. Kant had few dealings with women in his life; in his philosophy, he claims that respect for women is simply one example among others of the universal motive of respect for all rational agents. In contrast, Rousseau's relations with women were obsessive, even pathological, yet in his works, he accords a special moral place for holding women in respect.

Kofman announces that she will argue that both philosophers operate within a sexual economy in which respect operates as the inverse of an attitude of debasement (1982b, 15). Of Kant in particular she writes:

> As we will show, respect for women, far from being for [Kant] one example among others, is a necessary condition for the inception of morality, necessary for educating man to respect in general. Thus, it plays a privileged role, if not in the foundations or principles of morality, at least in its history or genealogy. And this privilege, in the last analysis[,] reveals above all a sexual economy. (Kofman 1982b, 17, my translation)

Kofman argues that, although Kant portrays respect for women as an application of the moral law, such respect in fact operates for Kant as its precursor, as the necessary condition for developing morality.

As a preliminary first analysis of Kofman's work in this section, I explore the rhetorical and connotative reverberations of Kofman's language in three related areas.[3] First, I investigate her use of epigrams to develop multiple senses of "respect"; then I discuss her starkest and simplest metaphor, that of the umbrella, revealing how it prefigures the role of respect for women in maintaining Kant's most crucial oppositions. Last, I analyze Kofman's subtle use of suggestive clusters of connotative terms: allusions to masks and veils suffuse the text, mingling with more localized allusions evoking the machinery of war and the activities of sewing fabric.

Kofman opens the introduction to *Respect*, "Tenir les femmes en respect" ("Holding Women in Respect"), with a lexical passage defining respect:

- Consideration, motive, regard, relation, communication.
- The deference that one has for someone or something. . . .
- "Excepting your respect[,]" said when one wants to excuse oneself of some shocking remark or of appearing too free.
- To assure someone of one's respects . . . [,] formulas of compliments.
- "I am with respect . . . [,]" formula by which one ordinarily ends letters to a superior.
- Without respect, without having regard to.
- Take in respect, in respect, to contain [oneself], to impose.
- Human respect; shameful badness.
- Said of the little stools which people of an inferior birth take to the homes of aristocrats. (Kofman 1982b, 11, my translation)

Among the nine definitions, I discern three loosely grouped and overlapping categories. The first simply denotes an unspecified relation, as in the English "with respect to" or "in regard to." The second, apparently close to the central meaning in Kant's usage, brings out the motive of deference but then emphasizes the respect of an inferior toward a superior. The third group comprises certain formulaic idioms of polite usage, for example, to close a letter, "Je suis avec respect . . ." (as in English, "Respectfully yours"), or to excuse a breach of decent speech, "sauf votre respect"). The latter example has a rather old-fashioned English parallel in the phrase "saving your presence," and the slang "pardon my French" alludes to this usage. Kofman herself makes no explicit references to this epigram; we shall see that she draws multiple relations between the distancing formulas of politeness, the breaching of standards of decency, the motives of deference, and relations of inferior and superior.

The epigram that opens "Kant: The Economy of Respect" also evokes the sense of a breach of decency: "Nec femina, amissa pudicita, alia abnuerit" (A woman, once losing her chastity, can refuse nothing) (Tacitus 1989, 3, my translation; cf. Kofman 1982b, 23).[4] Can it be that the respect due to women depends on their maintaining a proper modesty? What respite does such feminine propriety provide—for whom and with respect to whom?

"Respect" originates from the Latin *respectus, re + spectus*, to look back behind oneself; the term *respite, répit*, found in both French and English, is another derivative of the same Latin term. Kofman develops this etymological play: "Would respect not always permit the realization of a certain economy, the gaining of *respite* (one knows that *respect* and *respite* are both derived from *respicere*)?" (Kofman 1982a, 386; Kofman 1982b, 29).[5] We need respite from that which is overwhelming or distressing or oppressive. In each of its connotations, respect operates as a relation of distancing, of implementing conventions of decency, of providing a respite.

Kofman employs her most stark and simple metaphor—"Le respect est un parapluie" (Respect is an umbrella)—which reverberates in several later clusters of allusions (Kofman 1982b, 16). Let me develop Kofman's metaphor further: the umbrella protects and distances us from wet and unpleasant natural elements; it is made of cloth whose fabric can be torn but must be mended again to be effective; finally, it is a man-made artifact, a simple machine of levers, hinges, and spokes that can be opened and closed—a machine men can control.

Here, I have used "men" in the plural to indicate the gender-specific sense. I have preserved Kant's use of "man" to indicate the so-called generic sense of all humanity. Kofman herself continues to use "man" in this way, specifically in order to highlight the sense of ambiguity that she discovers in Kant's supposed sense of universal humanity. So except for a few occasions where context makes a gender-specific use clear, such as "the individual man or woman," "man" must be read in this chapter as making a double gesture, ostensibly including woman, but only differentially, and evoking the specifically male while denying that it does so.

Evoking both Nietzsche and Rousseau, Kofman reminds us of Freud's dictum (in fact, a joke he is analyzing) that if one's wife is an umbrella, one can still "procure a taxi" ("fiacre," or carriage—that is, a prostitute) (Kofman 1982b, 16, my translation; cf. Freud 1963, 78, 110–111; cf. Nietzsche 1974, 1984). Men seek to hold, keep, capture ("tenir") women in respect. To hold women in respect, thus, has multiple and conflicting connotations: it is done both to safeguard women and to keep them in check. Such kept women must be understood in complex relation to Kant's absolute moral law of respect (Kofman 1982b, 13).

Kofman explores a series of oppositions that shape Kant's discussions of women: for example, those between wife and whore, pursuit and resistance, and reverence and disgust (Kofman 1982a, 386ff.; Kofman 1982b, 29ff.; cf. Kant 1964, 1978). In Kant's use of these oppositions, Kofman discerns a sexual economy, an economy of subordination and domination, that cannot be explained as a mere example of universal respect among rational agents. Furthermore, the oppositions by which Kant distinguishes the precise nature of respect for moral law—nature and rational humanity, dignity and utility, reason and inclination—reiterate the specific economy of subordination and domination (Kofman 1982a, 393–395; Kofman 1982b, 40–44; cf. Kant 1956, 1969). Closing a paragraph of rhetorical questions by which she introduces "The Preliminary Respect or the Premium of Nonseduction," Kofman asks whether beneath the universal law of respect for all rational agents, "would morality not serve as a cover for an operation of a completely different order, an operation of mastery?" (Kofman 1982a, 385; Kofman 1982b, 28–29). Later, I will interpret more closely Kofman's arguments linking respect for women to the sexual economy and moral law; here, I am simply drawing out the connotations of her metaphors and their relation to her conclusions.

Several clusters of figurative language are prefigured in the intriguing metaphor of the umbrella. Throughout this section of *Respect*, Kofman evokes Kant's use of metaphors of masks and veils, linked in various ways to notions of mechanism or artifice. For example, women's respect-worthy decency operates also as a veil, a "disguise (*voile*) of sex and of language" (Kofman 1982a, 390; Kofman 1982b, 36). According to Kant, in the struggle for sexual domination, women's weakness and other feminine traits "are so many levers for controlling men," dominating "by indirect means, by the obliqueness of ruse" (Kofman 1982a, 386; Kofman 1982b, 30; cf. Kant 1978, 181). Kofman argues further that respect serves as a protective machine for men, a defensive weapon against women, an apotrope.[6]

In "Speculations concerning the Origins of Human History," Kant personifies instinct and inclination as a feminine Mother Nature, acting indirectly to inspire humans toward respect, toward the moral law, through "nature's ruse" ("la ruse de la nature") (Kofman 1982b, 38; Kant 1983b, 51).[7] In *Critique of Judgement*, Mother Nature is personified as a veiled goddess, Isis, while, elsewhere, Kant evokes the figure of the veiled goddess to represent the rational moral law itself (Kant 1969, 179; Kant 1993, 71; cf. Kofman 1982a, 390–393, 399ff.; cf. Kofman 1982b, 36–40, 49ff.). By unveiling

Kant's wary use of these aesthetic representations, Kofman traces the presence of the sexual economy that holds women in respect, in the relations between individual men and women; in the relation of human beings, but especially men, to their nature; and in the relation (perhaps again especially of men) to the moral law itself. A thematic unity pervades Kofman's figurative language; masks, machines, veils, and umbrellas suggest the hidden source by which Kant maintains his crucial theoretical distinctions.

By evoking metaphors of a fabric rent and mended, Kofman first indicates that the webwork of oppositions in Kant—between wife and whore, pursuit and resistance, dignity and utility, reason and inclination, nature and rationality—cannot be made in a cleanly cut or pure manner (Kofman 1982a, 386ff.; Kofman 1982b, 29ff.):

> In what manner would men have to try to "repair" ["reparer"] women whom they have always already torn ["dechirées"], sullied ["souillées"], debased ["rabaissées"], in the course of history, those whom they have already transformed into whores? What manner of darning ["repriser"], of sewing up ["recoudre"] the maternal body, of mending ["raccommoder"] women in order to try to patch things up with them ["se raccommoder avec elles," literally patch themselves (m.) up with them (f.)]. (Kofman 1982b, 17, my translation)

Just as "re-spect" is to look back/away in order to see differently, here, in Kofman's material metaphor, the fabric of women's nature—and of men's relation to them—is torn and "re-paired"; "woman" is doubled in order to construct the paired relation to men differently.

TO REND AND MEND THE FABRIC
OF SEXUAL ECONOMY

A skeptical technique of juxtaposing opposites is already at work here, specifically in the form of a deconstructive skepticism that reveals, overturns, and collapses oppositions and hierarchies.[8] As I read this section of Kofman's text, she juxtaposes two contrasting species of respect discussed by Kant: respect for women is supposedly an instance of the universal moral respect owed to all people, not that due to a superior. By elucidating the sexual economy at work in Kant's discussions of respect for women, Kofman overturns Kant's hierarchy; the mere instance of moral respect turns out to be its necessary precondition. Respect for women collapses Kant's distinction between two kinds of respect and hence undermines the foundation of moral law. Let me unfold this structure in greater detail.

Kant distinguishes two kinds of respect, only one of which operates as a principle of morality (Kant 1964, 116–117; cf. Kofman 1982a, 383–384; cf. Kofman 1982b, 26). As I interpret Kant, three key points of contrast distinguish the two kinds of respect. First, in keeping with his strict distinction between inclination and reason, what Kofman has called the comparative form of respect is based on inclination, emotion, and instinct, whereas the moral form of respect is based on reason. Second, the comparative respect, as emotional, may be differentially applied, whereas the moral form, as rational, must be applied universally. Kofman herself does not mention these points, but they directly inform the contrast of "distance" that she does make.

Third, the comparative respect "arises when we compare our value to that of another," whereby the inferior respects the superior, implying "a measurable and appreciable distance" between the value of one human being and another, even to the point of allowing the superior to use the inferior as a means (Kofman 1982a, 384; Kofman 1982b, 26; Kant 1964, 138). In contrast, the moral respect obliges us not "to deprive the other of any value to which his humanity gives him the right," implying, according to Kofman, "not so much the absence of a distance as an incommensurable distance" (Kofman 1982a, 384–385; Kofman 1982b, 26–27; cf. Kant 1964, 137). The comparative respect is emotion-based, contingent, and "grounded in part on arbitrary institutions" that distinguish those worthy of respect from those who are not (Kofman 1982a, 384–385; Kofman 1982b, 27–28; Kant 1964, 137). Clearly, it cannot serve as the rational principle of universal morality.

Respect for women would seem to be a form of this comparative respect, which is due to them, or due to some of them, because of specific differences between women and men, or between the virtues of different women. Yet having set aside these contingent forms of comparative respect, Kant argues that respect for women is simply a special case of the universal moral law requiring that we respect the dignity of all rational autonomous beings. So the comparative form of respect paradoxically reappears, supposedly subsumed under the moral law as an instance of the moral respect owed to all humanity (Kofman 1982a, 384–385; Kofman 1982b, 27–28; cf. Kant 1964, 137–140).

As I read her, Kofman argues two points here. First, she develops her claim that lurking within the respectful moral relation, the case of holding women in respect cloaks "an operation of mastery," a relation of war between the sexes (Kofman 1982a, 385–386; Kofman 1982b, 29–30).

Second, she further concludes that "this 'special case' [is] a model, a very prefiguration of moral respect" that must "come to stain by its empirical impurity the purity, if not of the principle, then at least of the motivation of the moral, the purity, that is, of respect for the moral law" (Kofman 1982a, 385; Kofman 1982b, 28).

Kofman concentrates on respect for women as problematic for universal moral respect. She seems not to realize that respect for women in Kant's system does not actually conform to the nature of comparative respect either. In the *Anthropology*, Kant describes the relations between the sexes as a struggle for domination, motivated not by universal respect but by fear of and desire for domination; women especially, although weaker, are motivated by "the tendency to dominate and the tendency to please" (Kofman, 1982a, 386; Kofman 1982b, 29; cf. Kant 1978, 216–225). Respect for women might seem to be simply "a measure of protection granted to the weak by the strong" (Kofman 1982a, 386; Kofman 1982b, 30). The comparative respect denotes deference of the lesser toward the greater, in this case of the weak toward the strong. But Kant's women are the weaker; indeed, as he describes women, there is no intrinsic respect-worthy superiority in women at all.

Kofman does argue that respect for women "cannot be simply reduced to a right accorded to the weak by the strong; it is the will to dominate that drives the arrogance of women, the desire to avert all importunity on the part of man" (Kofman 1982a, 387; Kofman 1982b, 30–31; cf. Kant 1964, 87–90). In this painfully familiar sexual economy of pursuit and resistance, Kofman summarizes Kant's view that "that which makes up the value of her sex and renders women as such respectable is, as for an entire tradition, her reserve, her modesty" (Kofman 1982a, 387; Kofman 1982b, 31; cf. Kant 1964, 87–90). This economy provides both men and women with "a certain respite" (Kofman 1982a, 387; Kofman 1982b, 31). Women's modesty protects them from debasement as mere means serving men's sexual ends, while it protects men from the debasement of the repugnant vice of succumbing to their own animal lust (Kofman 1982a, 387–388; Kofman 1982b, 31ff.). Notice that *women's* sexual ends have disappeared completely from Kant's picture. Rather, a woman "satisfies her will to dominate in educating man to chastity"; such an education in the restraint of inclinations constitutes a preliminary step toward developing the traditional restraint dictated by the moral law (Kofman 1982a, 387, 392; Kofman 1982b, 31, 38–39; cf. Kant 1964, 87–90).

On the one hand, Kant argues that these restrictive conditions can best be provided through marriage. On the other hand, Kant advocates celibacy for ensuring a long and happy life (Kant 1979, 185; cf. Kofman

1982a, 389; cf. Kofman 1982b, 33–34). What is the price of this even greater restraint of the natural passions? Kofman argues that the price is either "neurosis and misery" or procuring "substitute satisfactions by the route of sublimation"; she closes her chapter by saying, "This was no doubt the case with Kant[,] who, in spite of the theoretical importance accorded to marriage, managed to remain celibate. And died at a great age" (Kofman 1982a, 404; Kofman 1982b, 56). So we see that for Kant, men must strive for some level of restraint, for any relation with women seems to be associated with risk to the rational self and the danger of death.

Kofman points out another protection, in particular for men: women's modesty "also prevents man from having . . . disgust for the sex of woman, to which the full and entire satisfaction of man's inclinations inevitably leads him" (Kofman 1982a, 388; Kofman 1982b, 33; cf. Kant 1983b, 50–51). The full range of men's desires includes "perverse constituents" that could not be fulfilled within the confines of the respect for human dignity required by the categorical imperative; furthermore, Kant holds that "the sex of a woman, laid bare, without discretion, of all disguise, . . . cannot be looked upon as such without provoking disgust" (Kofman 1982a, 388, 403; Kofman 1982b, 32, 55; cf. Kant 1964, 87–90). So although respect, which distances feminine sexuality from both men and women, serves the needs of both men and women, it serves men better.

Even women's domination of men through their respect must be understood to serve this economy. As Kofman quotes Kant, the husband is like the deferential minister to a pleasure-seeking king (the wife): "This all-powerful master does what he wants on condition that his minister suggests his will"; if, like a queen, woman dominates, "it is man, the minister, who governs through his understanding" (Kofman 1982a, 389–390; Kofman 1982b, 35; cf. Kant 1978, 224; cf. Kant 1964, 140–143). Even when women dominate, the men, as rational, remain in charge.

To violate the restraints of respectful decorum is not held by Kant to be a wrong done against the woman at all. Kant holds that the exercise of lustful sensuality is a moral wrong against *oneself*, even more repugnant than suicide (Kofman 1982a, 388; Kofman 1982b, 32). The vehemence of Kant's disgust, claims Kofman, originates not solely from violation of moral law, but from the merged attraction to and abhorrence from female sexuality that Kant's texts have revealed.

Furthermore, Kofman argues that despite Kant's abhorrence, this sexual economy operates by distinguishing between women deemed worthy of respect and those who are not in order to keep respectable women at a safe distance while the unrespectable are available for use: "In this case, the respect men have for their wives in marriage, if it is a necessary preliminary to their morality, is also that of their immorality toward other women not worthy of the name of Mankind" (Kofman 1982a, 403–404; Kofman 1982b, 55). That this whole economy is rooted in ambivalence toward the powerful figure of the mother is attested to also by Kant's characterization of the return to nature both as a paradise and as a disgusting vice (Kofman 1982a, 390–393, 398; Kofman 1982b, 27–30; cf. Kant 1978, 224; cf. Kant 1964, 140–143).

We can see conflicting aspects of both forms of respect conflated in respect for women: "Women require, *in the very name of their sex,* consideration, even if they don't deserve it; that is what respect is" (Kofman 1982a, 387; Kofman 1982b, 31; cf. Kant 1964, 87–90). It is the moral respect that takes no account of distinguishing who deserves from who does not, but it is the comparative respect that attends to specific differences, for example, those between the sexes. Kofman argues that because Kant holds that respect for women is an application of the moral law, respect for women must be consequent to it. Yet this same respect also serves as an educational tool, leading men toward morality; it must be preliminary, stemming from the inclinations, instincts, and desires governing comparative rather than moral respect.

Combining Kofman's claims with my insight that respect for women also cannot be a straightforward form of comparative respect, I conclude that there are no intrinsic properties of women from which respect could follow in Kant's system. Kant's women have no intrinsic superiority that could evoke the comparative respect, nor can this educational respect be a result of the moral principle it inculcates. Kant's respect for women is bound up not with intrinsic but with relational properties, distancing relations of modesty, propriety, and decency, veiled in polite and formulaic language. It is not women but women with regard to men who garner Kant's respect.

MORAL LAW AND THE MACHINERY OF WAR

Clearly, Kofman wishes not only to analyze these Kantian texts but to psychoanalyze and diagnose Kantian ethics by a careful diagnostic genealogy, tracing the origins of Kantian ethics like those of a neurosis. The system of moral oppositions, the divisive categorization of women, and the double fascination all originate, she argues, from a split within the original fascination with the figure of the mother (Kofman 1982a, 393, 396; Kofman 1982b, 39, 44). Kofman asks whether, although Kant would not admit it, one should and could say that "the figure of the law and of its sublimity is a 'grandiose sublimation' of the figure of the mother" (Kofman 1982a, 396, 401; Kofman 1982b, 44, 51–52). Kofman argues that the same genealogy by which respect for women is a precondition to moral respect for an individual operates also for Kant on the level of the species. Furthermore, her analysis reveals this same sexual economy at work in Kant's descriptions of both nature and the moral law as sublime.

In his "Speculative Beginning of Human History," Kant speculates about how the sexual instincts of women and men give way to a distancing decency and respect (Kant 1983b, 51–52). In a quasi-parodic paraphrase of this passage, Kofman describes how Mother Nature uses women's and men's natural inclinations to bring them as a species through the preliminary comparative respect for women to reason and the moral law: "Through the device of the war between the sexes for domination, and hence through the device of what Kant calls human folly, nature directs the education of man toward morality" (Kofman 1982a, 390; Kofman 1982b, 35–36; cf. Alexander 1998).

Kofman's account brings to the forefront the double fascination Kant holds for nature/instinct/inclination. Just as with the fascination for women, this fascination combines a horror of servitude with an adulation of desire. She reveals how nature, like women, dominates only through indirection, such that "respect for women announces and prepares for respect for man" (Kofman 1982a, 392; Kofman 1982b, 39). And although Kofman's account does not explicitly make this point, it seems clear that nature as inclination and desire is like the pleasure-loving sovereign. She {wife/nature) gets her way as long as she decrees whatever the cabinet minister (husband/reason) suggests. Mother Nature is a conspirator in her own overthrow—her subordination to reason.

Kofman is now able to delve more deeply into the nature of respect, revealing it as a double fascination and linking it to Kant's analysis of the sublime. Unlike love, respect is a feeling that distances and protects one from that which remains an object of desire. Kofman summarizes Kant, who, "in bringing up the sentiment of the sublime, which always implies respect, describes it as an emotion comparable to a shock in which repulsion and attraction rapidly alternate, both having the same object" (Kofman 1982a, 394; Kofman 1982b, 41–42; cf. Kant 1969, 105–109). Similarly, Kant describes the moral law as a sublime and "holy and solemn majesty" that evokes a "frightening respect," revealing not only the unworthiness of humans as beings with inclinations toward evil but also the sublimity of humans as rational beings (Kofman 1982a, 394–395; Kofman 1982b, 42–43; cf. Kant 1969, 105–109). So in man's relation to the moral law, we find the same conflation of the moral and comparative respects as in man's respect for women, and the same double fascination of attraction and repulsion.

Furthermore, Kant's metaphoric descriptions of the moral law itself exhibit the same apotropaic function, the same veiled economy of sexual domination. This project of domination is both driven and camouflaged by an aesthetic device, an artifice of personification portraying human reason by an aesthetic (sensible) representation, devised precisely in order to deny that the sublime figure of moral law is a "grandiose sublimation" of the figure of the mother (Kofman 1982a, 397; Kofman 1982b, 44, 46; cf. Kant 1969, 94–98; cf. Alexander 1998).

In a discussion of the conditions for a morally acceptable representation of the moral law, Kant evokes as sublime the inscription to Isis as Mother Nature: I am all that which is, has been, and will be, and no mortal has ever lifted my veil. Kofman says, "It is impossible to completely dis-cover Mother Nature, she is inexhaustible, impenetrable. Behind one veil there will always be another veil" (Kofman 1982a, 399; Kofman 1982b, 49; cf. Kant 1964, 179). The physicist, in raising nature's veils, should feel a sublime reverence, a respect for the sublime inexhaustibility of nature that can never be fully mastered. Likewise, with respect to the moral law as Isis, Kant writes, "The veiled goddess before whom one way or another we kneel, that is the moral law in us in its invulnerable majesty" (Kant 1993, 71; cf. Kofman 1982a, 401; cf. Kofman 1982b, 51–52).[9] Kant insists on the apotropaic veiling function, the distancing function of respect. As with respect for women, one wonders what horror Kant is protecting himself from seeing about moral law.

Yet Kant sometimes explicitly prohibits representing moral law by means of sensible images such as the Isis image (Kant 1964, 49–51; cf. Kofman 1982a, 401; cf. Kofman 1982b, 51–52). As with the Jewish proscription of representations of God, which would inevitably limit and warp our apprehension of the inapprehensible, Kant at times proscribes representations of the moral law. He fears that man could be seduced away from reason by the pathological voice of the sensible representation itself. For example, one might identify the law too literally as the goddess Isis and lose sight of its nature as universal practical reason, an aspect of our own consciousness.

Furthermore, Kofman argues that the real danger of imaging the law as goddess is that one might be tempted to lift the veil in order to see what is under there; after all, the physicists do it. Kant warns against this desire to raise the veil, to master rather than submit to the law (Kant 1993, 68–69, 71; cf. Kofman 1982a, 399; cf. Kofman 1982b, 49). On the basis of Kofman's diagnosis, we may conclude that perhaps, as with the queen's minister, true mastery lies in a submission that bends the rule of law to one's specific purposes. The sublime, awesome, and solemn majesty of the moral law on which Kant insists keeps custody of the remnants ("les traces") of the original fascination with the mother as feminine (Kofman 1982a, 394; Kofman 1982b, 42).

Nevertheless, Kant himself continues to personify the law, both as the voice of reason and as the mother goddess Isis whose veil must not be lifted. According to Kofman, he sets two conditions for the moral (as opposed to the pathological) use of aesthetic representations to portray the moral law:

> In order to avoid the risks of mastery, Kant requires, and this is the minimal condition of a good personification, that an aestheticization be moral and not pathological, in other words that the personification should come after the ideal of the moral law and not before it. (Kofman 1982a, 401; Kofman 1982b, 51)

So on the one hand, a moral personification must come after the rational law, not before, in order not to stray beyond its rational limits in making a sensible representation. On the other hand, a moral personification must represent primarily the "in-sensibility" of the rational voice of law and the law's inexhaustible impenetrability by representation. Kofman summarizes Kant's second condition:

> The personification of the law in a figure must precisely figure its incommensurability, its unfigurability, in the sense in which no determinate figure could be adequate to it; that is to say that the figure must precisely figure its incommensurability, its unfigurability, that is to say sublimity. (Kofman 1982a, 397; Kofman 1982b, 46; cf. Kant 1969, 94–98, 175–182)

Putting the two criteria together, we see that Kant holds that the representation must be a consequence of a rational understanding of moral law in order to give life to the idea of moral law "by analogy" without attributing "to it other properties than those which the first method [reason] discovers" (Kant 1963, 71; cf. Kofman 1982a, 401; cf. Kofman 1982b, 50).

Kofman's arguments reveal that Kant's own descriptions properly meet neither of these conditions. Kant's metaphors invoke what is prior, not consequent, to moral law, and they attribute properties to the law that flow from its representation as a veiled, divine woman (Kofman 1982a, 402; Kofman 1982b, 53). First, "because there is a childhood of the individual and a childhood of peoples, moral respect certainly 'begins' with respect for women, for mothers." Kofman argues that, chronologically at least, the personification of the object of respect as mother, as woman, as goddess, must always come first (Kofman 1982a, 402; Kofman 1982b, 53). Such preliminary personification "risks the contamination of all subsequent 'representation' of the moral law" (Kofman 1982a, 402; Kofman 1982b, 53). The failure of the criterion that the personification of law must figure only the law's unfigurability illustrates the presence of this so-called contamination.

Second, far from exhibiting the pure, unfigurable universality of law or respect for universal human dignity, Kant's descriptions have revealed a very different economy at work: a distancing that protects and a submission that retains mastery, fueled by the sublime double fascination of attraction and repulsion. In other words, the sexual economy exhibited in respect for women is also at work in Kant's attitude toward the moral law itself. After all, as Kofman reminds us, Isis is the goddess who murdered Osiris and recovered (and, I add, mended) all his torn pieces, except his penis (Kofman 1982a, 400; Kofman 1982b, 51).[10] Isis, personification of the law, remains—behind the veil of her umbrella—the powerful, phallic, castrating mother goddess.

DIAGNOSING RESPECT

Throughout *Le respect des femmes*, Kofman has revealed the rend-and-mend sexual economy of reversal by which the originary fascination with one's own mother, Mother Nature, and Mother Isis is divided, distanced, sanitized, and denied. In this sense, men's holding women in respect is the sine qua non of morality, the foundation and origin of the law of laws (Kofman 1982a, 390; Kofman 1982b, 36). Kant's ethical theory veils again and again his horror of recognizing that the feminine infiltrates the masculine; that inclination, sexuality, and desire pervade reason; and that the hidden force driving moral law is feminine, sexual, and powerful.

In her overall diagnosis of Kant's ethic of respect, Kofman argues that "the economy realized by respect is that of the agony of castration, communicated with a gesture of fetishism" (Kofman 1982a, 403; Kofman 1982b, 54). It is the panic reaction of the child who both desires and fears the mother's sexuality. One must keep it at a distance; one must reject the powerful force of women's sexuality, both "on oneself and beyond oneself" (Kofman 1982a, 403; Kofman 1982b, 53). The power of feminine sexuality from which one might perish is dangerous for both men and women, who risk the loss of reason, of self, of life. Yet the economy through which Kant veils this power cannot altogether erase it. Such an attempt at erasure inaugurates Kant's economy of death (Kofman 1982a, 403; Kofman 1982b, 54).

In this chapter I have discussed Kofman's work in terms of the rhetorical texture and wit of her language, which can rarely survive translation, and have clarified both rhetorical and logical structures left implicit with a light touch in her own writing. Critics of Kant's ethics often attack the universalism of his moral law. While Kofman does expose the failure of this universality, her analysis undermines the often still cherished Kantian ideals of intrinsic worth, of human dignity. I find Kofman's critique disturbing, provocative, and insightful. She reveals that Kant can establish his universal moral respect only by excluding women in the same move by which he seems to include them. Critics of Kant will benefit from a close study of Kofman's skillful deployment of respect as a tool for collapsing the oppositions, especially those between desire and reason, that shore up Kant's ethical theory. The extension of Kofman's deconstruction by which I show that respect for women cannot be reduced to the comparative form of respect any more than to the universal may also prove fruitful. Finally, through this interpretation of Kofman's work I hope to unveil Sarah Kofman as a feminist source of carefully structured, insightful, and witty deconstructions. With these goals in mind, I close by returning to the heart of Kofman's text, with an overview of the divisive and defensive function she has revealed within Kant's economy, the strange umbrella-like device of "respect" for women.

Respect for women—implying an apotropaic, defensive machinery holding women at a distance—operates for the individual man or woman as a protective device, while nevertheless leaving plenty of room for gratification of men's desires. Within this deadly economy, in order not to be an object of disgust, woman must become not a rational subject but an object of propriety, of proper taste, and of proper language. She must hold herself under this umbrella of respect in order to mask her nature, in order to protect both herself and men from women's power, both dreaded and desired; woman is both umbrella and lightning rod. Kofman holds that as women realize how men's respectful "feminism" is always the inverse of their misogyny, ceasing their complicity with this debasing respect, women will refuse to serve as taxi, lightning rod, or umbrella (Kofman 1982a, 403; Kofman 1982b, 20, 54).

Respect for women—implying the refusal (or at least the endless veiling) of feminine sexuality—operates genealogically for both individual and species as a preliminary step in moral education; hence its economy suffuses that of morality. Kofman characterizes this notion of respect:

The word for "respect," if it is truly the one that fits this double sentiment which humiliates me at the same time that it elevates me, is like a "trace" of that first relation between an infant and that solemn and frightening majesty his mother is to him. (Kofman 1982a, 402; Kofman 1982b, 54)

Kofman's argument unmasks the insight that the purity and authority of Kant's moral law breaks down: reason is always infused with sensual figuration, the a priori with the a posteriori, universal respect with the desire of domination, the masculine with the feminine. And that this should be feared as a contamination is itself a symptom of the neurosis that both drives and camouflages moral respect.

Complicated Fidelity: Kofman's Freud (Reading The Childhood of Art with The Enigma of Woman)

PENELOPE DEUTSCHER

In an interview she gave in 1986, Sarah Kofman made some comments about autobiography that were later to place in a curious light the autobiographical work she wrote in 1994, *Rue Ordener, Rue Labat* (translated 1996). She declared that there was no self "Kofman" except for the multiple authors with whom she identified and aligned herself, and her assemblage of citations of diverse figures:

> I'm like [Hoffmann's] cat, Murr, whose autobiography is no more than an assemblage of citations of diverse authors. . . . This "myself," isn't that an illusion? Isn't it an illusion to believe I have any autobiography other than that which emerges from my bibliography? (Kofman with Jaccard 1986, 7)

One could think of *Rue Ordener* as compatible with Kofman's rejection of autobiography on the grounds that there is no "self" Kofman except for the multiple authors with whom she identifies. Through the biographical detail and the narrative of events recounted in *Rue Ordener, Rue Labat,* Kofman recounts a narrative of psychic division between structuring figures in the constitution of self: the division between maternal and paternal, and then the division of the maternal itself into "good" and "bad" figures. The self "Kofman" portrayed in her brief autobiographical pieces is caught in an economy of split identification and alliance.

In her interpretations of the history of philosophy, Kofman's particular methodology is seen in her deployment of this conception of the self. When Kofman acts as the interpretive self "Kofman" in her own corpus, she deploys a particular concept of the self as fragmented, mimetic, and plural. In this sense, it is particularly true that Kofman's autobiography—the autobiography of a fragmented, identificatory self—is at work in her bibliography.

KOFMAN'S MIMETIC METHODOLOGY

Kofman describes her work as a mimetic writing in which she identifies with philosophers such as Nietzsche, Freud, and Derrida (Kofman with Jaccard 1986, 7). Often the question of her fidelity to these philosophers has arisen. Is she too faithful, merely repeating, lacking inventive originality? For example, Kofman seems to be a disturbingly faithful Freudian critic, persistently locating Oedipal scenarios and castration anxiety in a series of philosophers—Rousseau, Comte, Freud himself. On the other hand, Kofman's identifications are never simply faithful. Consider *Camera obscura* as an example of one mode of Kofman's writing practice, and consider how faithful she is being in this example.

In *Camera obscura* Kofman moves across a body of male writers (Rousseau, Nietzsche, Freud, Marx) and across her own analyses of those writers in her other books (broadly referenced in footnotes), as well as across two key theoretical reference points: Derrida and Freud, both indicated in footnoted references that are usually very general, exaggerating the French style: "cf. *Of Grammatology,*" she broadly sketches, "cf. *Beyond the Pleasure Principle.*" Through this kind of broad ranging, she reconstructs a desire that fascinated her, a masculine desire, an ardent quest, to penetrate the depths of "bountiful nature" (Kofman 1973, 52). At one point, Kofman locates the expression of this desire in the writings of Leonardo da Vinci:

"I came to the threshold of a great cavern, before which I remained motionless, struck with a kind of stupor in front of this unknown thing. . . .

I leaned in toward the one side, toward the other several times, trying to make something out. . . . Two sentiments took hold of me, fear and desire, fear of the obscure and menacing grotto, desire to see it didn't conceal some wonder." (Kofman 1973, 52)

According to Kofman's reading of this passage, nature is the mother. The "darkness" veils ultimate knowledge concerning a much-feared discovery: the mother's nonpossession of the penis (Kofman 1973, 53). Kofman is frequently cutting about Freud's ascription of penis envy to women, but not about his ascription to men of castration anxiety. Castration anxiety is a theme that she appropriates—apparently with great fidelity—in her various accounts of masculine desire.

However, complicating the apparent fidelity of Kofman to Freud is the way in which the textual references ricochet. In this section of *Camera obscura*, for example, Kofman immediately passes from the reference to da Vinci to Jean-Jacques Rousseau. In his *Confessions*, Kofman reminds us, we see Rousseau similarly wanting to penetrate an inner depth and unveil all. Here, it's his own interior truth that Rousseau wants to penetrate and expose. And immediately, Kofman moves us on to the work of Freud. Freud often serves for Kofman as another instance of a theorist who wants to unveil secrets, for example, those of women's erotic life, which, he complains, are "still veiled in an impenetrable obscurity" (Freud 1905, 151).[1] In this case, however, Kofman cites Freud as an acute analyst of the economy of the secret behind the veil: fetishism. But immediately, Kofman also introduces Nietzsche, as another acute analyst of the desire to penetrate all. With the desire to reveal the hidden truth, proposes Nietzsche, it is the subject who projects and sustains the effect of an illusory truth behind the veil (Kofman 1973, p. 60). Behind the veil, Kofman's Nietzsche tells us, there would always be another veil (62). The illusion of the veil, we are then told, is a fetishizing denial of sexual difference, a denial of the mother's castration.

What might we say of Kofman's method here? Kofman's Nietzsche is no sooner cited than he dissolves into a Freudian account of fetishism. We frequently see this mode of transition in Kofman's work: the reverse move occurs in *The Enigma of Woman*, where Kofman introduces Nietzsche's discussion of women's silence into Freud's discussion of the profound silence of women. Also typical is the fact that she doesn't directly address the question of staging these juxtapositions, beyond comments of the genre: "One wonders whether Freud knew Nietzsche's wonderful text" (Kofman 1985a, 41).

The flickering across a stream of philosophers is one of the most operative elements in Kofman's work, and this is the kind of comment she often uses to facilitate the connectives between her male philosophers. Moving from Freud to Nietzsche, we might be told that Nietzsche was Freudian *avant la lettre*. Or moving from Rousseau to Gravesand, Kofman will muse, "One wonders if Rousseau had ever read Gravesand's treaty on perspective" (Kofman 1973, 55). The series of rhetorical questions used to connect and effect the transitions serves almost as a smoke screen, in the sense that the work this flickering is doing for Kofman is clearly not intended as a contribution to biographical or historical questions of who read what, nor a very serious contribution to the concept of the historical "forerunner."

One of the frequent dissolves at work for Kofman is that between Freud and Derrida. We might see broad references to Derrida in the midst of a discussion of Freud ("cf. *Spurs,*" "cf. *Glas*") or vice versa. A discussion of Freud's analytic discussions of literary texts might include comments on the distinction between what a text announces and what it actually does, as in the following passage from *Freud and Fiction:*

> Freudian texts are evidently complex, and must be read carefully, just as I showed in [*The Childhood of Art*]. By distinguishing what Freud *does* from what he *says*, we can see that his texts do indeed lead to the deconstruction of metaphysics. (Kofman 1991b, 8)

Just as Kofman fuses, or flickers between, a Freudian and a Nietzschean account of the economy of the veil, as she reconstructs these, she also flickers between her stylization of a Derridean distinction between the declared and the described content of a text and her stylization of a Freudian account of textual symptoms that might occur at the level of described content. Consider the following comment from *The Childhood of Art:*

> [We'll] distinguish what Freud declares in his discourse as a matter of strategy from what he masks more or less consciously. [We'll] do a symptomal reading of his text, making it say more or other than what it says literally, yet basing the reading on the literal sense alone. (Kofman 1988c, 1–2)

However, twenty pages later this has become a Derridean distinction. Kofman proposes reading Freud's texts by "using the deciphering method he himself taught us, distinguishing what he *says* from what he actually *does* in his discourse" (Kofman 1988c, 21–22), a comment then followed by a footnote: "See [cf.] Derrida's distinction between concept and discourse" (Kofman 1988c, 205).[2]

Though they exaggerate a conventional form, the "cf." footnotes aren't tongue in cheek, yet they can't be taken at face value. "Cf. *Of Grammatology*" is such a broad gesture, and besides, Kofman's work is quite specific and not much like Derrida's work. Furthermore, we would always have to read "cf. *Of Grammatology*" bearing in mind that in any text she's always also saying "cf. *The Genealogy of Morals*," "cf. *Studies in Hysteria*," and so on.

So what is the status of Kofman's fidelity? In *Freud and Fiction* she opens by explaining that she is pushing Freudian interpretation to the limit— but, she says, as loyally as possible (Kofman 1991b, 3). She reminds us in the Epilogue that her work could be interpreted as "remaining faithful" to the Freudian schema, merely "complicating" this schema. If we ask what "complication" means for Kofman, we find that she describes herself as emphasizing the deconstructive aspect of Freud (Kofman 1991b, 3), and above all the heterogeneity of his texts. Derrida has been patched onto Freud, then, but a Derrida always already as characterized by Kofman. For in *Lectures de Derrida,* she understands Derrida to have emphasized the heterogeneity of Freud. Similarly, at another point, Kofman refers to her project as a "grafting." Certainly, Freud is grafted, sometimes onto Nietzsche, sometimes onto Derrida. It's in the context of this patching onto, fusion, and flickering between that these theorists are particularly stylized, more Kofman's "masks" than anything else. That's how I interpret "cf.": as the indication of a stylized, often extraordinarily foreshortened reference point occurring when Kofman grafts herself onto a series of stylized figures and grafts them onto each other.[3]

In working in this fashion, is Kofman being faithful to Derrida? Well, to a kind of "Derrida," to the Derrida as she has stylized him (thus unfaithful), since Kofman emphasizes the Derrida who once declared, "To write means to graft" (Derrida 1981, 355), and who expresses himself, as she tells it, constantly *with* other authors (Kofman 1984b, 16–17, 53). So the Derrida she is appropriating is Derrida already become Kofman, Derrida as Kofman so particularly takes him—just a few threads and phrases of his, especially potent for her, put to work repeatedly. She *is* appropriating Freud and Derrida, but what is produced is neither faithful Freudianism nor diluted Derrideanism, because of the way in which she complicates appropriation as a project.

In sum, her fidelity to any one figure is complicated by three factors: the first is her identification with multiple authors: "When I take up Freud, I read him in the light of Nietzsche, that's to say, making a genealogical reading of psychoanalytic texts. When I'm interested in Nietzsche, all my analytic knowledge is engaged" (Kofman with Jaccard 1986, 7).[4] The second factor is the way in which she appropriates theorists in a starkly stylized or foreshortened form. This is entirely Kofman's project, her idiosyncrasy, since the authors she stylizes are figures to whom she has also devoted extremely close, fine, sustained studies, sometimes on a monumental scale.

The third factor is the question of how to reconcile—or at least read—her constant (multiple) deployment of masks of Nietzsche, Derrida, and Freud with her close, critical work on those figures. This is the project with which I'll conclude this chapter. I'll work toward considering one example of the relationship between Kofman's critical work *on* Freud and her critical work *with* Freud. The synthesis I want to look at in this context is the synthesis of Freud with Derrida. And the deployment—or "working with"—I want to consider is the use of Freudian concepts to interpret Freud's own account of the "enigma of woman." How is the Freudianism used to read that account affected by the deconstructive critical work Kofman also achieved on Freud? Put another way, how can texts such as *The Childhood of Art* and *The Enigma of Woman* be read together?

Kofman habitually slides, repetitively, across stylized identificatory figures such as Freud and Derrida. I wish to reclaim Kofman from a possible (mis)reading: that her fidelity to such figures is weak, or confused (for example, because she seems to confuse Freud with Derrida's reading of Freud or to confuse Freud with Nietzsche). I argue that rather than weakening Kofman's philosophy, this apparent "confusion" between philosophers is the source of its efficacy. I consider what this peculiarity in her method enables in Kofman's analysis. I have isolated a particular theme—the "enigma of woman"—in order to pursue this question. I suggest that although Kofman's versions of Freud and Derrida—not as she reads them (that's a different matter again), but as she deploys them—are rather simple, there is nothing simplistic about the product.

KOFMAN'S FREUD AND THE ENIGMA OF WOMAN

Interpreting philosophers such as Nietzsche, Rousseau, Comte, and Freud, Kofman locates images of women in their work as figures of mystery and enigma who fascinate and inspire fear, or the desire for distance.[5] Woman is a "spider woman," whom we should not approach or regard too closely.[6] We protect ourselves by refusing to look, by wearing a mask of blindness. We refuse to see, by being "respectful" of women, for example. In this economy woman also serves as a figure for that which is enigmatic; thus nature and truth often take on feminine connotations (Kofman 1985a, 95) or are described in the same terms: desire yet fear of penetrating, the secrets of nature, the hidden truth.[7]

Who is Kofman's Freud? He serves as one of Kofman's many examples of a male theorist whose desire is to penetrate secrets behind the veil, insofar as any psychic productions, "daydreams, dreams, slips of the tongue, bungled actions, art, and other social productions" (Kofman 1988c, 142), are seen as enigmas to be deciphered. This Freud describes his project as discovery ("Aufdeckung") or unmasking ("Entlarvtung") (55) or archaeological reconstruction (69). The declared intentions of a text or a subject should be seen as a facade (48) behind which Freud invites us to see the "real meaning" of a text through an analytic interpretation, by means of which nothing should remain enigmatic (49). For this Freud, there is often a distinction between the declared intentions and what the subject's text says at the level of discourse, a dream, a literary piece. For example, Freud claims that the story by Stefan Zweig, "Four-and-Twenty Hours in a Woman's Life," "ostensibly sets out only to show what an irresponsible creature woman is. . . . But the story tells far more than this. If it is submitted to an analytic interpretation, it will be found to represent . . . something quite different" (Freud 1928, 191, cited in Kofman 1988c, 48).

Freud goes on to call this "something different" the "hidden traces." Thus, glosses Kofman:

> The declared intentions are only a facade given to the story by the author to veil the analytic signification. The text is thus tissue that hides, or masks, its meaning: only certain details hidden in the woof of the material provide the thread that makes it possible to discover ["aufdecken"] the secret of the text. (Kofman 1988c, 48)

So Kofman locates a language of genesis and original meaning, original significance or hidden truth, in Freud's accounts of Oedipal desire. In "Four-and-Twenty Hours in a Woman's Life," the veiled secret turns out to be "every man's desire to be initiated into sexual life by his mother in order to fight against masturbation" (Kofman 1988c, 49). For the Freud who sees his project as unmasking or deciphering latent content, there exists an original meaning to the manifest content of psychic production. This is the Freud for whom the "fundamental signified" is the castration complex (Kofman 1991b, 159). Insofar as Kofman sees Freud as adhering to some projection of an original signified at the heart of an unconscious chain of signifiers and behind the veil of manifest content, she argues that Freud "is still tie[d] . . . to the traditional ideology of representation" (Kofman 1988c, 100).

KOFMAN'S FIDELITY

There are parallels between the forms of methodology and fidelity at work in *The Childhood of Art* and *The Enigma of Woman*. First, I will follow the thread of the critical work Kofman performs on Freud's texts, which she describes as reading Freud's texts "using the deciphering method he himself taught us" (Kofman 1988c, 21–22). One aspect of this project involves "deciphering" the figure of Freud. We see Kofman engage, in a way, in being Freudian with Freud, taking an analytic stance with him. This is one aspect of the project Kofman mentions: deciphering Freud according to a method she attributes to him.

The first form of Kofman's fidelity to Freud in *The Enigma of Woman*, then, is the most obvious. Kofman interprets a series of Freud's dreams and letters. She locates Freud's own castration anxiety (Kofman 1985a, 70), his anxiety about his own femininity (15, 30), and his desire/fear to unveil and penetrate the secrets of nature and women (29–30), a desire connected to his fear of being "blinded" (castrated). When Kofman dons the mask of Freudian analysis to interpret Freud's account of women, Freud's own dreams become the royal road followed by Kofman in analytic posture to Freud's desire: "This long detour by way of Freud's dreams will prove not to have been useless, for these dreams are the royal road that may lead to a better understanding of the status of female sexuality in Freud's theoretical texts" (32).

This is the most pseudo-Freudian of Kofman's Freudian masks. This is one form of fidelity to Freud—to Freudian method, as Kofman construes it when she describes the project Freud teaches us, distinguishing what a text *says* from what it really *does* (Kofman 1988c, 21–22). Kofman distinguishes the declared level of "Freud" from the level revealed by the posture of analytic interpretation, what this Freud (the Freud who positions unconscious meaning behind the veil) would have called the "secret trace," the something completely different one is thereby able to reveal. It is because of this guise that Kofman is often accused of repeating the mode of the dogmatic Freud she also criticizes, looking for the secret trace of the unconscious (in this case, Freud's unconscious).

But Kofman also distinguishes in a different fashion between levels of description and declaration. While still attributing the methodology to Freud, stating that she is following the method "Freud himself teaches us," she also invokes the same distinction and attributes it to Derrida. She pushes out of the declare/describe distinction, as she has located it in Freud's work, a method she locates in Derrida's work. She pushes out a Freud fused with other masks (those of Derrida, and also Nietzsche) from within her work on Freud's text, through the distinction between what Freud declares and describes. What occurs is the location of different Freuds to whom to be faithful.

Here, one has no need to locate secret traces. One simply needs to pay absolute attention to what Freud is really "describing." This is what Kofman describes several times as pushing Freud to the limit, and it is the text produced when Kofman "complicates" Freud (Kofman 1991b, 158–159) and reads his discourse as heterogeneous. Kofman is identifying with her version of Derrida at this point, the Derrida who locates the heterogeneous Freud (Kofman 1984b, 75). Kofman undertakes this project in both *Childhood* and *Enigma*.

In *Childhood*, the heterogeneity located by Kofman concerns psychic representation. Says Kofman, "One realizes that despite language that still belongs to the closure of metaphysics, Freud is not a prisoner of his ideology" (Kofman 1988c, 22). If we push Freud to the limit, she suggests, in fact we'll find him telling us that there is no original signified, but instead "a nonexistent originary text" (71), an "originary absence of meaning" (78), originary substitutes, and substitutes for substitutes (77). Kofman says that although in many ways Freud is still imprisoned in the logic of representation and the sign, "Freud's conception of truth is a new one" (100). Here, "truth is given only in its distortions and is constructed from those distortions" (100). Rather than an originary text that is supposedly "translated," there are "constructions after the fact" (100). Kofman reminds us that one could never arrive at an original signified because it is always fantasized by desire (78). A subject is nostalgic for a phantasmic, lost "full presence" or unity, but there never was a moment of original full presence or unity that is "represented" in a posterior time: "The archaic as such is nowhere in existence. . . . No vestiges of the past remain, but only subsequent elaborations of these vestiges" (64). So the imagination, or representation, should not be seen as an intermediary, but as original.

In *Childhood*, Kofman insists on the lack of an original signified, "the absence of originary meaning" (Kofman 1988c, 39), arguing that originary inscription is always already a symbolic substitute (78). In her reference to Freud's discussion of the Fort-da game, Kofman points out that in Freud's own account it is the game, the representation, that *constitutes* the absence of the mother to be represented (76–77). It is the representation that enables the absence of the mother to be constituted, rather than that absence temporally "preceding" its representation. It is thus the representation, and not that which one posits as having "been" represented, that is original. It is the supplement, glosses Kofman, that is original. It is for this reason that we can never aspire, in analytic interpretation, to retrieve the original signified at the heart of a chain of signification. This is not to say that we can't interpret, but that we have to reconsider the model of a psychic signifying structure in terms of which we interpret. We have to renounce the concept of "translated" or "transcribed" unconscious thoughts, latent content, or preexisting text in favor of a model of the psychic as a "single text," a "set of traces" (39). For Freud, "one is referred from construction to construction, from version to version, and from interpretation to interpretation without a nonexistent originary text ever being reached" (71).

In *Enigma*, we also see Kofman insisting on a complicated, heterogeneous Freud to whom she will be faithful by attending to what Freud's text "does" in contrast to what it says (Kofman 1985a, 103). In the case of the *Enigma* project, the heterogeneity in question concerns his phallocentrism. The Freud "pushed to the limit" discovers the "radical otherness" of woman (33).[8] Kofman locates the Freud for whom "it is no longer the woman who envies the man his penis, it is he who envies her" for her "narcissistic self-sufficiency and her indifference" (52), the Freud who emphasizes in his later work the "new importance of the preoedipal relation of daughter to mother and cast[s] doubt on the status of the Oedipus complex" (20). True, Freud also subordinates the importance of the pre-Oedipal phase (34). Kofman discusses Freud's "extreme restraint on the subject of women over a long period of time" (21), during which "[Freud] set up a simple parallelism and a simple symmetry between the girl's oedipal complex and the boy's; only later, with the preoedipal phase, came the discovery of the woman as *totally other*" (21).

Insofar as Freud reinstates this phase "within the process of a history which must lead to the Oedipus complex in every case," Kofman proposes, "one loses the specificity, the radical strangeness of the totally other, one overcomes the astonishing 'surprise' that the discovery of feminine sexuality elicited" (Kofman 1985a, 34). Nevertheless, to be true to the letter of Freud's text, the heterogeneous levels of declaration and of description, one must acknowledge that he is *both* "discovering" sexual difference and suppressing it in favor of a phallocentric account of female sexuality.

In the elaboration of the concept of a lack of an original signified, Freud has been synthesized with Derrida, not only at the level of the method ascribed to Freud/Derrida, but also in terms of the themes produced by reading Freud according to that method. Kofman ascribes to Freud the idea that the deformation of the text does not imply the presence of an original text; instead, the "substitution" or the supplement is original and there are not two separate systems, latent and manifest levels, but rather one "système énergétique" of psychic writing. However, she also references ("cf.") this interpretation of Freud to Derrida's "Freud and the Scene of Writing" (Kofman 1988c, 39, 66, 209, 211), which she has appropriated in her reading of Freud.

To *which* Freud, then, is Kofman faithful? Kofman's fidelity to Freud is complicated by the fact that her Freudian masks multiply. We've seen an analytic, a deconstructive, and a deconstructed Freud at work in Kofman.

Now, in *Enigma,* Kofman is faithful to the Freudian location of Oedipal narratives. In locating the "enacted" as opposed to the "declared" level of Freud's texts, she is faithful both to the deconstructive and deconstructed Freuds, since the method used to reveal a deconstructed Freud who discovers the radical otherness of woman is referenced interchangeably to Derrida and Freud. But there is one more Freud to whom Kofman is faithful, I'll suggest, and that is the Freud whom she has "deconstructed" in *The Childhood of Art,* who is heterogeneous on the question of representation. Thus, I'm suggesting that we think of *The Enigma of Woman* as a particularly dense intersection between the critical work achieved on, and with, Freud, between the Freud "destabilized" by Kofman and the Freud deployed by Kofman, producing the idiosyncratic methodology of Kofman's multiple masks.

BEHIND THE VEIL?

With one Freudian mask, Kofman discusses Freud's own castration anxiety; with another she discovers the Freud who discovers sexual difference. Another Freudian mask that Kofman dons is the Freud she has uncovered as a product of the project in *Childhood.* It is there that Kofman discovers a Freud who invents a new theory of truth, who renders questionable the concept of an original signified at which one could arrive at the heart of the chain of signification, producing a new Freudian mask that is a product of a synthesis with Derrida, as Kofman stylizes him, to whom she can be faithful in her mimetic deployment of Freudianism as a means of critically interpreting his account of femininity. Here, Kofman would be faithful to the Freud produced by a deconstructive (as Kofman appropriates it) reading, the Freud who insists on the lack of the original signified.

In *Childhood,* Kofman discusses the way in which latent unconscious meaning is constructed as a secret behind the veil, to be penetrated by the analyst. In *Enigma,* she discusses the way in which woman is constructed as an enigma behind a veil to be penetrated by the analyst. The language Kofman locates in *Childhood* that is used by Freud to discuss truth is the same structure of language he uses to discuss femininity and women, which Kofman locates in *Enigma.* Thus the economy of truth being a woman is constructed by Kofman at the Freudian site. But Kofman has also located the complicated Freud. In *Childhood* this is the Freud who "discovers" that there is no truth behind the veil. Most obviously, in *Enigma* this is the Freud who discovers sexual difference. My question is what this means for truths behind veils. If Kofman discovers the Freud who reinvents truth—and if she mimics Freudianism—is there a Freudian mask she dons in *Enigma* such that there is no truth behind the veil—the veil of woman? There is, and it is at this point that Kofman's Freudian text merges with her Derridean mask where she is faithful to the Freud who, she argues, invents a new concept of truth. To conclude, then, what is enabling one element of Kofman's critique of Freud's account of women is the way in which she slips between texts she appropriates, her own readings, and identificatory figures: Freud, Derrida, Nietzsche. Kofman picks up the Freud who emerges from *Childhood*, the theorist of the logic of supplementarity, for whom "one is referred from construction to construction, from version to version, and from interpretation to interpretation without a nonexistent originary text ever being reached" (Kofman 1988c, 71).

In "Ça cloche," Kofman discusses the implications of this element in Freud for the substitutive economy of fetishism. Here, the Freud she discusses is specifically referenced as Derrida's Freud.[9] For one Freud, the uncomplicated Freud, the fetish substitutes for—stands in the place of—the original, missing penis. But there is another Freud, and Kofman grafts herself onto Derrida here with minor disagreements in interpretation,[10] a complicated Freud, this time relating to fetishism. We see the same argument we've seen in *Enigma*, that there is a lack or aporia at the heart of the unconscious substitutive economy, this time specifically relating to fetishism, since, for the complicated Freud (in fact, the Freud Derrida locates), the fetish does not substitute for an object but for a phantasmic supposition on the part of the child. Suggests Kofman:

> Such a description [of fetishism] breaks with traditional metaphysics, that is to say with the idea of the penis as "thing itself," since this implies a fetish imagined by the infant, a belief that implies both the denial and the affirmation of castration. There had never been a "thing itself," only an *Ersatz*, a prosthesis, an originary supplement to the panicked reaction of infantile narcissism. (Kofman 1989a, 122)

Slipping across Derrida and across Freud, for neither of whom femininity is interrogated in these terms at this point, Kofman poses the question of the consequences for "la violence sexuelle, la différence entre les sexes" (Kofman 1984b, 69). The same temporal logic that applies to fetishism applies to the "discovery" of women as "castrated." One notices that sometimes Freud writes as if women really are castrated, as if this is a fact, an anatomical difference discovered by children at a certain point (Kofman 1985a, 142–143, 173–174). For this Freud, there is a sudden discovery of a brute fact, anatomical sexual difference. Freud passes from what, for him, children imagine to saying that what he thinks they imagine is also a simple fact (142). Thus there is a Freud to whom Kofman directs the question, "*Who* establishes a simple qualitative difference between the girl and the boy here, between the clitoris and the penis? Children? Science? Freud?" (140).

This is the Freud Kofman will sometimes "analyze" and sometimes "complicate." In the guise of analyzing Freud, Kofman claims that Freud's theory of women's penis envy is the product of his own castration anxiety.[11] In the guise of complicating him, Kofman locates the Freud who also wants to say that there is no brute anatomical difference to "discover," but only the retroactive effects of interpretation and construction, which are overdetermined by the influence of cultural forces and conventions.

Throughout *The Enigma of Woman*, we find Kofman citing, in this vein, a Freud for whom childhood and adult ideas about castration are often the result of "deferred action" (Kofman 1985a, 180), a Freud who destabilizes the "time" of the discovery of castration and childhood Oedipal desire, a Freud for whom the oral, sadistic, and phallic trends directed toward the mother are often "obscure instinctual impulses which it was impossible for the child to grasp psychically at the time of their occurrence" (Freud 1931, 237–238, cited in Kofman 1985a, 159). Here Kofman's claim is that the mother's sex cannot be directly looked at or directly accessed by observation; it is always the product of retroactive construction.

For this Freud, then, there is no original significance as "castration" of the discovery of a woman's sex, but rather the time of what it will come, retrospectively, to "have meant." And for this Freud, there is no brute anatomical meaning to women's lack of a penis; there is no truth to woman, just as there is no original truth behind the veil of fetishism. Thus Freud is heterogeneous; he discovers and disavows a "new theory of truth."

Now Kofman patches in the Freud she has "analyzed" in pseudo-Freudian guise. She locates Freud's own castration anxiety in his theory of penis envy, a theory that she describes as Freud's own substitute fetish object. The theory of penis envy, she suggests, is a screen used by Freud to hold women at a distance, so that he won't have to examine them too closely. The theory of penis envy, then, is Freud's mask of blindness:

Penis envy is one of these "screen solutions" that serve as a cover-up. It is like that supplementary mask that Oedipus called for after daring to look upon the unfathomable depths of nature: the very mask of *blindness*. (Kofman 1985a, 95)

Consider the number of Freudian masks Kofman has grafted together and put into play by the time she attributes to Freud's concept of penis envy the status of the fetish substitute. One of her Freuds is the one who destabilizes the logical time of fetishism, such that fetishism does not substitute for an original meaning. For Kofman to attribute to penis envy the status of substitute fetish is to suggest that Freud's theory of penis envy substitutes for something that never takes place: in this case, the recognition of sexual difference. Kofman operatively moves between different positions enabled by heterogeneous Freuds. She grafts onto the Freud whose fetish is his theory of penis envy the Freud who discovers sexual difference, which for Kofman means the discovery that there is no "parallelism and symmetry between boys and girls" (Kofman 1985a, 137). She grafts this Freud onto the Freud who denies sexual difference, inventing a substitute fetish object to displace his impotence onto her.

The result? Kofman draws out of Freud himself the philosophical position that at the heart of the acknowledgment/disavowal of sexual difference there is no original truth. Women will never have come to be different, to be figured in terms of alterity, argues Kofman. There is nothing but the product of retrospective time, and so women will come to "have been" castrated. But it is a masculine economy—indeed, it is in this sense "Freud himself," claims Kofman—that castrated woman (Kofman 1985a, 82). There is nothing behind the veil of fetishism. Through the multiple Freuds Kofman has grafted together, she does not mean that fetishism conceals the "shocking discovery" of the absence of the mother's penis, but that Freud's own "fetish," his theory of penis envy, conceals his own exclusion of the possibility of representing sexual difference.

For Kofman, the simultaneous avowal and denial involved in fetishism takes place in Freud's work around the recognition of sexual difference. Freud recognizes sexual difference, but in giving a phallocentric account of femininity, he disavows it. It is not surprising, then, that woman is also represented by Freud as mysterious, resistant, evasive, and inaccessible (enigmatic), since Freud is both recognizing and disavowing a sexual difference that exceeds his phallocentric representation. For an uncomplicated Freud, the issue of fetishism turns on an original lack of an object, a penis. But for the Freud complicated by Kofman, Freud's own "fetishism" turns around the original (and retrospective) lack of a concept of sexual difference that would enable women not to be represented as "lacking."

To which Freud is Kofman faithful? Which Freud is she appropriating, which destabilizing? The curiosity of Kofman's work is how she manages to deploy a heterogeneous Freudianism in her mimetically Freudian reading of Freud on women. She mimics multiple Freuds: the Freud who invites us to penetrate the "real meaning" of a text through submitting it to an analytic interpretation and the Freud who argues that there only seems to be a "real" original meaning, that the supplement is original, and that an enigma does not hide a truth, not even the truth of woman. *Enigma* is faithful to Freud in offering a pseudo-Freudian "analysis" of Freud. It is also faithful in attending to what Freud enacts: the "discovery" of phallocentrically conceived sexual difference (Kofman 1985a, 21, 137). And it is faithful to the Freud who (for Kofman) reinvented truth and so discovers, *tel* Nietzsche, the lack of truth behind the veil of woman. Thus, in *Lectures de Derrida,* Kofman makes Freud slide, via "Freud and the Scene of Writing," into a Nietzschean figure: "The mystic writing pad is in communication with the Nietzschean representation of life as a woman whose name is Baubô" (Kofman 1984b, 65).[12]

In *The Enigma of Woman,* Kofman grafts Freud onto Nietzsche again:

> And even supposing that Freud wished to speak "among men" of the enigma of femininity (which is not the case) . . . , that would not suffice to condemn him as a "metaphysician." One might interpret that gesture, indeed, in a Nietzschean sense: to speak of a riddle of femininity and to try to solve that riddle are a strictly masculine enterprise; women are not concerned with Truth, they are profoundly skeptical; they know perfectly well that there is no such thing as "truth," that behind their veils there is yet another veil, and that try as one may to remove them, one after another, truth in its "nudity," like a goddess, will never appear. (Kofman 1985a, 104–105)

Kofman's analysis is made possible only by her operative slippage across (or grafting between) Derridean, Freudian, and Nietzschean texts. This methodology enables a reading of Freud's "enigma of woman" in which Kofman *destabilizes* the truth of the very concept she deploys in apparent fidelity to Freud: castration anxiety.

Sarah Kofman's Queasy Stomach and the Riddle of the Paternal Law

KELLY OLIVER

I n *The Enigma of Woman* Kofman is critical of Freud's insistence on defining feminine sexuality and motherhood within a phallic economy. And in her early work on Nietzsche she reads the figures of woman and maternity outside of Freud's Oedipal drama and his phallic economy. In some of her later work on Nietzsche, however, she takes her reader back to the heart of Freud's phallic economy and Oedipal drama, his family romance.[1] My diagnosis of this transition is intended as a challenge to the traditional Oedipal structure. I read the case of Kofman against Oedipus in order to complicate the roles traditionally assigned to maternal and paternal functions.

PENIS ENVY AND MATRICIDE

Implicit in Kofman's *The Enigma of Woman: Woman in Freud's Writings* is a diagnosis of the restrictive phallic economy within which Freud describes feminine sexuality and the mother. One of the central theses of this chapter is that penis envy is a screen solution that serves to cover up man's incestuous and matricidal desires. It is only with the theory of penis envy that Freud can explain how men come to desire women. In fact, Kofman maintains that without the theory of penis envy, heterosexuality in men is necessarily pathological, while fetishism and homosexuality are normal consequences of the horror that the boy experiences at the sight of his mother's genitals.

Freud asserts that boys feel horror at the sight of female genitals because of castration anxiety. In his essay "The 'Uncanny,'" he also indicates that "neurotic men declare that they feel there is something uncanny about the female genital organs" (Kofman 1985a, 82). Departing from Kofman's analysis, I have identified elsewhere the *heimlich* and yet *unheimlich* experience described by Freud as his fear of birth, his fear that because they were once part of their mothers' bodies, men may be feminine. The mother's genitals are uncanny, both *heimlich* and *unheimlich,* because they recall the boy's original home in his mother's womb. The womb is the origin of his life, but an identification with the maternal body threatens castration and ultimately death. The physical identification with the maternal womb threatens to take away that which makes him different from the mother. The image of a return to the womb also threatens death inasmuch as for Freud death is figured as a type of return to the womb of nature. For the boy, the mother's womb promises both life and death.

Kofman takes up the connection between the mother and death. She suggests that Freud attempts to sublimate death by sublimating the mother. She begins by analyzing Freud's dream of the Three Fates, in which, after going to bed tired and hungry, Freud dreams of three women in a kitchen. One of them is making dumplings and tells him that he will have to wait; he is impatient and tries to put on his overcoat to leave, but the coat is too long, its fur trim and embroidery is suspicious, and it seems to belong to another man. It is as if he denies his own femininity, represented by fur trim and embroidery, which must belong to another man; perhaps his own identification with, and desire for, his mother is frustrated in that she belongs to another man.

In his analysis of the dream, Freud identifies the woman making dumplings with his mother. His dream appears to him as the wish fulfillment of the basic need for food and love, which he claims come together in the mother's breast. In his analysis, however, no sooner is the maternal figure in his dream associated with love and nourishment than she becomes a messenger of death. Freud associates the dumpling-making hand motion with an experience from his childhood when his mother convinced him that everyone dies and returns to the earth by rubbing her hands together as if making dumplings, to show him the "blackish scales of *epidermis* produced by the friction as a proof that we are made of earth" (Freud 1967, 238).

In Kofman's analysis, Freud's dream becomes representative of maternal pedagogy, whose primary lessons are death and deferral. Since the mother is associated with nature and therefore silent, the maternal pedagogy is always only a visual pedagogy later made scientific through male articulation (Kofman 1985a, 76). Science, including psychoanalysis, has its origin in this maternal pedagogy. In Freud's dream, the mother tells him that he will have to wait, thus teaching him the lesson of deferred gratification.[2] He will have to wait for a mother substitute in order to fulfill his wish for the life-giving maternal breast that brings together love and nourishment. Next, the mother shows him that the gift of life has to be paid for with death, death in the hands of his mother.

Kofman interprets Freud's interpretation of his dream of the Three Fates as his attempt to master the mother and thereby master death. By translating or sublimating the mother/death into his scientific discourse, Freud tries to claim as his own the lessons learned from his maternal pedagogy and thereby assume the position of master. The mother remains a silent image associated with natural bodily needs that are later sublimated through the intervention of paternal agency into socially acceptable forms of communication and love. The relation with the maternal body is forbidden and dangerous. It is associated with a return to nature that threatens murder and death. To deny the maternal pedagogy, however, is to try to insist that one is born without a mother; it is to try to insist that one gives birth to oneself. To deny that the mother knows or teaches the lessons of science is to commit matricide. But, as Kofman asks, can the mother/death be sublimated? Can science "re-present" either the mother or death, either the experience of birth or the experience of death?

The sight of the mother's genitals awakens the fear of experiences over which the boy is not the master, the experiences of birth and death, and ultimately incestuous desires. Freud compares the mother's sex to Medusa's head. Man cannot bear the sight of Medusa's head; it turns him to stone. It scares him stiff. Freud claims that the fear is the result of castration anxiety. The boy sees that his mother has been castrated and fears that he will suffer the same fate, but the sight of his mother's sex also awakens sexual desires that reassure him that he has not been castrated. Like the sight of Medusa's head, the sight of the mother's sex causes the boy's own sex to turn to stone, which reassures him that he is not castrated the way she is.

Kofman argues that penis envy is what completes masculine sexuality. Only penis envy can guarantee that the boy has not suffered castration. If women, including the mother, envy his penis, it proves both that they don't have one and that he does. It proves that women are castrated and men aren't. The sight of women's "castrated" genitals actually proves that man is not castrated. Kofman once again invokes Medusa:

> Penis envy, one might say, plays the same role as the hair on Medusa's head, so often represented by serpents substituted for the penis, the absence of which is the essential cause of horror. Penis envy is seen as equivalent in a way to the symbolic multiplication of man's penis. And if horror in the face of woman's genital organs always has as its *apotropaic* counterpart the erection of the male organ . . . we can then understand how what was *supposed* to draw man away from woman is always at the same time what brings him closer to her. (Kofman 1985a, 85, my emphasis)

Yet penis envy is merely a screen solution to Freud's more fundamental problem, incestuous desire for the mother and resulting matricide. Kofman suggests that the enigma of woman leads Freud back to the mother, but he stops short of uncovering the mother when he maintains that female sexuality is the bedrock and limit of psychoanalysis (Kofman 1985a, 94). Kofman claims that "to respond 'truly' to the riddle of female sexuality would have been in one way or another to dis-cover the mother, to commit incest" (94). Freud avoids revealing the mother by setting up screens to cover her nakedness, to cover her sex, not because of castration anxiety but because of incestuous and matricidal anxieties. Kofman suggests that unlike Oedipus, who uncovers his mother's sex and satisfies his incestuous desires (which lead to Jocasta's suicide), Freud cannot face the maternal sex because of his incestuous desires and his fear of *her* death (94–95). So he tries to sublate his incestuous desire into a desire for scientific research on sexuality, which leaves the fundamental riddle of feminine sexuality unanswered. The enigma of Freud's work is the way in which he devises complicated theories with which to *protect* his mother from death by castrating and killing her.

Taking Kofman's analysis one more turn, we can say that Freud learns too well the maternal lesson that the gift of life must be repaid with death. For he repays his mother's gift of life with death; he sacrifices her out of gratitude. He kills her so that she won't die. In a sense, by defining her in terms of a masculine phallic economy, the economy of the son, he tries to kill her off before he is born so that he won't have to love her and leave her, so that she won't leave him. He gives birth to himself out of the phallic economy that motivates the Oedipal drama and his family romance. Implicit in Kofman's criticism is the belief that Freud might have found a better way to repay his mother for the gift of life, and to protect her from his own incestuous desires, than castrating her and killing her.

But within the phallic economy, castration, fetishism, or matricide are the only alternatives. Either the boy admits the mother's castration and suffers castration himself by continuing to identify with her or he denies that she is castrated and puts fetishes, penis substitutes, in the place of her missing organ, which allows him to identify with a phallic mother. Or he denies any identification with the mother and commits matricide. Kofman suggests that insofar as the mother is defined within a phallic economy, matricide is unavoidable. In some of her early work on Nietzsche, Kofman presents an alternative to the castration, fetishism, or matricide entailed by Freud's phallic economy.

FETISHISM OR HAVING IT BOTH WAYS

In *Nietzsche et la scène philosophique* Kofman reads Nietzsche's Dionysus as an undecidable figure who "crosses himself out ('se rature') of the distinction between the veiled and unveiled, masculine and feminine, fetishism and castration" (Kofman 1988a, 198). Kofman relies on a passage from *The Gay Science* in which Nietzsche says, "Perhaps truth is a woman who has reasons for not letting us see her reasons? Perhaps her name is—to speak Greek—Baubô?" (Kofman 1974, 38). Baubô makes Demeter, the goddess of fertility, laugh by pulling up her skirts and showing Demeter a drawing of Dionysus on her belly. Kofman says:

> Whenever a woman lifts her skirts, she provokes laughter and flight, such that this gesture can be used as an *apotropaic* means. The belly of the woman plays the role of the head of Medusa. By lifting her skirts, was not Baubô suggesting that she go and frighten Hades, or that which comes to the same, recall fecundity to herself? By displaying the figure of Dionysus on her belly, she recalls the eternal return of life. (Kofman 1988a, 196–197, my emphasis)

Baubô represents fecundity and the eternal return of life. She is the female double of Dionysus (197).

Dionysus is both male and female but cannot be reduced to either one or the other. He is beyond this metaphysical distinction (197). He skirts both castration and fetishism by refusing to commit to the phallic economy of truth where it either is there or is not. He prefers masks and does not pretend to uncover or cover the secrets of nature/woman. Kofman identifies Nietzsche with Dionysus when she maintains that Nietzsche's reversal of the platonic notions of unchanging and changing is not only a reversal but also a challenge to this oppositional way of thinking (187). Nietzsche calls dogmatism into question and asserts perspectivism, which, according to Kofman, he can do only because he sees from a dual perspective, "having inherited from his father and his mother opposing evaluations" (187). Like Dionysus, "he is always his own double" (187).

Kofman suggests that by having it both ways, Nietzsche/Dionysus can give birth to himself without killing off the mother; rather, he gives birth to himself through his identification with her fertility. By having it both ways, he does not have to suffer castration nor set up fetishes as penis substitutes in order to identify with his mother.[3] He is his mother and his father. As Nietzsche says in *Ecce Homo:*

> The good fortune of my existence, its uniqueness perhaps, lies in its fatality: I am, to express it in the form of a riddle, already dead as my father, while as my mother I am still living and becoming old. This dual descent[,] as it were, forms both the highest and the lowest rung on the ladder of life. . . . I know both, I am both. (Nietzsche 1992, 222)

Appealing to Nietzsche's dual legacy again in her later work on him, *Explosion I: De l' "Ecce Homo" de Nietzsche,* Kofman prefers to read a later passage from *Ecce Homo* in which Nietzsche declares, "I consider it a great privilege to have had such a father: it seems to me that this explains whatever else I have of privileges—*not* including life, the great Yes to life" (Kofman 1992, 226). Relying on numerous passages in which Nietzsche identifies his mother with rabble, baseness, and decadence, Kofman concludes that the "venom" that Nietzsche "spits" at his mother indicates that he does not think that the privilege of life and the great Yes to life come from her. In Kofman's *Explosion I,* this Yes to life becomes Nietzsche's way to overcome his decadent mother and give birth to himself through his identification with his paternal morbidity. Kofman says that "a privilege is a right accorded to the nobility and to it alone: paradoxically, the source of Nietzsche's noble distinction is identified as paternal morbidity" (Kofman 1994a, 37).

Given the fact that Kofman reads Nietzsche's *Ecce Homo* as a family romance true to Freud's, it should not seem paradoxical that Nietzsche's nobility is his paternal morbidity (Kofman 1994a, 39). After all, Oedipus only becomes king by killing his father. Kofman explains that Nietzsche's horror at his mother is the flip side of an incestuous love (43).[4] He denies his incestuous desires by committing matricide. Kofman suggests that through his Dionysian version of the eternal return, Nietzsche imagines a selective return of active principles and difference that would exclude the return of rabble, baseness, and decadence; it excludes the return of the mother. In fact, she maintains that it is Nietzsche's horror at the idea of the eternal return of his mother that makes him recoil from the idea of the eternal return of the same and invent the idea of the eternal return of difference.

Kofman points to an early version of *Thus Spoke Zarathustra* in which Nietzsche associates the idea of the eternal return of the same with Medusa's head. Like Medusa's head, the concepts of the eternal return of the mother, the mother's sex, and incestuous desire turn men to stone. Kofman says, "This capital concept would threaten to decapitate Nietzsche if he did not defend himself immediately through the erection of another head, that of Dionysus, which functions *apotropaically*" (Kofman 1994a, 45, my emphasis). Only Dionysus, whose festivals include a celebration of the phallus, can displace Medusa and the fear of castration that she conjures.

On Kofman's reading, Nietzsche disassociates himself from his decadent maternal genealogy, and from an identification with the castrating mother, by substituting economic metaphors for a biological hypothesis (Kofman 1994a, 48). The eternal return is not the return of biological destiny in some historical cycle; rather, it acts as a principle of selection through which the great individual is born from "an accumulation of energy necessitating the buildup of capital that will burst forth or explode all the more strongly for the time it is kept in check" (49). Kofman says that "the individual undergoes a process of accumulation and selection that permits him to mature into himself, just as the accumulation and selection of forces over the course of time permit the coming into maturity, the explosion, of great men. . . . The great man is an outcome and an end point, and . . . a long work of accumulation was necessary for his coming" (49).

Although Kofman does not say as much, her analysis suggests that Nietzsche gives up his maternal genealogy, his biological destiny, in favor of a masculine genealogy through which he can give birth to himself. His self-birth is possible as the result of the sublimation of sexual energy, an accumulation of force that ends in an explosion where all that has been stored up bursts forth and the great man has come into himself. In this way, Kofman's Nietzsche, unlike Kofman's Freud, finds a way to insist that he is born without a mother; he can give birth to himself and avoid castration and fetishism, if not matricide. Kofman's Freud loves his mother too much to uncover her as the object of his desire, to uncover the key to the riddle of feminine sexuality, to uncover the possibility of maternal sexuality; unlike Oedipus, he refuses to answer the riddle of femininity and prefers to cover up his incestuous/matricidal desires with scientific theories. Kofman's

Nietzsche, on the other hand, the Nietzsche of her *Explosion I* and *Explosion II,* covers up his incestuous desires with hateful matricidal desires and a theory that denies his connection to his mother.

MOTHERS' SONS

In the case of both Freud and Nietzsche, by identifying them as sons of mothers, Kofman displaces her own paternal inheritance and debt to, or identification with, philosophical fathers. Instead she doubles their patronymics by creating a maternal genealogy, incestuous and matricidal though it may be. Compare Kofman's analysis of Freud and Nietzsche in relation to the mother to her interpretation of Oscar Wilde's *Picture of Dorian Gray* in "The Imposture of Beauty" (Chapter 1 in this volume). Once again Kofman positions the male object of her analysis as the son of a mother.

Here, Kofman reads Dorian's morbid solution to his inability to mourn his mother as his identification with her beauty. Dorian is sure that "he has inherited his beauty from his mother alone—a beauty that is utterly pagan and Dionysian, described as that of a bacchante affirming the sensuality and cheerfulness of life, the beauty of a loving mother who protected him with her smile" (see Chapter 1). In order to protect his protectress from the condemnation of his paternal grandfather and from the ravages of decay and death, Dorian incorporates her into his ideal of himself. He projects all of her sins and decay, along with his own, onto the painting so that he/she can remain eternally young and beautiful. He protects her love for him by making her into himself.

If, however, we go one step beyond Kofman's analysis, we could say that Dorian incorporates his mother, makes her into himself, in order to give birth to himself. He identifies with his mother and tries to save her from death in order to save himself from death. Kofman suggests that like Christ, Dorian takes on the wounds of his mother. In fact, she says that "art performs an inversion: it displays the bleeding body of the Son so as better to hide that of the mother, as if the Son, in order to 'save' the mother, were taking her wounds on himself" (Chapter 1). More than this, according to Kofman, the body is wounded not as the result of immorality and sin but as the result of morality and the mutilation of the passions.

Kofman's text hints that the passion of Christ is a screen for the mother's passion, a Dionysian passion too terrifying to view head-on. Behind the paternal Apollonian masks that reinscribe maternity and childbirth onto the male body and masculine psyche lies a creative force too powerful to imagine. Dorian Gray is not strong enough to look upon the face of the

Dionysian maternal force: "Though his mother was able to be a bacchante, following in the train of Dionysus, he himself is not really beautiful or strong enough to truly affirm life, to dare to reveal himself and look at himself naked. His fragility forces him to become an impostor and to hide behind the protecting mask of youth and beauty" (Chapter 1). The mother's face is the face that we can't face.

The riddle or enigma of Kofman's writing is why the trajectory of her work seems to lead both toward and away from the mother. Why does Kofman work so hard to leave the Oedipal model and family romance behind in her earlier work and embrace them so vigorously in some of her later work? Why does she both criticize and sympathize with Freud's refusal to confront the enigma of woman head-on as the enigma of the mother? Why, in her earlier work, does she praise Nietzsche's criticisms of the pervert's lack of respect for women's modesty, which he avoids through his dual genealogy, and then insist in her later work, in spite of passages to the contrary, that Nietzsche breaks with his maternal genealogy in favor of paternal morbidity?

Kofman seems fascinated with the figure of enigma or riddle in the texts that she analyzes. Her work on Freud and Nietzsche often touches on their enigmas and riddles. Her strategy is to identify what operates as an apotropaic figure or concept in their work. An apotropaic figure is one that displaces another or turns away in an attempt to avert evil. Kofman maintains that Freud's notion of penis envy operates apotropaically to displace the horror of the mother's sex; in Nietzsche, Baubô's stomach operates apotropaically to displace Hades' appropriation of fertility; and Dionysus' head operates apotropaically to displace Medusa or the mother's sex. In what way might Kofman's turning from the mother to the father in her later work on Nietzsche be an apotropaic move? Does the figure of the father function apotropaically in order to displace the mother? Is the figure of the father an enigma that covers up the mother? Or might the rejection of the mother cover up the rejection of the paternal law?

To begin to think through this enigma of Kofman's work, we might turn back to her reading of the enigma of Ariadne in Nietzsche's *Ecce Homo*. In *Explosion I*, Kofman, in passing, asserts that Nietzsche possesses the key to the enigma of Ariadne because he is the only one who has suspected that there is any enigma and that the key is Dionysus' suffering (Kofman 1994a, 47). The answer to Ariadne's riddle is Dionysus' suffering. Her riddle is an apotropaic figure for his suffering. Yet in the passage from *Ecce Homo* cited by Kofman, Dionysus' suffering is never explicitly linked to Ariadne's riddle. Nietzsche begins the section by identifying his writing with the suffering god Dionysus, then talks about possible redemption from nausea and riddles, and finally concludes with the exhortation to "become hard," because Dionysian creativity is hard. Against Kofman's reading, then, the key to Ariadne's riddle could be Dionysian hardness.[5]

Nietzsche suggests that *Ariadne is the answer to Dionysian solitude and suffering* and that only he knows what Ariadne is. Kofman reverses the riddle, saying that *Dionysus' suffering is the answer to the riddle of Ariadne.* In this section of *Explosion I,* Kofman reads Dionysus as a father figure who operates apotropaically to displace Medusa, the horrifying maternal sex. So the key to the riddle of Ariadne is the suffering of the father, Dionysus. In Kofman's reading, the father's suffering replaces his hardness, his phallic law, and this paternal suffering displaces the abject maternal body. For Kofman, it seems, the paternal is associated with suffering and compassion, which offer salvation from, and an answer to, the riddle of femininity (Ariadne), while the maternal is associated with the hardness of a law that threatens death.

Kofman seems to have identified with Nietzsche, perhaps with his suffering, perhaps with his dual genealogy. She wrote at least four volumes on his work. She committed suicide on the 150th anniversary of his birth. Like Nietzsche, she was sick most of her life, suffering from digestive problems from the time of her early childhood, and she lost her father when she was young. Might Kofman identify with what she calls Nietzsche's "fantastic genealogy"? Or perhaps her identification with Nietzsche, and her philosophical fathers, is her own fantastic genealogy, her own family romance, through which she attempts to give birth to herself.

In one of the last works published before her death, *Rue Ordener, rue Labat,* Kofman describes the experience of losing her father during the Nazi occupation of France. She begins her autobiographical essay:

> From him, only his pen remains with me. . . . I have used it during all of my scholarly work. It gave out on me before I could decide to abandon it. I have it in my possession always, fixed with Scotch tape, it is before my eyes on my work table and it compels ["contraint"] me to write, write. My numerous books have maybe been inevitable (or obligatory) ["obligées"] routes in order to reach the point to tell "it" ["ça"]. (Kofman 1994d, 9)

Her father's pen compels her to write; she writes from her paternal obligation. And all that she has written has been leading up to telling this story, the story of her father's death and her relationship with her mother during the war. Her writing obliges her to tell this story.

MATERNITY AND PATERNITY SPLIT
BETWEEN TWO MOTHERS

On July 16, 1942, Sarah Kofman's father, Rabbi Bereck Kofman, was taken from his Paris apartment by the police and never returned. Later, they heard that he was beaten with an ax by a "Jewish butcher" in Auschwitz and buried alive. During the war, Sarah's mother hid her and her five siblings with families in the country. Kofman tells the story of her refusal to eat pork, which she describes as an unconscious obedience to the paternal law as a pretext for returning to her mother: "This refusal[,] which appears as the pretext of obedience to the paternal law, comes also, without being completely conscious, to serve as a means to return me to the house, close to my mother" (Kofman 1994d, 30). Her obedience to the paternal law, which she calls earlier a "supplice paternal" (paternal burden), is practiced for the sake of the mother. For, as she says, "Le vrai danger: être séparée de ma mère" (the true danger: to be separated from my mother) (33).

Sarah returned to her mother and continued, now consciously, to use the obedience to the paternal law, refusing to eat, throwing up, along with crying, in order to remain with her mother. After hiding in various places in Paris, Sarah and her mother ended up staying with a former neighbor of the Kofman family who had moved two metro stops away to Rue Labat. Sarah called this woman, who became a second mother to her, "Mémé" (the English equivalent is something like "Grandma"). Kofman describes how she turned away from her mother and Judaism and became attached to Mémé. By the end of the war, Sarah preferred to stay with Mémé than be with her mother, who had become intensely jealous of Mémé's attentions to Sarah. Mémé introduced Sarah to new books, a new religion, a new diet, new clothes. In the street, Sarah passed as her daughter to avoid the Nazis. Out of her mouth, Sarah first heard of philosophy and various philosophers in the context of Mémé's anti-Semitic remarks about Judaism and Jews. After the war, Sarah's mother struggled violently to keep Sarah away from Mémé. And even though she loved Mémé or was in love with her, Sarah was relieved when, in spite of a court order that gave custody of Sarah to Mémé, her mother took her away.

Kofman says that after she testified against her mother in court, she felt as if she had committed a crime and was "wanted"; she uses the word "recherchée," which was the word used to refer to the Jews who were being sought by the Nazis. She describes feeling ashamed of preferring Mémé to her mother (Kofman 1994d, 55). Sarah felt guilty for abandoning her mother for another woman. She felt hunted by the Nazis because of her hatred for, and disobedience to, her mother. She felt guilty of loving (desiring) another more than her own mother. Yet she continued a clandestine relationship with Mémé until Mémé's death.

Toward the end of *Rue Ordener, rue Labat*, Kofman compares her relationships to her mother and Mémé, her two mothers, to two works of art: a da Vinci painting and an Alfred Hitchcock film. Da Vinci's painting "Carton de Londres" depicts the infant Christ with the Virgin Mary and St. Anne. Kofman quotes Freud's analysis of the painting at length. Freud maintains that the painting reflects the fact that da Vinci's stepmother replaces his real mother in his heart. The Hitchcock film *The Lady Vanishes* presents a more complicated comparison. Kofman says that this is one of her favorite films because of the visceral anxiety she experiences when the "good 'maternal' face of the old woman" on the train is replaced with the hard and threatening face of another woman, "the bad breast in the place of the good breast[,] . . . the one transforming itself into the other" (Kofman 1994d, 76–77). In the course of *Rue Ordener*, Kofman's mother undergoes a similar transformation. She begins as the mother without whom Sarah cannot live and will not eat, and she becomes the hard and threatening mother who beats Sarah and with whom she cannot live and will not eat. Mémé becomes the good mother, the desirable mother, close to whom Sarah experiences unfamiliar sensations in her body.

Several times Kofman describes her turning away from her mother and her turning away from Judaism as parts of one movement. She associates the law of her father with her mother, and just as she obeys the law in order to be close to her mother, she abandons the law as she abandons her mother. Compare the example of the Red Cross that Tina Chanter discusses in Chapter 11 of this volume: in an autobiographical essay, Kofman describes a time during the war when there was very little to eat and her family was on a train to Brittany. The Red Cross was distributing hot chocolate and ham and butter sandwiches. "'Don't eat that,' said my mother. 'Let the children eat,' my father intervened; 'it's wartime.' The ham and butter, once decreed impure, I found delicious, now purified by circumstances and paternal authority" (Kofman 1986a, 8). Here her mother is the voice of paternal law, while her father, through his paternal authority, is beyond the ritual protection of the paternal law. Her father's authority purifies, but her mother's contaminates.

She rejects her mother and the religion that she says she always found frightening and burdensome, the religion that keeps her mother prisoner on Rue Labat during the war and makes it necessary for her to hide. She says that the true danger is to be separated from her mother, because with her mother she is "saved." But she discovers that at the hands of the Nazis her mother cannot keep her safe; her mother becomes associated with danger. Her mother becomes the true danger. Mémé is the one who keeps her safe. Kofman ends her autobiographical essay with Mémé's death; in the last line of the essay, she tells a story recounted to her by the priest at Mémé's funeral: on Mémé's tomb it is written that she had saved a little Jewish girl during the war.

Like Kofman's Freud, Kofman both kills her mother and saves her by writing her story. Like Kofman's Nietzsche, Kofman associates her mother with everything that drags her down and keeps her from herself. And like Kofman's Nietzsche, who identifies with the suffering of his father-god, Dionysus, Kofman identifies with her father's suffering, which compels her to write. Like Nietzsche, her creative inheritance is her paternal morbidity.

Kofman's ambivalence toward her mother, and the split that she experiences between the good mother and the bad mother in *Rue Ordener*, might help to frame the enigma of the mother in Kofman's work and Kofman's fascination with the ambivalent maternal in both Freud and Nietzsche. Rather than identify with her abject mother, who, in both her good and bad forms, becomes associated with the pain of the war, Kofman identifies with her philosophical fathers. Whereas during the war, obedience to the law of her father threatened her safety but also returned her to her mother, obedience to her philosophical fathers provides a world safe from her mother. As Tina Chanter points out in Chapter 11, Kofman is caught between maternal and paternal authority. Her work is a display of the ambivalent position of woman in patriarchy; she must both deny and accept the paternal law.

Kofman's mother becomes associated with the paternal prohibitions, while her father is associated with suffering and sacrifice. He does not hide; he gives himself up. He is murdered for praying instead of working on the Sabbath. For Kofman, her father's pure relationship to the rites of his religion turns religion into art and law into morality, while her mother's relationship, sullied by the compromises of war and undermined by Mémé's anti-Semitism, turns the rites of religion into dangerous convention and arbitrary prohibition.

MIXED MESSAGES: TO EAT OR NOT TO EAT

I will conclude with a riddle of my own: what happens when the mother becomes a representative of paternal prohibition, when the separation from the mother is not the result of paternal prohibition, but the rejection of the paternal prohibition results in the separation from the mother? Can Kofman's fidelity to Freud's family romance actually help us to think about familial relations outside of the Freudian Oedipal model? I suspect that clues can be found in the stomach.

Recall Freud's dream of the Three Fates, which he describes as a wish fulfillment for the mother's breast, the place where love and nourishment meet. In his dream, nourishment associated with his mother, the dumplings, becomes a visual aid in the lesson of death. Like the dried dumpling dough, we turn to the earth. We become what we eat, flakes of dough. The dream that Freud interprets as a wish for the connection between food and love is really a dream about the connection between food and death. The mother is the link between food and love and between food and death. How can she be both what makes food love and what makes food death? How does she go from the good, nourishing maternal breast that Kofman associates with the kindly Miss Froy in Hitchcock's film *The Lady Vanishes* to the bad, threatening maternal breast?

It might seem that this transition can be explained with Freud's theories on how the infant separates from the mother: the transition from good to bad breast is a necessary step in weaning the child. But Kofman's case is not so simple. In fact, this case challenges Freud's notion of feminine identity. For Freud, the girl separates from her mother when, realizing that her mother is castrated and she too is castrated, she blames her mother. In the end, she identifies with her mother in the hopes that her father will give her a baby, which is now the symbolic instantiation for her missing penis. In Kofman's case, however, the girl refuses an identification with her mother in order to separate herself from her father and, in the end, identifies with her father.

At this point, it might seem that what we have is a girl who moves through the masculine Oedipal situation, refusing an identification with her mother and identifying with her father in the hope that someday she will have her mother or mother substitute as a love object. Yet in this case the prohibited mother becomes identified with the prohibition itself. The move away from the mother is at the same time a move away from the paternal prohibition. Rather than accept the paternal prohibition in the hope of receiving a mother substitute, Sarah rejects the paternal prohibition to receive her mother substitute, Mémé, with whom she identifies and whom she desires. Desire and identification are not the polar opposites that Freud describes.[6]

Food prohibitions are common in most cultures. Some things can be eaten and some should not be eaten. These prohibitions are usually prescribed on a cultural level through various paternal institutions such as churches, temples and other religious institutions, schools, health departments, and doctors' offices. But on the level of everyday life, they are enforced by maternal "institutions" involved in the food preparation and care of domestic life. It is not merely that these maternal institutions represent paternal authority or paternal regulation. Rather, control over the everyday practices of food preparation and dietary regulation invests the maternal with an authority that exceeds the paternal sanctions and prohibitions.

Yet if we take seriously Julia Kristeva's analysis of food prohibitions in *Powers of Horror* (1982), we see that when the mother enforces the paternal law in the kitchen, she is in an ambiguous position. Just as her commandment to eat while denying certain foods presents a riddle for the child, her position as the enforcer of paternal law is itself riddled with contradictions. Kristeva maintains that food prohibitions are always ultimately prohibitions against the maternal body. Prohibitions against the maternal body become ritualized and symbolized through religious food prohibitions. This means that mothers who are enforcing paternal law in their kitchens are enforcing a prohibition against their own bodies. In fact, the authority of the mother to enforce the paternal prohibitions is an authority that comes from her body. Thus, the maternal body is used in the service of a paternal law that outlaws the very body whose authority is invoked in order to enforce the law.

Kofman's life and work point to this impossible maternal body that sacrifices itself for the sake of a paternal law that demands matricide. Within this perverse patriarchal economy—the economy that demands that Freud kill his mother so that she won't die, that Nietzsche kill his mother so that he won't become her, and that Dorian Gray incorporate his mother to save her from death—the mother has to kill herself in order to get any recognition from a paternal law that demands her death through incorporation. Suicide seems the only act of self-assertion left for women within the restrictive confines of Freud's family romance (think of Jocasta) and patriarchy's fantastic genealogy that insists on the death of the mother so that the philosopher can give birth to himself.

The riddle of Sarah Kofman and her work, then, can be read as a tension between paternal and maternal authority. Her life and her work operate to displace the Freudian scenario, with its paternal active law and maternal passive deference. Indeed, even as she employs Freud's myth of the family romance in her analysis of Nietzsche, she exploits it. With Kofman, the Oedipal scenario can no longer explain sexual identity or sexual desire. Freud's riddle of femininity is riddled with Kofman's enigmatic mixing of maternal and paternal functions. Kofman's fidelity to her philosophical fathers has as its apotropaic counterpart her resistance to a paternal law that requires matricide and her own fantastic maternal genealogy that insists on turning her philosophical fathers into sons of mothers.

CHAPTER ELEVEN

Eating Words: Antigone as
Kofman's Proper Name

TINA CHANTER

Philippe Lacoue-Labarthe's "The Caesura of the Speculative"
(1989) is merely a dress rehearsal for an event that puts to the test the
idea that Antigone is at once the most Greek and the most modern of
tragedies. The event has spawned another text: spinning off on an angled
trajectory from the performance, Sarah Kofman begins her review of the
performance—a collaboration between Lacoue-Labarthe and Michel
Deutsch, performed on June 15 and 30, 1978, in Strasbourg—by re-
marking on the ceremony, the "ritual" preparations of theatergoing: the
architectural conventions of theaters, the classical style of the stage, the

I am grateful to Ewa Ziarek at the Department of English of Notre Dame University for inviting me to present this paper in March 1997 and to members of the Philosophy Department
at Vanderbilt University for inviting me to the "Styles of Piety" conference, also in March
1997. I am especially grateful to Joan Copjec of the comparative literature program at the
University of Buffalo, New York, for organizing the "Around Antigone: Psychoanalysis, Literature, and Film" conference in April 1997. The conference provided me with the impetus
for the paper and with the opportunity to revisit the figure of Antigone. A longer version of
this paper appears in *Differences, Eating and Disorder*, 9:2 (Summer 1997).

evening dress of the spectators—in short, the traditions that facilitate catharsis. "When you go to the theater," she says, in a remark that calls to mind Lacan's observations to the contrary, "you come to find [a way] of 'forgetting,' for the time of the spectacle, your daily cares" (Kofman 1978b, 1143); for Lacan it is the reverse: "When you go to the theater in the evening, you are preoccupied by the affairs of the day, by the pen that you lost, by the check that you will have to sign the next day." But, he adds, "You don't have to worry; even if you don't feel anything, the Chorus will feel in your stead." For Lacan, "The emotional commentary is done for you. The greatest chance for the survival of the classical tragedy depends on that" (Lacan 1992, 252).

Such a possibility is not admitted in Kofman's review of the 1978 production of *Antigone*, which is also a reading of Lacoue-Labarthe's "The Caesura of the Speculative." As theater critic and philosopher, a combination that fuses the two functions of dramaturgy and theory that Lacoue-Labarthe sees as inseparable for Hölderlin too, Kofman makes good on the suggestion that "this Greek tragedy par excellence, translated (repeated, rewritten), by Hölderlin, . . . is also, *as* tragedy, the most modern it could be" (Kofman 1978b, 1147). The production makes no pretense of being simply Greek: the scenic device uses "three languages, three rhythms, three epochs." The French does not eclipse the German or the Greek any more than the twentieth century encompasses the eighteenth century—in the style of which the actors dress—or ancient Greece, whose syntax is preserved along with "the infinite distance separating Hölderlin from the Greeks and distancing us from Hölderlin" (Kofman 1978b, 1147). Familiar with Hölderlin's poetic meditations on the near and the distant—and echoing Lacoue-Labarthe (cf. Lacoue-Labarthe 1989, 231)—Kofman does not hesitate to add that this distance does not exclude "extreme proximity" (Kofman 1978a, 1147) and to observe that neither Hölderlin nor Lacoue-Labarthe were ignorant of the "bankruptcy," the "untranslatability," of all translation, a lapse presented in the "interval" separating us from Hölderlin, and Hölderlin from Sophocles.

This separation, this interval marking off our modernity from Hölderlin's, and Hölderlin's Greek modernity from Sophocles' Greece, is taken up in a highly specific form by Kofman. If it is prepared for in some measure by Lacoue-Labarthe's affirmation of Girard's view that Hölderlin's "obstinate and oppressive questioning ('at the doors of madness') concerning tragedy and mimesis cannot be dissociated from his *biography*" (Lacoue-Labarthe 1989, 223), this endorsement of the relationship between the poet's encounter with the speculative and his life crisis does not anticipate the particular nature of the biographical crisis to which Kofman will, indirectly, allude. The allusion is made most directly in the paragraph immediately following this summary statement of the Greek modernity of *Antigone:* "*Antigone* is at once a Greek tragedy and a modern tragedy; it neither invents new tragic forms nor reconstitutes Sophocles' tragedy as it is. This is why the fragility of 'ruins,' of dilapidation, menaces you at every instant" (Kofman 1978b, 1147).

Kofman describes the "disused arsenal, a true military *ruin*" (Kofman 1978b, 1145), in which the production was staged and the impression that the building—"destined for imminent demolition"—gives of being in a "shantytown" (1145): the "charred walls, the broken windows[,] . . . the rubble" of the terrain that is reminiscent of a "house bombed in the last war" (1145–1146). She describes the "dilapidated stairs" that replace the "marble stairway" of more conventional theatergoing and the "rails" the audience is constrained to hold as they enter an "infernal world"—a "chthonic, nocturnal world," a "sinister space in which death roams, a death which would not be 'recovered' by some dialectical sublimation" (1146). She describes the debris that litters the stage, providing the setting for "the body of a soldier, Polynices," and then the reference toward which, one sees at once, this description has been leading: writing of the opening scene of the performance, Kofman says, "Antigone informs her sister of her wish to bury the brother she loves so much, Polynices who is outside the law. And perhaps because the 'plot' takes place in an attic, you think about Anne Frank, about all the Jewish women constrained to hide, to live clandestinely to survive the infernal night. And you think that a Greek tragedy thus *translated* can still today concern you" (1146).

The reference exposes the inadequacy of a theory of tragedy that constitutes the power and force of dialectical philosophy by "rendering tolerable the intolerable" (Kofman 1978b, 1144). Here, instead of providing a "*transfiguration* in *spectacle* of all that provokes horror and terror in 'real' life"; in place of "rendering supportable, and even agreeable[,] what cannot ordinarily be regarded head-on"; instead of "purifying the intolerable, making death *economic*" (1145), the theater exposes the audience to an abyss. If you are unlucky enough to be seated in the front row, Kofman reports, "during the whole spectacle your legs [would be] suspended in emptiness" (Kofman 1978b, 1147): "You are despite everything in a theater, but in a theater which opens onto an abyss, a gulf, a pit (this is where Antigone will descend to be enclosed forever in 'the obscure darkness of a crypt,' in this subterranean dwelling which will serve as a tomb and her wedding bed)" (1146–1147).

The dislocation effected by this "wholly other scenic space," (Kofman 1978b, 1145) as Kofman describes it, breaks with the "cathartic project" that Lacoue-Labarthe reads into the very tradition of German idealism that sought to distance itself from catharsis. Not that—as Lacoue-Labarthe points out repeatedly in relation to Hölderlin—the logic of the speculative is ever entirely broken: "A cathartic project commands the enterprise still, [but] it aims this time not to procure a *catharsis* through the speculative or the spectacular, but a *catharsis* of the speculative itself. By means of a certain caesura" (1145). This is a "place which singularly *displaces* the 'theater' . . . in the *space of the caesura,* which breaks [up] 'representation,' troubles it and singularly dislocates it" (1146).

KOFMAN'S IDENTIFICATION WITH ANTIGONE'S BURIAL RITUAL

A great deal more could be said about the operation by which the speculative is broken, fissured, rendered aporetic (only to be taken up again). But I want to pursue a biographical thread that will lead us away from this particular text, before returning us to it, making way for another cameo appearance that Antigone makes in an autobiographical text by Kofman—if not by name or direct representation, by an unmistakable image.

The text is a brief one, titled "Tomb for a Proper Name," in which Kofman relates a dream she had. In the dream, she reads on the cover of a book:

KAFKA
translated by
Sar . . . Ko(a)f . . .

Why, she wonders, had she become the translator of Kafka? She notices how, by associating the letter "o" with "a," the dream produces an "affinity between my name and Kafka's." She interprets the dream in terms of her shame about her proper name. This elision is an attempt to "reestablish what is held to be the correct way of writing my *proper* name" (Kofman 1986a, 9). She explains, parenthetically, *"The error of a city hall employee, which always delighted me, had distinguished Kofman from Kaufman, more common; and from Kaufmann, which can't help but suggest commerce, money, shit ['caca'], the Jew"* (9).[1] "Kof," she goes on, reminds her of "Ko(p)f" (head): "It allows me to bear a quite proper name, my head held high." And yet, since the proper name is that of a Jew, this " 'incorrect' spelling dissimulates what is low and dirty" (9).

She notices now that the last syllables of her name are omitted, observing that in Hebrew "ah" designates the feminine, while Man, Mann, designates the masculine. And now—this is where Antigone makes her cameo appearance—she asks, "Isn't the cutting 'elision' the equivalent of a double castration, punishment for the one who meant to deny her blood, to erase her lowly origins, to hold her head high?" (Kofman 1986a, 10). Antigone also suffered a double blow, being born of the incestuous union of Oedipus and Jocasta and being deprived of her mother, who committed suicide on discovering the true identity of her husband/son. Antigone will, like her mother, commit suicide—a fate she also shares with Kofman. But unlike Antigone, who never once denied her blood ties to Polynices and who from the beginning of the tragedy speaks out about her "lowly origins," Kofman's dream expresses her guilt for not wanting to admit to her true identity.

If Antigone speaks of her suffering repeatedly, from the opening lines of the play ("There's nothing grievous, nothing free from doom, not shameful, not dishonored, I've not seen"), Kofman's true identity is one that she was required to keep hidden.[2] The fact that—rightly or wrongly—Kafka, author of *The Trial,* has been proclaimed "the prophet of the Holocaust" (Langer 1996, 109) might help to explain Kofman's dream that she translated Kafka. Her hiding would then be necessitated by his truth, her translation an attempt to disguise the meaning of his words, just as she understands the alteration of her proper name. "Being hidden" (Kofman 1986a, 8) and being "locked in a dark closet" (13) continue the series of identifications that emerge between Kofman and Antigone.

In "Nightmare: At the Margins of Medieval Studies," Kofman interprets another dream, this one about the need to hide not only her name but also her body, her self. This is what she dreams:

> *I am in a room from my childhood, with my mother, my brothers and sisters, at night. A bird enters, a kind of bat with a human head, pronouncing in a loud voice: "Woe unto you! Woe unto you!"*
>
> *My mother and I, terrorized, run away. We are in tears in the Rue Marcadet; we know we are in very great danger and fear death.*
>
> *I awaken very anxious.* (Kofman 1986a, 12)

Kofman relates this dream in the context of a brief commentary on a book on medieval French in which the lexeme *mar* plays a prominent role. It is a "remnant, a relic, a segment of a vanished language," which appears at first to be "strange, *unheimlich,* unclassifiable, intractable, unmanageable, irreducible" (Kofman 1986a, 10) but which, through nuanced philosophical argument, the medieval scholar-author renders explicable.[3] Taking on this puzzling "*mar* phenomenon" (11), the author grapples with it until he can make sense of it. He makes it, says Kofman, "manageable and bearable by reducing it to a part of a mechanical toy that is pleasurable to manipulate" (11), locating it in a "rule-bound, codified game," exhibiting its place in language.

One can see the parallel between the medieval scholar making manageable the lexeme *mar* and Kofman's reading of "The Caesura of the Speculative." Just as death is rendered unbearable by German idealism, subjected to the mastery and domination of the dialectic, just as suffering becomes tolerable, this strange and apparently unclassifiable relic of language is fitted into a meaningful set of linguistic parameters and made to conform to the rules of language that can be mastered. Nor can one fail to notice the resonance of the Fort-da game in Kofman's account of the insertion of the lexeme *mar* into a linguistic system, in terms of the enjoyment of manipulating a mechanical toy. "*Mar*," Kofman tells us, as she learned from medieval linguistic scholarship—though she herself is neither a medievalist nor a linguist, as she points out—"'evokes the misfortune of an essentially dramatic fate[,] a word of hatred or anguish spoken quasi-ritually in certain texts.' . . . A masculine formula for love rejected, it is an especially important figure of the feminine lament" (Kofman 1986a, 11).

Kofman hears, in her nightmare, the utterance "Woe unto you!" and relates it to the particle *mar,* a "segment of a vanished language" (Kofman 1986a, 12); she thus distances herself from it. Still unmanageable, not yet bearable, she sees it as "belonging to an entirely other age, to my dark ages" (12), thereby establishing a connection between the medieval era and her own "buried past" (12), which allows her at first only a superficial reading of the dream. This she proceeds to give.

She was obliged to take a night flight on a plane on Tuesday (*mar*di). She was anxious. She associated this anxiety with a "sinister" event of her childhood. In 1943 a member of the Gestapo came to warn her and her mother (her five siblings were already hidden in the country) that they must go and hide: they were on the list to be picked up that night. She and her mother made haste along the Rue Marcadet. In her anxiety, she vomited her dinner onto the Rue Marcadet.

In this first (superficial) interpretation of the dream, which she takes back, reels in, replacing it with a more adequate theory, Kofman suggests that the dream served the purpose of allowing her to deal with the anxiety of having to take a night flight. She had survived before, in the worse situation in which she was deeply afraid, and she would survive now: "Only the spectacle of an old anxiety . . . could allow me to overcome the current anxiety" (Kofman 1986a, 13). Overcoming the spectacle of an old anxiety, Kofman sees herself as making bearable her present troubles. Although this fits seamlessly into the pattern of German idealism, the model of sublation that informs it is retracted in a second interpretation that does not follow the edict of repression. Kofman adds now that three months later she discovered that the Indo-European root of the word *mare* is *mer*—evocative of death, more precisely slow death by eating or suffocation. She tells us, "When I was bad my mother locked me in a dark closet where Maredewitch was supposed to come, if not to eat me, at least to take me far away from home" (13). She concludes that "the dream work was able to condense in one image the two terrifying figures of my childhood: the man from the Kommandantur, the bird of misfortune, and the old sorceress Maredewitch" (13). Allowing this to stand for what it is, let me suggest that Kofman's own biography, as she tells it in another biographical piece, "Damned Food," would seem to undermine it.

DEATH AND SACRIFICE: EATING HER WORDS

Kofman tells us, in "Damned Food" (Kofman 1986a, 8–9), about a double edict that cast a shadow over her childhood (as Creon's edict cast a shadow over Antigone's youth, reflecting the Oedipal curse under the sign of which her birth took place). She identifies this dual edict, first, as the maternal categorical imperative: "'You must eat,' said my mother. And she stuffed and stuffed and stuffed us. Not a chance of being deprived of dessert with her." Following her to school with a bowl of café au lait, her mother "tak[es] the teacher as witness of my crime: 'She didn't eat this morning!!!'"

While her mother engages a categorical imperative in the service of food—you must eat at all costs, at all times—her father tells her, "You must not eat everything[,] . . . not mix milk and meat, not eat just any meat." Kofman recalls the complication that the war introduced to this conflict of interest, when there was precious little to eat. On a train to Brittany, during the exodus that Kofman was forced to take, the Red Cross distributed cocoa and ham and butter sandwiches. " 'Don't eat that,' said my mother. 'Let the children eat,' my father intervened; 'it's wartime.' The ham and butter, once decreed impure, I found delicious, now purified by circumstances and paternal authority" (Kofman 1986a, 8). The circumstances of war purify the impurities of food; paternal authority sanctions the maternal taboo. Kofman's desire was facilitated as she delighted in precisely what was prohibited: she ate when her mother told her not to eat, but she was never hungry, had no appetite, and would not eat when her mother told her: eat, eat, eat!

This occasion of eating forbidden food is recalled as one in which her father—a man she remembers as a "ritual slaughterer, kill[ing] chickens in the toilet according to the law"—relented his strictly regulated discipline that stipulated which food was permissible and which was under interdiction. It is remembered as a relaxation of paternal authority—but as one that happened to contradict the reversal of the maternal categorical imperative: do not eat this! After relating this occasion, Kofman juxtaposes these two terse statements: "A few years later my father was deported. We could no longer find anything to eat" (Kofman 1986a, 8).

Just as she had been "saved" by the Red Cross from the maternal categorical imperative, she was now, she tells us, saved by a woman who looked after her in Paris until the end of the war. The substitute maternal figure "taught me what it was 'to have a Jewish nose'" and "put me on a totally different diet: the food of my childhood [her mother's food] was decreed bad for my health, held responsible for my 'lymphatic state.' . . . Put in a real double bind," Kofman continues, "I could no longer swallow anything and vomited after each meal" (Kofman 1986a, 9). The impossibility of obeying or enjoying any command made itself felt here, in the absence of both father and mother, and in response to a substitute maternal figure who declared her childhood food bad for her health, responsible for her illness, by implication responsible, perhaps, for the shape of her nose. The food of her mother, perhaps, was what made her identity illegitimate to the state.

If her desire was drawn along by the forbidden Red Cross food that her mother would not allow her to eat, if she wanted precisely what was forbidden because it was forbidden, she also wanted it because her father was constrained to relax his authority, was put outside the law by the war—a war whose circumstances purified the once- forbidden food, a war that was responsible for the paternal deportation, as well as for the exceptional paternal authority. When Kofman says, "I could no longer swallow anything," one thinks of Antigone's slow death.[4] What governs this double starvation? The death of the father, in both cases?

Kofman associates Hölderlin with Creon in her review of *Antigone,* making explicit a connection, a doubling, that Lacoue-Labarthe leaves unarticulated as such—although, insofar as his interest lies in Hölderlin's divine aspirations and what is conveniently called his "madness," Lacoue-Labarthe's entire discussion certainly points in this direction. Antigone, as we saw, brings to Kofman's mind an association with Anne Frank—an association that, there is no doubt, also stands for Kofman herself, as "a Jewish wom[a]n constrained to hide . . . in the infernal night" (Kofman 1978b, 1146). Kofman is thereby identified with Antigone—an association cemented by the references found in her autobiographical writings to her being hidden. Now if Hölderlin doubles with Creon, and Antigone doubles with Anne Frank—and with Kofman herself—it involves no great leap of imagination to extend the masculine series of associations to produce the connection Hölderlin, Creon, Hitler, an identification that Kofman would hardly be the first to make and one that is surely evoked by Kofman's description of Creon's maniacal and depressive tendencies, his "madness," his lust for "total power," a tyranny that she says Creon "noisily displays" in a "purely verbal" manifestation, but that also "camouflages under the flood of words and the choleric cries the vulnerability of a malady ready to collapse at the least menace." She adds, "His affirmation of the megalomaniacal, narcissistic 'self' would never have been that of a *subject,* for it is always already worked through . . . the pulsions of death, through a fragility which witnesses metaphorically the shaky scaffolding" (Kofman 1978b, 1150).

Nor does Antigone escape a certain madness: her appropriation of the divine position and of the right to establish the difference between the human and the divine plays the same somber note as Creon's pretensions (Kofman 1978b, 1150). And it is in this madness that Lacoue-Labarthe finds Hölderlin's identification with the *Antigone*'s heroic figures. Both Antigone and Creon are on ruinous courses; both are doomed. But their positions are not, for all that, symmetrical, although Lacoue-Labarthe's reticent silence about *Antigone*'s importance for Hölderlin also necessitates that he pass over in silence the asymmetry marking their fates.

It should not be forgotten that Antigone's doom is set in motion by her father's act and she has never escaped its reach. The patricide and incest committed by Oedipus structures Sophocles' Oedipal trilogy. Antigone's "feminine" and familial justice is opposed to Creon's kingly, political, "masculine" leadership, but so too Antigone's familial origins compromise her in a way that makes it difficult to imagine any family she might originate escaping from the doom of *ate* (fate or doom).Her choice to go to her death childless and unmarried not only represents the claims of divine familial justice; her premature death not only enacts her familial blood bond to her traitorous brother: these actions also bring to an end the twisted logic that seems destined to work itself through the members of her fated family. Her brothers have killed one another in a contest for political authority, and her father has married his mother, so that Jocasta is mother twice over: mother not only to Antigone, Ismene, Polynices, and Eteocles but also to their father, Oedipus. Antigone's father has murdered his own father, Laius, and her mother, Jocasta, has committed suicide, paving the way in this respect for her daughter, and her only remaining family member, Ismene, is afraid to contest their avuncular political figurehead's wishes.

It falls, then, to Antigone to draw to a close this tragedy of tragedies. She must act not only as the pious feminine daughter but also as the savior of her family. To save the name of her father, to rescue his sullied reputation, means in this extraordinary set of circumstances not to provide for the continuation of this familial line, not to ensure its progeny, but to cut off the life of this bloodline, sullied as it is by a father's incest and murder that has infected both the blood of her family and the heart of the city. Is it any wonder that Creon is so relentless in his exertion of an iron rule that forbids the burial of a traitor born of incest? And is it any wonder that Antigone is willing to forgo the possibility of marriage? Who would want to sanctify such a patrimony by entailing its continuation?[5]

When Kofman is presented with the double bind of living in a house presided over by a maternal figure who condemns her childhood diet (her mother) and defines for her the Jewish identity that her nose confirms—an identity that is responsible for her forced hiding, an identity that has condemned her father to death—she responds by a failure to eat, or rather by eating but being unable to keep down her food. The double bind of paternal and maternal authority informing this refusal of food, a refusal to sustain life, also orchestrates the rhythm of Kofman's speech elsewhere. Asked in a 1986 interview whether the inclusion of women in such institutions as the university and psychoanalysis will "help them to enter the twentieth-century canon, and if so, [if they will] be in the heart of this corpus or (still) in the footnotes?" (Jardine and Menke 1991, 106),[6] Kofman replies:

> That's my case, I'm a university professor but only a *maître de conférences* in spite of my nineteen books—this must be kept in mind. . . . The fact is that in this area few women have done work important enough or original enough to merit a place in any curriculum. That doesn't mean that I think the difference here comes from anatomy; it comes instead from the education women have received, which generally means that they are much more submissive to what they have read, more repetitive than innovative, more imitative of a master whom they need to stimulate their research. (Jardine and Menke 1991, 107)

Asked about women's new importance as producers of literary, philosophical, and psychoanalytic writings, and about whether the recent disciplinary fluidity will blur the categories of men and women, she responds:

It is important that both men and women be able to produce in the areas usually reserved for one sex or the other sex, and in this way to blur the boundaries. For example, I write an overwhelming number of philosophical texts in the manner described as masculine, but I also write psychoanalytic and autobiographical texts that are closer to literature.

As regards the psychoanalytic production of women, here too, it seems to me, all possible originality in the area is repressed. Lacan dominates in the Freudian school; this school has enormous editorial power; its numerous journals systematically eliminate reporting of work that is not strictly Lacanian or else criticize it because Lacan is not quoted. Only one of my books on psychoanalysis has been reviewed by *L'Ane*—*Un métier impossible*—only to be censured as "non-Lacanian." On the other hand, Lacan in person publicly recognized in his seminars the originality and importance of my work; for example, speaking of my *Quatre romans analytiques*, he said it was "entirely her own," and he telephoned me after the publication of each of my books—all the while remaining surprised that I did not go to his seminar and was not a "Lacanian." . . .

Among psychoanalysts I don't see any female writing of significance. . . . In France, all the women at all known in this area are philosophers as well: me, Monique Schneider, Monique David-Menard, for example; as for Kristeva, she came to psychoanalysis very late. Catherine Clément is likewise a philosopher, as is Luce Irigaray. (Jardine and Menke 1991, 109–110)

The rhythm of Kofman's assertions and counterassertions in the answers she gives to her interviewers swings between maternal and paternal authority, inhabiting this between, this interval: there are no original women philosophers; there are no women psychoanalysts who are not also philosophers; no psychoanalysts are permitted who are not Lacanians; she herself is not Lacanian, although Lacan phones her every time she publishes a book, to congratulate her but also to ask why she is not a Lacanian. Her need to quote the titles she has written, to quote the words of the master, and to cite herself as exemplary would be remarkable were it not for the fact that as the author of nineteen books—books on Sartre, Nietzsche, Freud, Nerval, Rousseau, and Kant—she was not, at the time of the interview, even the equivalent of a tenured professor. The universality of her judgments, and the way she undercuts their universality each time she utters them, would be extraordinary if this swinging to and fro in a double bind, trying to justify herself as on a par with the male establishment and yet not simply allowing herself to be assimilated into it, were not so very familiar.

Here is a woman who does not see herself recognized by her peers, who
has to point out to her feminist interviewers who ask her what she thinks
"as a Derridean" that she is not merely a Derridean, who writes with the
care of a critic who does the service of reading and rendering attentively
the authors she reads, who thinks that women in general remain too imi-
tative to be original thinkers yet quotes Lacan as having granted her "originality." In the face of this one wonders whether a tragedy concerning an
incestuous curse that overshadows Antigone's life, a tragedy named for
Antigone—a name that doubles for Kofman via Anne Frank's name—a
tragedy that opens in the wake of a double fratricide, a tragedy that depicts
Ismene's refusal to transgress the law, has lost any of its power or relevance.
Antigone's appeal may be in the fascination she provokes for those who
look on, prepared to be fascinated, but perhaps the tragedy of Antigone's
relevance lies in the apparently inescapable and unremitting work of identification, including that of dissociation, that the spectacle she presents so
insistently demands.

It is therefore unsurprising that Kofman is not alone in her complex series of identifications with Antigone. Irigaray's use of Antigone as a trope
has been labeled inconsistent (cf. Muraro 1994, 317–333); perhaps it is
less a matter of the inconsistency of Irigaray's reading than it is a question
of Antigone's waywardness—her resistance to philosophical categories or
literary conventions. Irigaray's engagement with and deployment of the
figure of Antigone can no more be dismissed as mistaken in the privilege
it accords to Hegel's reading of the play than Kofman's can for the privilege it accords to Lacoue-Labarthe's dramatization of it—unless we deny
our filiation to the modern era of tragic interpretation, which bears the
heavy stamp of Hegelian dialectics and the sons who follow in this line,
even as they seek to disrupt its continuity. And if Lacoue-Labarthe is right
when he insists on tracing this filiation through German idealism back to
Greek philosophy, not only to Aristotle but even to Plato, then to respond
to the Hegelian Antigone is also to read philosophy as the master discourse, a dialectical mastery that reflects Aristotle's catharsis.

Lacoue-Labarthe suggests that for Hölderlin the only modern tragedy
can be a translation of, or deconstruction of, the Greek, a re-performance
of Greek tragedy that does not seek to conceal the distance of modernity
from ancient Greece. Need we be reminded that the possibilities harbored
by such re-performances can be radical, given their reversal, for example
(and this is not just any example in the context of a study of Antigone), of
the convention observed by the ancients of having even the parts allotted
to women played by men? As Claire Nancy suggests, perhaps Antigone's
claim on us is a symbolic claim:

Sophocles did not go so far as to make Antigone a woman in the accomplished sense of the term. Neither married, nor mother, intact—in every sense of the word—better known to the dead than to the living, Antigone is more a voice than a spokeswoman for femininity, and it is perhaps this more symbolic than effectively incarnated status that lends her strength. Nonetheless, her opposition to Creon is, at least for him, perceived as coming from a woman because it is on these grounds that he challenges her, refusing to have his rules dictated by a woman who, by her sex, is allotted to submission. . . . She challeng[es] (according to the etymology of her name: she who is born to rise up against) man's unilateral institution of new laws. (Nancy 1996, 100)

Antigone's uprising consists in her insistence upon carrying out what Gillian Rose, in *Mourning Becomes the Law,* calls "that intense work of the soul, that gradual rearrangement of its boundaries, which must occur when a loved one is lost—so as to let go, to allow the other fully to depart, and hence fully to be regained beyond sorrow. To acknowledge and to re-experience the justice and the injustice of the partner's life and death is to accept the law, it is not to transgress it—mourning becomes the law" (Rose 1996, 36). That mourning becomes the law is not excluded by the dislocation that Lacoue-Labarthe marks with the caesura of the speculative. It is in this tragic dislocation that Antigone's symbolic importance lies. And it is in the space of this caesura, within a stage set that spirals around the abyss of Antigone's tomb, that Kofman allows a uniquely modern association to take place when she names Anne Frank an Antigone, thereby substituting yet another proper name for her own.

Unable to stomach anything, unable to introject permanently, to incorporate food, or to successfully sublate her father's death, a death that is abandoned by a nation-state that saw his/her religion, his/her race, his/her Jewish identity as unpalatable, Kofman vomits. What has been buried inside her mind cannot be sustained by her body. She vomits her food onto the Rue Marcadet in a symbolic refusal, a denial of her father's death. A melancholic symptom, mourning becomes not so much the law as its impossibility (which is not to deny that it is precisely the law).

Mourning "becomes" the law, in the decorative sense of adorning it, but it also becomes subject to it, undergoing transformation of and by it. Turning inside out Hegel's sublation of Antigone, one could say that woman occupies once more the position of a "jewel in the crown," the king's crown. She thus becomes nothing more than a precious stone, an object to be thrown around, albeit carefully and with the precision of a master craftsman. If Antigone decorates and beautifies the law by her insistent burial ritual, she also becomes the object of the law, subsumed by it, absorbed into it, eaten up by the king of Thebes; transfused through the texts of German idealism; transfigured from the one who oversees the hearth, the ashes, the spirit of the dead; eaten up and spewed out by the dialectical machine, a residue of the system, a mess, a little horror. Abjection.

As we gather up the pieces, cleaning up after Antigone, we find fragments among the remains she leaves to us, fragments we use to recollect ourselves, to piece ourselves back together. A continual process, this reconstituting of the flesh. As the body fails us, we overcome its frailty. We desperately hold together our disparate parts, we come back to ourselves, we impose order on chaos, we master the dispersion that threatens to overtake us again and again at every moment, we raise ourselves up, out of the dust of ruins, after Antigone, named eloquently by Carol Jacobs as "mother of the dust" (Jacobs 1996, 910). Between the grave and the light, between the dark crypt and the laws of the city: suspended, in an interval, a caesura, inhabiting the space of the between.

PART IV

JEWS AND GERMAN NATIONALISM

Kofman, Nietzsche, and the Jews

ALAN D. SCHRIFT

*If there is a finitude of memory, it is because there is something
of the other, and of memory as a memory of the other, which
comes from the other and comes back to the other.*
        —Jacques Derrida, *Memoires for Paul de Man*

*How does it happen that the human subject makes himself into
an object of possible knowledge, through what forms of rationality, through what historical necessities, and at what price? My
question is this: How much does it cost the subject to be able to
tell the truth about itself?*
—Michel Foucault, "How Much Does It Cost to Tell the Truth?"

*One might be tempted to say that identity categories are insuffi-
cient because every subject position is the site of converging relations of power that are not univocal. But such a formulation
underestimates the radical challenge to the subject that such
converging relations imply. For there is no self-identical subject
who houses or bears these relations, no site at which such relations converge. This converging and interarticulation is the
contemporary fate of the subject. In other words, the subject as a
self-identical identity is no more.*
        —Judith Butler, *Bodies That Matter*

This chapter was written originally for oral presentation at the commemorative conference
"Enigmas: On the Works of Sarah Kofman (1934–1994)," held at the University of Warwick,
U.K., March 16–18, 1995. Although I have made some changes from the original presentation, I have chosen to retain many of the initial formulations that were intended specifically
for that oral presentation.

I met Sarah Kofman only twice. On the first occasion, at the Nietzsche Society meeting in Swansea, Wales, in 1994, she was the keynote speaker and presented a shortened version of her most recent, and alas, what turned out to be her last, published work on Nietzsche, entitled *Le mépris des Juifs: Nietzsche, les Juifs, l'antisémitisme* (*Contempt for the Jews: Nietzsche, the Jews, Anti-Semitism*). While together in Swansea, she and I also talked about her autobiography, which had recently appeared to favorable reviews in Paris. Perhaps in part as a response to this strange textual confluence, she confided to my wife and me that I bore a resemblance to her father.[1] I didn't know at the time what to say in response, and my silence was even more pronounced when, six months later, I visited her in Paris and she showed me a photograph of her father, a photograph in which, I had to confess, I saw no particular resemblance to myself. It was only later still, after reading her autobiography *Rue Ordener, rue Labat*,[2] that I learned the fate of her father at the hands of the German occupiers of Paris in 1942.

Before I left Swansea, Sarah gave me a copy of her book on Nietzsche and the Jews. When I heard of her death, I thought back to this gift, a gift that now seemed so personal, linking me both to Sarah Kofman and to her father, Baruch Kofman. I thought about it again when Keith Ansell-Pearson invited me to attend a commemorative conference on the works of Sarah Kofman. Although I wanted to attend, I must admit that I also felt a bit obliged to accept his invitation in the sense that I wished to offer Sarah, in absentia, a countergift, a gift in honor of her works and, specifically, her works on Nietzsche. But perhaps, *pace* Mauss, it isn't so much the case that I felt obliged to reciprocate her gift—after all, two Nietzscheans should not feel obliged to one another, should they? Perhaps it was instead a question of desire: I *wanted* to honor her memory. That is why I felt so strongly that I not only should attend this gathering but also should write something for the occasion, inasmuch as writing was the gift Sarah seemed most comfortable giving.

But this raised another question, namely, what should I write about? Since my first encounter with her first textual productions on Nietzsche and metaphor, I have been an admirer of Sarah Kofman's work on Nietzsche. The last work of hers that I had encountered was the English translation by Duncan Large of "Contempt for the Jews." It is this curious work that I would like to recall here in order to raise an issue—an issue that Sarah's book on the Jews raised for me in a very personal way. So in honor of Sarah and her murdered father, whom she thought I resembled, I would like to take this opportunity to reflect on what it means to read Nietzsche "as a Jew."

This question has long struck me as an interesting one, not least because it has been raised so rarely. This is particularly noteworthy in the contemporary context of Nietzsche's highly self-reflexive scholarly audience. This self-reflexivity is particularly apparent in recent readings of Nietzsche by feminists, for whom the question of what it means to read Nietzsche "as a woman" has become a frequent topic. It certainly warrants notice, then, that for all the problematic associations between Nietzsche and Nazism, there has been no shortage of significant Jewish interpreters of Nietzsche. In addition to his first important English-language commentators, Walter Kaufmann and Arthur Danto, one might name, here, very selectively, Sarah Kofman, Jacques Derrida, Bernd Magnus, Alexander Nehamas, and Gary Shapiro.[3] Yet for all the important Jewish interpreters, the question of reading Nietzsche "as a Jew" rarely comes up. But it should, shouldn't it? It even came up for Nietzsche, didn't it? Didn't he note, not always with pleasure, that his "first" commentator, Georg Brandes, was a Jew? Are Nietzsche's supposedly anti-Semitic remarks any easier to pass over than his supposedly misogynistic remarks? I don't think they are. But then why do so many women who write on Nietzsche feel compelled to address such remarks as "You are going to woman? Do not forget the whip!" (Nietzsche 1967b, 179 ["On Little Old and Young Women"]) or "Everything about woman is a riddle, and everything about woman has one solution: that is pregnancy" (Nietzsche 1967b, 178 ["On Little Old and Young Women"]), while most of Nietzsche's Jewish readers pass over in relative silence remarks like "The *Jews* [in contrast with the Romans] were the priestly nation of *ressentiment par excellence*" (Nietzsche 1967a, 53 [I, sec. 16]) or "[the significance of the Jewish people is that] with *them* begins the *slave revolt in morals*" (Nietzsche 1966, 108 [sec. 195])?

Of course, this is not to say that all of Nietzsche's Jewish readers pass over remarks like these without noticing them. In fact, I can recall the surprise of my parents when I told them I was intending to write my undergraduate honors thesis on Nietzsche. "Wasn't he an anti-Semite?" I recall my mother asking. While I think I have explained to my parents' satisfaction that, in fact, the thinker on whose writings I've spent much of the past two decades working was neither a Nazi nor an anti-Semite nor what the Nazis thought him to be, I've never really thought seriously about why so many of Nietzsche's important commentators *are* in fact Jewish. And, more significantly, why are they, why are *we*, able to pass over remarks that would almost certainly cause offense were we, in another context, to hear them spoken in our presence? Why don't Nietzsche's remarks bother me? Or do they? And did they bother Sarah? Was this perhaps *why*, after spending so many years working on Nietzsche's autobiographical *Ecce Homo*, she chose to return to Nietzsche and address the question of his supposed "contempt for the Jews"?

Listening to her speak in Swansea, while reading Duncan Large's translation, I was struck by the rigor of her account, of her defense of Nietzsche against the charge of anti-Semitism. In fact, it does not seem inappropriate to regard her account as nothing less than "miraculous" in the sense that Bataille gives to that term. In the third volume of *The Accursed Share*, Bataille recounts his coming to understand why tears of happiness welled up in his eyes when he told the story of his cousin's miraculous assignment to another ship hours before the naval vessel on which he had served was sunk with all hands lost. The miraculous quality, Bataille remarks, "is conveyed rather exactly by the expression: *impossible and yet there it is*" (Bataille 1991, 206). It was something like this sense of the miraculous that I experienced when hearing Sarah present her talk: not only was Nietzsche *not* an anti-Semite but, according to Sarah, "The Jew who had become a great man—even more than the Renaissance man—could serve as a model for the '*Übermensch*' and bolster hope in the advent of that figure who until then had been purely 'ideal' and fictitious, with Zarathustra as his sole incarnation" (Kofman 1994c, 49). The true Sabbath, in whose advent Nietzsche takes delight, "will be a celebration not so much of the birth of a new Adam as [of] the return of the Jew of the biblical age, of the Jew who, at the peak of his power, was able to create in his own image and in the likeness of his prophets and of Moses a majestic, omnipotent, choleric, and jealous God" (Kofman 1994c, 47–48). Sarah Kofman, who when we met had impressed me as having as great a command over Nietzsche's texts as anyone I'd ever encountered, had come to these conclusions when reflecting on Nietzsche's supposed contempt for the Jews. Impossible, and yet there it is!

I must confess, however, that I was not completely persuaded, either on first hearing her speak or on subsequently rereading her text. Of course, Nietzsche was not the *reichsdeutsch* anti-Semite that his sister Elizabeth and others have wanted him to be and that too many readers on both sides of the Channel have thought him to be. But was he really such a great friend of the Jews? And is it really the case that in order for Nietzsche to become-Nietzsche, he had to become a Jew? For this is, after all, the ingenious conclusion to which Kofman's text leads as she argues that ultimately Nietzsche becomes who and what he is by settling accounts, once and for all, "with the Germany of the Reich, with his mother and his sister, and with the paternal substitutes who had been, among others, Wagner and Schopenhauer" (Kofman 1994c, 76). To settle these accounts meant settling accounts with the anti-Semitism that was perhaps their central unifying feature. Kofman suggests that this is the reason Nietzsche identified himself in *Ecce Homo*, the text that exercised such fascination over her, with precisely those characteristics—being clever (*klug*) and wise (*weise*)—that the people in Lessing's *Nathan the Wise* attribute to the Jews. A fascinating hypothesis, one that leads quite naturally to another: is this why Nietzsche concluded that he is a destiny? Is his destinal status and world-historical significance the final act of his identification with the "Chosen People"?

But do we want to go this far? Do we really want to claim that Nietzsche's decision to revalue all values led him to "necessarily and systematically" affirm in the Jews precisely those features that he should have despised had his family's and his mentors' anti-Semitic teachings successfully been instilled in him? While one must agree with Sarah Kofman's judgment that one can make Nietzsche the father of National Socialism and its racism "only at the cost of an interpretative violence" (Kofman 1994c, 73), there may nevertheless be more than a little textual blindness involved in attributing all of Nietzsche's hostility toward the Jews to his Wagnerian-Schopenhauerian youthful exuberance and the pernicious ideas of his family.

It is, therefore, particularly surprising to find Sarah Kofman noting, on the one hand, the plurality and complexity of Nietzsche's texts while on the other hand accusing those who conclude that Nietzsche was an anti-Semite of "bad faith and a self-satisfied blindness to the text's *strict literality*" (Kofman 1994c, 75, emphasis added). What are we to make of this notion of "strict literality"? Is what it means to be an anti-Semite so clear and unambiguous? And does *not* being anti-Semitic mean that one is necessarily, ipso facto, pro-Semitic? It might be worthwhile here to introduce a distinction, made much of by Hannah Arendt in *The Origins of Totalitarianism*, between being anti-Semitic and being anti-Jewish and to note that while Nietzsche is most definitely *not* anti-Semitic, his judgments concerning the worth of Jewish values remain ambivalent at best.[4] If Nietzsche's admiration of certain aspects of Jewish values and value judgments is conjoined with deep suspicion of and dissatisfaction with other aspects of Jewish valuation, what effect should this have on our own judgments concerning Nietzsche's "strict literality" on the "Jewish question"?

Let me be clear here about the point of these questions. It is absolutely apparent that Sarah Kofman was correct to point out that Nietzsche was a constant critic of both the politics of German nationalism and the politics of anti-Semitism, but it is no less apparent that Nietzsche's rhetorical "excesses" can and do leave him open to being interpreted in a wide variety of ways. And insofar as Nietzsche sanctions creative interpretation as an act of affirmative will to power, he can perhaps be held accountable—or at least more accountable than Sarah Kofman seemed to wish—for accommodating the

interpretations that allowed some of his more rhetorically charged and su-
perficially anti-Jewish remarks to eclipse his consistent and firm renunciation of the politics of anti-Semitism.[5]

This point has already been made by Jacques Derrida, among others, in
response to the Nazi appropriation of Nietzsche. In particular, one of the
points that emerges in the context of Derrida's reading in "Otobiographies" of Nietzsche's 1872 text *On the Future of Our Educational Institutions*
is that Nietzsche wrote some things that do in fact lend themselves to the
sort of use made of his works by the Nazis. As Derrida notes, while it may
be contrary to the intention of what he calls the "signatories of share-
holders in the huge 'Nietzsche Corporation,' . . . it cannot be entirely fortuitous that the discourse bearing his name in society, in accordance with
civil laws and editorial norms, has served as a legitimating reference for
ideologues. There is nothing absolutely contingent about the fact that the
only political regime to have *effectively* brandished his name as a major
and official banner was Nazi" (Derrida 1985, 30–31). Which is to say that
it is not just the result of an unfortunate coincidence or Nietzsche's bad
luck that his works, rather than the works of Kant or Leibniz, became
linked as they did with National Socialism.

Does this make Nietzsche a Nazi? Of course not. It does, however, say
something about his texts and the risks that all writers run when they allow
their works to enter the sphere of public discourse; namely, when they
make their writings public, they sanction, de facto, their work being appropriated and grafted onto other contexts. These risks, however, become
extreme when a writer chooses to write with the hyperbolic rhetoric that
one finds in Nietzsche. And no one knew this better than Sarah Kofman,
whose brilliant first book on Nietzsche, *Nietzsche et la métaphore* (1972) did
as much as any single text to draw attention to the *philosophical* significance
of Nietzsche's rhetorical skills.[6]

In contradistinction to an interpretative strategy like that of Heidegger,
which strives to isolate what is "essential" in Nietzsche's thought, Kofman
argued that we should avoid speaking of what Nietzsche's metaphors "really mean" or what his images "essentially" represent in favor of suggesting
that we can reread Nietzsche's text from the perspective of its strategic
metaphoric transformations. If Nietzsche had an "essential thought" to express, Kofman implied, he would have chosen a style of philosophical discourse more conducive to the task of its unambiguous expression. Unlike
Descartes, for example, whose method sought the metaphysical roots out
of which the tree of philosophical truth grows, Kofman saw Nietzsche as
providing us with an "arbre fantastique," one that would be the "best paradigm of the new philosopher, who affirms life in all its forms, multiplying

and displacing his perspectives without referring to any absolute and definitive center" (Kofman 1993b, 111). Rather than seeking the sturdy roots of the Cartesian tree in order to legitimate its fruits, Nietzsche prefers to play among the branches of this fantastic tree, tasting all the varied fruits that it brings forth. This fantastic tree, concludes Kofman, is life itself, and it has many offshoots that bear many different kinds of fruit, some ripe and others rotten.

By cultivating such a fantastic tree, Kofman noted, Nietzsche ran the risk of being misunderstood. And, she argued, Nietzsche not only accepted this risk; he *willed* it (Kofman 1993b, 112), claiming being misunderstood as a title of honor (Nietzsche 1974, 331–332 [sec. 371]). His aphorisms, the fruit born of his fantastic tree, are offered only to those who have the ears for them. His aristocratic style forsakes the goal of communicating with all in favor of communicating only with those few who know how his text should be read, the disciples of Dionysus. Only these readers will be able to follow Nietzsche's "dance with the pen," and they alone will be able to accept the invitation to dance that his aphorisms offer. These readers will elevate reading to the level of an art (Nietzsche 1967a, 23 [Preface, sec. 8]); they will recognize the aphorism as the "writing itself of the will to power" and "on every metaphor will ride to every truth" (Nietzsche 1967b, 295 ["The Return Home"]; cf. Nietzsche 1967a, 301 ["Zarathustra," sec. 3]). *Nietzsche et la métaphore* concluded on this note, suggesting that the ability to dance among aphorisms is another of Nietzsche's principles of selection that distinguish those with noble instincts from the *profanum vulgus*.

While I applauded this conclusion when I first read Kofman's work, the times have changed and I suppose I have changed. In looking back on her conclusion today, I find myself uncomfortable with remarks like this one: "Aphoristic writing and metaphorical style distinguish men from one another and keep at a distance the common run, the 'democratic' plebs, those who are not clean" (Kofman 1993b, 117). For although I still remain committed to viewing Nietzsche's texts as multiple, capable of multiplying meanings in the hands of multiple readers, I have become more sensitive to the uses that can be made of some of these multiple meanings. Which is only to say, playing with the metaphor Kofman herself provided, that some of the fruit born from Nietzsche's fantastic tree may be very rotten indeed.

As several recent works have shown, Nietzsche's fortunes have played themselves out among both the left and the right almost since his texts first appeared.[7] The recent turn to the right in Europe and the United States and the resurgence of nationalism often accompanying, if not driving, this turn have led to new associations between Nietzsche and the right that should concern those left-leaning intellectuals, in the English-speaking world and elsewhere, who will continue to turn to Nietzsche as a philosophical resource. Left-leaning readers of Nietzsche have legitimately criticized readings that make Nietzsche out to be a "simple" misogynist or a straightforwardly anti-Semitic or anti-Enlightenment thinker. But at the same time, there are problems with many of the readings that seek to "save" Nietzsche from charges of misogyny or anti-Semitism or to make him compatible with leftist or left-leaning liberal-democratic politics. Rather than directly confront and take account of Nietzsche's many crudely racist, sexist, or elitist remarks, those who attempt to package Nietzsche as a champion of the left often choose to overlook them as insignificant. With a writer whose prose is both as nuanced and as excessive as Nietzsche's, a certain amount of selective inattention may be unavoidable. But as philosophical and political centers are shifting to the right, which appears to be the case as we approach this *fin de millennium*, we overlook the less progressive of Nietzsche's remarks at our peril.[8]

Does this mean that one should give up on Nietzsche? I don't think so. For there is still reason to be optimistic about the future of Nietzsche's legacy, especially insofar as the identity politics that has produced ethnic nationalisms in Eastern Europe and Africa calls for a critical response in which the Nietzschean critiques of both identity and nationalism can be of value. For example, while much interpretative work is needed to show how Nietzsche can be used to support democratic pluralism, such work can be done. Consider, in this regard, the following comment from Ernesto Laclau:

> A democratic society is not one in which the "best" content dominates unchallenged but rather one in which nothing is definitely acquired and there is always the possibility of challenge. If we think, for instance, in [sic] the resurgence of nationalism and all kinds of ethnic identities in present-day Eastern Europe, then we can easily see that the danger for democracy lies in the closure of these groups around full-fledged identities that can reinforce their most reactionary tendencies and create the conditions for a permanent confrontation with other groups. (Laclau 1993, 292)

This, I would argue, is precisely the sort of leftist political position that a Nietzschean account of—and critique of—nationalism and identity can be used to support.

In fact, the grounds for such a Nietzschean account might be located in one of his passages on the Jews that, surprisingly, Sarah Kofman did not cite in *Le mépris des Juifs*. In Section 475 of *Human, All Too Human* (1986), Nietzsche offers one of his most powerful indictments of nationalism. In the context of rejecting the artificial and perilous separation of Europe into distinct nations through the "production of *national* hostilities," Nietzsche suggests that it is not the interests of the many but the interests of a few— "certain princely dynasties and certain classes of business and society"— that "impel to this nationalism." It is precisely at this point that Nietzsche situates the origins of modern anti-Semitism: "The entire problem of the *Jews*," he writes, "exists only in national states." He continues, in a passage that should refute definitively the charge of straightforward anti-Semitism:

> It is here that their energy and higher intelligence, their capital in will and spirit accumulated from generation to generation in a long school of suffering, must come to preponderate to a degree calculated to arouse envy and hatred, so that in almost every nation—and the more so the more nationalist a posture the nation is adopting—there is gaining ground the literary indecency of leading the Jews to the sacrificial slaughter as scapegoats for every possible public or private misfortune. (Nietzsche 1986, 175 [sec. 475])

Whether Nietzsche himself may succumb at times to an identity politics at the level of culture or ethnicity that his philosophical critique of nationalism should have distanced him from is, of course, a matter worth addressing. But insofar as he here provides tools for a critique of national identity in favor of the "production of the strongest possible European mixed race," there is reason to look to his critique as a possible resource for criticizing a politics of ethnic or cultural identity as well.

Similarly, the Nietzschean critique of dogmatism, grounded as it is in a perspectivist position that calls for multiplying points of view and avoiding fixed and rigid posturings, may be an important voice to heed in constructing a politics that can challenge the panoply of emerging fundamentalisms. At the same time, a thoroughgoing perspectivism can accommodate a notion of radical contingency that seems to be both theoretically desirable and pragmatically necessary at the present moment to many who—from the perspectives of feminism and women's studies, gender studies, queer theory, minoritarian studies, and cultural studies and, in general, from any oppositional perspective—hope to move from theory to action. That is, seeing the world with more and different eyes (cf. Nietzsche 1967a, 119 [III, sec. 12]) may become a political necessity if one hopes to succeed, paraphrasing Marx's eleventh thesis on Feuerbach, in not simply interpreting the world, but changing it as well.

With this in mind, I'd like to close by venturing a few final thoughts on the question of Nietzsche and the Jews. My response to this question differs from Sarah Kofman's in that, ultimately, I don't find any great love in Nietzsche for the Jews. In several recent discussions of Nietzsche and the Jews and Judaism, it has become common to distinguish between three phases of Judaism, toward each of which Nietzsche adopts a different response. To cite one example, Yirmiyahu Yovel summarizes the point nicely:

> Within historical Judaism, three . . . phases are to be distinguished: Old Testament Judaism, whose "grandeur" Nietzsche adored; the "priestly" Judaism of the Second Temple, which he profoundly despised and condemned as the parent of Christian culture; and the post-Christian Jews of the Diaspora and modern times, whom he defended, admired, and saw as a healing ingredient for his "new Europe." (Yovel, 1994, 214–215; cf. Duffy and Mittelman 1988)

While I agree that this distinction is to be found in Nietzsche's comments on the Jews, and while I think that Sarah Kofman would be sympathetic to such a typology, I still am not convinced that Nietzsche's *anti*-anti-Semitism is an active affirmation of Semitism or Jews. Rather, it seems to me that Nietzsche provides a reactive negation of anti-Semitism that is often motivated by something other than an unequivocally positive appraisal of Jews or Judaism.

In other words, I think that while Nietzsche might respect the severity and grandeur of pre-prophetic Old Testament or First Temple Judaism (cf. Nietzsche 1966, 65–66 [sec. 52]) and while he might admire certain Jewish individuals (Mendelssohn, Heine, Spinoza, perhaps even Jesus) (cf. Nietzsche 1986, 175 [sec. 475]), he is for the most part content to *use* the Jews and Jewish identity for his own rhetorical purposes. In that sense, I would agree with Kofman that Nietzsche champions the Jews in attacking the anti-Semitism of Elizabeth, Wagner, or Schopenhauer. We see this most clearly in *Der Antichrist,* a text whose title is perhaps better translated as *The Antichristian* than *The Antichrist.* But this text offers a good example, as well, of what I mean by Nietzsche's "using" of the Jews. There is little doubt that, as a text, *Der Antichrist* is a declaration of war on Christianity. And as a tactic within that battle, Nietzsche uses the Christian disdain for the Jews as a weapon against Christianity itself, showing that what is most Christian can be genealogically traced back to Jewish roots. His affirmation of the Jews in *Der Antichrist* is thus rhetorically charged primarily to insult Christians rather than affirm Jews. But to say that Nietzsche is anti-anti-Semitic or anti-Christian is not to say that he is pro-Semitic or pro-Jewish. It is therefore a mistake, I think, to conclude that Nietzsche's treatment of the Jews in *Der Antichrist* is in any way a genuine or authentic compliment: Judaism remains at bottom little more than the decadent soil out of which sprang what Nietzsche regarded to be that most rotten and poisonous of fruit: Christianity.

The case of *On the Genealogy of Morals* is perhaps even more problematic, for here one sees that for all of his admiration "in theory" for the Jews, so forcefully presented in Sarah Kofman's account, Nietzsche could quickly return to those anti-Semitic prejudices that Sarah Kofman and others want to attribute to his Wagnerian and Schopenhauerian youthful indiscretions. As we follow the references to Jews in Nietzsche's texts, we find the most noticeable hostility in *On the Genealogy of Morals*. And as one critic has argued, the answer to the question of why this is the case might be located in Nietzsche's human, all-too-human psychology. Rudolph Binion, in *Frau Lou: Nietzsche's Wayward Disciple* (1968), suggests that *On the Genealogy of Morals*, subtitled a "Streitschrift," a "Polemic," is a polemical rejoinder not just to Paul Rée's *Origin of the Moral Sensations* but to Rée himself and the role he played in the relations between Nietzsche and another Jew, Lou Salomé (see Binion 1968, 135–140).

And if this is the case, might it be that when all is said and done, Rée emerged for Nietzsche as little more than a Jew, whose Jewishness accounted for his less than noble behavior during the whole so-called "Lou affair." This was, after all, the judgment of Rée made earlier by the "other woman" in Nietzsche's life, Cosima Wagner, who wrote in reaction to Nietzsche's defense of the Jews in *Human, All Too Human* that "finally Israel intervened in the form of a Dr. Rée, very sleek, very cool, at the same time as being wrapped up in Nietzsche and dominated by him, though actually outwitting him—the relationship between Judea and Germany in miniature" (letter to Marie von Schleinitz, May 1878, quoted in Hayman 1980, 204).

If this hypothesis of transference has some plausibility, it would show Nietzsche, like all anti-Semites, to be guilty of essentializing his former friend's ethnic identity into his very definition in the most base and racist manner. That is to say, were this hypothesis an accurate reflection of Nietzsche's inner life, it would show him, perhaps at a moment of weakness, to be guilty of the paradigmatic racist gesture—*turning the multiplicity of an individual into a simple incarnation of a racial stereotype.*

But should we accept this rather crude psychological hypothesis that wants to analyze Nietzsche's criticism of Jews in *On the Genealogy of Morals* as a displacement of his hostility toward Paul Rée for sabotaging Nietzsche's advancements toward Lou? Put this way, it seems rather ridiculous and, aside from the fact that such a hypothesis most likely could not be proven, there is, I think, some significant evidence that stands against it. This evidence, which like Binion's is circumstantial at best, I would locate in Nietzsche's drafts of letters from mid-July 1883 to Rée and to his brother George Rée, in which he accuses Paul Rée of having behaved "behind [his] back as a sneaking, slanderous, mendacious partner" ["als schleichender, verleumderischer, verlogener Gesell"] and suggests that he would "take great pleasure in giving [Rée] a lesson in practical morality with a few bullets" (Nietzsche 1981, div. 3, vol. 1, 398–402). Had Nietzsche really been guilty, as Binion suggests, of a sort of psychoanalytic transference from Rée's Jewishness to his criticisms of Jews in *On the Genealogy of Morals*, one might expect to find this tendency previewed in these almost hysterical letters of 1883. But in these letters, there is not the slightest allusion to Rée's being Jewish, nor is there any hint of anti-Semitic generalization or stereotype in Nietzsche's language. Similarly, one might expect to find some negative reference or connotation to Rée's or Lou's being Jewish in *Ecce Homo* but, on the contrary, Nietzsche's references to them both in this text are even-tempered and positive, even as his criticisms of Germans, particularly his mother and sister, are not.

This, of course, leaves open the question of why Nietzsche is so critical of the Jews in *On the Genealogy of Morals*, a question left open by Kofman's text as well. My suspicion, and it is only a suspicion, is that although he was never driven primarily by anti-Semitism, Nietzsche did not really care for Jews and certainly did not have many dealings with Jewish people. As a result, while he was consistently critical of the politics of anti-Semitism, he made use of Judaism as an analytic category when it suited him to do so. In his earliest works, under the influence of Wagner and Schopenhauer, although he distanced himself from their more overtly anti-Semitic political determinations, he largely accepted their judgments concerning the Jews.[9] During his middle period, when he was quite friendly with Paul Rée among others, he wanted to sever his earlier personal commitments, and toward that end he actively extolled the virtues of Judaism and certain Jews. But when, at the end of his productive life, the time came to make war on Christianity, he used the Jews and Judaism as a weapon in this war.

Thus, in *Der Antichrist*, where the battle involved a direct assault on Christianity, Semitism made an attractive weapon by which to point out the life-negating attributes of Christianity and further the contrast between Jesus' life and Paul's (mis)interpretation of it. But in *On the Genealogy of Morals*, where the case against Christianity is made on "historical/genealogical" grounds, Judaism and the Jews stand not as a contrast but as the diseased origin out of which Christianity grew. As Sarah Kofman correctly points out, Nietzsche is not inconsistent or contradictory in this treatment of the Jews. Rather, like a *bricoleur*, he uses them as they are called for in furthering the ultimate goal of his argument.

This puts the Jewish reader of Nietzsche, like the woman reader of Nietzsche, in a sometimes very awkward and uncomfortable position. For no matter how much one refuses to identify with the caricature that is offered by Nietzsche when he says some of his more outrageous things about Jews or women, these caricatures teach us something important about what it means to not be of the majority, namely, that one's identity is not always freely adopted but is sometimes imposed. This was a lesson that the "assimilated" and "nonreligious" Jews of Europe tragically learned during the reign of Nazism, and it is a lesson that all minorities need to recognize if they wish to avoid similar tragedies.

This brings me to my final point, offering a hypothesis concerning why so many Jewish scholars are attracted to Nietzsche. This hypothesis appeals to what is perhaps one of the most Semitic of values, namely, that the enemy of my enemy is my friend. Nietzsche's enemy is clearly the hegemonic value system of modernity, a value system that he identifies most closely with Christianity. Inasmuch as Jews as a persecuted minority have been suffering at the hands of Christians for much of the past two thousand years, perhaps there is more than a little vicarious pleasure to be derived by a Jewish scholar from citing Nietzsche's vitriol directed against the ethico-theological hegemony of Christianity. But it is not *just* vicarious pleasure, I would hasten to add; nor is it mere *ressentiment,* for at least in the United States these days, where more than a few people are seeing in the Christian fundamentalist right the signs of a coming jihad against all who think differently and against many of the values and programs that have long been taken for granted by both social welfare state leftists and social democratic centrists, it may not only be the Jews who will find critical resources in Nietzsche's declaration of war against a fundamentalist Christianity.

Over a century ago, Nietzsche noted the posthumous character of his work, predicting that a century hence, he would find his rightful readers. To be the sort of reader Nietzsche himself sought, we must recall, one does not have to receive his words as truths or follow him as a disciple, two situations he openly tried to forestall. Instead of calling for an aesthetics of reception, Nietzsche's works call for a performative hermeneutics in which one furthers the project of transvaluing values by making Nietzsche's writings one's own. Sarah Kofman was one of Nietzsche's rightful readers. Her last two works, *Le mépris des Juifs* and *Rue Ordener, rue Labat,* perhaps her two most personal, show how one might return to the personal as one confronts the question of whether, at this moment in history, it is yet possible for a Jew, or for a woman, to escape an identity that others will not let them escape. For these books, Sarah Kofman's last two gifts of herself, I find myself again wishing to thank her, this time for raising for me a question that until now I have chosen and been able to avoid, namely, the question of Nietzsche and the Jews.

CODA

In rereading this essay several years after Sarah Kofman's death, it seems clear to me that I am perhaps guilty of a certain transference—from myself to Sarah—as I project an answer to the question of why she wrote her book on Nietzsche and the Jews and whether the question of being a Jewish reader of Nietzsche may have been one that haunted her through all the years she worked on Nietzsche. It is equally clear that with her death, not only did the Nietzsche community lose a major voice, but I lost the opportunity to broaden the conversation that was just beginning between us concerning the reading of Nietzsche to the very personal question, which perhaps indeed had haunted us both for a long time, of reading Nietzsche as a Jew.

"Made in Germany": Judging National Identity Negatively

DIANE MORGAN

"**M**ade in Germany" is a quotation from Freud's essay "Negation," an essay that is analyzed by Kofman in her text *Un métier impossible*. Freud writes:

> Die Verurteilung ist der intellektuelle Ersatz der Verdrängung, ihr "Nein" ein Merkzeichen derselben, ein Ursprungszertifikat etwa wie das *"Made in Germany."* (Freud 1989, 374)

> A negative judgment is the intellectual substitute for repression; its "no" is the hallmark of repression, a certificate of origin—like, let us say, "Made in Germany." (Freud 1984, 438)

The phrase "Made in Germany," in English in the original text, printed in italics and bordered by quotation marks, presents itself as more than just a foreign expression: it is represented as being an absolute and pure sign that guarantees one the truth.

Before the Second World War, in France, people were exposed to a publicity campaign that aimed to teach them not to buy German products; the message was "Il ne faut pas acheter du '*Made in Germany.*'"[1] Here the expression has become a formula to be learned by heart; the translation "des

produits fabriqués en Allemagne" does not suffice: consumers should instinctively refuse to purchase the product once this label of origin is recognized. As Freud states, this phrase points to an origin—but a highly complex one—that is, for example, not directly translatable from the medium
of the English language in which it is suspended. The English is essential:
when it is not misused in this way for disputes between national states—in
this case between France and Germany—it is the neutralizing and appeas-
ing language of commercial exchange, the bridge between differences,
self-effacing, transparent, liberal, open to everyone, international, but yet
parochial: no real culture, only quaint heritage. Visible everywhere in the
world and yet not to be found anywhere in particular. Sickening.

All too quickly, we have arrived at the main topics of this chapter: negative judgments, the mechanisms of the psyche, and notions of national
identity. As Kofman herself points out in *Explosion,* her mammoth two-vol-
ume commentary on Nietzsche's *Ecce Homo,* such vituperative disclaimers
of psychological and physiological affinity are most dubious, too indicative
of disavowal to be taken at face value. She draws our attention to Nietzsche's overdetermined insistence on his absolute disdain and abhorrence
for the *canailles*—his mother (German through and through) and his sister (busy founding an Aryan fatherland out in Paraguay). Both these figures epitomize for him the collapsing of the realm of culture under the
bulky weight of the political, beer-bloated Reich. What Nietzsche's disavowal hides, or rather draws attention to, is the traumatic articulation between this "realm of culture"—not tied down to a particular place, free to
choose, to invent its alliances—and an ineluctable belongingness determined from birth by locality, nationality, and politics.[2] What Nietzsche
wants to repress is the conspicuous label of his origin, "Made in Germany."[3]

Let us return to Freud and Kofman's *Un métier impossible:* negation is presented as offering the analyst an easy road into the unconscious, a dependable way of reaching the "Aufklärung" (enlightenment) he desires
about the repressed material still locked up in the psyche. Negation is a
sign of a loosening up of the mechanisms of defense. Freud says, "Negation is a way of taking cognizance of what is repressed; indeed it is already
a lifting of the repression, though not, of course, an acceptance of what is
repressed" (Freud 1984, 438).

The barriers of censure are still in place but foregrounded in such an obvious way that the analyst can "permit himself the freedom of disregarding
the negation" and, Freud says, just "pick out the 'pure content' preserved
within the association." The example used by Freud to illustrate the me-
chanics of negation ("You ask who this person in the dream can be. It's *not*
my mother"), is not unrelated to Nietzsche (Freud 1984, 437). Indeed,

Kofman finishes *Explosion II* with the hypothesis that the mother is the disavowed object of desire for Nietzsche; his far too successful death wish against his younger brother resulted in the irremediable loss of an agonistic identification with him that, once victory had been secured, could have bestowed upon him an exceptional status—sure of his mother's love and admiration, blissfully reassured about where he belonged, and untouchable in his confirmed sense of rootedness (Kofman 1993a, 377–384).

That the mother should provide the answer to the enigma is no surprise; it is even a bit of a disappointment. As Kofman herself writes, when Freud, like her, again pulls the mother from the hat—this time in "Constructions in Analysis" (Freud 1937, 361)—the example is so "typical" that specificity tends to be smothered under the generalizable (Kofman 1983b, 91). A more slippery instance of negation and disavowal would be "I'm not German," the symbol for such a negation still being "Made in Germany." Does the label announcing a country of origin simply coincide with the disclosed affirmation of indeed being German?

Thomas Mann, like Kofman,[4] is someone who repeatedly read Nietzsche and Freud together. His reading of Nietzsche's disavowal presents us with no definite answer to our question as to whether the German is to be equated with Germany. In "Nietzsches Philosophie im Lichte unserer Erfahrung" ("Nietzsche's Philosophy in the Light of our Experience"), he points to "the despairing cruelty with which Nietzsche spoke about so many things, actually about everything that he venerated, about Wagner, music in general, Christianity, and, I almost added, about 'Deutschtum,' things German" (Mann 1990c, 683). *Deutschtum* (Germanness) is then not not Germany, but not necessarily Germany.[5]

To advance our inquiries into one's sense of an identity and things national, it is essential to decide whether such negative judgments are copatriots of the pleasure principle or not. It is this instinct, which here Freud equates with Eros and the destructive drives, that compels the subject either to move toward union with selected strangers or to break away from, or even eliminate, outsiders perceived to be a threat, to be unpleasurable.[6] The general aim is always to work for what appears to be the best interests of the subject. Now the act of judgment is indeed presented by Freud as being just another more effective and mature, more intellectual way of getting what one wants. It marks a progress from the primitive "What is good is what I want to incorporate into me; what is bad, what threatens me, is what I want to expel from me."

This rather unsophisticated and impulsive method of deciding has many inconveniences. It prematurely disallows the encounter with new material, the foreign, the unknown. The external is prejudged. The maturer faculty of judgment permits thought to enrich itself with new materials ("bere-ichert sich um Inhalte"), to draw on new territory otherwise cordoned off by the reactionary forces of repression (Freud 1984, 439).[7] The ego is a capitalist, amassing riches, and a colonialist, prepared to go on dangerous ventures to secure riches for itself. Freud explains that "the repressed is for-eign territory to the ego—internal foreign territory—just as reality (if you will forgive the unusual expression) is external foreign territory" (Freud 1975, 88). In "Freud and the Future," Thomas Mann glosses this passage as follows: "As for the ego itself, its situation is pathetic, well-nigh alarming. It is an alert, prominent, and enlightened little part of the id—much as Eu-rope is a small and lively province of the greater Asia" (Mann 1947, 417).[8]

The conscious vigilance of "Europe" is constructed out of terrain won from the expanse of "Asia," which stands in geographically for "external foreign territory" and psychically for "internal foreign territory." The bridge between the latter and enlightened "Europe" is the label "(Made in) Germany," which indicates a point of entry into the traumas of the re-pressed. The ego, or "Europe," is besieged on both sides, not by hostile strangers but by belligerent relations. It is precariously and artificially carved out of the very forces to which it belongs and that threaten to un-dermine its constitution. Freud writes: "The ego is *that portion of the id* which was modified by the proximity and influence of the external world, which is adapted for the reception of stimuli and as a protective shield against stimuli" (Freud 1975, 108, emphasis added).

"Europe": when is the right moment to remove the (censuring? post-poning?) quotation marks, when shall we put an end to the deferral, the *Aufschub,* and pass judgment, move into action, move into the political—remembering that Freud defines judging as "the intellectual action which decides the choice of motor action, which puts an end to the postpone-ment due to thought, and which leads over from thinking to acting" (Freud 1984, 440)?[9] "Europe," this artificial, vulnerable entity, suspended in doubt over a geopolitical entity, is "culture," on which all humanist hopes are hung. Mann continues:

> The ego [that is, "Europe"] takes cognizance of the outer world, it is mindful, it honorably tries to distinguish the objectively real from what-ever is an accretion from its inward sources of stimulation. It is entrusted by the id with the lever of action[,] but between the impulse and the ac-tion it has interposed the delay of the thought process, during which it summons experience to its aid and thus possesses a certain regulative su-periority over the pleasure principle that rules supreme in the uncon-scious, correcting it by means of the principle of reality. But even so, how

feeble it is! Hemmed in between the unconscious, the outer world and what Freud calls the superego, it leads a pretty nervous and anguished existence. Its own dynamic is rather weak. (Mann 1990b, 486)

By the end of his essay—which was actually a speech delivered in Vienna in 1936 on the occasion of Freud's eightieth birthday—Mann comes clear about his meaning. Confronted with what is being "Made in Germany" at that very time by the unleashed "powers of the lower world," Mann in desperation is turning to Freud's work. Faced with the ever-increasing wave of fear and hate that is emanating from Germany and infectiously spilling into the rest of Europe, Mann hangs on to Freud's brave explorations into the machinations of the psyche as a foundation stone for "the future dwelling of a wiser and freer humanity" (Mann 1947, 427). The "colonizing spirit" driving Freud's work—winning territory from the id and turning it into productive, progressive consciousness—is a "cultural labor" that epitomizes the long-term destiny of Europe (428).

The ego and "Europe" or, since the conflation has already been made for us, Europe's ego, is "mindful" and "honorable." It has therefore been "entrusted" with a certain responsibility. Because of its "superiority" (over "Asia" and over that which is "Made in Germany"), it has a duty to "regulate" what is going on, to pass judgment in a way that is mature and not impulsive. However, despite his faith in European consciousness, Mann is nevertheless aware that his humanist investment in the "civilizing" process is jeopardized by the fundamental "feebleness" of Europe's ego. The ego still runs the risk of being taken over, ventriloquized by the "primitive," of which it is a part.

In "Negation," Freud does at times seem to lend support to Mann's hope that the ego can break away from the infantile, potentially self-destructive—because they are unrealistic—demands of the psyche. A certain objectivity does accompany one's ability to judge and this is marked by its independence from the pleasure principle: "In this stage of the development [i.e., the formation of the capacity to judge] regard for the pleasure principle has been set aside" (Freud 1984, 439). However, despite this decisive separation of the more mature judgment from the primitive pleasure principle, Freud then proceeds to define judgment as just a more refined and disciplined ruse for teaching the desirable:

Experience has shown the subject that it is not only important whether a thing (an object of satisfaction for him) possesses the "good" attribute and so deserves to be taken into his ego, but also whether it is there in the external world, so that he can get hold of it whenever he needs it ["so dass man sich seiner nach Bedürfnis bemächtigen kann"]. (Freud 1984, 439)

Freud appears to collapse any qualitative difference between mature, responsible consciousness and self-centered preoccupation with pleasure. What we have here is the difference between an impulsive smash and grab of things I like or want and thoughtful window-shopping for things I like and will want in the future when the time and price are right. Kofman comments:

> It is still the demand of pleasure, of a pleasure which is repeatable and lasting, which drives one to posit the existence of an object independent of the subject, so that the subject can always find it again in the real. That is to say, to be able "to seize it according to his need," "really" to satisfy himself, not just in a hallucinatory way. (Kofman 1983b, 54)

In this scenario all judgment is a saying no to the uneconomical demands of the pleasure principle—any negativity is affirmative inasmuch as it bolsters the resilience of the ego. The intellectual faculty is in control, but it works for the best long-term interest of the pleasure principle. There does not seem to be much scope for harnessing the survival of the ego to the nobler aims sought by Mann for Europe's (that is, for him and for culture's and humanity's) sake.

Indeed, more ominous overtones creep in as Kofman's exegesis progresses. Glossing Freud's proposition that "the negation is an *Ersatz* of repression," she writes:

> The *Satz* is an *Ersatz,* the "no" is a label indicating the source of the product, its unconscious and instinctual origin. A commodity which, as an *Ersatz* of repression[,] is worth less than it inasmuch as it fails to reject all that causes displeasure, but which still has a positive function, as it liberates the symbolic function of thought. If one emphasizes the nature of the substitute, of the *Ersatz,* the judgment is disqualified in relation to repression; it is a mere superficial result ["un simple résultat de surface"] at the level of secondary processes relating to what is produced elsewhere. The "*Made in Germany*" which labels the commodity signals that, beyond the *Aufhebung* performed by judgment, this noble intellectual function is nevertheless a product which emanates from the depths of the unconscious. (Kofman 1983b, 48–49)

The "Made in Germany" is not to be taken as a denotative sign of a homely (*heimisch*) origin—this would be a superficial judgment of the situation. It should rather be read as a symbol for a symptom that emerges from a somewhere that is elusive, unnameable, and unsettling to the intellect's claim to be in control. This release of displeasing and disruptive forces is constitutive of one's capacity to think and articulate. The question to be addressed later will be whether all this negativity is compliant enough to be press-ganged into an economy of underlying affirmation.

The negativity that is in question at the moment is the one that fuels an economy of an empowering recognition of the repressed through negation and is driven by an underlying affirmation that is liberating. In his essay on negation, which is quoted by Kofman, Hyppolite explains the benefits of this sophisticated economy: "Tout le refoulé peut à nouveau être repris et réutilisé dans une espèce de suspension . . . et il peut se produire une marge de la pensée" (All the repressed elements can be taken back and reused in a kind of suspension and a margin of thought can be produced) (Hyppolite 1966, 886).

There is negativity, but it can be put to work for the advantage of the thinking ego. Interestingly enough, Jacqueline Rose, in her book *Why War?* glosses and translates this passage as follows:

> What Freud's article shows is that this capacity [to symbolize] emerges in a "*space of* suspension" [(emphasis added); i.e., *dans un espace de suspension,* not *dans une espèce de suspension*] from a "margin of thinking" where thinking and being can only emerge through what they relegate to non-being, to the not-thought: "what one is in the mode of *not* being it." (Rose 1993, 155)

Since our themes are negativity, the psyche, and space understood as a particular cultural forum or as political entity, this slippage from *espèce* to *espace* is most helpful. It highlights the way that in the economy of affirmation and denial, suspended denotation takes place, circulates, within a sort of spatiality. It is this search for and the necessity of spatial delimitation that encourages me to venture a quick sortie into Kant's first *Critique.*

Kant begins his chapter "Phenomena and Noumena" in the following manner:

> We have now not merely explored the territory of pure understanding and carefully surveyed every part of it, but have also measured its extent, and assigned to everything in it its rightful place. This domain is an island, enclosed by nature itself within unalterable limits. It is the land of truth—enchanting name!—surrounded by a wide and stormy ocean, the native home of illusion. (Kant 1983a, 257)[10]

Kant's argument is that there is no sense in the intrepid traveler setting off on such a perilous journey in search of the land of noumena, since in searching for things-in-themselves he would undo the very delimitations that permit thought in the first place. The term *noumenon* should be treated as an "indeterminate concept" of something intelligible that is "not an object of our sensible intuition" (Kant 1983a, 268). If this absolute difference, or its absolute indifference to and for us, is respected, then this noumenal negativity can have a positive significance for us inasmuch as it provides a nonoriginary basis from which understanding can orient itself within the field of possible experience (Philonenko 1983, 132).

However, there is another all too tempting approach to things noumenal. In Kant's analysis of the negative judgment of the noumenon, that is, the formula "noumenon is an object of nonsensible intuition," the presupposed term "intuition" juts out into the unknown to form a bridging device that the negation just straddles.[11] The result of such rashness is the transcendental illusion, whose effects are devastating. Driven on by transcendent principles, we are "incited to tear down all those boundary fences and to seize possession of an entirely new domain which recognizes no limits of demarcation" (Kant 1983a, B352). This is, however, no exhilarating trespassing on private property but rather a dangerous trip into something not bound by the pure forms of sensible intuition, space, and time. Out there, a "there" that cannot exactly be designated, into which Kant's homely metaphor of the stormy seas is absorbed without trace, there is nothing for us.

It is only from within the area delimited by the "guardian of possible experience," Philonenko's term for the noumenon, which is always already represented by the pure forms of sensible intuition, that we can carve out notions of outer and inner sense, of space and time. To return to our theme, "Europe" and "Germany," with and without quotation marks, only have meaning for us within this preformed negotiation with negativity. This is the "space of suspension" I mentioned earlier in relation to Freud, within which we can think and affirm all the more "purely" the more rigorously we repudiate whatever threatens our fragile boundaries.[12]

Freud recognized that Kant's transcendental aesthetic was most probably significant for his work on the psyche. In "Beyond the Pleasure Principle," he writes cryptically:

At this point I shall venture to touch for a moment upon a subject which would merit the most exhaustive treatment. As a result of certain psychoanalytic discoveries, we are today in a position to embark on a discussion of the Kantian theorem that time and space are "necessary forms of thought." We have learned that unconscious mental processes are in themselves "timeless." This means in the first place that they are not ordered temporarily, that time does not change them in any way and that the idea of time cannot be applied to them. These are negative characteristics which can only be clearly understood if a comparison is made with conscious mental processes. On the other hand, our abstract idea of time seems to be derived from the method of working of the system Perception-Consciousness and to correspond to a perception on its own part of that method of working. This mode of functioning may perhaps constitute another way of providing a shield against stimuli. I know that these remarks must sound very obscure, but I must limit myself to these hints. (Freud 1984, 299)

This association of our abstract idea of time with conscious mental processes that function as a "shield against stimuli" further underlines the fact that something has to be shut out in order to generate a space for thought to circulate.

In "Civilization and Its Discontents," Freud initially uses an architectural metaphor to describe the psyche but abandons it with the following conclusion:

If we want to represent historical sequence in spatial terms we can only do it by juxtaposition in space: the same space cannot have two different contents. Our attempts seem to be idle game. It has only one justification. It shows us how far we are from mastering the characteristics of mental life by representing them in pictorial terms. (Freud 1987, 258)

He later adds: "The fact remains that only in the mind is such a preservation of all the earlier stages alongside of the final form possible, and that we are not in a position to represent this phenomenon in pictorial terms ['anschaulich zu machen']" (Freud 1987, 259).

The psyche, with its primitive drives, foils attempts to pin it down within space by a human, all too human image, that of architecture as the concretization of human cultural achievement. We cannot represent or intuit what the psyche is because it cannot be spatialized. Geographic metaphors like the one used by Thomas Mann, with the id symbolizing Asia and the ego representing Europe, are emblematic of a desperate attempt to defend the humanist faith in rationality and progress. When Mann describes Freud's lifework as "the cornerstone for the building of a new anthropology," he is desperately trying to arm himself to face the crisis that is his contemporary Europe (Mann 1947, 427).

Such a reaction is most understandable, but its humanist packaging— faith in consciousness as all-conquering reason—sits uncomfortably together with many of Freud's speculations. For instance, Freud asks whether the psyche, that volatile bundle of contradictory drives, actually belongs to this human world. He unflinchingly replies, also in "Civilization and Its Discontents," that there is nothing, no evidence, that can underwrite the risky assumption that it does:

> The idea of men's receiving an intimation of their connection with the world around them through an immediate feeling which is from the outset directed to that purpose [i.e., the oceanic feeling] sounds so strange and fits in so badly with the fabric of our psychology that one is justified in attempting to discover a psychoanalytic—that is[,] a genetic—explanation of such a feeling. (Freud 1987, 252)

The oceanic feeling, the intimation that one "cannot fall out of this world," becomes, paradoxically, the demolition of "this world." Our world, bound by the pure intuitions of space and time that provide us with the foundations we need to build and construct (Kant 1983a, 69), is undermined, undone, by the search for absolute identity, for total unity, which is the death drive, a return to the at-oneness of the inorganic state.

To summarize the argument so far, we have isolated two sorts of negativity that are intimately related. The first works together with the pleasure principle by expelling or denying elements that threaten the stability of the thinking subject; these economical processes of negation provide the human with a "space of suspension" that can be seized and colonized as a geopolitical belongingness or grasped and affirmed as a cultural forum for identification that is not necessarily tied down to an empirical entity. The second sort of negativity is in fact a prolongation of the first, but here the instinct for mastery has detached itself from the economical instinct for self-conservation and turned its negativity against the subject himself or herself. This is what Freud calls the "Triebentmischung" (Freud 1989, 376; Freud 1984, 441), which has been strangely translated as the "defusion of the instincts." Instead of defusing the danger, this distinction of the instincts produces something highly explosive.[13] Here the search for identity undoes the safeguards of the region circumscribed by the a priori intuitions of space and time, decimating the subject in its uncontrolled descent into the absolute indifferentiability of inorganic matter, the not-human, beyond our reach.

Kofman concludes her analysis of Freud's "Negation" with a discussion of these two forms of negativity:

> The passage from the unconscious to consciousness necessitates the mediation of negation (therefore of the death drive). The negation is an *Aufhebung* which involves the disintrication of the death drive. But the death drive, which permits the lifting ["relève"] of judgment[,] cannot in

itself be sublated [it is "irrelevable"]: this process of *Aufhebung* cannot be assimilated to the Hegelian *Aufhebung*[;] neither can the death drive, which works away in silence, be equated with the work of the negative. (Kofman 1983b, 62)

In her later work on Nietzsche, *Explosion I, Explosion II,* and *Le mépris des Juifs,* Kofman returns to this preoccupation with negativity, the psyche, and its negotiation with spatialization.[14] What Kofman stresses perhaps most of all in relation to Nietzsche is his invention of his own " 'fantasmatic' genealogy," which substitutes for physiological ties a family of elective affinities that purports to override questions of race, nationality, and class (Kofman 1992, 191, 209). He is the "sans patrie." In *Le mépris des Juifs,* this fantasy is used to distance Nietzsche from anti-Semitism. Anti-Semitism belongs to the realm of petty-minded politics of national states. All that is left behind by the espousal of a cultural entity called Europe, which promises to be not merely international but "übernational," full of nomads no longer tied down by geographic and biological determinations.

In her defense of Nietzsche, Kofman curiously appeals to something she calls the "strict literality" of his text, which can only be misread and distorted by persons of bad faith out to accuse him of being racist (Kofman 1994c, 75). This is a bewildering statement because it suggests that there is an integral textual truth and clarity that shines through any misinterpretation, as if the act of writing took place in a preserved sphere detachable from the contingencies of its reception. There are, however, no guarantees that the apparent celebration of a European race and culture that will have become pure will not be seized upon and permanently sullied by a political instance that reads Nietzsche's words as a statement advocating empirical European hegemony, or indeed German dominance on a larger scale. Indeed this dangerous eventuality must be taken into account, though it can never be entirely anticipated or preempted. As Derrida writes in a passage quoted by Kofman in "Un philosophe 'unheimlich'":

Every sign, linguistic or nonlinguistic, spoken or written[,] . . . can be cited, put between quotation marks; in so doing it can break with every given context, engendering an infinity of new contexts in a manner which is absolutely illimitable. This does not imply that the mark is valid outside of a context, but on the contrary that there are only contexts without any center or absolute anchoring. (Kofman 1984b, 20)

Indeed, the economy of disavowal and selective recognition that is the focus in this chapter cannot be "in itself" an innocent projection of a better world exempt from violence and the will to mastery. As Nietzsche pointed out, "Every drive is tyrannical: and it is as such that it tries to philosophize" (Nietzsche 1990, 37). One can never be entirely sure whether the "Made in Germany" is merely a contingent metaphor that is interchangeable with any other, or whether it is an innuendo encouraging us to act, to take the initiative and liberate an empirical, geopolitical referent from its artificial suspension within a negation. The dangerous, destructive potential of Nietzsche's economical conversion of negation/denial into affirmation is exactly what is explored by Kofman in *Explosion I* and *Explosion II*. Here the price of presenting "negation as a simple prelude to a presupposed affirmation" is examined in psychic terms (Kofman 1993b, 346).

Nietzsche's preoccupation with national identity and culture is paradoxical and complex. Thought must be allowed to circulate freely, without being trapped by what can only be provincial concerns. However, it also requires sustenance and continuity, some sort of protective tradition to belong to and identify with. This is encapsulated by the proposition in *Human, All Too Human* that "to be a good German means to de-Germanize oneself" (Nietzsche 1986, 287).[15] This suggests that the good German, such as Goethe, moves gracefully away from his embarrassing national roots into the eternal, reified air of a "Europe" but, curiously, in so doing he remains typically German and helps to further the aims of the despised tradition whose shackles he was supposed to have discarded. The *Volk* need a demolition man to smash down the otherwise petrifying and debilitating crust that builds up on their forms of self-representation; in repudiating his origins he thereby liberates them, obliging them to outgrow the imprisoning stereotypes that determine them and to imitate his new model.

Some sort of shelter is also needed to protect the fragile economy of the creative mind itself. One of the problems posed by modern man living in an age of accelerated change is how to build up a conserving framework that is not outgrown too quickly, that does not become a mausoleum encasing him alive (Nietzsche 1986, 24). However, in *Ecce Homo*, Nietzsche actually advocates a "walling oneself in" ("eine Art Selbst-Vermauerung"), which serves to protect the self from excessive outer stimuli by disavowing their relevance (Nietzsche 1992, 26). This permits an inner circulation of refreshing sources of inspiration (authors, philosophers, musicians, and others) with whom the voluntary prisoner can identify. It is the adoption and subsequent discarding of these identifications—Nietzsche's set being Wagner, Paul Rée, Schopenhauer, and so on—that Kofman analyzes so convincingly (Kofman 1992, 189–213). These are the various disguises one assumes, the "furtive paths" ("Schleichwege") one adopts in order to creep up on truth (Nietzsche 1992, 36). On the condition that one continues to employ these ruses, investing in one and subsequently swapping it for another, the air within the mausoleum remains fresh enough to breathe and create in.

Germans, especially those from Thüringen, are adepts at this devious art of manipulating *Schleichwege* (Nietzsche 1992, 36). There is, however, a terrible danger. Just as in *On the Genealogy of Morals*, forgetting is necessary for survival but hampers cultural development if it is taken too far, likewise, memory is essential for cultural advancement but risks poisoning the self when it becomes bad conscience. So too do *Schleichwege* present us with a double bind. In *Beyond Good and Evil*, Nietzsche writes, "The German understands himself on the furtive paths to chaos" (Nietzsche 1990, 175, translation modified). These devious tactics are the best way to protect the self, but the concomitant risk is that they will drag one too far. All one can do is look back just before reaching the abyss and understand one's self retrospectively—autobiography as "thanatography" (double heritage of life and death), suggests Kofman (Kofman 1992, 334).

Kofman provides us with an analysis of this "chaos" and of how the adoption of devious, identificatory ruses can break down in such a way that the destruction of the subject is inevitable. She suggests that Nietzsche's "madness" can be attributed to his collapsing of the economy *identification* into absolute *identity*, his claim *actually to be* Wagner, Zarathustra, Rée, and so on (Kofman 1992, 143). This can be understood if we return to our previous reference of the mausoleum that one wants to be walled up in for personal security: the air remains life-supporting if it is encouraged to circulate by the stimulating adoption of different identificatory figures. If this strategy is abandoned and identification is collapsed into undifferentiated identity, the air is compressed. This leads to an explosion, the decimation of the subject into an absolute negativity outside of any libidinal economy.

This is an encounter with a negativity that cannot be put to work in the service of a restricted economy that takes place within a "space of suspension." This is the negativity that cannot be spatialized, on which we cannot pin labels of national identity and that we cannot use to carve an ethereal cultural sphere that is apparently immune from the problematic nastiness of nationality. This is the negativity of the death drive that, having sought an outlet in the external world and been thwarted, returns to crush the subject. It overrides any human consideration in its blind, relentless pursuit of the inorganic.

Kofman's last book to be published before her suicide, *Rue Ordener, rue Labat,* provides us with the culmination of this study of negativity, national and cultural belongingness, and the psyche. In it, Kofman's analysis of volatile negativity—which, handled correctly, can help to preserve the self but which all too quickly can career out of control, resulting in its destruction—is brought to a head. However, before we conclude with a look at this traumatizing, autobiographical "confession," I want to underline the insistent themes uniting the texts by Freud, Nietzsche, and Kofman discussed so far.

In *Un métier impossible*, Kofman points out that Freud, in "Constructions in Analysis"—one of his last texts before his death—is anxious to gather his oeuvre together, to protect it as a way of warding off his own destruction:

> It is as though, at the end of his life, faced with the disintegration which threatens him, faced with the work of the death drive, he felt the need to erect a reassuring "construction" in which everything would be unified, which would hold everything together. As if, at the moment when everything is collapsing within himself, he felt the need to feel that the analytic home at least was still standing[,] . . . as if he felt the need also to make contact with the past, with the happy period of his youth: . . . if the sick suffer from reminiscences, Freud by contrast seems to no longer be able to enjoy life without his reminiscences. (Kofman 1983b, 131)

Freud's desperate attempt to unify his lifetime's work is shared by Nietzsche in *Ecce Homo*. Both these texts analyzed by Kofman are in this sense autobiographical, indeed confessional. This eventuality is openly recognized by Nietzsche: "It has gradually become clear to me what every great philosophy has hitherto been: a confession on the part of its author and a kind of involuntary and unconscious memoir" (Nietzsche 1990, 37; Kofman 1992, 73).

Kofman's contribution is to have recognized that this attempt to unify; to sweep together disparate aspects of a personality, of a life's work; and to collapse ambivalence, contradiction, and diversity into an identity is not only illusory but dangerous. Kofman demonstrates how, instead of Nietzsche's being able to tell the cumulative story of his becoming a self, *Ecce Homo* charts the "death of the *autos* as a stable and substantial subject" (Kofman 1992, 29). Death also hangs over the traumatic articulation between the weight of biological belongingness and the freer realm of "culture" wherein one can invent identifications: "There is also the death of the *bios*, if one understands by that that the 'life' of a living being has as its origin two parents to whom he is attached by blood" (Kofman 1992, 29).

Nietzsche's desperate attempt to reinvent himself, to equip himself with a " 'fantasmatic' genealogy" requires a lacerating act of absolute separation from his family, and most particularly from his mother. Kofman suggests that this inability to come to terms with this demonized mother can in turn help to explain his bad mothering of his own offspring. Zarathustra and the other identificatory figures Nietzsche conceives risk being smothered by the wish of their "mother" for undifferentiated identity with them, a fantasy that is madness itself (Kofman 1992, 143).

Rue Ordener, rue Labat is a disarmingly blatant account of the rejection of a mother, the *bios,* in the search for a freer cultural identification with another. The Jewish mother in Rue Ordener is bad, restrictive, and suffocating. The French mother in Rue Labat provides access to a higher, less backward-looking cultural realm. That which is "made in France" is modern, European; by contrast, the Jewish *bios* is archaic, hampered by strange and frightening customs that belong to some dark and unenlightened world. Her separation from her family and her adoption by her French "Mémé," which the war permitted, allowed the young Sarah to liberate herself from this biological drag on her development. She admits to dreading the end of the war, which would put a stop to her happiness (Kofman 1994d, 67).

The separation from her father turned out to be absolute. The book opens with the following passage about him:

All that remains of him in my possession is the pen. I took it one day from my mother's bag where she kept it with the other mementos of my father. A pen of the type that is no longer produced, that one had to fill with ink. I used it throughout my schooling. It packed up on me before I could decide to abandon it/him [or, alternatively, exploiting the ambiguity of this sentence in French ("Il m'a 'lâchée' avant que je puisse me décider de l'abandonner"), "He walked out on me before I could decide to abandon him"]. I've still got it, patched up with Scotch tape[;] it is in front of me on my table and forces me to write, to write.[16]

Here Kofman is suggesting more than the idea, which is already traumatic enough, that her writing pours out of her pain, the loss of her father, who died at Auschwitz. The pen substitutes for her father and he walked out on her. Here all questions of free will are irrelevant; the fact that he was forcibly deported has no bearing on this logic. Her father walked out on her before she could make her mind up to abandon him, just like the pen. The pen would have offered her the possibility of economizing the loss, but it too packed up on her before she could take control of the situation and decide to chuck it away.

Kofman's work on Freud and Nietzsche, together with this last, most harrowing of texts, provides us with an exhaustive, even exhausting, analysis of negativity and the self. She amply demonstrates how " 'the becoming of oneself' prepares itself in the unconscious depths which operate more inevitably ["avec plus de sûreté"] than the Cartesian ratio and the rules of the method that it advocates" (Kofman 1992, 367). The label "Made in Germany" provides us with just an inkling of what goes on in those murky depths and just how far away we are from being able to equate the ego with responsible consciousness and with Europe as civilizing "culture."

Notes

Chapter 1. The Imposture of Beauty: The Uncanniness of Oscar Wilde's *Picture of Dorian Gray*

1. According to Hegel's *Aesthetics*, the difference between the body of an animal and the human body is that the latter is expressive in its entirety, whereas in the animal's case the outside does not betray any inside: "The *human* body . . . stands in this respect at a higher stage, since in it there is everywhere and always represented the fact that man is an ensouled and feeling unit" (Hegel 1975, 1:146). The *Encyclopaedia* (sec. 411) establishes between the inside and the outside a relation of sign to signified, and the actual soul is this identity of inside and outside, insofar as the latter is subject to the former. Yet according to Hegel one cannot raise physiognomy to the rank of science. The figure in its externality is something immediate and natural: it can therefore only be an indefinite and imperfect sign for the mind. There are limits to the expressivity of the human body, and deficiencies in it. The soul, the inner life, does not manifest itself in all the reality of the human form. Physiognomic and pathognomic determination represent something contingent to mind. There is something accidental about expressivity that explains the differences in appearance of the human organism depending on race, family, occupation, profession, temperament—all distinctive features lacking the character of mind. The finitude of human existence is specified so that according to chance, particular physiognomies are produced, each of which ultimately finds permanent expression (Hegel 1971, 147f.).

Wilde does not allude to Hegel in his text, but to Giordano Bruno, Darwin, Haeckel, and Gall (when Dorian Gray gives himself over to endless speculations on the soul and the body, the mystery of their unity or of their representation; cf. 58, 106, 133).

2. Without being displayed as a *painting*, since, as Mallarmé pointed out, *The Picture of Dorian Gray* is not a picture but a book (Mallarmé 1973, 328, quoted in Gattégno 1992, 9). The first transformation of the portrait is brought about by writing, which exhibits the picture in words alone: words that, at the same time as they display it, conceal it from view, thus making tolerable the intolerable and monstrous metamorphosis. And the blasphemous laying bare of a soul.

3. This fatal first meeting of the eyes can be compared to the one that takes place with the same fatality between the two leads, man and woman, in Louis Malle's film *Fatale*.

4. Translator's Note (hereafter "TN"): Cf. Alcibiades' speech in Plato's *Symposium* and Kofman's analysis of it in "Socrate et ses doubles (Les Socrate(s) du *Banquet* de Platon)" (Kofman 1989c, 25–52).

5. This loss of total self-control is also indicated in Louis Malle's film. Cf. also 114: "I was dominated, soul, brain, and power by you. You became to me the visible incarnation of that unseen ideal whose memory haunts us artists like an exquisite dream. I worshipped you. I grew jealous of every one to whom you spoke. I wanted to have you all to myself. I was only happy when I was with you. . . . I only knew that I had seen perfection face to face, and that the world had become wonderful to my eyes."

6. "Was it not Plato, that artist in thought, who had first analyzed it? Was it not Buonarotti who had carved it in the coloured marbles of a sonnet-sequence?" (36).

7. Ronsard is alluded to several times in the text, even though he is never directly named or quoted. TN: The allusion is to Ronsard's most famous poem, "Mignonne, allon voir," from 1553, which expresses a sentiment similar to Herrick's "Gather ye rosebuds while ye may" and concludes: "Pick, pick your youth: / Like that flower's, old age / Will tarnish your beauty" (Ronsard 1963, 86).

8. This scene is depicted in the Uccello predella, "Miracle of the Desecrated Host," at the Galleria Nazionale delle Marche, Urbino, Italy.

9. According to Voltaire's *Philosophical Dictionary*, Sybil means "god's council" (Voltaire 1971, 375).

10. The whole text emphasizes the importance and power of words. Words do not describe a preexistent reality but magically create it. Wilde is opposed to realism in literature: "Names are everything. I never quarrel with actions. My only quarrel is with words. That is the reason I hate vulgar realism in literature. The man who could call a spade a spade should be compelled to use one. It is the only thing he is fit for" (194).

11. "The moment one sits down to think, one becomes all nose, or all forehead, or something horrid. Look at the successful men in any of the learned professions. How perfectly hideous they are! Except, of course, in the Church. But then in the Church they don't think" (3).

There is a whole tradition relating the wrinkles and blemishes on a face to thoughts that are too weighty and make it bow toward the ground, like a flower wilting and crumpling. Cf., for example, Jean Paul in his "Praise of Stupidity":

> Consider the happy mortal whose stomach has never been troubled by his head during digestion and who has never squandered his nervous humor in fertilizing the slightest thought: his body is the image of health. Admittedly you do not see on his face the signs of profound thought, but precisely for the same reason there is no trace either of a soul laid waste. . . . Set beside this image that of the wise man. You can see that he has a soul, for it is often doubtful whether he has a body. This body has been worn out in its constant service of the mind, and in wasting away it seems to be approaching the incorporeality of the being that thinks inside it. The face is marked by wrinkles, those scars borne by all who combat Stupidity, and the head, as if weighed down by so much knowledge and filled with the strength stolen from the other limbs, bows toward the ground. (Jean Paul 1928, 295)

12. In the same way, primitive man is afraid of having his picture "taken," because for him it is not a likeness but a magical and malign object (cf. Francastel and Francastel 1969, 47). For him the image does not represent. It is above all an object capable of

producing effects and of being subject to an action performed by others. It can also serve as an intermediary and transmit good and evil spells over a distance. Cf. also "Animism, Magic, and the Omnipotence of Thoughts" (Freud 1913, 75–99).

13. This knife thrust that makes a corpse of the model on seeing his double has a parallel in some of Balthus's pictures (cf., for example, "The Golden Days," 1944–1949), where a young girl is looking in a mirror, trying to view her undefined identity, and this look is likened to a knife thrust, which makes a corpse of her and marks the loss of her innocence. Cf. Kofman 1985b, 93.

14. The double does not therefore function for Dorian Gray as it does for primitive man in Otto Rank's book *The Double* and Freud's essay "The 'Uncanny'": as an insurance against the destruction of the ego and a denial of the power of death. Freud notes that such a representation, which has its origin in the primary narcissism of the child and primitive man, is transformed once this stage has been surmounted. The double, the assurance of an afterlife, becomes an uncanny harbinger of death. The double, which at first had a benevolent meaning, is transformed into a terrifying image, "just as, after the collapse of their religion, the gods turned into demons" (Freud 1919, 236).

15. Cf. "Animism, Magic, and the Omnipotence of Thoughts": "It is easy to perceive the motives which lead men to practice magic: they are human wishes. All we need to suppose is that primitive man had an immense belief in the power of his wishes. . . . The principle governing magic . . . is the principle of the 'omnipotence of thoughts'" (Freud 1913, 83, 85).

"We appear to attribute an 'uncanny' quality to impressions that seek to confirm the omnipotence of thoughts and the animistic mode of thinking in general, after we have reached a stage at which, in our *judgment*, we have abandoned such beliefs" (Freud 1913, 86 n. 2).

"At the animistic stage men ascribe omnipotence to *themselves*. At the religious stage they transfer it to the gods but do not seriously abandon it themselves, for they reserve the power of influencing the gods in a variety of ways according to their wishes" (Freud 1913, 88).

16. "What [the artist] does in play produces emotional effects—thanks to artistic illusion—just as though it were something real. People speak with justice of the 'magic of art' and compare artists to magicians. . . . There can be no doubt that art did not begin as art for art's sake. It worked originally in the service of impulses which are for the most part extinct today" (Freud 1913, 90).

17. At the end of "The 'Uncanny'" ("Das Unheimliche"), Freud refers to Wilde—not to *The Picture of Dorian Gray* but to "The Canterville Ghost," in which the ghost does not inspire any feelings of terror, he argues, because the writer makes a mockery of him. Earlier on, he might have cited *Dorian Gray* in corroboration. In fact, Freud writes, "*A great deal that is not uncanny in fiction would be so if it happened in real life; and . . . there are many more means of creating uncanny effects in fiction than there are in real life*" (Freud 1919, 249). Whether or not the author has left behind the world of reality, we follow him in every case. Uncanniness cannot arise "unless there is a conflict of judgment as to whether things which have been 'surmounted' and are regarded as incredible may not, after all, be possible; and this problem is eliminated from the outset by the postulates of the world of fairy tales" (Freud 1919, 250).

We adapt our judgment to the conditions of the writer's fictive reality. If he "pretends to move in the world of common reality": "in this case he accepts . . . all the conditions operating to produce uncanny feelings in real life. . . . He is in a sense betraying us to the superstitiousness which we have ostensibly surmounted; he deceives us by promising to give us the sober truth, and then after all overstepping it. . . . He can keep us in the dark for a long time about the precise nature of the presuppositions on which the world he writes about is based" (Freud 1919, 250f.).

For *Unheimlichkeit* and the double, cf. Kofman 1991b, 119–162.

18. Laughter has a devilish resonance in the text. The first exchange of glances between Dorian and Lord Henry is followed by laughter.

19. Here one should recall the very fine text by Bataille, "The Language of Flowers":

After a very short period of glory the marvelous corolla rots indecently in the sun, thus becoming, for the plant, a garish withering. Risen from the stench of the manure pile—even though it seemed for a moment to have escaped it in a flight of angelic and lyrical purity—the flower seems to relapse abruptly into its original squalor: the most ideal is rapidly reduced to a wisp of aerial manure. For flowers do not age honestly like leaves, which lose nothing of their beauty, even after they have died; flowers wither like old and overly made-up dowagers, and they die ridiculously on stems that seemed to carry them to the clouds. . . . The appearance of leafy stems generally gives the impression of strength and dignity. . . . No crack, it seems[,] . . . conspicuously troubles the decisive harmony of vegetal nature. (Bataille 1983, 12–13)

An "inevitable seductiveness" is "produced by the general thrust from low to high. And in order to destroy this favorable impression, nothing less is necessary than the impossible and fantastic vision of roots swarming under the surface of the soil, nauseating and naked like vermin" (Bataille 1983, 13).

20. A designation reminiscent of fairy tales. Wilde was himself the author of *The Happy Prince and Other Tales,* published in 1888, not long before *Dorian Gray.*

21. Cf. also Basil, who cannot believe the scandalous rumors that are being spread about Dorian Gray, for "sin is a thing that writes itself across a man's face. It cannot be concealed. People talk sometimes of secret vices. There are no such things. If a wretched man has a vice, it shows itself in the lines of his mouth, the droop of his eyelids, the moulding of his hands even. . . . With your pure, bright, innocent face, and your marvellous untroubled youth—I can't believe anything against you" (149f.).

Cf. also 175: "Those finely-shaped fingers could never have clutched a knife for sin, nor those smiling lips have cried out on God and goodness. He . . . for a moment felt keenly the terrible pleasure of a double life."

22. Modeled on *A rebours* (*Against Nature*) by Huysmans, published in 1884 and described by Arthur Symons as "the breviary of the decadence."

23. Some of Hoffmann's heroes also have this feeling, among others Leonardo in *The Devil's Elixirs.*

24. TN: "To exist is to be perceived" (Berkeley, *Principles of Human Knowledge,* sec. 3).

25. Cf. 91: "The painted image of himself . . . would alter. . . . Its gold would wither into grey."

26. The etching concerned depicts one of the temptations of St. Anthony: St. Anthony is praying before a crucified Christ, who is transformed into the vision of a crucified woman. Cf. Freud 1907, 35.

27. Lord Henry says, for example, that art has no influence upon action, that it annihilates the desire to act and is superbly sterile, for the books that the world calls immoral are books that show the world its own shame (218). And in the Preface to the book, Wilde writes: "There is no such thing as a moral or an immoral book. Books are well written, or badly written. That is all." And again: "No artist has ethical sympathies.

... The artist can express everything. ... Vice and virtue are to the artist materials for an art. ... All art is quite useless" (xxiiif.). Moreover, he says that it is the spectator and not life that art really mirrors (xxiv).

For his part, Théophile Gautier, in his Prefaces to *Enamels and Cameos* and *Albertus*, makes a principle out of the split between art and politics; in the Preface to *Mademoiselle de Maupin*, he states that the only things that can really be beautiful are those that serve no purpose whatsoever and are superfluous. And in *Albertus*, sec. XIII, after the description of the witch's hut: "Yet to an artist a hell like this is a paradise" (Gautier 1903, 222).

28. The poem "Variations on the Carnival of Venice," II: "On the Lagoons" (Gautier 1903, 54–55).

29. Cf., for example, "Art," in *Enamels and Cameos:*

> Things perish. Gods have passed.
> But song sublimely cast
> Shall citadels outlast. (Gautier 1903, 181)

And "Tombs and Funeral Pyres":

> No grim cadaver sets its flaw
> In happy days of pagan art,
> And man, content with what he saw,
> Stripped not the veil from beauty's heart.
>
> . . . .
>
> Then death concealed its visage gaunt,
> Whose sockets deep, and sunken nose,
> And railing mouth our spirits haunt,
> Past any dream that horror shows.
>
> . . . .
>
> Gods, whom Art ever must avow,
> Ruled the marmoreal sky's demesne. (Gautier 1903, 118–120)

(With the death of Pan and the advent of Christianity, dusk deepens and the skeleton gleams out.)

> Come back, come back, O ancient Art!
> And cover with thy marble's gleam
> This Gothic skeleton! Each part
> Consume, ye flames of fire supreme!
>
> . . . .
>
> Immortal form! Rise thou in flame
> Again to beauty's fount of bloom,
> Let not thy clay endure the shame,
> The degradation of the tomb! (Gautier 1903, 123)

Cf. also the text taken from *Albertus*, sec. LXXII, quoted in my epigraph.

30. The continuation of the poem is worth quoting, since one can infer from it that the idea of *The Picture of Dorian Gray* as the writing or the scratched hieroglyphics of vice is an implicit "quotation" from Gautier:

> There every vice and passion's whim
> Had seamed the flesh abundantly

> With hideous hieroglyphs and grim,
> That headsmen read with fluency.
> . . . .
> There plainly writ in furrows fell,
> I saw the deeds of sin and soil,
> Scorchings from every fiery hell
> Wherein corruptions seethe and boil.
> . . . .
> There was a track of Capri's vice,
> Of lupanars and gaming-scores,
> Fretted with wine and blood and dice,
> Like ennui of old emperors. (Gautier 1903, 50)

More generally, Wilde perhaps borrows from Gautier the idea that "the outside makes known the inside," which Gautier owes to Gall; cf. *Albertus*, sec. LIX: "a brow which Gall ecstatically would have felt for six months, and taken for base for a dozen treatises" (Gautier 1903, 247). The description of the witch Veronica in *Albertus*, sec. VI, is based on the same principle: "bowed her back, her foot misshapen, and her legs yet worse, harsh her voice, and her soul more repulsive even than her frame. The Devil himself more hideous could not be" (Gautier 1903, 218).

31. In *Albertus*, sec. LXXX, there is also a portrait—of a Venetian woman stabbed to death by her jealous husband—which the painter Albertus hides from the eyes of strangers with a thick curtain (Gautier 1903, 258); in sec. LXXXIV, he sees the Venetian woman's head move inside the frame and her mute mouth stir and open as though she were about to speak (Gautier 1903, 260). For the final description of the corpse, Wilde is perhaps also borrowing from Gautier's in "Sea-Gloom," where a drowned man's corpse is described as "bluish, swollen, unrecognizable."

32. In *Albertus*, sec. XCIX, we find: "Chaste like Adam before the Fall, they onward freely go in their sainted nudity, free from all vice, and showing without fear all that the hypocrite world so carefully conceals" (Gautier 1903, 267f.).

33. Here again, cf. *Albertus*, sec. LXXI: "Our hero, like Eve his ancestress, had, by the serpent urged, tasted the bitter fruit. A god he desired to be. When naked he beheld himself and possessed in full of knowledge human, he longed for death" (Gautier 1903, 253). And in sec. LXXII: "Woe! Woe! unto him who the fathomless ocean of man's heart imprudently seeks to sound! Too oft the sounding lead, instead of golden sand and pearly shells that lovely shine, brings up foul and stinking mud.—If I could live another life again, certes I should not within it all search out as hitherto I have done. What matters after all, whether the cause be sad, if the effect produced be sweet?" (Gautier 1903, 253f.). And in sec. CI: "God alone the mighty Master is; His secret well he keeps, and none may make it out; in vain we strive" (Gautier 1903, 269).

34. Here again in *Albertus*, sec. LVIII, "Painting, God rivaling, and His equal, sublime deception, wondrous imposture, that life restorest and nature doublest" (Gautier 1903, 246).

35. This is no doubt the verse referred to by Hawthorne in *The Scarlet Letter*, where the heroine, a second Eve, bears on her bosom the mark of a scarlet letter, a magnificently embroidered letter *A*, which fills people with terror, surprise, and wonder, representing sin and marking out the sinner.

In *The Picture of Dorian Gray*, the first mark of sin is the appearance of a "tiny scarlet speck that makes men mad" (91), and in general scarlet is the color that signs the loss of Dorian's soul: "He was trying to gather up the scarlet threads of life, and to weave them into a pattern; to find his way through the sanguine labyrinth of passion through which he was wandering" (95).

In Latin antiquity, red is likewise the most striking color that fixes things in the memory. In the *Rhetorica ad Herennium*, III, 22, Cicero writes that red marks out everything that is exceptionally shameful, dishonorable, horrifying, or laughable. His recommended way of intensifying an image is to make it red. Faces will be more memorable "if we somehow disfigure them, as by introducing one stained with blood or soiled with mud or smeared with red paint, so that its form is more striking" (Cicero 1954, 221).

36. His appreciation of the beauty and the personal appearance of other people was originally quickened by Basil's portrait (73).

37. "Like Gautier, he was one for whom 'the visible world existed.' . . . To him Life itself was the first, the greatest, of the arts" (129). He is fascinated by Dandyism, which is an attempt to assert the absolute modernity of beauty. He wants to elaborate a scheme of life that would find in the spiritualizing of the senses its highest realization. Lord Henry remarks that Dorian has never done anything, never carved a statue, or painted a picture, or produced anything outside of himself: "Life has been your art. You have set yourself to music" (217).

38. On Dorian Gray's sexual ambivalence, many pages could be analyzed. Let us note the reference to Gautier's sonnet "Contralto," in *Enamels and Cameos,* where the subject is an enigmatic statue, disturbing in its beauty, of uncertain sex and a double voice, that of the contralto, man and woman combined: "thou fantastical of birth, / The voice's own Hermaphrodite thou art!" (Gautier 1903, 71). A "bell in whose alloy of mighty mold / Are voice of bronze and voice of silver blent" (Gautier 1903, 72). This voice—of "doubtful" sex—to which Dorian is so sensitive might be Lord Henry's, simultaneously sweet and low (maternal and paternal?).

39. Cf. the unpublished note from 1881 on "that which is *aesthetically* offensive about the insides of man without his skin": "Where he lacks shape ["Gestalt"], man finds himself disgusting—he does everything he can *not to think about it*" (Nietzsche 1980, 9:460).

Diderot, too, invites the artist to remain on the surface of things, and he denounces internal observation as indecent, perfidious, and perverse: "In painting as in morality, it is highly dangerous to look beneath the skin" (Diderot 1959, 815). TN: Cf. Kofman 1985b, 65–67, for a development of this parallel in the context of a more extended analysis of Diderot's aesthetics.

40. Cf. Freud 1915, 291.

Two films by Resnais, *Smoking* and *No Smoking* (set under the emblem of Kierkegaard and his *Either/Or*) put on permanent display the ludic possibility of starting over, beginning again from square one, playing new roles, contrary to what happens in irreversible "real" time, where every move makes its mark and it is not a matter of indifference whether one decides to smoke or not to smoke. Only in the cinema are Players cigarettes that can be played with without irreversible consequences.

41. As all beauty is. Fatality, it is said, always dogs anything physically or intellectually distinguished. It spares the mediocre, all those who do not stand out from the rest. The fatality of beauty is its necessary defeat, the price every exceptional being has to pay to the jealousy of the gods: at least this is what Basil says when he foresees that he, Henry, and Dorian will all suffer terribly for this gift of the gods (3).

42. Freud writes of Hoffmann's *Devil's Elixirs* what could also apply to *The Picture of Dorian Gray:*

These themes are all concerned with the phenomenon of the 'double,' which appears in every shape and in every degree of development. Thus we have characters who are to be considered identical because they look alike. This relation is accentuated by mental processes leaping from one of these characters to another . . . , so that the one possesses knowledge, feelings, and experience in common with the other. . . . In other words, there is a doubling, dividing, and interchanging of the self. And finally there is the constant recurrence of the same thing—the repetition of the same features or character traits or vicissitudes, of the same crimes. (Freud 1919, 234; cf. Kofman 1975)

43. TN: The allusion is to a line in Nietzsche's last letter, written to Jacob Burckhardt in January 1889 after his collapse in Turin: "The unpleasant thing, and one that nags my modesty, is that at root every name in history is I" (Nietzsche 1969, 347). Cf. Kofman 1992, 26.

44. Cf. Barande 1977 and Kofman 1979, where I developed this point in relation to Gérard de Nerval.

45. TN: Cf. the third essay of Nietzsche's On the Genealogy of Morals, "What Is the Meaning of Ascetic Ideals?" (Nietzsche 1967a, 97—163).

46. In a letter of February 12, 1894, to Ralph Payne, Wilde writes: "I am so glad you like that strange coloured book of mine: it contains much of me in it. Basil Hallward is what I think I am: Lord Henry what the world thinks me: Dorian what I would like to be" (Wilde 1962, 352, quoted in Gattégno 1992, 39f.).

47. "We degenerate into hideous puppets, haunted by the memory of the passions of which we were too much afraid, and the exquisite temptations that we had not the courage to yield to" (23).

48. TN: For a fuller analysis of Nietzsche's figurations of Oedipus, cf. Kofman (1979) 1986b.

49. It would be interesting to read Wilde's Portrait of Mr. W. H., written the year before The Picture of Dorian Gray. There the narrator undertakes a reading of Shakespeare's sonnets that stresses the lover's wish to see his beloved remain eternally young and beautiful. One can also find in this text a direct reference to Plato's Symposium, which Wilde considered the most admirable of the dialogues.

Chapter 3. Kofman's Hoffmann

1. Her second essay on Freud's reading of Jensen's Gradiva, "Delusion and Fiction: Concerning Freud's Delusions and Dreams in Jensen's Gradiva" (Kofman 1988c, 175–199), was written at the same time as Quatre romans analytiques and first published in 1974.

2. Gerhard R. Kaiser's authoritative overview of Hoffmann criticism (Kaiser 1988), which makes no mention of Kofman's work, is typical in this respect, although Autobiogriffures has been translated into German complete (Kofman 1985c).

3. On Freud's predilection for literature, cf. Kofman 1988c, 201 n. 6; on the "scientific" status of psychoanalysis, cf. Kofman 1994b, 99–107.

4. Cf. Kofman with Jardine 1991, 108 ("It is to Nietzsche that we owe the idea that philosophy and literature are not inherently heterogeneous to each other"); on Nietzsche's own heterodox "literary" philosophical style, cf. Kofman 1993b, 1–5.

5. Cf. the group interview on the collective work Mimesis: Des articulations (Agacinski et al. 1976) and the manifesto of the Groupe de recherches sur l'enseignement

philosophique: "For the GREPH—there isn't such a thing as 'philosophy' [*'la* philoso-phie']" (Groupe de recherches sur l'enseignement philosophique 1977, 5). On the problems of categorizing her own work, cf. Kofman with Jardine 1991, 111: "My book on Nerval is classified in France as literature, but it could also be classified as psycho-analysis. It's the same for my recent *Conversions*, which concerns *The Merchant of Venice* but is also a critical rereading of Freud's theme of 'the three caskets.' "

6. The quotation marks around "'Uncanny'" are not Freud's but were added by James Strachey for the English translation in the *Standard Edition*—an interlinguistic in-dication, already, of the term's disturbing reach. Other languages have in general found it difficult to settle for a satisfactory term to translate it: the French translation that Kof-man works with uses the unhappy formulation "inquiétante étrangeté" ("disquieting strangeness").

7. Freud's only other publication on Hoffmann seems to have been the short anec-dote from *The Devil's Elixirs*, on consciousness as a customs officer, recounted (by "S. F.") in the *Zeitschrift für Psychoanalyse* (cited by Strachey in Freud 1919, 233 n. 1).

8. Cf. the similar methodological principle that opens *The Childhood of Art:* "They [Freud's texts] urge us, therefore, to do a symptomal reading of his text, making it say something more or other than what it says literally, yet basing the reading on the literal sense alone" (Kofman 1988c, 2).

9. This analysis is developed in a Nietzschean context in the first chapter of *Nietzsche et la scène philosophique*, "Le complot contre la philosophie" (Kofman [1979] 1986b), a discussion of the passage in Nietzsche's "Philosophy in the Tragic Age of the Greeks" where he analyzes the eclipse of the "ancient masters of philosophy" at the hands of later thinkers. In "Nietzsche and the Obscurity of Heraclitus" (Kofman 1987a), Kofman focuses on one particular case.

10. As Kofman points out, on one level Freud's essay is a polemic, intended to be doubly corrective not only by focusing on a topic that had hitherto been neglected in aesthetics, but also by providing a better explanation of the effect than that provided by Jentsch in the only other paper on the topic he had come across. Although this goes some way toward explaining the restrictedness of his approach, Kofman's point is that it is by no means a justification.

11. In Freud's defense, it should be noted that, at least in the title of his essay, he sub-stantivates *unheimlich* as "Das Unheimliche" (literally, "that which is uncanny") and not as the abstract concept of "Unheimlichkeit" ("uncanniness"). In other words, Strachey's English translation, despite the added quotation marks, is more accurate in rendering it as "The 'Uncanny'" than is the French translation Kofman uses, where it is rendered as "L'inquiétante étrangeté" (cf. note 6). Although in her early works Kofman rightly observes the nicety of this distinction, she herself later "forgets" it, referring to Freud's essay by the title "Die Unheimlichkeit" (Kofman 1985a, 82) or, perhaps by unconscious analogy with "Vergänglichkeit" ("On Transience"), simply "Unheimlichkeit" (Kofman 1995b, 21 n. 1, 23 n. 1).

12. Cf. "Summarize, Interpret (*Gradiva*)" (Kofman 1991b, 83–117), especially 91: "The text-summary is a text already selected by the future interpretation: thus it is hardly surprising that this interpretation can make it intelligible."

13. The association between the uncanny and repetition is one made by Freud him-self, not only preempting his analysis of the repetition-compulsion in *Beyond the Plea-sure Principle*, but also (a point that Kofman leaves uncommented) alluding in passing to the Nietzschean doctrine of "eternal recurrence" ('ewige Wiederkehr des Gle-ichen'), as he refers to "the constant recurrence of the same thing ['beständige

Wiederkehr des Gleichen']—the repetition of the same features or character traits or vicissitudes, of the same crimes, or even the same names through several consecutive generations" (Freud 1919, 234).

14. Here the English version gives the unfortunate mistranslation "atropaic" (Kofman 1991b, 161).

15. The number of different permutations of possible reading strategies proliferates further in Kofman's remarks on her study during the group interview for *La Quinzaine Littéraire*: here the Nietzschean perspective undermines a "hegelo-theologico- psychoanalytic" reading (Agacinski et al. 1976, 21).

16. Cf. Kofman 1988a, 184: "The *problem of hierarchy* is Nietzsche's problem," paraphrasing *Human, All Too Human*, vol. 1, Preface, sec. 7 (Nietzsche 1986, 10).

17. For a philosopher working on Freud in Paris throughout the period of Lacan's lionization there, Kofman remained remarkably resistant to Lacan's doctrines, and to his reading of Freud. A sense of this resistance can be gained from the debate that followed her 1980 paper on Derrida, "Ça cloche," in which François Raux-Filio remarks: "It is never only a question of imaginary castration," and Kofman retorts: "That is not in Freud but in Lacan" (Kofman 1989a, 138). In general, references to Lacan are conspicuous by their absence in her works, and what few references there are are almost exclusively, as here, to his most celebrated paper, "The Mirror Stage as Formative of the Function of the I" (Lacan 1977). Cf. also Kofman 1988c, 219 n. 15; Kofman 1985b, 93; Kofman 1995b, 19–23. For Kofman on her relation to Lacan, cf. Kofman with Jardine 1991, 109.

18. Kofman's remarks here are associated with the painter Francesko in *The Devil's Elixirs*: in *Autobiogriffures* she turns her attention to the painter Ettinger in *Life and Opinions of Murr the Tomcat*, and beyond her Hoffmann studies she explores the question of painterly mimesis in a number of other texts, particularly *Mélancolie de l'art* (1985b). On the "Unheimlichkeit" of painting, cf. "La mélancolie de l'art" (1985b, 15–20); on painting as a "double mimesis," cf. "La ressemblance des portraits: L'imitation selon Diderot" (1985b, 52–61). The link between literary and painterly mimesis is already established in *The Childhood of Art*, where Kofman addresses "Freud's Method of Reading: The Work of Art as a Text to Decipher" (1988c, 53–103), and the "imposture" of portraiture (1975, 120) will of course become the subject, much later, of "L'imposture de la beauté" (1995b, 9–48).

19. It is significant that one of the few Hoffmann commentators sympathetic to a deconstructive approach, Manfred Momberger, closes his study with a chapter entitled "The Place of Laughter" (Momberger 1986, 178–209), taking an epigraph on laughter from Nietzsche (178) and following Kofman in concentrating on "B/S" in *The Devil's Elixirs* (188–199).

20. Again, Kofman will later expand her catalog of examples to include painterly representations of cats, by Balthus (Kofman 1985b, 94–101).

21. The texts in square brackets here are my own graftings. One could, of course, continue such a game more or less indefinitely—by reference, for example, to the "GREPH," the "Grif," and so on.

22. The term is ultimately derived from Plato: cf. Kofman 1988b, 18; Kofman 1989c, 34–39.

23. Although Freud writes a whole book entitled *Jokes and Their Relation to the Unconscious*, it is not in itself a funny book (cf. Kofman 1986c); for Kofman, it is Nietzsche's "generalized unmasking" that actually provokes laughter (cf. Kofman with Degoy 1994).

24. Nietzsche's familiarity with Hoffmann was in fact surprisingly slight. He makes only two passing references to the writer, both of them in unpublished notes and both in the context of Hoffmann's literary influence on German composers (although Hoff-

mann, like Nietzsche himself, was a minor Romantic composer). In summer–autumn 1884 (Nietzsche 1980, 11:250), he writes of Wagner's having gone through a "Schauer-Hoffmann" phase; in 1887 or 1888, again in a musical context, he notes that "Schumann has in himself Eichendorff, Uhland, Heine, Hoffmann, Tieck" (*The Will to Power,* sec. 106 [Nietzsche 1968b, 67; Nietzsche 1980, 13:133).

Chapter 4. Suffering Contradiction: Kofman on Nietzsche's Critique of Logic

1. Tragedy, then, is a process of imitating an action that has serious implications, is complete, and possesses magnitude; by means of language that has been made sensuously attractive, with each of its varieties found separately in the parts; enacted by the persons themselves and not presented through narrative; through a course of pity and fear that completes the purification of tragic acts that have those emotional characteristics.

Chapter 5. Nietzsche and Metaphor

1. This is a translation of the second edition of *Nietzsche et la métaphore* (Paris: Galilée, 1983), originally published in 1972. Earlier versions of material included in this book first appeared in 1971: "L'oubli de la métaphore," a review of *Das Philosophenbuch/Le livre du philosophe: Études théoriques,* trans. Angèle Kremer-Marietti (Paris: Aubier-Flammarion, 1969), appeared in *Critique* 27 (August–September 1971); "Nietzsche et la métaphore" appeared in *Poètique* 5 (Spring 1971), along with the second part of Derrida's "La mythologie blanche: La métaphore dans le texte philosophique," Lacoue-Labarthes's "Détour (Nietzsche et la rhétorique)," and translations of selections from Nietzsche's notebooks on rhetoric and language.

2. I have discussed some similarities between Derrida and Deleuze on concept and metaphor in Patton 1996.

3. Kröner ed Leipzig: Naumann, 1901–1913, 12:1, p. 79.

Chapter 6. Schemata of Ideology in *Camera obscura* and *Specters of Marx*

1. *L'enfance de l'art,* Kofman's first book, on Freudian aesthetics, had appeared in 1970. *Nietzsche et la métaphore* appeared in 1972.

2. This was the first introduction to appear to one of Kofman's English editions. Large also provides us with a complete bibliography of Kofman's work.

3. Interview with Alice Jardine. Excerpts from the Kofman interview, translated by Janice Orion, and several other of the *Shifting Scenes* interviews had first appeared in "The Politics of Tradition: Placing Women in French Literature," *Yale French Studies* 75 (1988).

4. As examples of this sparse citation, one might note the exergue quotation of *Comment s'en sortir?* taken from Blanchot's *La folie du jour,* or "Ça cloche," in Kofman 1984b, 141–151. In the latter, Blanchot is cited in the context of a discussion of *Glas.* The English translation of "Ça cloche," appearing in Kofman 1989a, omits two footnote references to Blanchot.

5. Cf. Duncan Large's introduction to Kofman 1993b and Penelope Deutscher's "Complicated Fidelity: Kofman's Freud," Chapter 9 in this volume. And indeed Deleuze's troika of Nietzsche/Freud/Marx forms the core of *Camera obscura* and stands

adjacent to the Nietzsche/Heidegger diad that animates so much of Derrida's work, particularly in the 1960s and 1970s.

6. *Nietzsche et la métaphore* had been presented in a Derrida seminar on metaphor in 1969–70. Though the general issue of metaphor is weighing heavily on Derrida at this time ("White Mythology" will become the fruit of this contact), nonetheless *Nietzsche et la métaphore* clearly bears the original mark of Kofman's early engagement, "in isolation," with Nietzsche.

7. For a good account of the genesis of the concept of ideology, see Eagleton 1991.

8. Not even in the ironic sense of Derrida: "What is certain is that I am not a Marxist, as someone said, in a witticism reported by Engels. Must we still cite Marx as an authority in order to say 'I am not a Marxist?'" (Derrida 1994, 88). Kofman settles her accounts with Marx in *Camera obscura* and will not discuss him again.

9. The general trend is to dismiss the reading from *The German Ideology* as a naive and simplistic conception of ideology as an illusory, chimerical reflection of the material basis of society that is directly analogous to the simple, specular inversion carried out by the lens of the camera obscura. Althusser, for example, in *Lenin and Philosophy*, dismisses this reading outright as "not Marxist," which for Althusser is equivalent to saying "pre-*Capital*." Terry Eagleton supports the notion that Marx offers a far subtler, more sophisticated conception of ideology in *Capital*, as against *GI*, in the Introduction to *Ideology* (Eagleton 1994, 5–12). John Mepham, in "The Theory of Ideology in *Capital*" in the same volume (211–237), also suggests a strict divergence between the two accounts, while suggesting that the reading from *GI* is largely inadequate.

10. The theme of the textual play of metaphors, of "metaphors correcting metaphors," is a distinct feature of Kofman's interpretative methodology, seen particularly in *Nietzsche and Metaphor*, and is crucial to the readings given in all three main chapters of *Camera obscura:* on Marx, Freud, and Nietzsche. Kofman also makes careful and prudent use of extensive quotation in *Camera obscura*, a practice that is linked to what is, disparagingly and I believe unfairly, referred to as her "mimeticism."

11. See Kofman 1973, 40, 48 n. 31. Cf. Freud 1912, 264; Nietzsche 1967a, II sec. 1.

12. Cf. Marx and Engels 1996, 23.

13. With regard to this last point, cf. the earlier quotation from "Theses on Feuerbach" (Kofman 1973, 19) and a reference from *Capital* that Kofman inserts into her text (Kofman 1973, 29–30; Marx and Engels 1996, 90–91). If ideological mystification could be overturned, if the inversion could be inverted, by the mere exposure of its contradictions, then there would be no need for the social conditions that are the "product of a long and painful process of development" as a necessary precondition of demystification (Kofman 1973, 30). Both theoretical, polemical critique and practical struggle are required to carry out the labor of the revolution. Marx's insistence on the necessity of their simultaneity effaces any strict opposition between theory and praxis.

14. The footnote reads: "On the relation between fetishism and ideology, cf. Sarah Kofman *Camera obscura—de l'idéologie*, in particular what precedes and follows 'La table tournante.'"

15. The paper is something of a response to Aijaz Ahmad's largely critical, though admittedly provisional, analysis given in the previous *New Left Review* (Ahmad 1994). This reading is in response to the second chapter of *Specters*, "Conjuring-Marxism," which had first appeared under the title "A Lecture on Marx" in *New Left Review* 205.

16. Cf. Foucault 1979, 222–223:

> Historically, the process by which the bourgeoisie became . . . the politically dominant class was masked by the establishment of an explicit, coded, and formally egalitarian ju-

ridical framework. . . . But the development and generalization of disciplinary mechanisms constituted the other, dark side of these processes. The general juridical form that guaranteed a system of rights that were egalitarian in principle was supported by these tiny, everyday, physical mechanisms, by all those systems of micro-power that are essentially non-egalitarian that we call the disciplines. . . .

The acceptance of a discipline may be underwritten by contract; the way in which it is imposed, the mechanisms it brings into play, the nonreversible subordination of one group of people by another, the "surplus" power that is always fixed on the same side[—]all these distinguish the disciplinary link from the contractual link, and make it possible to distort the contractual link systematically from the moment it has as its content the mechanism of a discipline. We know, for example, how many real procedures undermine the legal fiction of the work contract.

17. Who is afraid of ghosts here? Derrida is "bound to" the specter of an ontologized Marx "in a troubling way" (Derrida 1994, 139).

18. Aijaz Ahmad is not impressed with Derrida's sketch of the new International, referring to it as "defined in terms of what it is not" and having the "quality, more or less, of a Masonic order" (Ahmad 1994, 103–104). Jameson, also somewhat suspicious, refers to it as a "subterranean Utopianism" (Jameson 1995, 81).

19. Benjamin's weak messianism is maintained by the sober remembering of the historical materialist who, in the moment of revolutionary action, acts in remembrance, redeeming past generations. Derrida clearly wants to remember, can't help but remember, a particular specter of Marx, who appears, truly, to be the specter of Walter Benjamin. He cannot easily settle his metaphysical accounts with this particular ghost.

And here, let us recall Kofman's analysis of the forgetfulness of ideology, which should reawaken us to the tension between the active forgetting of Kofman's Nietzsche and the remembering of Benjamin's historical materialism—a tension that I suggest urgently announces itself in this chapter.

Chapter 7. How a Woman Philosophizes

1. To save thought also to the detriment of the writing: why do philosophers not write (Socrates) or write poorly (Auguste Comte)?

2. Because "the modesty of a god is nothing other than nudity," says Nietzsche. But nudity is not confused with exhibition.

3. Just as in Auguste Comte the depressive episode functions as theoretical operator. Cf. Sarah Kofman, "Le bénéfice de la maladie" in *Aberrations* (Kofman 1978a, 181–184).

Chapter 8. Rending Kant's Umbrella: Kofman's Diagnosis of Ethical Law

1. *Le respect des femmes (Kant et Rousseau)* discusses themes familiar to American feminists engaged in the analysis of cultural systems, including, for example, the role played by gestures of respect in supporting oppression; the association of the masculine with culture, the feminine with nature; and the identity of woman's protector with the predator. Usually these themes emerge from analyses of cultural systems or specific social institutions. Kofman's work provides a genealogical perspective on these issues by tracing their operation in the influential early modern philosophies.

Few American feminist treatments of Kant achieve the same depth of insight. Early second-wave feminists dismissed Kant's personal attitudes toward women in his life and in his a posteriori works as revealing a culturally limited bias, a mere aberration from his ethical universalism; later feminists criticized that very universalism as an antifeminist way of thinking, but without returning to his specific writings (Gilligan 1982). In contrast to these treatments, more recent works, for example, Robin Schott's detailed, cogent study of asceticism in Kant's philosophy, have made just such a return. Schott's excellent book argues from a Marxian perspective to give a comprehensive and insightful treatment of Kant in terms of alienation and commodity fetishism (Schott 1988).

2. In this chapter, I am largely concerned with the introductory section of *Respect* and the first chapter, which focuses on Kant. For the introductory section, I have provided my own translations; for Kofman's chapter on Kant, while providing page references to the original text (Kofman 1982b), I have cited an existing translation (Kofman 1982a).

3. Christopher Norris has successfully debunked an overly aesthetic interpretation of deconstruction (Norris 1987, 13–20, 194ff.). See also Derrida's most explicit response to American literary critical readings of deconstruction as aestheticism in *Otobiographies* (1984). Nevertheless, developing sensitivity to the rhetorical connotations of a deconstructive text remains a useful first entry to such texts, before moving on to more sophisticated readings.

4. Kofman's citation of Tacitus is followed by Rousseau's translation and commentary: " 'Quand une femme a perdu sa pudeur, elle n'aura plus rien à refuser.' Cité par Rousseau dans *Emile*, . . . accompagné du commentaire suivant: 'Jamais auteur connutil mieux la coeur humain dans les deux sexes que celui qui a dit cela?' " ("When a woman has lost her decency, she can no longer refuse anything.") (Kofman 1982b, 23). Cited by Rousseau in *Emile*, accompanied by the following comment: "Was there ever an author who knew the human heart in the two sexes as well as the one who has said this?" (my translation).

This passage is also cited in part in translation (Kofman 1982a, 383). Cf. Tacitus (1989); Rousseau (1993).

5. "Respite" originates as a legal plea for delay in order to take a second look at the case or contract, evoking both a temporal distancing and a transformed relation.

6. From the Greek, a turning away or averting, a prevention or deterrent. Used by Cixous (1975) of Perseus' defense against the Medusa.

7. The title "Speculative Beginning of Human History" is more commonly translated as "Conjectures on the Origins of Human History."

8. Recently the skeptical reading of deconstruction has come under scrutiny, notably in Ewa Ziarek's *Rhetoric of Failure* (1995), which criticizes the assimilation of Derridean deconstruction into a skeptical model from a Levinasian approach. While I find much of her work compelling, I note that the commentators she discusses usually make the move from a skeptical reading back to the overworked aestheticized one in order to debunk deconstruction wholesale. In another work, "The New Pyrrhonians: Taking Deconstructive Skepticism Seriously" (Alexander, n.d.), I have argued that, if it is not done with a reductive agenda, reading a deconstructive text as a latter-day skepticism can be tremendously fruitful, although not perhaps the last word in interpretation.

9. An excerpt of Kant's essay is also available (Kant 1963).

10. In most common versions of the myth, Seth, not Isis, murders and dismembers Osiris.

Chapter 9. Complicated Fidelity: Kofman's Freud

1. Expressing Rousseauist suspicions about women, Freud comments that this is partly due to their conventional secretiveness and insincerity (Freud 1905, 151).

2. Derrida's discussion of the difference between what a text declares, or "would like to say," and what the text actually describes is to be found in his discussion of Rousseau in *Of Grammatology* (Derrida 1976, 229). The translator of *The Childhood of Art* adds to Kofman's footnote that a discussion of the distinction between concept and discourse is to be found in "Différance" in Derrida's *Margins of Philosophy* (1982).

3. I have discussed elsewhere Nietzsche's foreshortening of figures such as "Rousseau," and "feminism" (Deutscher 1993, 164). Perhaps Kofman's own foreshortening of the philosopher is another of her Nietzschean masks?

4. Comments in a similar vein are made by Kofman at the conclusion of *Explosion II:*

Il y apparaîtrait que, pour moi, auront joué les rôles de "Wagner" et de "Schopenhauer," Freud et Nietzsche, ces deux "génies" rivaux que j'ai toujours eu besoin de tenir ensemble . . . (lisant Freud, je le lis avec la troisième oreille nietzschéene, lisant Nietzsche, je l'entends de ma quatrième oreille freudienne). C'est peut-être ce qui fait la spécificité de ma lecture: au plus près du texte de Nietzsche, je le féconde pourtant et le déplace légèrement grâce à mon écoute freudienne. (Kofman 1993a, 371–2)

5. On this theme, see in particular Kofman's book on the theme of respect for women in Rousseau and Kant, *Le respect des femmes* (1982b, partially translated in Kofman 1982a and 1989b). See also her essay on Nietzsche and Baubô (Kofman 1988a). In both essays, Kofman suggests that respect for women's distance "permits the male to desire a woman without being petrified ["médusé"]; it is a veil[,] . . . a spontaneous defense" (Kofman 1988a, 191, discussed in Deutscher 1993, 167).

6. See, for example, Kofman's gloss on Freud in *The Childhood of Art:* "Woman is enigmatic because she lacks a penis. Freud reminds us that it is she who invented weaving (*weben*) in order to veil her nudity; that is, to hide the fact that she has nothing to hide: to cover over a hole (*verdecken*). In Freud's view, the spider (*Spinne*) that weaves is a symbol of the phallic mother" (Kofman 1988c, 57). As we will see, in *Enigma of Woman* Kofman suggests that Freud prefers to close his eyes before the enigma constituted by his mother and by all women, and so he attributes to them a spurious and in fact entirely speculative concept: penis envy (Kofman 1985a, 95).

7. Again, see in particular Kofman's *Le respect des femmes* (1982b) for these themes. Here, Kofman also "thematizes" the divided *Respect des femmes* figure that woman often represents: adored and vilified, idealized and feared. She argues that this division sometimes serves to protect an ideal image of woman, or of the mother, by displacing onto the concept of the "other" woman concepts of degradation or impurity that threaten to jeopardize the idealized image. It is in these terms that Kofman analyzes Rousseau, for example, for whom the figure of "woman" is represented by the exaggerated opposites of the virtuous Sophie and the deceitful, worldly Parisienne. Thus in Kofman's analysis, woman—to use the figure she often employs—is often the Janus figure with opposite but inseparable faces: the good and the bad mother, or the virgin and the prostitute.

8. Kofman uses the term "sexual difference" in this context to refer to the asymmetry of men and women.

9. She references Derrida's discussions of Freud in "To Speculate—on 'Freud'" in *The Postcard* (Derrida 1987), in *Glas* (Derrida 1986), and, briefly, in "The Double Session" in *Dissemination* (Derrida 1981).

10. For Kofman's criticism that Derrida's account of the undecidability of fetishism gives Freud both too much and too little of the benefit of the doubt, see "Ça cloche" (Kofman 1989a, 121ff.).

11. Freud desires to unveil all, but he also fears the process of unveiling. In "Il n'y a que le premier pas qui coûte" (Kofman 1991c), Kofman considers Freud's reservations about philosophy, speculation, about trying to know all. Although he is tempted, Freud considers that he shouldn't transgress the limits of his proper terrain of work, a reserve that Kofman relates to his fear of being punished with blindness (42–43). Now it is Freud himself, she points out, who connects fear of blindness with fear of castration (56, see also 68).

12. Here, Kofman references Derrida's *Spurs* (1979) and her own essay on Nietzsche and Baubô (Kofman 1988a).

Chapter 10. Sarah Kofman's Queasy Stomach and the Riddle of the Paternal Law

1. See Kofman [1979] 1986b; cf. Kofman 1992.

2. Freud indicates that he is not sure that she actually *said* this in the dream, but in the dream she *shows* him that he will have to wait.

3. In my *Womanizing Nietzsche,* I argue that "having it both ways" is the logic of fetishism. I analyze Derrida's notion of undecidability as a form of fetishism. There I am critical of Kofman's suggestion that by having it both ways Nietzsche escapes fetishism (Oliver 1995).

4. For an alternative reading of Nietzsche's ambivalent relationship to the mother, see Oliver 1994, 53–67.

5. I am reminded of a passage in *Beyond Good and Evil* where Nietzsche says that good and bad women alike want a stick (Nietzsche 1966, "E&I," sec. 147).

6. For both boys and girls, Freud describes an original identification with, and desire for, the mother that the Oedipal situation effectively splits. Post-Oedipus, identification and desire lie at opposite poles. The boy discontinues his identification with the mother, identifies with the father, and desires a mother substitute. The girl is forced to identify again with her mother, even after the betrayal of castration, and now desires her father. What Oedipus ensures is that desire and identification are split. You desire what you are not and you identify with what you are. As I have argued elsewhere, Freud's description of the desire for the feminine is not a description of a desire for something that the masculine is not; rather, Freud's feminine is always defined within a masculine economy as castrated or phallic (see Oliver 1995). It could be said, then, that Freud splits identification and desire, insisting that he desire what he is not, the feminine, so that he can ensure that he is himself masculine. (For a more developed analysis of the relationship between identification and desire, see Oliver 1997.)

Chapter 11. Eating Words: Antigone as Kofman's Proper Name

1. Later the story is amended; see Frances Bartowski's introduction to Kofman 1986a.

2. Antigone recalls her suffering again before going on to specify her relationship to Polynices with reference to her mother: "Who lives in sorrows many as are mine how shall he not be glad to gain his death? And so, for me to meet this fate, no grief. But if

I left that corpse, my mother's son, dead and unburied I'd have cause to grieve as now I grieve not" (Sophocles 1954, 463–468).

3. Kofman's use of the word "unheimlich" recalls Heidegger's designation of Antigone's essence as "unheimlich," to which he translates *to deinon*, in his reading of Hölderlin's poem, *Der Ister*. See Heidegger 1996.

4. One thinks too of the food that Creon orders to be left outside Antigone's tomb-cave in a fruitless attempt to absolve himself of the guilt of her death.

5. As Derrida observes in ironic understatement, this is not just any family: "Antigone's parents are not some parents among others" (Derrida 1986, 165; Derrida 1974, 186). Antigone is born of the incestuous embraces of Oedipus with his mother, Jocasta. The law that binds Antigone to her brother Polynices is thereby doubly marked by the ties of kinship binding her to a mother who is also her father's mother. Antigone's duty to her brother is indelibly imprinted on her mind by the terrible circumstances of their birth—or, as Irigaray calls it—the "dreadful paradigm of a mother who is both wife and mother to her husband" (Irigaray 1985, 219; Irigaray 1974, 272).

6. Alice Jardine and Anne Menke conducted the interview as one of a series that they held between May 1986 and November 1987.

Chapter 12. Kofman, Nietzsche, and the Jews

1. When someone who knows the texts of Freud as well as Sarah Kofman makes such a comment, one is tempted to bring the machinery of psychoanalytic decoding to bear on such a remark. I have chosen, however, to avoid this temptation.

2. When we met, I was not familiar with Kofman's *Paroles suffoquées* (1987b). Had I been, I would have recalled immediately its first dedication: "À la mémoire de mon père, mort à Auschwitz."

3. It warrants recalling as well that two of this century's most important critical analysts of anti-Semitism, Frankfurt School founders Theodor Adorno and Max Horkheimer, also offer significant reflections on Nietzsche's works that similarly overlook the "Jewish question" in Nietzsche.

4. Arendt herself notes that while Nietzsche correctly estimated "the significant role of the Jews in European history," his affirmation of the " 'good European' . . . saved him from falling into the pitfalls of cheap philosemitism or patronizing 'progressive' attitudes" (Arendt 1951, 23).

5. A similar point could be made about Marx, whose early anti-Jewish writings, while they should not be confused with the anti-Semitic writings of some of his contemporaries, may bear some responsibility for the twentieth-century anti-Semitism of some supposed "Marxists."

6. For a discussion of Kofman's *Nietzsche and Metaphor*, see Schrift 1990, 85–94, 166–168.

7. Nietzsche's cultural and political reception in Germany is discussed in a number of recent works, including Aschheim (1992) and Taylor (1990). An earlier and more narrowly focused discussion of Nietzsche's reception by the German left is to be found in Thomas (1983).

8. This and several of the following paragraphs are taken, with minor alterations, from the concluding pages of Schrift (1995).

9. Sarah Kofman cites several of these remarks in the closing chapter of *Le mépris des Juifs* (1994c).

Chapter 13. "Made in Germany": Judging National Identity Negatively

1. Paul Valéry provides us with further confirmation of the menacing potency of these three words, "Made in Germany," in his essay "Souvenir actuel" (Valéry 1994, 93–94):

> M. Williams avait eu l'idée d'examiner de fort près la situation du commerce et des industries britanniques, et l'avait trouvée dangereusement menacée par la concurrence allemande. Dans tous les domaines de la production, de la consommation, des moyens de transport et de la publicité, grâce à une information extraordinairement précise et pénétrante qui centralisait d'innombrables renseignements, l'entreprise réalisait systématiquement l'éviction des produits anglais sur tous les marchés du monde, et parvenait à dominer jusque dans les colonies même de la Grande Bretagne. Tous les traits de cette vaste et méthodique opération étaient relevés un à un, décrits avec le plus grand soin par Williams, et présentés à la manière anglaise: le moins possible d'idées et le plus possible de faits. Le titre même que Williams avait donné à l'ensemble de ses articles était en train de faire fortune, un bill célèbre allait l'incorporer dans la législation, et ces trois mots Made in Germany s'incrustèrent du coup dans le têtes anglaises.

Germany is at once a symbol of an ultramodern, streamlined efficiency that scientifically applies itself to the economic market, thereby undermining the out-of-date and cumbersome regime of the Empire, and of primitive fears of unknowable and elusive powers, evoked by the incantatory formula of "Made in Germany." Lars von Trier's 1991 film *Europa* also uses Germany explicitly as the symbol of Europe's unconscious. The journey into postwar Germany, divided up into Allied zones and fitfully resisting "denazification," is also the journey into the depths of the psyche.

2. See, for example, Nietzsche 1992, 12:

> One is least related to one's parents: it would be the most extreme sign of vulgarity to be related to one's parents. Higher natures have their origins infinitely further back, and with them much had to be assembled, saved, and hoarded. The greatest individuals are the oldest: I don't understand it, but Julius Caesar could be my father—or Alexander, this Dionysus incarnate.

3. Folkloric costumes are also horrifically conspicuous national labels, to be replaced as quickly as possible by modern dress. In Nietzsche 1986, 365, "modernity" and "Europe" are coterminous. Indeed, in the same passage, Nietzsche highlights the distinction to be drawn between "Europe" as culture and "Europe" as geographic location:

> Here where the concepts "modern" and "European" are almost equivalent, what is understood by Europe comprises much more territory than geographic Europe, the little peninsula of Asia: America, especially, belongs to it, insofar as it is the daughterland of our culture. On the other hand, the cultural concept "Europe" does not include all of geographic Europe; it includes only those nations and ethnic minorities who possess a common past in Greece, Rome, Judaism, and Christianity.

4. "Freud et Nietzsche, ces deux 'génies' rivaux que j'ai toujours eu besoin de tenir ensemble pour qu'aucun d'eux ne l'emportât définitivement sur l'autre ni sur 'moi' . . . (lisant Freud, je le lis avec la troisième oreille nietzschéenne, lisant Nietzsche, je l'entends de ma quatrième oreille freudienne). C'est peut-être ce qui fait la spécificité de ma lecture" (Kofman 1993a, 371–372).

5. Elsewhere it becomes clear that *Deutschtum* is nothing other than Thomas Mann himself:

Verdient oder nicht, mein Name hatte sich nun einmal für die Welt mit dem Begriff eines Deutschtums verbunden, das sie liebt und ehrt; dass gerade ich der wüsten Verfälschung klar widerspräche, welche dies Deutschtum jetzt erlitt, war eine in alle freien Kunstträume, denen ich mich so gern überlassen hätte, beunruhigend hineintönende Forderung. (Mann 1990a, 788).

Mann carries the portable cultural burden of *Deutschtum* with him to Pacific Palisades, California, where he then becomes that burden: he has to represent this heritage, no longer determined by national ties but upheld by its international, supranational audience. It speaks through him as he broadcasts his messages back to Germany during the war.

6. "De plus, alors qu'Eros et la pulsion de mort sont dans les autres textes posés comme des principes d'unification et de désintrication au-delà du principe de plaisir, en rattachant l'affirmation à l'introjection qui introduit en soi ce qui fait plaisir, Freud ne fait-il pas dépendre à leur tour Eros et la pulsion de la destruction du principe de plaisir" (Kofman 1983b, 60).

7. See Kofman 1983b, 47: "Seule la négation et son symbole 'non' [or 'Made in Germany'] permettent d'établir une indépendance de la pensée à l'égard du refoulement, lui permettent d'utiliser le 'contenu' inconscient indispensable à son fonctionnement tout en maintenant le refoulement."

8. "Was nun das Ich selbst und überhaupt betrifft, so steht es fast rührend, recht eigentlich besorgniserregend damit. Es ist ein kleiner, vorgeschobener, erleuchteter und wachsamer Teil des 'Es'—ungefähr wie Europa eine kleine, aufgeweckte Provinz des weiten Asiens ist" (Mann 1990b, 486).

9. "Das Urteilen ist die intellektuelle Aktion, die über die wahl der motorischen Aktion entscheidet, dem Denkaufschub ein Ende setzt und vom Denken um Handeln überleitet" (Freud 1989, 376).

10. Derrida's book *The Other Heading* (1992) provides an interesting complement to this discussion of the limits of navigation, the fate of Europe, and possible negativity. See, for example, page 6, where he poses the question of whether Europe's future face will be monstrous.

11. See the helpful section, "The Object of the Indefinite Judgement," in Žižek 1993, 108–114.

12. See Rose 1993, 153: "What 'Negation' offers is a way of theorizing a subject who comes into being on the back of a repudiation, who exists in direct proportion to what it cannot let be."

13. Hence our interest in Kofman's *Explosion I* and *Explosion II,* which can be regarded as a 770-page exploration of Nietzsche's claims in *Ecce Homo:* "I am no man, I am dynamite" and "How I understand the philosopher—as a terrible explosive, endangering everything" (Nietzsche 1992, 58, 96).

14. These themes are also of major importance for her last book, *Rue Ordener, rue Labat* (Kofman 1994d).

15. Derrida talks about this "nonidentity to itself," this "difference *with itself,*" as being indicative of cultural identity per se; see Derrida 1992, 9–10.

16. "De lui, il me reste seulement le stylo. Je l'ai pris un jour dans le sac de ma mère où elle le gardait avec d'autres souvenirs de mon père. Un stylo comme l'on n'en fait plus, et qu'il fallait remplir avec de l'encre. Je m'en suis servie pendant toute ma scolarité. Il m'a 'lâchée' avant que je puisse me décider de l'abandonner. Je le possède toujours rafistolé avec du scotch, il est devant mes yeux sur ma table de travail et il me contraint à écrire, écrire" (Kofman 1994d, 9).

Consolidated Bibliography

Adorno, T. W. 1972. "Parataxis." In *Notes to Literature*. Trans. S. W. Nicholsen. Vol. 2. New York: Columbia University Press.

Agacinski, S., et al. 1976. "Six philosophes occupés à déplacer le philosophique à propos de la 'mimesis.'" *La Quinzaine Littéraire* 231 (16–30 April): 19–22.

Ahmad, A. 1994. "Reconciling Derrida: *Specters of Marx* and Deconstructive Politics." *New Left Review* 208 (November–December): 88–106.

Alexander, N. 1998. "Sublime Impersonation: The Rhetoric of Personification in Kant." In *Language and Liberation: Feminism, Philosophy and Language*. Ed. C. Hendricks and K. Oliver. Albany, N.Y.: SUNY Press.

———. n.d. "The New Pyrrhhonians: Taking Deconstructive Skepticism Seriously." Unpublished manuscript.

Arendt, H. 1951. *The Origins of Totalitarianism*. Cleveland: World Publishing Company.

Aristotle. 1967. *Poetics*. Trans. G. F. Else. Ann Arbor: University of Michigan Press.

———. 1971. *Metaphysics*. Trans. C. Kirwan. Oxford: Oxford University Press.

Armengaud, F. 1997. "Sarah's Lachen." *In Sie ist gegangen- Geschichlen vom Abschied für immer*. Ed. T. Bührmann. Berlin: Orlanda Frauen verlag.

Artaud, A. 1956. *Oeuvres complètes*. Vol. 14. Paris: Gallimard.

Aschheim, S. E. 1992. *The Nietzsche Legacy in Germany 1890–1990*. Berkeley: University of California Press.

Barande, I. 1977. *Le maternel singulier: Freud et Léonard de Vinci*. Paris: Aubier-Montaigne.

Bataille, G. 1983. "The Language of Flowers." In *Georges Bataille: Visions of Excess. Selected Writings, 1927–1939*. Ed. A. Stoekl. Trans. A. Stoekl, with C. R. Lovitts and D. M. Leslie, Jr. Minneapolis: University of Minnesota Press.

———. 1991. *The Accursed Share*. Trans. R. Hurley. Vols. 2 and 3. New York: Zone Books.

Beaufret, J. 1962. "Hölderlin et la question du père." *Les Temps Modernes* 18 (July–December): 147–161.

Beauvoir, S. de. 1962. *The Prime of Life*. Trans. P. Green. Cleveland: World Publishing Company.

Benjamin, W. 1968. "Theses on the Philosophy of History." In *Illuminations*. Ed. H. Arendt. Trans. H. Zohn. New York: Schocken Books.

———. 1996. *Selected Writings*. Cambridge, Mass.: Belknap Press.

Binion, R. 1968. *Frau Lou: Nietzsche's Wayward Disciple*. Princeton, N.J.: Princeton University Press.

Blanchot, M. 1973. *Le pas au-delà*. Paris: Gallimard.

———. 1982. "Hölderlin's Itinerary." In *The Space of Literature*. Trans. A. Smock. Lincoln and London: University of Nebraska Press.

Cicero. 1954. *Rhetorica ad Herennium*. Trans. H. Caplan. London: Heinemann; Cambridge, Mass.: Harvard University Press.

Cixous, H. 1975. "Le rire de la Méduse." *L'Arc* 61:39–54.

Clark, M. 1990. *Nietzsche on Truth and Philosophy*. Cambridge: Cambridge University Press.

Collin, F. 1997. "L'impossible diététique: Philosophie et récit." *Les Cahiers du Grif* 3 (new series): 11–26.

Dancy, R. M. 1975. *Sense and Contradiction: A Study in Aristotle*. Dordrecht, Netherlands: D. Reidel.

David-Menard, M. 1993. *La folie dans la raison pure*. Paris: Vrin.

Deleuze, G., and F. Guattari. 1987. *A Thousand Plateaus: Capitalism and Schizophrenia*. Trans. B. Massumi. Minneapolis: University of Minnesota Press.

Derrida, J. 1974. *Glas*. Paris: Galilée.

———. 1976. *Of Grammatology*. Trans. C. G. Spivak. Baltimore and London: Johns Hopkins University Press.

———. 1979. *Spurs: Nietzsche's Styles*. Trans. B. Harlow. Chicago and London: University of Chicago Press.

———. 1981. *Dissemination*. Trans. B. Johnson. Chicago and London: University of Chicago Press.

———. 1982. *Margins of Philosophy*. Trans. A. Bass. Brighton, U.K.: Harvester Press.

———. 1984. *Otobiographies*. Paris: Galilée.

———. 1985. "Otobiographies." In *The Ear of the Other: Otobiograph, Transference, Translation*. Ed. C. V. McDonald. Trans. P. Kamuf. New York: Schocken Books.

———. 1986. *Glas*. Trans. J. P. Leavey and R. Rand. Lincoln: University of Nebraska Press.

———. 1987. *The Postcard: From Socrates to Freud*. Trans. A. Bass. Chicago: University of Chicago Press.

———. 1988. *Limited Inc*. Trans. S. Weber and J. Mehlman. Evanston, Ill.: Northwestern University Press.

———. 1992. *The Other Heading*. Trans. P. A. Brault and M. Nass. Bloomington: Indiana University Press.

———. 1994. *Specters of Marx*. Trans. P. Kamuf. New York and London: Routledge.

———. 1997. "Les dons de Sarah Kofman." *Les Cahiers du Grif* 3 (new series): 131–165.

des Forêts, L.-R. 1960. "Les grands moments d'un chanteur." In *La chambre des enfants*. Paris: Gallimard.

———. 1963. *Le bavard*. Paris: Gallimard.

——. 1988. *Poèmes de Samuel Wood*. Paris: Fata Morgana.

——. 1997. *Ostinato*. Paris: Mercure de France.

Deutscher, P. 1993. " 'Is It Not Remarkable That Nietzsche ... Should Have Hated Rousseau?' Woman, Femininity: Distancing Nietzsche from Rousseau." In *Nietzsche, Feminism and Political Theory*. Ed. P. Patton. London and New York: Routledge.

Diderot, D. 1959. "Pensées détachées sur la peinture." In *Oeuvres esthétiques*. Ed. P. Vernière. Paris: Garnier.

Duffy, M. F., and W. Mittelman. 1988. "Nietzsche's Attitude Toward the Jews." *Journal of the History of Ideas* 49 (2): 301–317.

Eagleton, T. 1991. *Ideology: An Introduction*. London: Verso Press.

——, ed. 1994. *Ideology*. New York: Longman.

Fermon, N. 1997. *Domesticating Passions: Rousseau, Woman and Nation*. Hanover, N.H., and London: Wesleyan University Press.

Foucault, M. 1962a. "Jean Laplanche: Hölderlin et la question du père." *Nouvelle Revue Française* 19 (January–June): 125–127.

——. 1962b. "Le 'non' du père." *Critique* 176 (January): 195–209.

——. 1979. *Discipline and Punish*. Trans. A. Sheridan. New York: Vintage Press.

Francastel, G., and P. Francastel. 1969. *Le portrait: 50 siècles d'humanisme en peinture*. Paris: Hachette.

Freud, S. 1905. "Three Essays on the Theory of Sexuality." In *The Standard Edition of the Complete Psychological Works of Sigmund Freud*. Vol. 7. Trans. and ed. J. Strachey. London: Hogarth Press and Institute of Psychoanalysis, 1953–1966.

——. 1907. "Delusions and Dreams in Jensen's *Gradiva*." In *The Standard Edition of the Complete Psychological Works of Sigmund Freud*. Vol. 9. Trans. and ed. J. Strachey. London: Hogarth Press and Institute of Psychoanalysis, 1953–1966.

——. 1910. "Leonardo da Vinci and a Memory of His Childhood." In *The Standard Edition of the Complete Psychological Works of Sigmund Freud*. Vol. 11. Trans. and ed. J. Strachey. London: Hogarth Press and Institute of Psychoanalysis, 1953–1966.

——. 1912. "A Note on the Unconscious in Psychoanalysis." In *The Standard Edition of the Complete Psychological Works of Sigmund Freud*. Vol. 12. Trans. and ed. J. Strachey. London: Hogarth Press and Institute of Psychoanalysis, 1953–1966.

——. 1913. "Totem and Taboo: Some Points of Agreement between the Mental Lives of Savages and Neurotics." In *The Standard Edition of the Complete Psychological Works of Sigmund Freud*. Vol. 13. Trans. and ed. J. Strachey. London: Hogarth Press and Institute of Psychoanalysis, 1953–1966.

——. 1915. "Thoughts for the Times on War and Death." In *The Standard Edition of the Complete Psychological Works of Sigmund Freud*. Vol. 14. Trans. and ed. J. Strachey. London: Hogarth Press and Institute of Psychoanalysis, 1953–1966.

——. 1916. "On Transience." In *The Standard Edition of the Complete Psychological Works of Sigmund Freud*. Vol. 14. Trans. and ed. J. Strachey. London: Hogarth Press and Institute of Psychoanalysis, 1953–1966.

——. 1919. "The 'Uncanny.' " In *The Standard Edition of the Complete Psychological Works of Sigmund Freud*. Vol. 17. Trans. and ed. J. Strachey. London: Hogarth Press and Institute of Psychoanalysis, 1953–1966.

———. 1925. "Negation." In *The Standard Edition of the Complete Psychological Works of Sigmund Freud.* Vol. 19. Trans. and ed. J. Strachey. London: Hogarth Press and Institute of Psychoanalysis, 1953–1966.

———. 1926. "Dostoevsky and Parricide." In *The Standard Edition of the Complete Psychological Works of Sigmund Freud.* Vol. 21. Trans. and ed. J. Strachey. London: Hogarth Press and Institute of Psychoanalysis, 1953–1966.

———. 1931. "Female Sexuality." In *The Standard Edition of the Complete Psychological Works of Sigmund Freud.* Vol. 21. Trans. and ed. J. Strachey. London: Hogarth Press and Institute of Psychoanalysis, 1953–1966.

———. 1937. "Constructions in Analysis." In *The Standard Edition of the Complete Psychological Works of Sigmund Freud.* Vol. 23. Trans. and ed. J. Strachey. London: Hogarth Press and Institute of Psychoanalysis, 1953–1966.

———. 1963. *Jokes and Their Relation to the Unconscious.* Trans. J. Strachey. New York: Norton.

———. 1967. *The Interpretation of Dreams.* Trans. J. Strachey. New York: Avon Books.

———. 1975. "The Dissection of the Psychical Personality." Trans. J. Strachey. In *New Introductory Lectures on Psychoanalysis.* Penguin Freud Library, vol. 2. Harmondsworth, U.K.: Penguin.

———. 1984. *On Metapsychology: The Theory of Psychoanalysis.* Trans. J. Strachey. Penguin Freud Library, vol. 11. Harmondsworth, U.K.: Penguin.

———. 1987. "Civilization and Its Discontents." In *Civilization, Society and Religion.* Trans. J. Strachey. Penguin Freud Library, vol. 12. Harmondsworth, U.K.: Penguin.

———. 1989. "Die Verneinung." In *Psychologie des Unbewussten.* Studienausgabe, vol. 3. Franfurt am Main: Fischer.

Gattégno, J. 1992. "Préface." In O. Wilde, *Le portrait de Dorian Gray.* Trans. and ed. J. Gattégno. Paris: Gallimard.

Gautier, T. 1903. "Enamels and Cameos and Other Poems." Trans. A. Lee and F. C. de Sumichrast. In *The Works of Théophile Gautier.* Trans. and ed. F. C. de Sumichrast. Vol. 24. London: Harrap.

Gilligan, C. 1982. *In a Different Voice: Psychological Theory and Women's Development.* Cambridge, Mass.: Harvard University Press.

Groupe de recherches sur l'enseignement philosophique (GREPH). 1977. *Qui a peur de la philosophie?* Paris: Flammarion.

Habermas, J. 1971. *Knowledge and Human Interests.* Trans. J. J. Shapiro. Boston: Beacon Press.

Hayman, R. 1980. *Nietzsche: A Critical Life.* New York: Penguin Books.

Heckman, P. 1991. "Nietzsche's Clever Animal: Metaphor in 'Truth and Falsity.' " *Philosophy and Rhetoric* 24 (4): 301–321.

Hegel, G. W. F. 1952. *Phänomenologie des Geistes.* Ed. J. Hoffmeister. Hamburg: Felix Meiner.

———. 1971. *Hegel's Philosophy of Mind.* Trans. W. Wallace and A. V. Miller. Oxford: Clarendon Press.

———. 1975. *Aesthetics: Lectures on Fine Art.* Trans. T. M. Knox. 2 vols. Oxford: Clarendon Press.

———. 1979. *Phenomenology of Spirit.* Trans. A. V. Miller. Oxford: Clarendon Press.

Heidegger, M. 1959. *An Introduction to Metaphysics*. Trans. R. Manheim. New Haven: Yale University Press.

———. 1996. *Hölderlin's Hymn "The Ister."* Trans. W. McNeill and J. Davis. Bloomington and Indianapolis: Indiana University Press.

Hölderlin, F. 1804. *Die Trauerspiele des Sophokles*. Frankfurt am Main: Friedrich Wilmans.

———. 1984. *Hymns and Fragments by Friedrich Hölderlin*. Ed. R. Sieburth. Princeton, N.J.: Princeton University Press.

———. 1994. *Poems and Fragments*. 3d ed. Ed. M. Hamburger. London: Anvil Press Poetry.

Hyppolite, J. 1966. "Commentaire parlé sur la 'Verneinung' de Freud." In J. Lacan, *Écrits*. Paris: Seuil.

Irigaray, L. 1974. *Speculum de l'autre femme*. Paris: Editions de Minuit.

———. 1985. *Speculum of the Other Woman*. Trans. G. C. Gill. Ithaca, N.Y.: Cornell University Press.

Jacobs, C. 1996. "Dusting Antigone." *MLN* 111: 889–917.

Jameson, F. 1995. "Marx's Purloined Letter." *New Left Review* 209 (January–February): 75–110.

Jardine, A. A., and A. M. Menke, eds. 1991. *Shifting Scenes: Interviews on Women, Writing, and Politics in Post–68 France*. New York: Columbia University Press.

Jean Paul [Richter, J. P. F.]. 1928. "Das Lob der Dumheit." In *Jean Pauls Sämtliche Werke: Historisch-kritische Ausgabe*. Ed. E. Behrend. Vol. 2/1. Weimar: Hermann Böhlaus Nachfolger.

Kaiser, G. R. 1988. *E. T. A. Hoffmann*. Stuttgart: Metzler.

Kant, I. 1956. *Critique of Practical Reason*. Trans. L. W. Beck. New York: Liberal Arts Press.

———. 1963. "On a Noble Tone in Philosophy [Excerpt]." In *Kant*. Trans. and comp. G. Rabel. Oxford: Clarendon Press.

———. 1964. *The Doctrine of Virtue*. Trans. and intro. M. J. Gregor. Philadelphia: University of Pennsylvania Press.

———. 1969. *Critique of Judgement*. Trans. J. C. Meredith. Oxford: Clarendon Press.

———. 1978. *Anthropology from a Pragmatic Point of View*. Trans. V. L. Dowdell. Intro. by F. P. Van de Pitte. London: Feffer and Simons.

———. 1979. *The Conflict of the Faculties*. Trans. M. J. Gregor. New York: Abaris.

———. 1983a. *Critique of Pure Reason*. Trans. N. K. Smith. London: Macmillan.

———. 1983b. "Speculative Beginning of Human History." In *Perpetual Peace and Other Essays on Politics, History, and Morals*. Trans. T. Humphrey. Indianapolis: Hackett.

———. 1991. *The Metaphysics of Morals*. Trans. M. J. Gregor. Cambridge: Cambridge University Press.

———. 1993. "On a Newly Arisen Superior Tone in Philosophy." In *Raising the Tone of Philosophy*. Trans. and ed. P. Fenves. Baltimore: Johns Hopkins University Press.

Kofman, S. 1972. *Nietzsche et la métaphore*. Paris: Payot.

———. 1973. *Camera obscura: De l'idéologie*. Paris: Galilée.

———. 1974. *Quatre romans analytiques*. Paris: Galilée.

——. 1975. "Vautour rouge: Le double dans *Les élixirs du diable* d'Hoffmann." In S. Agacinski et al., *Mimesis: Des articulations.* Paris: Aubier-Flammarion.

——. 1978a. *Aberrations: Le devenir-femme d'Auguste Comte.* Paris: Aubier-Flammarion.

——. 1978b. "L'espace de la césure." *Critique* 379 (December): 1143–1150.

——. 1979. *Nerval: Le charme de la répétition. Lecture de "Sylvie."* Lausanne: L'Age d'Homme.

——. 1981. "No Longer Full-Fledged Autobiogriffies." *SubStance* 29: 3–22.

——. 1982a. "The Economy of Respect: Kant and Respect for Women." *Social Research* 49 (2): 383–404.

——. 1982b. *Le respect des femmes (Kant et Rousseau).* Paris: Galilée.

——. 1983a. *Comment s'en sortir?* Paris: Galilée.

——. 1983b. *Un métier impossible.* Paris: Galilée.

——. [1976] 1984a. *Autobiogriffures: Du chat Murr d'Hoffmann.* 2d ed. Paris: Galilée. Originally published Paris: Christian Bourgois.

——. 1984b. *Lectures de Derrida.* Paris: Galilée.

——. 1985a. *The Enigma of Woman: Woman in Freud's Writings.* Trans. C. Porter. Ithaca, N.Y.: Cornell University Press.

——. 1985b. *Mélancolie de l'art.* Paris: Galilée.

——. 1985c. *Schreiben wie eine Katze: Zu E.T.A. Hoffmann's "Lebens-Ansichten des Katers Murr."* Trans. M. Buchgeister and H.-W. Schmidt. Graz and Vienna: Böhlau.

——. 1986a. "Autobiographical Writings" ("Nightmare: At the Margins of Medieval Studies"); "Damned Food"; "Tomb for a Proper Name"; and "Prometheus, the First Philosophe." *SubStance* 49 and 50: 6–13, 26–35.

——. [1979] 1986b. *Nietzsche et la scène philosophique.* 2d ed. Paris: Galilée. Originally published Paris: Union Générale d'Éditions ["10/18"].

——. 1986c. *Pourquoi rit-on? Freud et le mot d'esprit.* Paris: Galilée.

——. 1987a. "Nietzsche and the Obscurity of Heraclitus." *Diacritics* 17 (3) (Fall): 39–55.

——. 1987b. *Paroles suffoquées.* Paris: Galilée.

——. 1988a. "Baubô: Theological Perversion and Fetishism." In *Nietzsche's New Seas: Explorations in Philosophy, Aesthetics and Politics.* Ed. M. A. Gillespie and T. B. Strong. Chicago and London: University of Chicago Press.

——. 1988b. "Beyond Aporia?" In *Poststructuralist Classics.* Ed. A. Benjamin. London and New York: Routledge.

——. 1988c. *The Childhood of Art.* Trans. W. Woodhull. New York: Columbia University Press.

——. 1989a. "Ça cloche." In *Continental Philosophy II: Derrida and Deconstruction.* Ed. H. J. Silverman. New York and London: Routledge.

——. 1989b. "Rousseau's Phallocratic Ends." *Hypatia* 3 (3): 123–136.

——. 1989c. *Socrate(s).* Paris: Galilée.

——. 1990a. "Conversions: *The Merchant of Venice* under the Sign of Saturn." In *Literary Theory Today.* Ed. P. Collier and H. Geyer-Ryan. Cambridge: Polity Press.

——. 1990b. *Séductions: De Sartre à Héraclite.* Paris: Galilée.

——. 1991a. "Descartes Entrapped." In *Who Comes after the Subject?* Ed. E. Cadava, P. Connor, and J.-L. Nancy. New York and London: Routledge.

——. 1991b. *Freud and Fiction.* Trans. S. Wykes. London: Polity Press.

———. 1991c. *"Il n'y a que le premier pas qui coûte": Freud et la spéculation*. Paris: Galilée.

———. 1992. *Explosion I: De l' "Ecce Homo" de Nietzsche*. Paris: Galilée.

———. 1993a. *Explosion II: Les enfants de Nietzsche*. Paris: Galilée.

———. 1993b. *Nietzsche and Metaphor*. Trans. D. Large. London: Athlone.

———. 1994a. "A Fantastical Genealogy: Nietzsche's Family Romance." In *Nietzsche and the Feminine*. Ed. P. Burgard. Charlottesville: University of Virginia Press.

———. 1994b. " 'It's Only the First Step That Costs.' " In *Speculations after Freud: Psychoanalysis, Philosophy and Culture*. Ed. S. Shamdasani and M. Münchow. London and New York: Routledge.

———. 1994c. *Le mépris des Juifs: Nietzsche, les Juifs, l'antisémitisme*. Paris: Galilée.

———. 1994d. *Rue Ordener, rue Labat*. Paris: Galilée.

———. 1995a. "Accessories (*Ecce Homo*, 'Why I Write Such Good Books,' 'The Untimelies,' 3)." In *Nietzsche: A Critical Reader*. Ed. P. R. Sedgwick. Oxford and Cambridge, Mass.: Blackwell.

———. 1995b. *L'imposture de la beauté et autres textes*. Paris: Galilée.

———. 1996. *Rue Ordener, Rue Labat*. Trans. A. Smock. Lincoln and London: University of Nebraska Press.

Kofman, S., with L. Degoy. 1994. "Le mot d'esprit, l'humour, la mort et Freud selon Sarah Kofman." *L'Humanité* 25 (January): 19.

Kofman, S., with E. Ender. 1993. "Interview avec Sarah Kofman 22 mars 1991: Subvertir le philosophique *ou* Pour un supplément de jouissance." *Compar(a)ison* 1: 9–26.

Kofman, S., with J. Hermsen. 1992. "La question des femmes, une impasse pour les philosophes." *Les Cahiers du Grif* 46: 65–74.

Kofman, S., with R. Jaccard. 1986. "Apprendre aux hommes à tenir parole: Portrait de Sarah Kofman." *Le Monde* 27–28 (April): 7.

Kofman, S., with A. A. Jardine. 1991. "Sarah Kofman." In *Shifting Scenes: Interviews on Women, Writing, and Politics in Post–68 France*. Ed. A. A. Jardine and A. M. Menke. New York: Columbia University Press.

Kofman, S., and J.-Y. Masson. 1991. *Don Juan ou le refus de la dette*. Paris: Galilée.

Kristeva, J. 1982. *Powers of Horror*. Trans. L. Roudiez. New York: Columbia University Press.

Lacan, J. 1977. "The Mirror Stage as Formative of the Function of the I." In *Écrits: A Selection*. Trans. A. Sheridan. London: Tavistock; New York: Norton.

———. 1992. *The Ethics of Psychoanalysis 1959–1960: The Seminar of Jacques Lacan Book VII*. Ed. J.-A. Miller. Trans. D. Porter. London: Tavistock and Routledge.

Laclau, E. 1993. "Power and Representation." In *Politics, Theory, and Contemporary Culture*. Ed. M. Poster. New York: Columbia University Press.

Lacoue-Labarthe, P. 1987. "L'antagonisme." In *Nietzsche, Hölderlin et la Grèce: Actes du colloque organisé par le Centre du recherches d'histoire des idées à Nice*. Ed. E. Gaède. Nice: Centre du recherches d'histoire des idées.

———. 1989. "The Caesura of the Speculative." In *Typography: Mimesis, Philosophy, Politics*. Ed. C. Fynsk. Cambridge, Mass.: Harvard University Press.

———. 1995. "La naissance est la mort." *Séquences* 2, Théâtre National de Strasbourg.

Langer, L. L. 1996. *Admitting the Holocaust: Collected Essays*. New York and Oxford: Oxford University Press.

Laplanche, J. 1969. *Hölderlin et la question du père*. Paris: Presses Universitaires de France.

Large, D. 1995. "Double 'Whaam!' Sarah Kofman on *Ecce Homo.*" *German Life and Letters* 48 (4) (October): 441–462.

Lernout, G. 1994. *The Poet as Thinker: Hölderlin in France.* Columbia, S.C.: Camden House.

Levinas, E. 1991. *La mort et le temps.* Paris: L'Herne.

Mallarmé, S. 1973. *Correspondence 1890–1891.* Vol. 4/1 of *Correspondance de Stéphane Mallarmé.* Ed. H. Mondor and L. J. Austin. Paris: Gallimard, 1959–1985.

Mann, T. 1947. "Freud and the Future." In *Essays of Three Decades.* Trans. H. T. Lowe-Porter. London: Secker and Warburg.

———. 1990a. "Briefwechsel mit Bonn." In *Reden und Aufsätze I.* Frankfurt am Main: Fischer.

———. 1990b. "Freud und die Zukunft." In *Reden und Aufsätze I.* Frankfurt am Main: Fischer.

———. 1990c. "Nietzsches Philosophie im Lichte unserer Erfahrung." In *Reden und Aufsätze I.* Frankfurt am Main: Fischer.

Marx, K. 1977. *Karl Marx: Selected Writings.* Ed. D. McLellan. Oxford: Oxford University Press.

Marx, K., and F. Engels. 1996. *Collected Works.* Vol. 35. Trans. S. Moore and E. Aveling. New York: International Publishers.

Maurel, J. 1997. "Enfances de Sarah." *Les Cahiers du Grif* 3 (new series): 55–68.

Miller, J. H. 1985. "Dismembering and Disremembering in Nietzsche's 'On Truth and Lies in a Nonmoral Sense.' " In *Why Nietzsche Now?* Ed. D. T. O'Hara. Bloomington: Indiana University Press.

Møller, L. 1991. " 'The Sandman': The Uncanny as Problem of Reading." In *The Freudian Reading: Analytical and Fictional Constructions.* Philadelphia: University of Pennsylvania Press.

Momberger, M. 1986. *Sonne und Punsch: Die Dissemination des romantischen Kunstbegriffs bei E. T. A. Hoffmann.* Munich: Fink.

Muraro, L. 1994. "Female Genealogies." In *Engaging with Irigaray.* Ed. C. Burke, N. Schor, and M. Whitford. New York: Columbia University Press.

Nancy, C. 1996. "The Tragic Woman." In *On The Feminine.* Ed. M. Calle. Trans. C. McGann. Atlantic Highlands, N.J.: Humanities Press.

Nietzsche, F. 1966. *Beyond Good and Evil: Prelude to a Philosophy of the Future.* Trans. W. Kaufmann. New York: Random House.

———. 1967a. *On the Genealogy of Morals and Ecce Homo.* Ed. W. Kaufmann. Trans. W. Kaufmann and R. J. Hollingdale. New York: Random House.

———. 1967b. *Thus Spoke Zarathustra: A Book for Everyone and No One.* In *The Viking Portable Nietzsche.* Trans. and ed. W. Kaufmann. New York: Viking Press.

———. 1968a. *Twilight of the Idols and the Anti-Christ.* Trans. R. J. Hollingdale. New York: Penguin.

———. 1968b. *The Will to Power.* Trans. W. Kaufmann and R. J. Hollingdale. New York: Vintage Books.

———. 1969. *Selected Letters.* Trans. and ed. C. Middleton. Chicago: University of Chicago Press.

———. 1974. *The Gay Science.* Trans. W. Kaufmann. New York: Vintage Books.

———. 1979. *Philosophy and Truth: Selections from Nietzsche's Notebooks of the Early 1870s.* Trans. and ed. D. Breazeale. New York and London: Humanities Press.

——. 1980. *Friedrich Nietzsche: Sämtliche Werke. Kritische Studienausgabe in 15 Einzelbänden.* Ed. G. Colli and M. Montinari. Munich: dtv; Berlin and New York: de Gruyter.

——. 1981. *Briefwechsel: Kritische Gesamtausgabe.* Ed. G. Colli and M. Montinari. Berlin and New York: de Gruyter.

——. 1982. *Daybreak: Thoughts on the Prejudices of Morality.* Trans. R. J. Hollingdale. Cambridge: Cambridge University Press.

——. 1984. *Human, All Too Human: A Book for Free Spirits.* Trans. M. Faber. Lincoln: University of Nebraska Press.

——. 1986. *Human, All Too Human: A Book for Free Spirits.* Trans. R. J. Hollingdale. Cambridge: Cambridge University Press.

——. 1990. *Beyond Good and Evil: Prelude to a Philosophy of the Future.* Trans. R. J. Hollingdale. Harmondsworth, U.K.: Penguin.

——. 1992. *Ecce Homo: How One Becomes What One Is.* Trans. R. J. Hollingdale. 2d ed. Harmondsworth, U.K.: Penguin.

Norris, C. 1987. *Derrida.* Cambridge: Cambridge University Press.

Oliver, K. 1994. "Nietzsche's Abjection." In *Nietzsche and the Feminine.* Ed. P. Burgard. Charlottesville: University Press of Virginia.

——. 1995. *Womanizing Nietzsche: Philosophy's Relation to the "Feminine."* New York and London: Routledge.

——. 1997. *Family Values: Subjects between Nature and Culture.* New York and London: Routledge.

Patton, P. 1996. "Strange Proximity: Deleuze and Derrida dans les parages du concept." *Oxford Literary Review* 18 (1–2): 117–133.

Philonenko, A. 1983. *L'oeuvre de Kant.* Paris: Vrin.

Proust, F. 1997. "Impasses et passes." *Les Cahiers du Grif* 3 (new series): 5–10.

Richter, J. P. F. *See* Jean Paul.

Ronsard, P. de. 1963. *Poésies choisies.* Ed. P. de Nolhac. Paris: Garnier.

Rose, G. 1996. *Mourning becomes the Law: Philosophy and Representation.* Cambridge: Cambridge University Press.

Rose, J. 1993. *Why War?* Oxford: Blackwell.

Rousseau, J.-J. 1993. *Emile.* Trans. B. Foley. London: Rutland.

Russo, A. 1987. "Le respect des femmes: Le retour du père. Quelques réflexions sur le discours philosophique de Sarah Kofman." *Dalhousie French Studies* 13: 105–115.

Ryan, M. 1982. *Marxism and Deconstruction.* Baltimore: Johns Hopkins University Press.

Schneider, M. 1997. "Le regard et la femme." *Les Cahiers du Grif* 3 (new series): 39–52.

Schott, R. M. 1988. *Cognition and Eros: A Critique of the Kantian Paradigm.* Boston: Beacon Press.

Schrift, A. 1990. *Nietzsche and the Question of Interpretation: Between Hermeneutics and Deconstruction.* New York: Routledge.

——. 1995. *Nietzsche's French Legacy: A Genealogy of Poststructuralism.* New York: Routledge.

Smock, A. D. 1996. "Translator's Introduction." In S. Kofman, *Rue Ordener, Rue Labat.* Trans. A. Smock. Lincoln and London: University of Nebraska Press.

Sophocles. 1954. *Antigone.* In *Sophocles I.* Ed. D. Grene and R. Lattimore. Trans. E. Wyckoff. Chicago: University of Chicago Press.

———. 1978. *L'Antigone de Sophocle.* Paris: Christian Bourgois.

Szondi, P. 1986. "The Notion of the Tragic in Schelling, Hölderlin and Hegel." In *On Textual Understanding and Other Essays.* Trans. H. Mendelsohn. Minneapolis: University of Minnesota Press.

Tacitus. 1989. *Annals, Book IV.* Trans. R. Martin and A. J. Woodman. Cambridge: Cambridge University Press.

Tahon, M.-B. 1997. "Kofman lectrice de Rousseau: La tenue à distance." *Les Cahiers du Grif* 3 (new series): 71–85.

Taylor, S. 1990. *Left-Wing Nietzscheans: The Politics of German Expressionism 1910–1920.* Berlin and New York: de Gruyter.

Thomas, R. H. 1983. *Nietzsche in German Politics and Society 1890–1918.* Manchester, U.K.: Manchester University Press.

Valéry, P. 1994. *Regards sur le monde actuel.* Paris: Gallimard.

Voltaire. 1971. *Philosophical Dictionary.* Trans. and ed. T. Besterman. Harmondsworth, U.K.: Penguin.

Wilde, O. 1962. *The Letters of Oscar Wilde.* Ed. R. Hart-Davis. London: Rupert Hart-Davis.

———. 1981. *The Picture of Dorian Gray.* Ed. I. Murray. Oxford: Oxford University Press.

Williams, H. L. 1989. *Hegel, Heraclitus and Marx's Dialectic.* Hemel Hempstead, U.K.: Harvester Wheatsheaf.

Yovel, Y. 1994. "Nietzsche, the Jews, and *Ressentiment."* In *Nietzsche, Genealogy, Morality: Essays on Nietzsche's Genealogy of Morals.* Ed. R. Schacht. Berkeley: University of California Press.

Ziarek, E. 1995. *The Rhetoric of Failure: Deconstruction of Skepticism, Reinvention of Modernism.* Albany, N.Y.: SUNY Press.

Žižek, S. 1993. *Tarrying with the Negative: Kant, Hegel and the Critique of Ideology.* Durham, N.C.: Duke University Press.

Sarah Kofman: Bibliography, 1963–1998

This revised and updated version of "Sarah Kofman: A Complete Bibliography, 1963–1993" (Kofman 1993c, 191–207) is limited to original-language publications and English translations. Conventions observed are as follows: all books are published in Paris unless otherwise indicated; within each year, books precede articles and interviews; and square brackets indicate that the title or subtitle has been added by the compiler.

1963

"Le problème moral dans une philosophie de l'absurde." *Revue de l'enseignement philosophique* 14/1 (October–November): 1–7. Reproduced in *Séductions* (1990a), 167–181.

1968

"Métamorphose de la volonté de puissance du Judaïsme au Christianisme d'après 'L'Antéchrist' de Nietzsche." *Revue de l'enseignement philosophique* 18/3 (February–March): 15–19. Reproduced in *Le mépris des Juifs* (1994a), 85–95.

1969

"Freud et Empédocle." *Critique* 25/265 (June): 525–550 [review article on Jean Bollack, *Empédocle* (Minuit, 1965), and Sigmund Freud, *Analyse terminée et analyse interminable*, trans. A. Berman, *Revue Française de Psychanalyse* 2 (1939)]. Revised republication in *Quatre romans analytiques* (1974a), 31–66.

1970

a. *L'enfance de l'art: Une interprétation de l'esthétique freudienne.* Payot ("Bibliothèque scientifique"). 2d ed.: "Petite bibliothèque Payot," coll. "Science de l'homme,"

Compiled by Duncan Large with the assistance of Sarah Kofman and Alexandre Kyritsos.

250, 1975. 3d ed.: Galilée ("Débats"), 1985, includes "Délire et fiction (à propos de *Délire et rêves dans la* Gradiva *de Jensen* de Freud)," 251–281 (cf. 1974c). English: *The Childhood of Art: An Interpretation of Freud's Aesthetics.* Trans. Winifred Woodhull. New York: Columbia University Press ("European Perspectives"), 1988.

b. "Généalogie, interprétation, texte." *Critique* 26/275 (April): 359–381 [review article on Jean Granier, *Le problème de la vérité dans la philosophie de Nietzsche* (Seuil, 1966)]. Revised republication in *Nietzsche et la métaphore* (1972a), 173–206.

1971

a. "Nietzsche et la métaphore." *Poétique* 5 (Spring) (special number: "Rhétorique et philosophie"): 77–98. Revised and extended republication in *Nietzsche et la métaphore* (1972a).

b. "L'oubli de la métaphore." *Critique* 27/291–292 (August–September): 783–804 [review article on Friedrich Nietzsche: *Das Philosophenbuch/Le livre du philosophe: Études théoriques,* trans. Angèle Kremer-Marietti (Aubier-Flammarion, 1969); *La naissance de la tragédie,* trans. Geneviève Bianquis, 12th ed. (Gallimard, 1949); *La naissance de la philosophie à l'époque de la tragédie grecque,* trans. Geneviève Bianquis, 7th ed. (Gallimard, 1938)]. Revised and extended republication in *Nietzsche et la métaphore* (1972a).

c. "Judith, ou la mise en scène du tabou de la virginité." *Littérature* 3 (October): 100–116. Revised republication (as "Judith") in *Quatre romans analytiques* (1974a), 67–98.

1972

a. *Nietzsche et la métaphore.* Payot ("Bibliothèque scientifique"). 2d ed.: Galilée ("Débats"), 1983. Includes "Appendice: Généalogie, interprétation, texte," 173–206 (cf. 1970b).

English trans. of "Métaphore, symbole, métamorphose" (15–37): "Metaphor, Symbol, Metamorphosis." Trans. David B. Allison. In *The New Nietzsche: Contemporary Styles of Interpretation.* Ed. David B. Allison, 201–214. New York: Dell, 1977; 2d ed. Cambridge, Mass., and London: MIT Press, 1985.

English trans. of "Architectures métaphoriques" (87–117): "Metaphoric Architectures." Trans. Peter T. Connor and Mira Kamdar. In *Looking after Nietzsche.* Ed. Laurence A. Rickels, 89–112. Albany, N.Y.: SUNY Press ("Intersections: Philosophy and Critical Theory"), 1990.

English: *Nietzsche and Metaphor.* Trans. Duncan Large. London: Athlone Press; Stanford, Calif.: Stanford University Press, 1993.

b. "Résumer, interpréter." *Critique* 28/305 (October): 892–916 [review article on Sigmund Freud, *Délire et rêves dans la* Gradiva *de Jensen* (Gallimard ["Idées"], 1971)]. Revised republication (as "Résumer, interpréter [*Gradiva*]") in *Quatre romans analytiques* (1974a), 99–134.

1973

a. *Camera obscura: De l'idéologie.* Galilée ("La philosophie en effet").
English trans. of "Nietzsche: La chambre des peintres" (47–69) and "L'œil de bœuf: Descartes et l'après-coup idéologique" (71–76): "Nietzsche and the Painter's Chamber" and "The Ox's Eye: Descartes and the Ideological After-Effect." Trans. Will Straw. *Public* 7 ("Sacred Technologies," 1993): 153–170.
English: *Camera Obscura: Of Ideology.* Trans. Will Straw. London: Athlone Press, 1998.

b. "Le/les 'concepts' de culture dans les 'Intempestives' ou la double dissimulation." In *Nietzsche aujourd'hui?* [Proceedings of the Colloque de Cerisy-la-Salle, July 1972]. 2 vols. Union Générale d'Éditions ("10/18"), II ("Passion"), 119–146 (discussion to 151; further SK interventions: I, 180, 182f., 215, 288, 367; II, 85 and 181). Reproduced (without the discussion) in *Nietzsche et la scène philosophique* (1979b), 337–371.

c. "Un philosophe 'unheimlich.'" In Lucette Finas, Sarah Kofman, Roger Laporte, and Jean-Michel Rey, *Écarts: Quatre essais à propos de Jacques Derrida,* 107–204. Fayard ("Digraphe"). Revised republication in *Lectures de Derrida* (1984a), 11–114.

1974

a. *Quatre romans analytiques.* Galilée ("La philosophie en effet"). Includes "Freud et Empédocle," 31–66 (cf. 1969); "Judith," 67–98 (cf. 1971c); "Résumer, interpréter (*Gradiva*)," 99–134 (cf. 1972b); "Le double e(s)t le diable: L'inquiétante étrangeté de *L'homme au sable (Der Sandmann)*," 135–181 (cf. 1974b).
English: *Freud and Fiction.* Trans. Sarah Wykes. Boston: Northeastern University Press; Cambridge: Polity Press, 1991.

b. "Le double e(s)t le diable: L'inquiétante étrangeté de *L'homme au sable (Der Sandmann).*" *Revue Française de Psychanalyse* 38/1 (January–February): 25–56. Revised republication in *Quatre romans analytiques* (1974a), 135–181.

c. "Délire et fiction (à propos de *Délire et rêves dans la* Gradiva *de Jensen* de Freud)." *Europe* 539 (March) (special number: "Freud"): 165–184. Reproduced in *L'enfance de l'art* (3d ed., 1985, 251–281) (cf. 1970a).

1975

a. "Vautour rouge (Le double dans *Les élixirs du diable* d'Hoffmann)." In Sylviane Agacinski, Jacques Derrida, Sarah Kofman, Philippe Lacoue-Labarthe, Jean-Luc Nancy, and Bernard Pautrat, *Mimesis: Des articulations,* 95–163. Aubier-Flammarion ("La philosophie en effet").

b. "Les Femmes-Écrivains et leur colloque" [letter cosigned by Chantal Chawaf, Hélène Cixous, Catherine Clément, Françoise d'Eaubonne, Viviane Forrester, Xavière Gauthier, Sarah Kofman, Annie Leclerc, and Victoria Therame]. *Le Monde* 9422 (3 May): 15.

c. "Baubô (Perversion théologique et fétichisme chez Nietzsche)." *Nuova Corrente* 68–69 (1975–76) (special number: "Nietzsche"): 648–680. Revised republication (as "Baubô. Perversion théologique et fétichisme") in *Nietzsche et la scène philosophique* (1979b), 263–304.

English (with new Postscript): "Baubô: Theological Perversion and Fetishism." Trans. Tracy B. Strong. In *Nietzsche's New Seas: Explorations in Philosophy, Aesthetics, and Politics.* Ed. Michael Allen Gillespie and Tracy B. Strong, 175–202. Chicago and London: University of Chicago Press, 1988.

1976

a. *Autobiogriffures.* Christian Bourgois. 2d ed.: *Autobiogriffures: Du chat Murr d'Hoffmann.* Galilée ("Débats"), 1984.

English trans. of "La perte des plumes" (89–141): "No Longer Full-Fledged *Autobiogriffies.*" Trans. Winnie Woodhull. *SubStance* 29 (1981): 3–22.

b. "'Ma vie' et la psychanalyse (Janvier 76: Fragment d'analyse)." *Première Livraison* 4 (February–March). Reproduced in *Trois* 3/1 (Autumn 1987): 18 (cf. 1987c), *La Part de l'Œil* 9 (1993) (special number: "Arts plastiques et psychanalyse II"): 83, and *Les Cahiers du Grif* (new series): 3 (1997) (special number: "Sarah Kofman"), 171–172 (cf. 1997).

c. "Six philosophes occupés à déplacer le philosophique à propos de la 'mimesis.'" *La Quinzaine Littéraire* 231 (16–30 April): 19–22 (SK, 19–21) [group interview with Sylviane Agacinski, Jacques Derrida, Sarah Kofman, Philippe Lacoue-Labarthe, Jean-Luc Nancy, and Bernard Pautrat; questions from Jean-Louis Bouttes, Roger Dadoun, Christian Descamps, Gilles Lapouge, and Maurice Nadeau].

d. "Tombeau pour un nom propre." *Première Livraison* 5 (April–May). Reproduced in *Trois* 3/1 (Autumn 1987): 20 (cf. 1987c), *La Part de l'Œil* 9 (1993) (special number: "Arts plastiques et psychanalyse II"): 84 (with "Post-scriptum—1992"), and *Les Cahiers du Grif,* (new series): 3 (1997) (special number: "Sarah Kofman"), 169–170 (cf. 1997).

English: "Tomb for a Proper Name." Trans. Frances Bartkowski. In "Autobiographical Writings." *SubStance* 49 (1986): 6–13 (9–10).

1977

a. "Philosophie terminée, philosophie interminable." In GREPH [Groupe de recherches sur l'enseignement philosophique], *Qui a peur de la philosophie?* 15–37. Flammarion ("Champs"). Revised republication in *Lectures de Derrida* (1984a), 153–184.

b. "Sarah Kofman" [interview]. In François Laruelle, *Le déclin de l'écriture, suivi d'entretiens avec Jean-Luc Nancy, Sarah Kofman, Jacques Derrida et Philippe Lacoue-Labarthe,* 260–266. Aubier-Flammarion ("La philosophie en effet").

1978

a. *Aberrations: Le devenir-femme d'Auguste Comte.* Aubier-Flammarion ("La philosophie en effet").

b. "Qui a peur de la philosophie?" *Noroît* 224–227 (January–April) [roundtable discussion with Sylviane Agacinski, Roland Brunet, Jacques Derrida, and Sarah Kofman].

c. "L'espace de la césure." *Critique* 34/379 (December): 1143–1150 [review article on Philippe Lacoue-Labarthe, *Hölderlin: L'Antigone de Sophocle, traduction française suivie de "La césure du spéculatif"* (Christian Bourgois ["Première livraison"], 1978)]. Revised republication in *Mélancolie de l'art* (1985a), 71–86.

1979

a. *Nerval: Le charme de la répétition. Lecture de "Sylvie."* Lausanne: L'Age d'Homme ("Cistre Essais" 6).

b. *Nietzsche et la scène philosophique*. Union Générale d'Éditions ("10/18"). 2d ed.: Galilée ("Débats"), 1986. Includes "Annexe: Baubô. Perversion théologique et fétichisme," 263–304 (cf. 1975c); "Appendice: Le/les 'concepts' de culture dans les *Intempestives* ou la double dissimulation," 337–371 (cf. 1973b).
   English trans. of "Descartes piégé" (227–261): "Descartes Entrapped." Trans. Kathryn Aschheim. In *Who Comes after the Subject?* Ed. Eduardo Cadava, Peter Connor, and Jean-Luc Nancy, 178–197. New York and London: Routledge, 1991.

c. "Nerval sur le divan" [interview with Lucette Finas on *Nerval: Le charme de la répétition* (1979a)]. *La Quinzaine Littéraire* 306 (16–31 July): 17.

1980

a. *L'énigme de la femme: La femme dans les textes de Freud*. Galilée ("Débats"). 2d ed., 1983; 3d ed. (Librairie Générale Française ["Le livre de poche," coll. Biblio/essais 4194]), 1994.
   English trans. of "La relève des mères" (84–97): "The Sublation of Mothers." Trans. Cynthia Chase. *Enclitic* 4/2 (1980): 17–28.
   English trans. of "Supplément rhapsodique" (253–272): "Freud's 'Rhapsodic Supplement' on Femininity." Trans. Christine Saxton. *Discourse* 4 (Winter 1981–82): 37–51.
   English: *The Enigma of Woman: Woman in Freud's Writings*. Trans. Catherine Porter. Ithaca, N.Y., and London: Cornell University Press, 1985.
   English trans. of excerpts from "L'autre" (39–42) and "Criminelle ou hystérique" (77–80): "The Other" (248) and "Criminal or Hysteric" (249f.). In *Feminisms: A Reader*. Ed. Maggie Humm. Hemel Hempstead, U.K.: Harvester Wheatsheaf, 1992.

b. "La mélancolie de l'art." In *Philosopher: Les interrogations contemporaines. Matériaux pour un enseignement*. Ed. Christian Delacampagne and Robert Maggiori, 415–427. Fayard. Revised republication in *Mélancolie de l'art* (1985a), 9–33.

c. "Sacrée nourriture." In *Manger*. Ed. Christian Besson and Catherine Weinzaepflen, 71–74. Liège: Yellow Now; Chalon-sur-Saône: Maison de la Culture. Reproduced in *Trois* 3/1 (Autumn 1987): 17 (cf. 1987c), *La Part de l'Œil* 9 (1993) (special number: "Arts plastiques et psychanalyse II"): 85, and *Les Cahiers du Grif* (new series): 3 (1997) (special number: "Sarah Kofman"), 167–168 (cf. 1997).

English: "Damned Food." Trans. Frances Bartkowski. In "Autobiographical Writings." *SubStance* 49 (1986): 6–13 (8–9).

d. "La femme narcissique: Freud et Girard." *Revue Française de Psychanalyse* 44/1 (January–February): 195–210. Revised republication in *L'énigme de la femme* (1980a), 60–80.

English: "The Narcissistic Woman: Freud and Girard." Trans. Catherine Porter. *Diacritics* 10/3 (Fall 1980): 36–45. Reproduced in *French Feminist Thought: A Reader*. Ed. Toril Moi, 210–226. Oxford and New York: Blackwell, 1987.

1981

a. "Ça cloche." In *Les fins de l'homme: A partir du travail de Jacques Derrida* [Proceedings of the Colloque de Cerisy-la-Salle, 23 July–2 August 1980]. Ed. Philippe Lacoue-Labarthe and Jean-Luc Nancy, 89–112. Galilée. (Discussion to 116; further SK interventions: 16, 47, 86, 87, 184, 196f., 199, 310, 341, 365, 391, 392, 410, 480, 497, 650, 651.) Revised republication (without the discussion) in *Lectures de Derrida* (1984a), 115–151.

English: "'Ça cloche.'" Trans. Caren Kaplan. In *Continental Philosophy II: Derrida and Deconstruction*. Ed. Hugh J. Silverman, 108–138. New York and London: Routledge, 1989.

b. [2 illus.]. In Françoise Metz, "Ombrelles, ou la puissance fantastique de l'écriture" [review article on *Aberrations: Le devenir-femme d'Auguste Comte* (1978a), *Nerval: Le charme de la répétition* (1979a), and *Nietzsche et la scène philosophique* (1979b)]. *Avant-Guerre* 2 (1981): 91.

1982

a. *Le respect des femmes (Kant et Rousseau)*. Galilée ("Débats").

English trans. of "L'économie du respect: Kant" (21–56): "The Economy of Respect: Kant and Respect for Women." Trans. Nicola Fisher. *Social Research* 49/2 (Summer 1982): 383–404. Republished in *Feminist Interpretations of Immanuel Kant*. Ed. Robin May Schott. University Park: Pennsylvania State University Press ("Re-Reading the Canon"), 1997.

b. "La femme autrement dite." *Les Nouveaux Cahiers* 70 (Autumn): 80 [review article on Catherine Chalier, *Figures du féminin: Lecture d'Emmanuel Levinas* (La Nuit surveillée, 1982)].

1983

a. *Comment s'en sortir?* Galilée ("Débats").

English trans. of "Cauchemar: En marge des études médiévales" (101–112): "Nightmare: At the Margins of Medieval Studies." Trans. Frances Bartkowski. In "Autobiographical Writings." *SubStance* 49 (1986): 6–13 (10–13).

English trans. of "Prométhée, premier philosophe" (71–94): "Prometheus, the First Philosopher." Trans. Winnie Woodhull. *SubStance* 50 (1986): 26–35.

English trans. of "Aporie" (9–100): "Beyond Aporia?" Trans. David Macey. In *Post-structuralist Classics*. Ed. Andrew Benjamin, 7–44. London and New York: Routledge ("Warwick Studies in Philosophy and Literature"), 1988.

b. *Un métier impossible: Lecture de "Constructions en analyse."* Galilée ("Débats").

1984

a. *Lectures de Derrida*. Galilée ("Débats"). Includes "Un philosophe 'unheimlich,'"
11–114 (cf. 1973c); "Ça cloche," 115–151 (cf. 1981a); "Annexe: Philosophie
terminée. Philosophie interminable," 153–184 (cf. 1977a).

b. "La ressemblance des portraits (A propos du *Salon de 1767* consacré à *La Tour*)."
L'Esprit Créateur 24/1 (Spring): 13–32. Reproduced in *Rencontres de l'École du
Louvre* (September 1984) (special number: "L'imitation"): 215–230. Revised
republication (as "La ressemblance des portraits: L'imitation selon Diderot") in
Mélancolie de l'art (1985a), 35–70.

c. "Il y a quelqu'un qui manque." *Le Temps de la Réflexion* 5, 430–441 [review article on Denis Hollier, *Politique de la prose: Jean-Paul Sartre et l'an quarante* (Gallimard, 1982)]. Revised and extended republication (as "Sartre: Fort! ou Da?")
in *Séductions* (1990a), 139–166.

    English: "Sartre: Fort! ou Da?" Trans. Arthur Denner. *Diacritics* 14/4 (Winter
1984): 9–18.

1985

a. *Mélancolie de l'art*. Galilée ("Débats"). Includes "La mélancolie de l'art," 9–33
(cf. 1980b); "La ressemblance des portraits: L'imitation selon Diderot," 35–70
(cf. 1984b); "L'espace de la césure," 71–86 (cf. 1978c); "Balthus ou la pause,"
87–101.

b. *Rousseau und die Frauen*. Trans. Ruthard Stäblein. Tübingen: Rive Gauche
(Konkursbuchverlag Claudia Gehrke) ("Wegweisende Worte"). Includes 4 illus. by SK.

    French: "Les fins phallocratiques de Rousseau." *Cahiers de l'ACFAS* 44 (1986)
(special number: "Égalité et différence des sexes"): 341–358.

    English: "Rousseau's Phallocratic Ends." Trans. Mara Dukats. *Hypatia* 3/3
(Winter 1989): 123–136. Reproduced in *Revaluing French Feminism: Critical
Essays on Difference, Agency, and Culture*. Ed. Nancy Fraser and Sandra Lee
Bartky, 46–59. Bloomington and Indianapolis: Indiana University Press,
1992.

1986

a. *Pourquoi rit-on? Freud et le mot d'esprit*. Galilée ("Débats").

b. "Apprendre aux hommes à tenir parole" [interview with Roland Jaccard]. *Le
Monde* (27–28 April) ("Le monde aujourd'hui"): vii.

c. "Entrevista com Sarah Kofman conduzida por Chaké Matossian." *Revista
de comunicação e linguagens* 3 (June) (special number: "Textualidades"):
143–147.

d. "Nietzsche et l'obscurité d'Héraclite." *Furor* 15 (October): 3–33. Revised and
extended republication in *Séductions* (1990a), 87–137.

    English: "Nietzsche and the Obscurity of Heraclitus." Trans. Françoise Lion-
net-McCumber. *Diacritics* 17/3 (Fall 1987): 39–55.

1987

a. *Paroles suffoquées.* Galilée ("Débats"). Extract (61–63) reproduced in "Les 'mains' d'Antelme" (1994d). English: *Smothered Words.* Trans. Madeleine Dobie. Chicago: Northwestern University Press, 1998.

b. *Conversions:* Le Marchand de Venise *sous le signe de Saturne.* Galilée ("Débats"). English: "Conversions: *The Merchant of Venice* under the Sign of Saturn." Trans. Shaun Whiteside. In *Literary Theory Today.* Ed. Peter Collier and Helga Geyer-Ryan, 142–166. Cambridge: Polity Press, 1990.

c. "Trois textes." *Trois* 3/1 (Autumn): 16–20. Includes "Sacrée nourriture," 17 (cf. 1980c); " 'Ma vie' et la psychanalyse," 18 (cf. 1976b); "Tombeau pour un nom propre," 20 (cf. 1976d). Also includes 2 illus. by SK: "Surmoi," 16, and "La mort ou l'autisme," 19.

d. [Interview with Christa Stevens]. *Stoicheia* 4 (December).

e. "Sarah Kofman: De verleiding van een legendraads filosofe" [interview with Christa Stevens]. *Katijf* 42 (December 1987–January 1988): 26–29. Includes illus. by SK, 28.

1988

a. "Gesprek met de Franse filosofe Sarah Kofman: 'De vrouw is de skeptika, zij weet dat er geen waarheid achter de sluiers is' " [interview with Karen Vintges]. *De Groene Amsterdammer,* 22 June: 20–21.

b. "Miroir et mirages oniriques: Platon, précurseur de Freud." *La Part de l'Œil* 4 (special number: "VOIR: Les procès métonymiques de l'image"): 127–135. Revised republication in *Séductions* (1990a), 61–86.

c. "Sarah Kofman" [excerpted interview with Alice Jardine]. Trans. Patricia Baudoin. In Alice Jardine and Anne M. Menke, "Exploding the Issue: 'French' 'Women' 'Writers' and 'The Canon'? Fourteen Interviews." *Yale French Studies* 75 (special number: "The Politics of Tradition: Placing Women in French Literature"): 229–258 (SK, 246–248). Republished in *Displacements: Women, Traditions, Literatures in French.* Ed. Joan DeJean and Nancy K. Miller. Baltimore and London: Johns Hopkins University Press, 1990. Full interview in *Shifting Scenes* (1991c).

d. "Shoah (ou la Dis-Grâce)." *Les Nouveaux Cahiers* 95 (Winter 1988–89): 67. Reproduced in *Actes* 67–68 (September 1989) (special number: "Droit et humanité"): 1.

1989

a. *Socrate(s).* Galilée ("La philosophie en effet").
English trans. of "Les Socrate(s) de Nietzsche: 'Qui' est Socrate?" (291–318): "Nietzsche's Socrates: 'Who' is Socrates?" Trans. Madeleine Dobie. *Graduate Faculty Philosophy Journal* 15/2 (1991): 7–29.
English: *Socrates: Fictions of a Philosopher.* Trans. Catherine Porter. London: Athlone Press; Ithaca, N.Y.: Cornell University Press, 1998.

b. "Autour de *Socrate(s)*: Rencontre avec Sarah Kofman" [interview with Ghyslaine Guertin]. *La Petite Revue de Philosophie* 10 (Spring) (special number: "Psychologie et connaissance de soi"): 117–129.

c. "L'efficace du simulacre." *Autrement Dire* 6 (special number: "Simulacres"): 141–149. Extract from "Séductions: Essai sur *La Religieuse* de Diderot" in *Séductions* (1990a).

1990

a. *Séductions: De Sartre à Héraclite*. Galilée ("La philosophie en effet"). Includes "Séductions: Essai sur *La Religieuse* de Diderot," 9–60 (cf. 1989c); "Miroir et mirages oniriques: Platon, précurseur de Freud," 61–86 (cf. 1988b); "Nietzsche et l'obscurité d'Héraclite," 87–137 (cf. 1986d); "Sartre: Fort! ou Da?" 139–166 (cf. 1984c); "Appendice: Le problème moral dans une philosophie de l'absurde," 167–181 (cf. 1963).

English: *Seductions: From Sartre to Heraclitus*. Ithaca, N.Y.: Cornell University Press, 1998.

b. "Un battu imbattable: Sur *Larmes de clown* de Victor Sjörström." *Théâtre/Public* 92 (March–April): 55. Reproduced (as "Un battu imbattable: À propos de *Larmes de clown* de Victör Sjöström") in *L'imposture de la beauté et autres textes* (1995a), 129–137.

c. "Au-delà de la mélancolie" [reply to a questionnaire on Sartre]. *Libération* (23–24 June): 25.

1991

a. Sarah Kofman and Jean-Yves Masson, *Don Juan ou le refus de la dette*. Galilée ("Débats"). Includes Sarah Kofman, "L'art de ne pas payer ses dettes (Molière)," 63–121.

b. *"Il n'y a que le premier pas qui coûte": Freud et la spéculation*. Galilée ("Débats"). English: "'It's Only the First Step That Costs.'" Trans. Sarah Wykes. In *Speculations after Freud: Psychoanalysis, Philosophy and Culture*. Ed. Sonu Shamdasani and Michael Münchow, 97–131. London and New York: Routledge, 1994.

c. "Sarah Kofman" [interview with Alice Jardine]. Trans. Janice Orion. In *Shifting Scenes: Interviews on Women, Writing, and Politics in Post–68 France*. Ed. Alice A. Jardine and Anne M. Menke, 104–112. New York and Oxford: Columbia University Press ("Gender and Culture"). Republished (as "Sarah Kofman: An Interview") in *New Political Science* 30/31 (Summer–Fall 1994) (special number: "Bodies and Nations"): 23–31.

d. "Schreiben ohne Macht: Ein Gespräch mit Sarah Kofman" [interview with Ursula Konnertz]. Trans. Ursula Beitz. *Die Philosophin* 3 (April 1991) (special number: "Weimarer Republik und Faschismus: Eine feministische Herausforderung"): 103–109.

English: "Writing without Power: A Conversation with Sarah Kofman." Trans. Monique Rhodes-Monoc and Akosua Adomako. *Women's Philosophy Review* (June 1995): 5–8.

e. "Tot, unsterblich." *Die Philosophin* 3 (April 1991) (special number: "Weimarer Republik und Faschismus: Eine feministische Herausforderung"): 111–112.
f. "Eonoito wo miyo" [interview with Takashi Minatonichi]. Trans. Sumie Koyama. *Gendai-Shiso* 19/11 (November) and 19/12 (December).

1992

a. *Explosion I: De l' "Ecce Homo" de Nietzsche.* Galilée ("La philosophie en effet").
   English trans. of "Introduction" (9–43): "Explosion I: Of Nietzsche's *Ecce Homo.*" Trans. Duncan Large. *Diacritics* 24/4 (Winter 1994): 51–70.
   English trans. of "Une généalogie fantastique" (189–213): "A Fantastical Genealogy: Nietzsche's Family Romance." Trans. Deborah Jenson. In *Nietzsche and the Feminine.* Ed. Peter J. Burgard, 35–52. Charlottesville and London: University of Virginia Press, 1994.
b. "La question des femmes: Une impasse pour les philosophes" [interview with Joke Hermsen]. *Les Cahiers du Grif* 46 (Spring) (special number: "Provenances de la pensée: Femmes/philosophie"): 65–74.
c. "Nietzsche et Wagner: Comment la musique devient bonne pour les cochons." *Furor* 23 (May): 3–28 (slightly modified version of 1993b). Republished in *L'imposture de la beauté et autres textes* (1995a), 75–103.
   English: "Wagner's Ascetic Ideal according to Nietzsche." Trans. David Blacker and Jessica George, revised by Alban Urbanas and by Richard Schacht and Judith Rowan. In *Nietzsche, Genealogy, Morality: Essays on Nietzsche's Genealogy of Morals.* Ed. Richard Schacht, 193–213. Berkeley, Los Angeles, London: University of California Press, 1994.

1993

a. *Explosion II: Les enfants de Nietzsche.* Galilée ("La philosophie en effet").
   English trans. of "Le psychologue de l'Éternel féminin" (49–72): "The Psychologist of the Eternal Feminine (Why I Write Such Good Books, 5)." Trans. Madeleine Dobie. *Yale French Studies* 87 (1995) (special number: "Another Look, Another Woman: Retranslations of French Feminism"): 173–189.
   English trans. of "Accessoires" (158–174): "Accessories (*Ecce Homo,* 'Why I Write Such Good Books,' 'The Untimelies,' 3)." Trans. Duncan Large. In *Nietzsche: A Critical Reader.* Ed. Peter R. Sedgwick, 144–157. Oxford and Cambridge, Mass.: Blackwell, 1995.
b. "L'idéal ascétique de Wagner selon Nietzsche." In *L'art moderne et la question du sacré.* Ed. Jean-Jacques Nilles, 43–65. Le Cerf. First version of 1992c.
c. "Interview avec Sarah Kofman 22 mars 1991. Subvertir le philosophique *ou* Pour un supplément de jouissance" [interview with Evelyne Ender]. *Compar(a)ison* 1 (January): 9–26.
d. "'Naissance et renaissance de la tragédie' suivi de 'Sagesse tragique.'" *La Métaphore* 1 (Spring): 77–114. Prepublication of two chapters from *Explosion II* (1993a): "Renaissance" (77–99) and "Le premier philosophe tragique" (105–116).

e. "Un autre Moïse ou la force de la loi." *La Part de l'Œil* 9 (special number: "Arts plastiques et psychanalyse II"): 70–81. Revised republication in *L'imposture de la beauté et autres textes* (1995a), 49–73.

1994

a. *Le mépris des Juifs: Nietzsche, les Juifs, l'antisémitisme.* Galilée ("La philosophie en effet"). Includes "Annexe: Métamorphose de la volonté de puissance du Judaïsme au Christianisme d'après 'L'Antéchrist' de Nietzsche," 85–95 (cf. 1968).

b. *Rue Ordener, rue Labat.* Galilée.
   English: *Rue Ordener, Rue Labat.* Trans. Ann Smock. Lincoln and London: University of Nebraska Press ("Stages" 7), 1996. Includes illus. by SK: "Sarah Kofman self-portrait 1991," vi.

c. "Le mot d'esprit, l'humour, la mort et Freud selon Sarah Kofman" [interview with Lucien Degoy]. *L'Humanité* (25 January): 19.

d. "Les 'mains' d'Antelme: Post-scriptum à *Paroles suffoquées.*" *Lignes* 21 (January) (special section: "Robert Antelme: Présence de *L'Espèce humaine*"): 159–163. Includes extract (61–63) from *Paroles suffoquées* (1987a).

e. "Et pourtant, elle tremble! (Nietzsche et Voltaire)." *Furor* 26 (September) (special number: "Voltaire"): 135–154. Reproduced in *L'imposture de la beauté et autres textes* (1995a), 105–127.

f. "L'imposture de la beauté." *Autrement* (série "Mutations") 148 (October) (special number: "Le visage: Dans la clarté, le secret demeure," ed. Catherine Chalier): 191–214. Revised and extended republication (as "L'imposture de la beauté: L'inquiétante étrangeté du *Portrait de Dorian Gray*, d'Oscar Wilde") in *L'imposture de la beauté et autres textes* (1995a), 9–48.

1995

a. *L'imposture de la beauté et autres textes.* Galilée ("La philosophie en effet"). Includes "L'imposture de la beauté: L'inquiétante étrangeté du *Portrait de Dorian Gray*, d'Oscar Wilde," 9–48 (cf. 1994f); "Un autre Moïse, ou la force de la loi," 49–73 (cf. 1993e); "Nietzsche et Wagner: Comment la musique devient bonne pour les cochons," 75–103 (cf. 1992c); "Et pourtant elle tremble! (Nietzsche et Voltaire)," 105–127 (cf. 1994e); "Un battu imbattable: À propos de *Larmes de clown* de Victör Sjöström," 129–137 (cf. 1990b); "Angoisse et catharsis: Ou comment l'angoisse naît et disparaît (à propos de *The Lady Vanishes*, d'Alfred Hitchcock)," 139–145.
   Extract from manuscript of "Angoisse et catharsis" reproduced in facsimile in *Les Cahiers du Grif* (new series): 3 (1997) (special number: "Sarah Kofman"), 69–70 (cf. 1997).
   English trans. of "L'imposture de la beauté: L'inquiétante étrangeté du *Portrait de Dorian Gray*, d'Oscar Wilde" (9–48): "The Imposture of Beauty: The Uncanniness of Oscar Wilde's *Picture of Dorian Gray*." Trans. Duncan Large. In

Enigmas: Essays on Sarah Kofman. Ed. Penelope Deutscher and Kelly Oliver, Chapter 1 of this volume.

b. "La mort conjurée: Remarques sur *La leçon d'anatomie du docteur Nicolas Tulp,* 1632 Mauritshuis, La Haye." *La Part de l'Œil* 11 (special number: "Médecine et arts visuels"): 41–45.

1997

[3 illus.]. In *Les Cahiers du Grif* (new series): 3 (1997) (special number: "Sarah Kofman"), 27, 53, 166. Also includes extract from manuscript of "Angoisse et catharsis" (cf. 1995a) reproduced in facsimile, 69–70; "Sacrée nourriture," 167–168 (cf. 1980c); "Tombeau pour un nom propre," 169–170 (cf. 1976d); and " 'Ma vie' et la psychanalyse," 171–172 (cf. 1976b).

About the Contributors

Natalie Alexander is assistant professor of philosophy at Truman State University. She has published articles on Kant and Derrida. Her current research interests involve developing a postmodern reading of Sartre's *Being and Nothingness* and further exploring the works of Sarah Kofman.

Tina Chanter is an associate professor of philosophy at Memphis State University. She is the author of *Ethics of Eros: Irigaray's Rewriting of the Philosophers* (1995) and numerous articles on philosophy and feminist theory.

Penelope Deutscher is a lecturer in the Department of Philosophy at the Australian National University. She is the author of *Yielding Gender: Feminism, Deconstruction, and the History of Philosophy* (1997) and of many articles on feminist philosophy.

Françoise Duroux teaches in the Centre des études féminines at the Université de Paris VIII. She is the author of *Antigone encore: Les femmes et la loi* (1993) and of essays in the area of feminist philosophy.

Sarah Kofman lived from 1934 to 1994. She held a teaching post in philosophy at the Université de Paris I for most of her professional life. She was coeditor, with Jacques Derrida, Philippe Lacoue-Labarthe, and Jean-Luc Nancy, of the series La philosophie en effet, published by Galilée, and the author of over twenty books.

Pierre Lamarche is a doctoral candidate in the Department of Philosophy at The University of Texas at Austin. He has published on Hellenistic skepticism and is currently completing his thesis project, entitled "Ontology of Boredom."

Duncan Large is a lecturer in German at the University of Wales, Swansea, and chairman of the British Nietzsche Society. He has published translations of Kofman's *Nietzsche and Metaphor* (1993) and Nietzsche's *Twilight of the Idols* (1998), as well as various articles on Kofman, Nietzsche, Proust, and Musil.

Mary Beth Mader holds a doctoral degree in philosophy from The University of Texas at Austin. She is the translator of Luce Irigaray's *The Forgetting of Air* (1998).

Diane Morgan is senior lecturer in literary and cultural studies at Nene College, Northampton, United Kingdom. She has published articles on Kant, Hamann, and Buechner.

Jean-Luc Nancy teaches philosophy at the Université des Sciences Humaines de Strasbourg. He is the author of many books, including *The Inoperative Community* and *The Birth to Presence* and, with Philippe Lacoue-Labarthe, *The Literary Absolute.*

Kelly Oliver is an associate professor of philosophy at The University of Texas at Austin. Her books include *Family Values: Subjects between Nature and Culture* (1997), *Womanizing Nietzsche: Philosophy's Relation to "the Feminine"* (1995), and *Reading Kristeva* (1993). She has edited *The Portable Kristeva* (1997) and *Ethics, Politics and Difference in Kristeva's Writing* (1993).

Paul Patton is associate professor in philosophy at the University of Sydney. He has translated *Deleuze's Difference and Repetition* (1994) and edited *Nietzsche, Feminism and Political Theory* (1993) and *Deleuze: A Critical Reader* (1996).

Alan D. Schrift teaches philosophy at Grinnell College. His books include *Nietzsche and the Question of Interpretation* (1990), *The Hermeneutic Tradition: From Ast to Ricoeur* (1990), *Transforming the Hermeneutic Context: From Nietzsche to Nancy* (1990), and *Nietzsche's French Legacy: A Genealogy of Poststructuralism* (1995).

Ann Smock teaches French literature at the University of California, Berkeley. She is the translator of Sarah Kofman's *Rue Ordener, rue Labat* and *L'espace litteraire* and *l'écriture du desastre* by Maurice Blanchot. She is the author of *Double Dealing* (1985) and is working on a book about speech and speechlessness in the works of Louis-René des Forêts, Blanchot, Herman Melville, and other writers.

Index

Aberrations: Devenir-femme d'Auguste Comte,
viii, 4, 136, 138
Adam, 37
Adorno, Theodor, 131, 251n.3 (chapt.12);
Negative Dialectics, 131
Aeschylus, 79
Ahmad, Aijaz, 130, 246n.15, 247n.18
Alcibades, 26, 236n.4
Alexander, 252n.2
Alexander, Nathalie, 5, 17-8; "The New
Pyrrhonians: Taking Deconstructive
Skepticism Seriously," 248n.8
Althusser, Louis, 122-3, 126, 128, 246n.9;
Lenin and Philosophy, 246n.9
Anna Fercovitz, 60, 62-63, 65-66
Ansell-Pearson, Keith, 206
Antigone, 19-20, 189, 192-3, 195-196,
198, 201-202, 250n.2 (chapt.11),
251n.4 (chapt.11), 251n.5 (chapt.11)
Apollo, 55
Arendt, Hannah, 134, 209, 251n.4; *The
Origins of Totalitarianism,* 209
Ariadne, 138, 182-3
Aristotle, 87-89, 91, 93-96; *Metaphysics,* 88
"Aristotle and the 'Pre-Socratics,'" 70
Armengaud, Françoise, 8
Artaud, Antonin, xiii
Aurelia, 40, 76
Autobiogriffures, 11, 13, 68, 78, 81, 244n.18

Balthus, 237n.13, 244n.20
Barthes, Roland, 81

Basil, Hallward, 26-29, 34-35, 37-38, 43,
45-46, 238n.21, 241n.36, 241n.41,
242n.46
Bartowski, Frances, 250n.1 (chapt.11)
Bataille, George, 208, 237n.19; *The Ac-
cursed Share,* 208; "The Language of
Flowers," 237n.18
Baubô, 16, 22, 178, 182, 250n.12
Baudrillard, Jean, 125
Benjamin, Walter, 122, 128-129, 131,
247n.19; "Theses on the Philosophy
of History," 130
Binion, Ralph, 215-6; *Frau Lou: Nietzsche's
Wayward Disciple,* 215
Blanchot, Maurice, x, xiii, 1, 64, 110,
245n.4 (chapt.6); *La folie du jour,*
245n.4 (chapt.6)
Bologna, Sergio, 131
Borges, Jorge, 80, 125
Bruno, Giordano, 235n.1
Burckhardt, Jacob, 242n.43

"Ça Cloche," 170, 244n.17, 245n.4
(chapt.6), 250n.10 (chapt.9)
Caeser, Julius, 252n.2
Camera obscura: De l'ideologie, 8, 15-16,
109-110, 112, 124-126, 160-161,
246n.8, 246n.10; "The Photographic
Apparatus," 121; "Nietzsche: The
Chamber of Painters," 121
Campbell, Alan, 36, 43
Chanter, Tina, 7, 18-20, 185-186

The Childhood of Art, 2, 6–8, 18, 68–69, 82,
    164–165, 167, 169, 170, 244n.18,
    245n.1 (chapt 6), 249n.2, 249n.6;
    "Freud's Method of Reading: The Work
    of Art as a Text to Decipher," 244n. 18
Christ, 21, 32, 46, 181, 238n.26
Cicero, 241n.35; *Rhetorica ad Herennium,*
    241n.35
Cixous, Hélène, 248n.6
Clark, Maudemarie, 99, 102
Clément, Catherine, 199
Collin, Françoise, 2
Comment s'en sortir?, 8, 245n.4 (chapt.6)
Comte, Auguste, 1, 4–5, 14, 17, 82, 136,
    138–9, 160, 164, 247n.1 (chapt.7),
    247n.3 (chapt.7)
"Contempt for the Jews," 206
Coppelius, 71
Coppola, 71
Cordelia, 40
Corneille, 79
Count Viktorin, 75
Creon, 195–196, 198, 251n.4

"Damned Food," 195
Danto, Arthur, 207
Darwin, Charles, 235n.1
David-Ménard, Monique, 136, 199
da Vinci, Leonardo, 160, 185
de Beauvoir, Simone, 134–135, 139
de Fontenay, Elisabeth, 8
de Gandillac, Maurice, 135
de Sade, Marquis, 8
de Vaux, Clotilde, 4
Deleuze, Gilles, 1, 14, 98, 104–105, 108,
    110, 245n.2 (chapt.5)
Demeter, 178
Derrida, Jacques, xi, 1–2, 7–8. 13–16, 18,
    69–70, 77–78, 80, 82, 97–98,
    104–105, 108–110, 115–116,
    120–121, 123, 125, 128, 130–133,
    141, 160–164, 166–170, 173, 200,
    207, 210, 229, 244n.17, 245n.1,
    245n.2 (chapt.5), 246n.6, 246n.8,
    247n.17, 247n.18, 247n.19, 248n.3,
    248n.8, 249n.2, 250n.10, 250n.12,
    250n.3 (chapt.10), 251n.5, 253n.10,
    253n.15, *Glas,* 162, 245n.4, 249n.9;
    "To Speculate–on 'Freud,'"249n.9;
    The Postcard, 249n.9, *Dissemination,*
    249n.9; "La double session," 249n.9;

Spurs: Nietzsche's Styles, 162, 250n.12;
    Specters of Marx, 15–16, 110, 123, 129,
    131–132, 246n.15; "Apparition of the
    Inapparent," 124, "Freud and the
    Scene of Writing," 168; *Of Grammatol-*
    ogy, 160, 162–163, 249n.2; "Plato's
    Pharmacy," 77; "Signature, Event, Con-
    text," 80; "White Mythology," 98, 104,
    245n.1 (chapt.5), 246n.6; "Force of
    Law," 129; *The Other Heading,* 129,
    253n.10; "Otobiographies," 210,
    248n.3; "A Lecture on Marx," 246n.15;
    "Différance," 249n.2; *Margins of Philoso-*
    phy, 249n.2
des Forêts, Louis-Réné, 11–12, 49, 51,
    54–55, 57, 61, 63; *Ostinato,* 54, 61
Descartes, Réné, 79, 135, 210–211, 234
Desdemona, 40
Destutt de Tracy, Antoine, 111
Deutsch, Michel, 19, 189
Deutscher, Penelope, 18
"The Devil's 'Pharmacy,'" 77
Diderot, Denis, 1, 41, 56, 241n.39; *Paradox*
    on Acting, 41
Dionysus, 21–22, 178–180, 182–183, 186,
    211, 252n.2
Dom Juan, 49–51
Don Juan ou le refus de la dette, 11
Don Giovanni, 12, 49, 51–59, 62
Don Juan, 19, 49–51, 54, 56, 62
Dorian Gray, 9–12, 18, 26–31, 33, 35–48,
    55, 63, 181, 188, 235n.1, 237n.18,
    238n.21, 241n.35, 241n.37, 241n.38,
    241n.41, 242n.46
"Le double dans les elixirs du diable
    d'Hoffman," 75
"The Double is/and the Devil: The Uncan-
    niness of the Sandman," 68–72
Duroux, Françiose, 16–17

Eagleton, Terry, 246n.9; *Ideology,* 246n. 9
Eckermann, J. P., 69; *Conversations with*
    Goethe, 69
Empedocles, xiii, 68
"L'enchevêtrement," 74
Ender, Wolfram, 69
Engels, Friedrich, 246n.8
The Enigma of Woman, 2–3, 18, 161, 164–
    171, 174, 249n.6
Eteocles, 197
Ettlinger, 244n.18

Explosions I: De L' "Ecce Homo" de Nietzsche,
    xv, 6, 14, 81–82, 138, 179, 181–183,
    220, 229–230, 253n.13
Explosions II: Les Enfants de Nietzsche, 6, 8,
    14, 68, 81–82, 138, 181, 220, 221,
    229–230, 249n.4, 253n.13

Förster-Nietzsche, Elizabeth, 208, 214
Foucault, Michel, 126–127
Francesko, 76–77, 244n.18
Frank, Anne, 191, 196–197, 200–201
Frédéric Molieri, 11–12, 49, 51–66
Freud, Sigmund, xii–xiii, xv, 1–3, 5–6,
    8, 10, 13, 18–19, 21, 31, 36, 41–43,
    67–76, 82, 105–106, 109, 112, 115,
    117, 120, 127, 132, 135, 138, 141,
    146, 160, 162–170, 172–177,
    179–182, 186–188, 199, 220,
    222–227, 232, 234, 237n.14, 237n.17,
    241n.42, 242n.1, 242n.2, 243n.6,
    243n.11, 244n.17, 244n.23, 246n.10,
    249n.1, 249n.4, 249n.6, 250n.11,
    250n.6 (chapt.10), 251n.1 (chapt.12),
    252n.4; *Jokes and Their Relation to the
    Unconscious,* xii, 244n.23; "On Tran-
    sience," 41–42; "Mourning and
    Melancholia," 43; "Negation," 21,
    219, 223, 228; "The Uncanny," 69,
    72, 78, 110; "Leonardo da Vinci and
    a Memory of His Childhood," 70;
    The Interpretation of Dreams, 72; *Beyond
    the Pleasure Principle,* 73, 160, 226,
    243n.13; "Constructions in Analysis,"
    221, 232, *Civilizations and Its Discon-
    tents,* 227–228; "A Note on the Uncon-
    scious in Psychoanalysis," 117; *Studies
    on Hysteria,* 163; "Animism, Magic,
    and the Omnipotence of Thoughts,"
    237n.12, 237n.15; *Delusions and
    Dreams,* 242n.1
Freud and Fiction, 67, 70, 162–163, 199
Fukuyama, Frances, 123, 126; *The End of
    History and the Last Man,* 123

Gall, Andre, 235n.1
Gattégno, Jean, 235n.2
Gautier, Théophile, 36–37, 44, 239n.27,
    240n.30, 240n.31, 241n.37; *Enamels
    and Camels,* 36, 239n.27, 239n.30,
    241n.38; *Albertus,* 239n.27, 240n.30,
    240n.31, 240n.32, 240n.33, 240n.33,

240n.34; *Mademoiselle de Maupin,*
    239n.27; "Sea-Gloom," 240n.31
Goethe, Johann Wolfgang, 80; *Egmont,* 80
Gravesand, 162
Guattari, Felix, 98, 104–105
Guéroult, 135

Habermas, Jurgen, 89, 131
Haeckel, Ernst, 235n.1
Hawthorne, Nathaniel, 240n.35; *The Scar-
    lett Letter,* 240n.35
Hebbel, Friedrich, 68
Heckman, Peter, 103
Hegel, G.W.F., 26, 76, 78, 114, 135,
    200–201, 229, 235n.1; *Aesthetics,*
    235n.1, *Encyclopaedia,* 235n.1
Heidegger, Martin, 139, 210, 251n.3
    (chapt.11); *Der Ister,* 251n.3 (chapt.11)
Heraclitus, 88, 92–95
Hermsen, 3
"Heterogeneity: Is This Not the Very Char-
    acter of Every Text," 76
Hitchcock, Alfred, 185, 187; *The Lady Van-
    ishes,* 185, 187
Hitler, Adolf, 197
Hobbes, Thomas, 113
Hoffman, E.T.A., 1, 12–14, 18, 58, 67–
    79, 81–83, 159, 238n.23, 241n.42,
    242n.2, 243n.7, 244n.18, 244n.19,
    244n.24; *Life and Opinions of Murr
    the Tomcat,* 13, 58, 68, 78–81, 83,
    244n.18; "The Sandman," 13, 18,
    68–71, 74, 81, 83; *The Devil's Elixirs,*
    68, 74–79, 83, 241n.42, 243n.7,
    244n.18, 244n.19
Hölderlin, Friedrich, 190, 192, 196–197,
    200, 251n.3 (chapt.11)
Horkheimer, Max, 251n.3 (chapt.12)
Husserl, Edmund, xi
Huysmans, J.K., 238n.22; *Against Nature,*
    238n.22
Hyppolite, Jean, 135, 225

"Il n'y a que le premier pas qui côute,"
    250n.11
Imogen, 40
L'imposture de la beauté et autres textes, 9, 11,
    67, 82, 181
Irigaray, Luce, 135, 199–200, 251n.5
    (chapt.11); *Speculum de l'autre femme,*
    135; *Éthique de la différence sexuelle,* 135

Isis, 147, 154–156, 248n.10
Ismene, 197–198, 200

Jacobs, Carol, 202
Jameson, Frederic, 124–125, 127, 247n.18
Janus, 249n.7
Jardine, Alice, 109–110, 242n.4, 245n.3 (chapt.6), 251n.6 (chapt.11); *Shifting Scenes*, 124, 245n.3 (chapt.6)
Jensen, Wilhem, 68, 72; *Gradiva*, 72, 242n.1
Jentsch, 71–72, 77
Jesus, 214
Jocasta, 19, 177, 188, 193, 251n.5 (chapt.11)
Johannes Kriesler, 79–80
Juliet, 40

Kafka, Franz, 192–193, *The Trial*, 193
Kaiser, Gerhard, 242n.2
Kant, Immanuel, 1, 4, 6, 17–18, 69, 90, 95, 99, 136–139, 144–146, 148–158, 199, 210, 224, 226, 248n.1, 248n.2, 248n.9, 249n.5; *Anthropology from a Pragmatic Point of View*, 150; *Metaphysical Foundations of Morals*, 137; *Critique of Judgment*, 147; "Speculations Concerning the Origins of Human History," 147, 153, 248n.7; *Critique of Pure Reason*, 225
Kaufmann, Walter, 207
Kierkegaard, Søren, 241n.40; *Either/Or*, 241n.241
Kofman, Bereck Rabbi, 184, 206
Kremer-Marietti, Angele, 245n.1
Kristeva, Julia, 188, 199; Powers of Horror, 188

Lacan, Jacques, 77, 190, 199–200, 244n.17; "The Mirror Stage as Formative of the Function of the 'I,'" 244n.17
Lacenaire, P. F., 44, 37
LaClau, Ernesto, 212
Lacoue-Labarthe, Phillipe, xiii, 1, 19, 109, 189, 190, 192, 196–197, 200, 245n.1 (chapt.5); "The Caesura of the Speculative," 189–190, 194; "Detour," 245n.1 (chapt.5)
Lady Hamilton, 45
Laius, 197
Lamarche, Pierre, 15–17
Large, Duncan, 13, 109, 206, 208, 245n.2 (chapt.6); *Conversions*, 243n.5

Lectures de Derrida, 110, 163, 173
Leibniz, G.W.F., 135, 210
Leporello, 54
Leonardo, 238n.23
Lessing, G. E., 209; *Nathan the Wise*, 209
Levinas, Emmanuel, xi, xii, 129, 248n.8
Lewis, 80, *The Monk*, 80
Lord Henry, 9, 26–30, 34, 36, 39, 40, 44–47, 237n.18, 238n.27, 241n.37, 241n.38, 241n.41, 242n.46
Lucretius, 80

Mader, Mary Beth, 14
Maeterlinck, Maurice, xiv, *Life of the Ants*, xiv
Magnus, Bernd, 207
Mallarmé, Stephane, 235n.2
Malle, Louis, 235n.3; *Fatale*, 235n.3, 236n.5
Mann, Thomas, 221–224, 227, 252n.5; *Nietzsche's Philosophy in the Light of Our Experience*, 221; *Freud and the Future*, 222
Marini, Marcelle, 124
Marx, Karl, 15–16, 110–115, 118, 120, 121–123, 127–133, 138, 213, 246n.8, 246n.9, 246n.10, 248n.1, 251n.5 (chapt.12); *Capital*, 5, 113, 115, 118–120, 124–125, 246n.9, 246n.13, 247n.17, 247n.19; "The Fetishism of Commodities and the Secret Thereof," 119; *German Ideology*, 15, 112–115, 118–120, 124–125, 133, 246n. 9; "Theses on Feuerbach," 117, 246n.13
Matheron, Alexandre, 137
Maurel, Jean, 8
Mauss, Marcel, 206
Medardus, 75–78
Medusa, 22, 176–177, 180, 182–183, 248n.6
Mélancolie de l'art, 11, 244n.18
Mémé, 184–187, 233
Mendelssohn, B. F., 214
Menke, Anne, 251n.6 (chapt.11)
Mepham, John, 246n.9; "The Theory of Ideology in *Capital*," 246n.9
Le mépris des juifs, 20–21, 206, 212, 217, 229, 251n.9
Métier impossible, 21, 199, 219–200, 232
Mimesis: Des articulations, 68, 74, 242n.5
Miss Froy, 187
Molière, 49–50, 67; *Dom Juan*, 49, 50, 53

Møller, Lis, 68, *The Freudian Reading*, 68
Momberger, Manfred, 244n.19; "The
    Place of Laughter," 244n.19
Morgan, Diane, 21–22
Mozart, Wolfgang Amadeus, 11, 49,
    51–52, 54, 57–59, 61; *Don Giovanni*,
    11, 51–52, 57, 59
Murr, 78–80, 159

Nancy, Claire, 200
Nancy, Jean-Luc, 1–2, 7, 109
Napoleon, Bonaparte, 111
Narcissus, 29
Nathaniel, 13, 18, 71–72
Negri, Tony, 131
Nehamas, Alexander, 207
Nerval, Gérard, 1, 14, 40, 67, 82, 199,
    Sylvie, 40
Nietzsche, Friedrich, xii–xiii, xv, 1, 5–6, 8,
    10, 13, 18–22, 45, 48, 50, 63, 67–70,
    73, 76, 78–80, 82–83, 87–103, 105–
    109, 112–113, 115, 117, 120–122, 125,
    132, 138–141, 146, 160–164, 166,
    170–171, 173–174, 178–183, 186, 188,
    199, 206, 208–211, 213, 217–220, 230,
    230, 232–234, 242n.43, 242n.48,
    242n.4, 244n.15, 244n.19, 244n.24,
    246n.6, 247n.19, 247n.2 (chapt.7),
    249n.3, 249n.4, 250n.12, 250n.4
    (chapt.10), 250n.5 (chapt.10), 251n.3
    (chapt.12), 251n.4 (chapt.12), 251n.7,
    252n.2, 252n.3, 252n.4, 253n.13; *Thus
    Spoke Zarathustra*, 180; *The Birth of
    Tragedy*, 11, 41, 55, 101–102; *Ecce Homo*,
    14, 79, 81, 139, 179, 182, 207, 209, 216,
    220, 230, 232, 253n.13; *On Truth and
    Lies in a Nonmoral Sense*, 15, 79, 98–99,
    101, 103, 108; *The Will to Power*, 90, 94;
    Twilight of the Idols, 93; *Human, all Too
    Human*, 93, 212, 215, 230; *Werke*, 99, *The
    Gay Science*, 101; *On the Genealogy of
    Morals*, 106, 117, 163, 178, 215–216,
    231; *Philosophenbuch*, 112, *Beyond Good
    and Evil*, 231, 250n.5 (chapt.10); *The
    Antichrist*, 214, 216; *On the Future of Our
    Educational Institutions*, 210; "Philosophy
    in the Tragic Age of the Greeks," 243n.9
Nietzsche and Metaphor, 6, 14, 68, 74, 81,
    83, 97, 100, 107, 109, 210, 245n.1
    (chapt.5), 245n.1 (chapt.6), 246n.6,
    246n.10, 251n.6 (chapt.12)

Nietzsche et la scène philosophique, 14, 87,
    243n.9; "The Presuppositions of
    'logic,'" 87; "Le complot contre
    philosophie," 243n.9; "Nietzsche and
    the Obscurity of Heraclitus," 243n.9
"Nightmare: At the Margins of Medieval
    Studies," 193
Norris, Christopher, 248n.3

Oedipus, 48, 63, 177, 179–180, 193, 197,
    242n.48, 251n.5 (chapt.11)
Oliver, Kelly, 7, 18–20; *Womanizing Nietz-
    sche*, 250n.3 (chapt.10)
Olympia, 71
Ophelia, 40
Orion, Janice, 245n.3 (chapt.6)
Osiris, 156, 248n.10
"L'oubli de la métaphore," 245n.1 (chapt.5)

"Painting and Eloquence–The Abuses of
    Resemblance," 78
Patton, Paul, 6, 14–17
Paul, Jean, 236n.11; "Praise of Stupidity,"
    236n.11
Perseus, 248n.6
*Das Philosophenbuch/Le livre du philosophe:
    Études Théoretiques*, 245n.1 (chapt.5)
"Un philosophie 'unheimlich,'" 69, 72, 78,
    110
Pietro Belcampo/Peter Schöenfeld, 13, 78
Plato, 1, 27, 137, 200, 236n.6, 244n.22,
    Symposium, 27, 236n.4, 242n.49 *Repub-
    lic*, 137; *Phaedo*, 125; *Timaeus*, 125
Plutarch, 93
"The Politics of Tradition: Placing
    Women in French Literature," 245n.3
    (chapt.6)
Polynices, 191, 193, 197, 250n.2
    (chapt.11), 251n.5 (chapt.11)
Pourquoi rit-on? Freud et le mot d'esprit.,
    xv
Prorsa, x
Proudhon, P. J., 113
Proust, Marcel, 2, 8

"Rhapsodic Supplement," 68
Rank, Otto, 75
Raux-Filio, François, 244n.17
Rée, George, 216
Rée, Paul, 215–216, 230–231; *Origin of the
    Moral Sensations*, 215

Le Religieuse, 55
Les Respect des Femmes, 5, 17, 144–145, 156, 247n.1 (chapt.8); "Tenir les femmes en respect," 145, 249n.5
Resnais, Alain, 241n.40; *Smoking*, 241n.40; *No Smoking*, 241n.40
Ricoeur, Paul, 82
Ronsard, Pierre, 33
Rops, Félicien, 36
Rosalind, 40, 236n.7
Rose, Jacqueline, 225
Rose, Gillian, 201; *Mourning Becomes the Law*, 201
Rousseau, Jean-Jacques, 1, 4–5, 17–18, 137–139, 144, 146, 160–162, 164, 199, 248n. 4, 249n.2, 249n.5, 249n.7; *Social Contract*, 137; *Emile*, 137, 248n.4; *The New Heloise*, 137; *Confessions*, 137, 161
Rue Ordener, Rue Labat, xiii, 7, 17–18, 22, 138, 159–160, 183, 185, 206, 217, 231, 233, 253n.14
Ryan, Michael, 132,; Marxism and Deconstruction, 132

St. Anthony, 238n.26
Salomé, Lou, 215
Sartre, Jean-Paul, 135, 199
Schelling, W. J., 70, 76
Schneider, Monique, 2–3, 8, 199
Schopenhauer, Arthur, 21, 69, 208, 214–216, 230, 249n.4; *The World as Will and Representation*, 69
Schott, Robin, 248n.1
Schrift, Alan, 6, 20–21, 251n.8
Séductions: De Sartre à Héraclite, 11
Seth, 248n.10
Sgnarelle, 50
Shakespeare, William, 1, 67, 79, 242n.49; *The Merchant of Venice*, 243n.5
Shapiro, Gary, 207
Sibyl Vane, 29, 33, 35, 40, 41
Silenus, 33
Smock, Ann, 8, 11–12, 19
"Socrate et ses doubles," 236n.4
Socrates, 26–27, 33, 48
Sophie, 249n.7
Sophocles, 190–191; *Antigone* 19, 190–191
Spinoza, x, 136–137, 214; *Ethics*, 137; *Political Treatise*, 137

Stirner, Max, 125–127
Strachey, James, 243n.6, 243n.11
Sybil, 236n.9
Symons, Arthur, 238n.22

Tieck, Ludwig, 79–80; *Puss and Boots*, 79–80
Tourneur, Cyril, 40
Trilling, Lionel, xiv

Uccello, 236n.8; "Miracle of the Desecrated Host," 236n.8

Valéry, Paul, 252n.1, "Souvenir actuel," 252n.1
"Vautour Rouge," 13, 68, 74–75, 83
Venus, 36
Veronica, 240n.30
Voltaire, 236n.9; *Philosophical Dictionary*, 236n.9
von Trier, Lars, 252n.1; *Europa*, 252n.1

Wagner, Cosima, 215
Wagner, Richard, 21, 208, 214–216, 221, 230–231, 249n.4
Webster, Benjamin, 40
Weininger, Otto, 134
Wilde, Oscar, 1, 9–11, 15, 18, 20, 22, 31, 33, 36, 41, 43, 46, 63, 67, 235n.1, 236n.10, 237n.17, 238n.20, 240n.31, 242n.49; *Picture of Dorian Gray*, 9, 15, 20, 36, 47, 55, 67, 181, 235n.2, 237n.17, 238n.20, 239n.30, 240n.35, 241n.42, 242n.49; "The Canterville Ghost," 237n.17; *The Happy Prince and Other Tales*, 238n.20; *Portrait of Mr. W. H.*, 242n.49
Woodhull, Winnie, 81

Xenophon, 48

Yovel, Yirmiyahu, 214

Zarathustra, 21, 208, 231, 233
Ziarek, Ewa, 248n.8, *Rhetoric of Failure*, 248n.8
Žižek, Slavoj, 253n.11; "The Object of Indefinite Judgment," 253n.11
Zweig, Stefan, 165; *Four and Twenty Hours in a Woman's Life*, 165